Fast Tanks and Heavy Bombers

Excerpt from "Losses" from *The Complete Poems* by Randall Jarrall.
Copyright © 1969 by Mrs. Randall Jarrall. Reprinted by permission
of Farrar, Straus & Giroux, Inc., and Faber and Faber Ltd.

First published 1998 by Cornell University Press
First Printing, Cornell Paperbacks, 2003

Printed in the United States of America

Cornell University Press strives to use environmentally responsible suppliers and
materials to the fullest extent possible in the publishing of its books. Such
materials include vegetable-based, low-VOC inks and acid-free
papers that are also recycled, totally chlorine-free,
or partly composed of nonwood fibers.

Library of Congress Cataloging-in-Publication Data

Johnson, David E. (David Eugene), 1950–
Fast tanks and heavy bombers : innovation in the U.S. Army,
1917–1945 / David E. Johnson.
p. cm. — (Cornell studies in Security affairs)
Includes bibliographical references and index.
ISBN 0-8014-3458-0 (cloth : alk. paper)
ISBN 0-8014-8847-8 (pbk. : alk. paper)
1. United States. Army—Weapon systems—History—20th century.
2. United States. Army—Operational readiness.   I. Title.
II. Series
UF503.J65   1998
355'.07'097309041—dc21   98-16418

1   2   3   4   5   6   7   8   9   10   Cloth printing
1   2   3   4   5   6   7   8   9   10   Paperback printing

To Wendy

Tables

Acknowledgments

This book is the product of an intellectual odyssey that started in 1987, when the U.S. Army gave me, a serving officer at the time, the extraordinary opportunity to enter the graduate program in history at Duke University. During three wonderful years at Duke, I enjoyed the privilege of working with a community of scholars who took quite seriously their obligations as educators. My development as a historian is the direct result of the efforts of Joel Colton, Calvin Davis, W. A. B. Douglas, Larry Goodwyn, I. B. Holley Jr., Tim Lomperis, Kristen Neuschel, Alex Roland, Theodore Ropp, Bill Scott, and Peter Wood. I thank them all.

I am particularly indebted to Alex Roland, I. B. Holley Jr., and Larry Goodwyn. Alex Roland subtly challenged me to grow out of my preconceptions and introduced me to colleagues who have fundamentally influenced my work. Finally, Alex helped me gain and maintain control over this project. I. B. Holley gave me the rigorous grounding in research methodology and scholarship that enabled me to conceptualize and write this book. Larry Goodwyn introduced me to social history, helped me understand institutions, and in the process significantly influenced the way I have come to view my work and the world.

Many institutions and individuals have been particularly helpful. The staff of Perkins Library at Duke University provided every possible assistance. Stuart Basefsky and Ken Berger were always there when I needed help. Marty Andresen, John Slonaker, Richard Sommers, and David Keough led me through the holdings of the U.S. Army Military History Institute at Carlisle Barracks, Pennsylvania. Richard Morse, Tim Johnson, Robert Johnson, and Archie DiFante provided similar support at the U.S. Air Force Historical Research Agency at Maxwell Air Force Base, Alabama. These people made the use of their institutions' resources an enjoyable experience.

Later I had the good fortune to work in the U.S. Army Center of Military History in Washington, D.C. My colleagues there, particularly Jeffrey Clarke, Harold Nelson, Roger Cirillo, Kavin Coughenaur, Edward Drea, John Elsberg, John Greenwood, Roger Kaplan, Jim Knight, and Frank Schubert, gave steadfast assistance and encouragement.

I continued revising this book while serving at the National Defense University, first as a member of the faculty of the School of Information Warfare and Strategy, then as the director of academic affairs. David Alberts, Ken Allard, Brad Barriteau, John Carabello, Karen Carleton, Rob Cox, Tom Czerwinski, Jim England, Fred Giessler, Gerry Gingrich, Alan Gropman, Dan Kuehl, Martin Libicki, Michael McDevitt, Ervin Rokke, Rudy Rudolph, Jim Stafford, Susan Studds, and Dave Tretler all helped me bring the book to closure. John Alger provided useful critiques and invaluable editorial assistance. By challenging some of my assertions, my students at the National War College and the Information Resources Management College helped me tighten my arguments.

I finished this book in my new life as a civilian. Four colleagues at Science Applications International Corporation (SAIC), Bill Owens, Jim Blaker, Dr. Ed Frieman, and Wendy Frieman, listened to my arguments about military innovation and RMAs (revolutions in military affairs) and offered valuable insights.

The long process of writing this book was immeasurably aided by Roger Haydon, my editor at Cornell University Press. Roger worked with me over several years and showed extraordinary patience when the demands of my life forced delays in the completion of the manuscript.

Five other people have made this work possible. My late father, Eugene E. Johnson Jr., fostered my interest in World War II. Like many other men who served in that war, he became an armchair historian in an effort to understand his personal experience. This book originated in his interests and doubts, often expressed as asides as we watched motion pictures about the war. I thank Tim Tyson for reading this book in an earlier incarnation and being a friend in every sense of the word. Whenever the frustrations of the process approached the unendurable, I could always turn to Tim.

The freedom to devote an extraordinary measure of my time and energies to this project was made possible by the sacrifices of Sharon Johnson and our son, Sean Johnson. It took me seven intense months to write the first draft of this book—and seven years of stolen weekends to complete it. Without their support and understanding, I could not have completed it.

Finally, I want to thank Wendy Frieman—the woman who has changed my life. To her I dedicate this book.

D. E. J.

Washington, D.C.

Introduction

"History is lived forward," the English historian C. V. Wedgwood perceptively noted, "but it is written in retrospect. We know the end before we consider the beginning and we can never wholly recapture what it was like to know the beginning only."[1] This cognitive constraint is particularly compelling in a study of the U.S. Army between the two World Wars. Conditioned by the reality of World War II and some fifty years of a large, standing postwar army, we find it too easy to assume we know what needs to be analyzed.

The most familiar version of the Army's fate during the interwar era suggests that although it endeavored to maintain its readiness, the Army was unprepared for the enormous demands of World War II. A miserly Congress, supported by a peace-minded and isolationist American public, denied it the funds and personnel needed to maintain an adequate military establishment. The official history of the U.S. Army emphasized that this public and official malaise had dire consequences. The Army "became tragically insufficient and . . . incapable of restoration save after the loss of many lives and the expenditure of other resources beyond man's comprehension."[2] In short, as a contemporary historian has noted: "Although many dedicated individual professional soldiers had during the 1920s and 1930s conscientiously studied to be ready for the next war, decline, neglect, and stagnation marked America's military forces."[3]

This view of the origins of the Army's unpreparedness at the beginning of World War II is important for at least three reasons. First, the successes of World War II are the bedrock on which existing American military doctrines are constructed. Second, the high costs of American unpreparedness at the beginning of World War II served to justify large standing military forces and their associated defense budgets in the postwar years. Third, the

[1]

"lessons" of the interwar era provide compelling arguments to avoid the dismantling and neglect of American defense institutions at the end of the cold war. Thus, the interwar period is frequently cast as one analogous to the present post–cold war era, with its ambiguous threats to American security and concomitant demands for cuts in defense spending and smaller military forces.[4]

In this book I present a different perspective on the interwar Army. I argue that internal barriers to change and the myopic vision of single-issue constituencies contributed significantly to the Army's unpreparedness for World War II—perhaps more so than the external challenges. Even though the Army faced severe resource constraints, it also had intellectual and institutional deficits that exacerbated shortfalls in money and personnel.

I focus on the adaptation of the U.S. Army to the realities of modern war by analyzing how the Army responded to two technologies that had demonstrated their military utility in World War I—the tank and the airplane. The military forces of France, Great Britain, Germany, and the United States had all experimented with tanks and airplanes on the western front. During the two decades that followed the Great War, these nations and others grappled with the implications of these new weapons and debated the means by which the technologies would be assimilated into their military institutions. From the conceptual choices, tank and airplane doctrines and designs emerged. The results varied from country to country.

FRANCE

In the aftermath of World War I, France "was a victim of her own historical experience, geography, and political and military institutions."[5] The French, although exhausted by World War I and dreading another conflict, focused considerable energy on creating a strategic security environment that would provide protection from the ever-present threat of Germany.[6] The French also studied what they perceived to be the lessons of World War I. The result was a defensive strategy that relied on fortifications (the Maginot Line) and on a military establishment staffed by short-term and therefore relatively poorly trained conscripts. In this establishment the Army was clearly ascendant; and within the Army the infantry was dominant, because it formed the focal point of a doctrine that stressed defense, firepower, and the methodical battle.[7] The methodical battle reflected the French views of the lessons of World War I and a belief that "fire rather than movement dominated the modern battlefield."[8] Consequently,

> the French preferred rigid centralization and strict obedience. Their doctrine
> stressed the necessity of avoiding an encounter battle in which moving armies

unexpectedly collided and had to fight in an impromptu and spontaneous fashion. They thus opted for a time-consuming, intricate process that prized preparation rather than improvisation. As a consequence of this approach, French doctrine envisaged first the weakening of an attacker by a defender's fire, and then his destruction by a massive but tightly controlled "battering-ram" attack.[9]

Hence, "the methodical battle was the centerpiece of French doctrine" because "it resolved the tension between the manifest tactical superiority of defensive firepower and the imperative that . . . the French Army had to be ready to undertake offensive operations." The methodical battle rested on three fundamental tenets: centralized control, massive artillery support of infantry attacks, and offensives divided into subordinate efforts with clear objectives.[10] Thus, the French Army viewed technology from an evolutionary perspective supportive of its existing doctrine. The focus on the strategic defensive and the methodical battle created the environment that shaped the evolution of the tank and the airplane in France during the interwar era.

In the French Army, the tank existed to support the methodical battle. The 1929 manual governing tank employment stressed that tanks, although valuable, supported the infantry but did not replace it.[11] This is not to imply that the French did not put considerable effort into the development of tanks; in fact, in 1940 they had more tanks than the Germans, and some were better than those in the German Army.[12] Indeed, the French Char B1bis was perhaps the finest tank in the world in 1940. Unfortunately for the French, those who developed French armored doctrine did not take full advantage of the excellent tanks available to them. In the French Army, the tank was inextricably tied to the methodical battle. As one historian wrote, "More ambitious doctrine would have required a different army, but the mission of the French high command was to heed the nation's political, economic, and psychological limitations and to develop simple, stable, and credible methods appropriate for a nation in arms."[13]

Some French officers, however, envisioned a different kind of army and an expanded role for the tank. Charles de Gaulle was perhaps the most vocal. In 1934 he called for the creation of a professional French army built around an armored corps.[14] This "rapid reaction force" would complement the French Nation in Arms and would "be used before the nation completed its mobilization." De Gaulle's ideas were denounced by both the civilian and military hierarchies; France did not begin to form armored divisions until January 1940.[15]

The publication of de Gaulle's ideas did, however, have an effect on French doctrine. In 1935 General Maurice Gamelin, chief of the French general staff, dictated that henceforth all writings by French officers would be vetted by the high command before publication to ensure their adherence to doctrine.[16] This decision clearly had a stultifying effect. One French general later recalled: "Everyone got the message, and a profound silence reigned until the awakening of 1940."[17]

The airplane suffered a similar fate. Even after the French Air Force was granted independence in 1933, it remained strongly subordinated to the Army. Although officers in the Armée de l'Air had a "modest preference for the counter-city strategic bombing advocated by Giulio Douhet," they were "not fanatical" about it. Furthermore, to counter the emerging threat of Germany in the late 1930s, the French Air Force turned to the production of fighter aircraft.[18] This decision was made late, and although the French produced an excellent fighter, they had too few of them to stem the tide in 1940.

The focus was clearly on supporting ground forces, and mobilization plans placed the nominally independent Air Force under the command of the Army.[19] Not surprisingly the French Air Force focused on close air support and air defense as its primary missions.[20]

GREAT BRITAIN

In Great Britain, the experience of World War I greatly influenced the environment in which the tank and the airplane developed. In the wake of the horrors of the Great War, Britain became determined to avoid a heavy ground involvement in another protracted Continental war. The widely supported concept of "limited liability" in future Continental wars became national policy when Neville Chamberlain was elected prime minister in 1937. It was a return to the past. The Royal Navy would provide a shield to guarantee the island's security, as it had always done. The Army was largely confined to the role of a colonial police force. Not until February 1939 did the British government authorize the Army to prepare for war on the Continent.[21]

Britain's postwar aversion to Continental engagement diminished the resources made available to the armed forces, particularly to the Army. In September 1938 the Army had only two poorly prepared infantry divisions available to deploy the Continent.[22] Furthermore, the Cardwell system, which required an army equally balanced between the imperial and home defense missions, constrained the Army's ability to focus on the requirements of modern war. The Army was particularly limited in the development of armored formations because a colonial police force had little use for armored divisions.[23] Finally, the inherent conservatism of the British Army, centered on the regiment and tradition, created formidable barriers to innovation, and these institutional realities were exacerbated by a general anti-intellectual bent that pervaded the Army's culture.[24]

This anti-intellectualism is reflected in the fact that the Army did not begin a formal effort to study the lessons of World War I until 1932. The Kirke

Committee report that resulted was critical of the Army's performance and suggested improvements that could have led to reform in doctrine and military education. General Archibald Montgomery-Massingberd, chief of the Imperial General Staff (CIGS) when the report was completed, suppressed the report. He restricted its distribution to the Army's senior commanders. A highly edited version—one that gave a favorable and distorted version of the Army's performance in the war—was given general circulation. Innovators, particularly B. H. Liddell Hart and J. F. C. Fuller, were so publicly and loudly critical of the Army that they alienated professional soldiers. Consequenly, their voices were marginalized in the Army preparedness debate.[25]

Nevertheless, between 1926 and 1934 the British Army conducted innovative experiments with armored warfare, mainly during General George Milne's tenure as CIGS.[26] The Royal Tank Corps became a permanent part of the Army in 1923, thus creating a body of officers with an institutional reason to champion the tank.[27] Still, it was an uphill struggle to prove the worth of armor in a conservative army that focused on the traditional infantry, artillery, and cavalry branches. Ironically, even though an experimental armored force performed well in maneuvers in 1927 and 1928, its success hurt the cause of the armor advocates.[28] General Montgomery-Massingberd was commander of the area where the maneuvers were held, and after the 1928 exercise he noted his belief that the experimental armored force

> although invaluable for experimental purposes . . . was definitely affecting adversely the morale and training of the Cavalry and Infantry. . . . What should have been done was to gradually mechanize the Cavalry Division and the Infantry Division and not to introduce an entirely new formation based on the medium Tank. Nor was it sound to pit the new formation with its modern armament, against the older formations, in order to prove its superiority. What was wanted was to use the newest weapons to improve the mobility and fire power of the old formations. . . . What I wanted, in brief, was evolution and not revolution.[29]

Instead of concentrating on the armored force, Montgomery-Massingberd believed that the entire Army should be mechanized and motorized. His arguments, when coupled with a shortage of resources, were persuasive in the Army, and the experimental armored force was disbanded until 1931.

In that year Milne assembled the Army's four tank battalions into the First Brigade, Royal Tank Corps. This unit had a mixed legacy. Although it did innovative work with radios and proved the flexibility of armored formations in making moderately deep attacks, it reinforced in the minds of tank officers the validity of all-tank units rather than units of combined arms. Finally, the British Army authorized the creation of a permanent tank brigade in 1934.[30]

Milne's successors were less progressive, and reforms languished. Montgomery-Massingberd, CIGS from 1933 to 1936, had a particularly pernicious impact on innovation. In addition to suppressing the Kirke Committee report, he "imposed rigid centralization on the army . . . and perpetuated the notion that the next European war would be merely an updated version of the experience of 1914–1918."[31]

From 1934 until the beginning of the war in 1939, the Army attempted to form a mobile division. By 1938 the division was little more than an unbalanced aggregation of units, of which two-thirds were cavalry light tank units. This structure was likely the result of Montgomery-Massingberd's belief that the mission of the mobile division in a war on the Continent would be the same as that of the calvary division in 1914—to cover the advance of the British Expeditionary Force.[32] The mobile division eventually evolved into the 1st Armored Division. When the Germans invaded France in 1940, however, this division remained in England and was "still more a basis for argument than an instrument of war."[33] Conservatism within the British Army, coupled with a strategy of limited liability, constrained budgets, and the Cardwell system for imperial defense, ensured that the Army in 1937 "had no tank in production, its artillery was antiquated, its antitank gun obsolete, and its vehicular support inadequate."[34]

Not until February 1939 did the British government begin serious efforts to prepare the Army for war—a war that would clearly require deploying to the Continent. It was a very late start, and thus, "when the Germans invaded France and Belgium in 1940, the only British armored units, other than the divisional cavalry regiments, were two battalions of the Royal Tank Regiment assigned to the 1st Army Tank Brigade."[35]

The British air arm fared somewhat differently than the Army. In the aftermath of World War I, Great Britain's Royal Air Force (RAF) was the only independent air service in the world. Its leadership during the interwar period were focused largely on maintaining that independence.[36]

In the early postwar years the RAF, searching for a mission that would justify its existence, embraced "air control." Air control, or the "concept of using aircraft, either independently or in conjunction with mobile columns of troops and armored cars, as an efficient and economical means of controlling the Empire, saved the RAF."[37] Nevertheless, air control, although vital to the preservation of the RAF in its early years, was peripheral to the thinking of British air officers. As one officer noted:

> In the past, we have been glad to take over the responsibility of control, sometimes in none too favorable circumstances, because we had no other chances of showing what we could do. The rearmament of Germany, which has emphasized with dramatic suddenness the problems involved in Home Defence

and European war, has relegated the subject of small wars to its proper place in our microcosm.[38]

Thus, although air control served to guarantee the survival of the RAF in the short term, British air officers embraced another role—strategic bombing—that they believed would guarantee their independence. Quite simply, missions that did not support an independent RAF, such as close air support, received little attention.[39] This parochialism on the part of the RAF was not particularly surprising in a defense establishment that operated from independent ground, sea, and air philosophies of war.[40]

The independent strategic offensive mission was vital to a RAF deeply embroiled in budgetary battles with the Navy and the Army. Air officers sought the counter to the question that "if the RAF missions were only to support the army on the ground and the navy at sea, then why should Britain allocate resources to a service that had no independent mission?"[41] The answer was strategic bombing. Additionally, the RAF demonstrated its belief "that the past had *no* relevance to the future, and [it] was comfortable with manipulating the evidence to support conclusions that were in line with current doctrine." Consequently, its official history of World War I in the air "was a masterpiece of propaganda to justify its continued existence" rather than a critical analysis of its wartime experience.[42]

The need for an independent RAF was also buttressed by the change brought to Great Britain's strategic position by the advent of air power. During World War I England was bombed by Germany and thus was vulnerable to a threat against which the Royal Navy could not provide a defense. During the interwar years, many believed that England was vulnerable to a "knockout blow" from the air by bombers "that would always get through." The people's fears were heightened by "civilian propagandists who wrote voluminously about the air threat."[43] Stanley Baldwin's views, expressed to the House of Commons in 1934, captured the new strategic reality: "Let us not forget this: since the day of the air, the old frontiers are gone. When you think of the defense of England, you no longer think of the White Cliffs of Dover; you think of the Rhine."[44]

The British response to the new strategic reality resulting from the rise of air power occurred on two levels. First and foremost, the RAF focused on strategic bombing. Strategic bombing was attractive as both a deterrent and a retaliatory option. Thus,

> Britain would try to maintain a bombing capability that would frighten others into not starting a war. . . . If the more extreme predictions of the bombing advocates proved wrong, if "knock-out blows" were unachievable, strategic bombing would at least give the British a way to attack their adversaries with-

out recourse to the feared, casualty intensive, ground operations of World War I. Bombing would be an addition to Britain's blockade strategy.[45]

Second, as the Luftwaffe steadily grew as a threat in the late 1930s, the RAF was increasingly seen to have the important role of defending England from air attacks by Germany.

As the threat from Nazi Germany increased, so too did funding for the RAF's Fighter Command. In 1937 the Chamberlain government chose to fund Fighter Command, a sophisticated air defense system that depended on radar and new fighters. The fighters that resulted, Hurricanes and Spitfires, were among the best in the world, but this decision was made at the expense of Bomber Command's program for a new generation of bombers.[46] Predictably, the air staff, wanting the focus to remain on bombers, opposed this plan.[47] As Sir Thomas Inskip, the minister of coordination of defense, noted in 1937 when he rejected the expansion of Britain's bomber force, "at the outset of war our first task is to repulse a knock-out blow within the first few weeks, trusting thereafter to defeat the enemy by a process of exhaustion, resulting from our command of the sea, in the later stages."[48] Although this decision likely saved England during the Battle of Britain, it also created a situation that "insured until 1943 Bomber Command failed to receive technologically up-to-date aircraft needed to wage a strategic bombing campaign."[49]

GERMANY

Germany's armed forces developed in a dramatically different interwar context than those of either Great Britain or France. As a defeated nation, Germany faced the immediate—and significant—constraints of the Versailles treaty. In the new Weimar Republic, the German Army was restricted to 96,000 soldiers and 4,000 officers. The general staff was dissolved. Only seven infantry divisions and three cavalry divisions could be formed, and their size was restricted. Fixed fortifications in the west were forbidden. And Germany was denied possession of any heavy artillery, tanks, or military aircraft.[50] In the realm of military doctrine and military planning the Weimar Republic and the Nazi Third Reich responded similarly to these constraints.

Reform-minded General Hans von Seeckt's selection as the German Army's commander in chief significantly influenced army doctrine. Von Seeckt, who headed the army from 1919 to 1926, was responsible for major reforms in the German Army, or Reichswehr. When the size of the Reichswehr was reduced by the Treaty of Versailles, Seeckt filled the 4,000 officer positions with general staff officers, placing them in all of the important command and staff positions. In so doing, he broke the hold traditionalists had had on the Army during the war and created "a very different officer corps from that which had existed before World War I, one whose cultural ethos emphasized intellectual as well as tactical and operational excellence."[51]

Von Seeckt's doctrinal reforms were grounded in a thorough critical analysis of World War I. Numerous committees were formed, and eventually more than 500 war-experienced German officers were involved in developing a modern German military doctrine and organization. This effort included nearly 100 air service officers, who examined the war from the perspective of air warfare. The result of the work of the committee was Army Regulation 487, *Leadership and Battle with Combined Arms*, published in 1921 and 1923.[52] The regulation showed that the Germans' conclusions about the lessons of World War I were very different from those of the French or British. As opposed to the French strategic defensive and methodical battle, or the British strategy of a protracted war of attrition and limited liability, the Germans stressed offense and maneuver. The regulation also emphasized the decentralization of operations and the use of judgment and initiative by battlefield leaders. Finally, "*all* officers had to be thoroughly familiar with army doctrine and that doctrine was to form a coherent framework within which the whole army operated."[53]

An important point of departure for the German Army's development of doctrine was the experience with infiltration tactics (called "Hutier Tactics" after General Oskar von Hutier, who developed the concept on the eastern front), employed in the latter years of World War I. This approach was an effort to end the stalemate of trench warfare through large-scale breakthroughs. At the heart of the new tactical doctrine was the belief in the necessity for combined arms operations. Additionally, the general staff created special battalions of Storm Troops well armed with mobile weapons, to lead the attack. The mission of the Storm Troops was to penetrate enemy defenses at weak points and then attack enemy strong points from the flank and rear. The normal large artillery preparation was abandoned for a short intense barrage so as not to warn the enemy of the attack. Once the Storm Troops created a breach, German reserves would exploit this tactical success and create a strategic victory. And strategic victory would come with Kesselschlacht, or the encirclement of the enemy and his annihilation.[54]

In 1917 German units employing this new doctrinal scheme created a fifty-mile breakthrough on the Italian front at Caporetto, and in the spring of 1918 General Erich Ludendorff employed the new tactics on the western front. After initial success and the creation of a forty-mile penetration into Allied lines, the offensive ground to a halt because German artillery and logistical support could not keep up with the attacking forces.[55]

[9]

Von Seeckt believed that the logistical and supporting arms failures experienced in 1918 would be corrected through motorization.[56] He also emphasized a well-trained, professional force as the core of the German military. He was convinced that "the whole future of warfare . . . lies in the employment of mobile armies, relatively small but of high quality and rendered distinctly more effective by the addition of aircraft."[57] The professional army would be poised to attack immediately at the onset of a war, while militia would defend the borders and to train and serve as replacements for the regular officers.[58] Thus, the German Army would take the initiative and strike before its enemies could mobilize.[59] Finally, von Seeckt stressed war games and maneuvers as means to establish the professional force and to validate evolving doctrine.[60]

The tank became a key element in the German Army's doctrine despite the Versailles treaty's prohibition against tanks. First, the Germans learned vicariously by studying the experiences of other armies with tanks, most notably the British Army.[61] Second, Germany trained its armored forces, in violation of the Versailles treaty, in the Soviet Union. From 1929 to 1933 the Reichswehr trained officers, tested equipment, and conducted exercises at the secret armor center at Kazan.[62] Moreover, "German doctrinal conceptions, by emphasizing exploitation, speed, leadership from the front, and combined arms, provided a solid framework for thinking through not only how the *Reichswehr*, if it possessed tanks, might employ them against an enemy, but how a potential opponent might utilize armor against German forces."[63] Experimental armored units performed well in the Wehrmacht's 1935 maneuvers, and three panzer divisions were authorized. Not surprisingly, these divisions were combined-arms units that contained—in addition to tank units—infantry, artillery, and support elements motorized to give them the necessary mobility to keep pace with the tank elements.[64]

Opinions differ over the origins of the German panzer force. Some contend that the panzer force and blitzkrieg tactics were revolutionary and resulted from the efforts of maverick officers, most notably Heinz Guderian, and the critical support of Adolf Hitler. Indeed, one scholar has written that in the absence of Hitler's intervention, "it seems likely that normal organizational dynamics would have been determinative" and that Guderian's "ideas would have been suppressed and the German Army would have entered World War II with a much more traditional doctrine."[65] Guderian claimed that General Ludwig Beck, chief of the general staff, was "thoroughly hostile to armored warfare."[66] Guderian's memoirs are frequently cited as evidence for his contention that traditionalists opposed the development of the panzer force.[67]

Another view is that General Beck was not, in fact, a reactionary but concerned with the development of the entire Wehrmacht. Indeed, Beck had chaired the committee that rewrote Army Regulation 487, which became

Army Regulation 300, *Troop Leadership,* a regulation centered on combined-arms armored commands and motorized infantry, artillery, and support elements.[68] *Troop Leadership* also noted that "tanks should attempt deep penetrations of the enemy's position in order to put out of action the hostile units ... and they should be finally employed with the infantry and supporting artillery to encircle and destroy the enemy."[69] Furthermore, by 1935 Beck was advocating using independent panzer divisions for attacking long-range objectives.[70] Finally, it appears that the Germans were tolerant of outspoken officers—even "Hammering Heinz" Guderian, as he was known in the German Army. Guderian "at one time or another antagonized virtually every senior officer in the army with little discernible impact on his career, at least until he ran afoul of his Führer in December 1941."[71]

This is not to say that there was not "considerable skepticism among senior officers" about "whether mechanized formations could make the deep penetrations that advocates like Guderian claimed." Most generally believed, however, that tank forces "could substantially aid infantry and armor in pushing their way through enemy defensive positions and making possible the infantry exploitation that had occurred in the attacks in spring 1918."[72] As one historian has noted, "even the cavalry, the most conservative branch of the army, was eager to motorize and mechanize."[73] From this perspective, "the new panzer divisions merely extended basic principles on which all German doctrine rested, an evolutionary rather than a revolutionary change." Additionally, the massive military expansion ordered by Hitler after he came to power gave the Wehrmacht the resources it needed to wage a blitzkrieg. The success of the blitzkrieg in Poland in 1939 ensured that the German "officer corps as a whole began to grasp the potential of armored exploitation on the operational level of war."[74]

The German Air Force, or Luftwaffe, was a key component of the blitzkrieg, but, as one historian argued in 1981, "the prevailing historical picture of a *Luftwaffe* tied closely to the army's coattails is no longer tenable."[75] Indeed, a recent assessment of the Luftwaffe contends that

> German air power theory of the interwar period is remarkable for its broad and comprehensive approach to air power. To the German airmen, air power meant a doctrine of strategic bombing, but it also meant a concept of conducting joint operations with ground forces, a theory of homeland defense and passive defense against a bombing campaign, the creation of a paratroop force capable of seizing and holding vital objectives behind the enemy lines, the creation of a large air transport force and a mobile logistics system for keeping one's forces supplied in the field, and the development of a strong antiaircraft artillery arm that could defend the homeland and provide support to the armed forces. In virtually all these aspects of air power, the Luftwaffe was ahead of the British and the Americans in the interwar period.[76]

[11]

Although the German air arm was disestablished by the Versailles treaty, German air officers remained within the Reichswehr and participated in the postwar analyses under von Seeckt's leadership. As with the armor center in Kazan, the Germans established a secret training and testing program in the Soviet Union at Lipetsk. Between 1925 and 1933 the Lipetsk air base "ensured the maintenance of a proficient cadre of fliers, and a thorough research and development program for aerial weaponry."[77]

In 1935 the Luftwaffe became an independent service when Hitler denounced the Treaty of Versailles.[78] Consequently, it had only some four years to organize, train, and equip before World War II started with the invasion of Poland in 1939.

The Luftwaffe issued Luftwaffe Field Manual no. 16, *The Conduct of the Air War*, in 1935. The manual articulated four major offensive air missions: air superiority, strategic or independent air operations, interdiction of the battlefield, and close support. Notably, close air support of ground forces was the last priority. Field Manual no. 16 also stressed that "decision in war could be brought about only through the combined efforts of all three branches of the military forces."[79] Hence, Germany fielded ground and air forces that operated jointly rather than separately as they did in Great Britain and the United States. Indeed, it appears that "most German officers seem to have felt that the lives of aircrews and ground troops, and the successful completion of military operations, were more important than the narrow concerns of their own service."[80]

The Luftwaffe's difficulties were immense, however. Like the German Army, the Luftwaffe carefully analyzed its operational experiences in World War I, the Spanish civil war, and the invasion of Poland to improve its performance.[81] Nevertheless, the German aircraft industry's capabilities were marginal in the early 1930s, particularly in engine development. Although the Germans tried to field a four-engine heavy bomber to support their strategic bombing concepts, "the inadequacy of power plants" and the "lack of resources as well as inadequate long-range planning rendered the German aircraft industry incapable of sustaining a heavy bomber program." Still, the Luftwaffe fielded the best medium bombers and dive bombers of their day, and its fighter aircraft were formidable until the end of the war. Additionally, it recognized the importance of fighter escorts for bomber formations and the need for navigational and blind bombing aids—insights British and American airmen would ignore until well into World War II. Thus, "when war came in 1939, the Germans possessed more broadly based conceptions of air power, and hence the *Luftwaffe* intervened in military operations more effectively during the first two years."[82]

Within the armed forces of the United States, the Army's air arm was the only one fixated on strategic bombing as the principal mission. Marine Corps aviators were committed to supporting "small wars," occupying the

Marine Corps through much of the interwar period, and "amphibious land-ing operations upon hostile shores." The general sense in the Marine Corps was "that aviation was best employed in support of ground troops."[83] The Marine airmen's attitude was summed up by a Marine officer: "Marine avi-ation is not being developed as a separate branch of the service that consid-ers itself too good to do anything else. Unlike the army air service, we do not aspire to be separate from the line or to be considered as anything but regu-lar marines."[84]

Similarly, the Navy fought efforts, led by Army General Billy Mitchell, to create a unified air force that would include naval aviation. The Navy, in the person of Adm. William A. Moffett, Navy Bureau of Aeronautics chief from 1921 to 1933, "set out to bind naval aviators to the navy, rather than see them subsumed into a unified air force."[85] Although there was some resentment of the "ingrained technological conservatism of the capital ship navy . . . the overwhelming majority [of naval aviators] held that for the time being the chief function of naval aviation was to support the battle-line."[86] In short, Marine Corps and Naval aviators, unlike the majority of Army aviators, re-mained loyal to their services and worked within them.

The differing national experiences raise an interesting theoretical ques-tion: Why did each of these nations derive different solutions for the tank and the airplane, when each had largely the same empirical base (World War I) as a starting point for innovation? A number of scholars have at-tempted to deal with the question of innovation in military organizations.

Conceptually, the literature on military innovation is broad. Some argue that military innovation results from civilian intervention, or "outsiders," while others assert that only military "insiders" can have a significant im-pact. The influence of bureaucratic politics, military culture, institutional norms, paradigm theory, and organization theory also provide insights into the complex subject of military innovation.

Edward Katzenbach's "The Horse Cavalry in the Twentieth Century" was one of the earliest scholarly efforts to understand military innovation. Katzen-bach argued that culture, tradition, and conservatism resulted "in the strange and wonderful survival of the horse cavalry" well into the twentieth century, despite the appearance of modern weapons that should have challenged its utility. Katzenbach ultimately concluded that the very need for "discipline, for hierarchy, for standardization within the military structure . . . create pres-sures for conformity, and conformity, too, is the enemy of change." Finally, he believed that "the greatest instigation of new weapons development has in the past come from civilian interest plus industrial pressure."[87]

Barry R. Posen's *The Sources of Military Doctrine* analyzed the interwar military doctrines of France, Britain, and Germany from the perspectives of organization theory and balance of power theory. His principal assertion was that military doctrine is changed by civilian intervention. He qualified this conclusion, however, and noted that because "civilians do not necessarily have the expertise to directly change military doctrine to bring it into conformity with overall grand strategic design . . . they must rely upon mavericks within military organizations for the details of doctrinal and operational innovation." Posen relied mainly on two examples in reaching this conclusion: (1) the role of civilians in forcing the RAF to focus on the air defense mission, with the assistance of Air Chief Marshall Sir Hugh Dowding, and (2) the intervention of Hitler, aided by Guderian, in the creation of the blitzkrieg.[88] His conclusions may be accurate in the case of the RAF, where civilians used budget allocations to fund fighter and air defense network procurement over bomber production. However, significant evidence suggests that the blitzkrieg was a logical evolution of an innovative Reichswehr doctrinal base, nurtured under General von Seeckt, and that Guderian's role as a maverick was exaggerated.

Stephen Peter Rosen's *Winning the Next War* examines twenty-one cases of American and British experiences in peacetime, wartime, and technological innovation in the military. Rosen's approach recognizes that "different kinds of innovation occur for different reasons in the same organization, and that different organizations will handle innovation very differently."[89]

Rosen concludes that "peacetime innovation has been possible when senior military officers with traditional credentials, reacting not to intelligence about the enemy but to a structural change in the security environment, have acted to create a new promotion pathway for junior officers practicing a new way of war." He asserts that "wartime innovation . . . has been most effective when associated with a redefinition of the measures of strategic effectiveness employed by the military organization, and it has generally been limited by the difficulties connected with wartime learning and organizational change, especially with regard to time constraints." Rosen notes about technological innovation that "the problems of choosing new technologies seem to have been best handled when treated as a matter of managing uncertainty." Rosen also concludes, in contrast to Posen, that "civilian political leaders . . . do not appear to have had a major role in deciding which new military capabilities to develop, either in peacetime or in war, although they did help protect or accelerate innovations already in progress."[90]

Rosen's view is echoed by Brian Bond and Martin Alexander in an essay that examined Liddell Hart's and Charles de Gaulle's influence on the military establishments in Great Britain and France, respectively. They concluded:

> In practice "outsiders" can seldom exert a direct influence on military reform because they lack full knowledge of the difficulties and of options available. . . . On the other hand, the responsible military authorities tend to be all too

well aware of the problems and to accept that only piecemeal or compromise measures are feasible. . . . Most important of all, the interwar period bears out the Clausewitzian perception that political attitudes, priorities, and constraints exert a dominating influence on the development of armed forces and strategic doctrines.[91]

Carl Builder's *The Masks of War* provides insights into how service cultures, or, as Builder calls them, personalities, influence American military innovation. He believes that to understand these service personalities is "to understand much that has happened and much that will happen in the American military and national security arenas." Most useful are his view that "the dominant concepts of war held by military institutions have a significant effect upon the kinds of forces they acquire and train and, therefore, upon the kinds of wars they are prepared to fight" and the notion that "the services' dominant concepts of war probably serve their peacetime institutional interest better than they serve their preparedness for the next war."[92]

Other useful studies that deal with bureaucracy's impact on military innovation include Morton Halperin's *Bureaucratic Politics and Foreign Policy*, James Q. Wilson's *Bureaucracy: What Government Agencies Do and Why They Do It*, and Michael H. Armacost's *The Politics of Weapons Innovation: The Thor Jupiter Controversy*.[93] Additionally, doctrine is in many ways a paradigm, and Thomas Kuhn's *The Structure of Scientific Revolutions* is an invaluable tool in understanding how paradigms are formed and change and their implications for communities.[94]

Finally, the anthology *Military Innovation in the Interwar Period* attempts to provide insights "into the nature of the processes involved in major innovation and change in military organizations during the interwar period and to highlight those factors that encourage success as well as those that inhibit innovation."[95] In the concluding essay in *Military Innovation in the Interwar Period*, Williamson Murray and Barry Watts note that "given . . . the degree to which military innovation in peacetime is unavoidably nonlinear, contingent, and infected with serendipity, it seems best to avoid theoretical generalizations in probing for answers."[96] The story of the development of tanks and airplanes in the U.S. Army in the interwar era is extremely complex and defies any prescriptive answers. In the pages that follow, I examine the Army's experience with these technologies and attempt to explain what happened and why.

PART I

SOLDIERS AND MACHINES:
1917–1920

In some ways it was like the debate of a group of savages as to how to extract a screw from a piece of wood. Accustomed only to nails, they had made one effort to pull out the screw by main force, and now that it had failed they were devising methods of applying more force still, of obtaining more efficient pincers, of using levers and fulcrums so that more men could bring their strength to bear. They could hardly be blamed for not guessing that by rotating the screw it would come out after the exertion of far less effort; it would be a notion so different from anything they had ever encountered that they would laugh at the man who suggested it.

—C. S. Forester, *The General*

[1]

America, the Army, and the Great War

On April 2, 1917, President Woodrow Wilson stood before a special session of the U.S. Congress and asked for a declaration of war against the German Empire. Almost overnight, public opinion shifted from cautious, albeit increasingly pro-Allied, neutrality to overwhelming enthusiasm for intervention to stamp out the evils of "Prussianism." Americans' idealism was shared by their president, whose words before Congress echoed their sentiments: "The world must be made safe for democracy."[1] Wilson, who was convinced that only the United States could ensure a just peace, framed the war as a crusade, one worthy of American intervention:

> We shall fight for the things which we have always carried nearest our hearts—for democracy, for the right of those who submit to authority to have a voice in their own governments, for the rights and liberties of small nations, for a universal dominion of right by such a concert of free peoples as shall bring peace and safety to all nations and make the world itself at last free.[2]

Wilson's speech was enthusiastically received by Congress; its members voted for war by a margin of 82 to 6 in the Senate and 373 to 50 in the House. On April 6 the United States went to war with Germany. This event, perhaps more than any other in American history, marked a turning point in American foreign policy. For better or worse, the United States had entered into an association with the Allied powers, a major departure from its tradition of avoiding involvement in European affairs. This radical shift also had immense implications for the U.S. Army.

The Army on the eve of World War I was a reflection of the tasks long assigned to it by the civil government. Until late in the nineteenth century, its principal missions were to repress Native American opposition against continental expansion and to guard national coasts and borders. The excursions during the Mexican-American, Civil, and Spanish-American wars were anomalies; the Army quickly reverted to its traditional role as a frontier constabulary after each conflict. When it reached the West Coast the United States briefly tried to establish an overseas empire; after its victory over Spain, the Army merely shifted its garrisons from the western frontier to colonial outposts in the Philippines, Cuba, and Puerto Rico. Nevertheless, as the United States entered the twentieth century as a major economic and industrial power, some saw the need for change in its army.

Elihu Root, secretary of war from 1899 to 1904, was foremost among the individuals trying to drag the Army into the twentieth century. Root had analyzed the findings of a commission examining the conduct of the Spanish-American War and realized that many of the Army's problems in planning and supply were attributable to institutional weaknesses. His attempts at reform hinged on replacing the Army's tenured position of commanding general with a limited-term chief of staff, replacing the cumbersome branch-oriented bureaus of the War Department with a functional general staff, and revitalizing the Army educational system by establishing a war college.[3] Although Root was able to push through the establishment of a war college and a chief of staff office, his plans for a general staff met stiff resistance. American political leaders were wary of any kind of central war planning group, which many saw as similar to the Prussian autocratic state. Thus, when America entered World War I, only twenty General Staff officers were assigned to Washington, and the bureaus were still firmly entrenched.[4]

The small planning staff was constrained by more than numbers. President Wilson, committed to American neutrality, was enraged when he learned in 1916 that the War Department was developing contingency plans for a war with Germany and ordered a halt to such activity. Furthermore, the planners on the General Staff were busy trying to support the latest American foray into Mexico under the command of Gen. John J. Pershing. Lack of planning, however, was only one of the challenges the Army faced when confronted with the actuality of entering into a modern war in Europe. Other serious problems, particularly in personnel and industrial mobilization, soon became apparent.

On the eve of its entry into World War I, the U.S. Army was unprepared for a twentieth-century war. The most obvious deficiency was its size. On April 1, 1917, only 213,557 Regular Army and National Guard soldiers were active in federal service. The inadequacy of this force was made clear by the French offensive on the Aisne, which began with 800,000 men. By May 15, when the slaughter finally stopped, the French had suffered nearly 130,000 casualties and the Germans 163,000—losses equal to twice the size of the active-duty U.S. Army.[5] Moreover, the French Army almost disintegrated in the aftermath of the offensive; elements of fifty-five divisions mutinied, weakening the Allied position.[6] When the French mission arrived in Washington late in April, Marshal Joseph Joffre concisely stated what the Allies needed from the United States: "We want men, men, men."[7]

The challenge for the U.S. Army, however, was much more complex than recruiting enough soldiers. Gone were the days when the small Regular Army could be rapidly expanded with haphazardly trained volunteers for a temporary emergency against a minor power such as Spain or Mexico. The Great War demanded a mass army trained and equipped to fight a powerful opponent that was on the verge of defeating the Allies. The War Department had attempted to improve personnel mobilization through the provisions of the 1903 Dick Act and the more comprehensive National Defense Act of 1916. The latter, however, allowed for only 175,000 regular servicemen and 457,000 National Guardsmen—figures woefully inadequate in the context of the war in Europe.

Conscription was the answer to twentieth-century personnel mobilization problems. After passage of the Selective Service Act of May 18, 1917, American ranks began to swell almost immediately, and by the end of the conflict the Army numbered 3,685,458 officers and enlisted men. But forging these men into a viable army proved a difficult task. Although token American forces arrived in France in the summer of 1917, it was late May 1918 before the American Expeditionary Forces (AEF) in France were able to execute even limited offensive operations.[8]

The war on the western front was one not only of mass armies but also of mass firepower and increasing technological complexity. Supplies of artillery, machine guns, airplanes, poison gas, tanks, and—above all—munitions were necessary for modern warfare. Design and quantity production of this matériel required specialized research and industrial bases, and the United States had neither when it entered the war. Its army had traditionally relied on the War Department's limited technical services for its modest and unsophisticated munitions needs. The frontier constabulary had little demand for large numbers of machine guns and heavy artillery, much less poison gas.

The officers' attitude toward technological research and development also influenced the Army's state of preparedness. Most lacked confidence that civilian scientists would observe basic security measures and questioned even the military practicality of their efforts. Additionally, the powerful bureaus controlled military research and development and jealously guarded their prerogatives. Before the war they had focused on developing and testing proven designs—largely offered by independent inventors—rather than systematic research and development. The results of their efforts were disappointing. By early 1917 the Army still lacked a standardized machine gun and a field artillery piece equivalent to the French 75, which had been introduced in France in 1897.

[21]

The Army's lack of matériel preparedness also stemmed from the types of officers assigned to the technical services, a post many regarded as detrimental to their careers. Most positions in the technical services were filled through four-year details of officers from combat arms, such as the infantry. This policy tended to keep the most ambitious officers—those eager to make a mark in their own branches—out of the specialized technical services.[9] Nevertheless, the Army, although admittedly conservative, was not far behind the national trend in industrial research. Industrial research was in its infancy, and the government had done little to support or acknowledge it. Still, among government agencies, the Army was particularly backward.[10]

Finally, the bureaus also dominated the manufacture and procurement of military weapons and equipment, with little reference to private industry. The model 1903 Springfield rifle is a good example of the problems the Army encountered because of its almost exclusive reliance on government arsenals. By 1917 the Army had received 600,000 Springfields from federal manufacturers. When it became clear that this stockage and the limited production capacity of the government arsenals were inadequate to equip the rapidly swelling ranks of a national army, the Army had to turn to civilian industry for help. But American arms manufacturers were not tooled for producing Springfields, and modification of their assembly lines promised long delays. Fortunately, two American companies, Remington and Winchester, were producing Enfields for the British. As a stopgap measure, the government contracted with them to produce Enfields modified to fire American ammunition.

Similar difficulties were encountered with almost every aspect of military munitions and matériel procurement. The production facilities for the massive quantities of ordnance and equipment needed to supply the U.S. Army in 1917 could not be improvised, particularly for more sophisticated weapons such as tanks and airplanes. In the end, the Allies had to make up the difference.[11] By this point in the war, however, British and French war industries were running at full capacity and could compensate for American matériel shortfalls.

By early 1918 it was painfully apparent that the semiautonomous bureaus were capable of neither staying abreast of the demands of mobilization nor supporting General Pershing's growing AEF. In February 1918 Secretary of War Newton D. Baker finally addressed the need for centralized control of the War Department by reorganizing the General Staff and installing a new chief of staff. From this point forward the General Staff grew enormously in size and power, numbering 1,072 people before the end of the war. The new chief of staff, General Peyton C. March, had been Pershing's chief of artillery in France before returning to the United States at Baker's request. March was vigorous and efficient, if somewhat tactless, and rapidly gained control of the bureaus. By August 1918, using the temporary wartime authority of the May 20, 1918, Overman Act, he had structured a General Staff of four divisions: Operations; Military Intelligence; Purchase, Storage, and Traffic; and War Plans. He had also created the Air Service, Tank Corps, and Chemical Warfare Service.

March made the new arrangement work by ruthless—many said high-handed—tactics. He made some powerful enemies, particularly in Congress, and ultimately came into conflict with Pershing over the relationship between the War Department and General Headquarters in France. With Baker's support he tried to rein in the AEF.[12] Nevertheless, despite this controversy, March's leadership and management of the War Department provided Pershing with the tools to fight the war.

Given the prevailing conditions when the United States entered the war, the accomplishments of the War Department in support of the AEF were impressive: more than two million soldiers were mobilized, trained, and deployed overseas and nearly six million tons of supplies were procured and shipped to France.[13] These American forces were decisive in the Allied victory over Germany. Although not nearly as sophisticated in the ways of modern war as the Europeans, the Americans made up for their lack of experience and training with their enthusiasm, a quality long since bled out of the other war-weary armies.

The turning point in the war came in July 1918, when the Allies contained General Erich Ludendorff's offensive in the Second Battle of the Marne. The German attack, after some initial success, faltered under the weight of 800,000 casualties. The Allies held the initiative for the remainder of the war. But the German Army had lost more than momentum: the horrendous losses sapped morale and destroyed discipline in both the Army and the German civilian population.[14] It was in this regard that the American forces probably played their greatest role in the Allied victory:

> It was the Americans—not the handful of divisions in the line, but the huge and growing reserve of well-fed, unwearied, and unshaken men they supplied. Whereas in August the average field strength of a German battalion had sunk to 660–665 men, and the only fresh reserves were 300,000 men of the 1900 class called up in June, the American army in France had risen to 1,473,190. It was not the present that was impossible; it was the future. The British and French had won the battles of 1918, but it was the Americans who won the war.[15]

When the Armistice finally stopped the carnage on November 11, 1918, the U.S. Army faced two major tasks: demobilizing and developing a viable policy for the peacetime military establishment. Demobilization, in keeping with American tradition, was rapid. Within ten months of the Armistice, 3,280,000 soldiers returned to civilian life.[16] A postwar military policy, however, proved a thornier issue.

[23]

New legislation was vital, and even though consensus existed on the need for reorganization to correct the obvious deficiencies encountered during the war, there was little agreement on how the restructuring should proceed. Not surprisingly, General Pershing and General March were the key players in the congressional hearings on Army reorganization.

Pershing's perspective on the lessons of the war was largely informed by the proceedings of a board of officers he had appointed at his headquarters in Chaumont, France. Pershing's Superior Board met from April 27 to July 1, 1919. Available for its perusal were the proceedings of earlier boards of AEF experts on staff organization, Field Artillery, Heavy Artillery, Cavalry, Infantry, Signal Corps, Engineer Corps, and Medical Corps. Although the board had been chartered to examine only organization and tactics, it carried its inquiry much further. Its final report was divided into five main sections: the directing head, the separate arms of the combat forces, the arms combined, the administrative services, and the supply services.[17]

In the section on the directing head, the board stated its views on command and staff relationships. It stressed particularly that "no greater lesson can be drawn from the World War than that *Unity of Command* is absolutely vital to the success of military operations. All the activities of a separate military organization, large or small, must be controlled by the mind of the commander."[18] This statement probably alluded to the dispute between the AEF and the War Department General Staff over whether General Pershing or General March had precedence during the war, with the board predictably siding with Pershing. But the board did not stop with generalizations.

Major General Joseph T. Dickman, president of the Superior Board, and his colleagues delineated the functional lines along which all Army staffs should be organized, from the War Department down to battalions in the field; they called for separate directorates for personnel (G-1), intelligence (G-2), operations (G-3), and logistics (G-4). They further proposed that chiefs of arms for the infantry, artillery, cavalry, and aeronautics would be responsible for the development of tactics, training, equipment, organization, and doctrine in their branches. Finally, the board outlined the responsibilities of the chiefs of services, and made it clear that they would work under the supervision of the appropriate staff section, whether at the War Department or in the field. Apparently Dickman and company, all senior officers of the line, had little more affection for the bureaus than General March did.

The report emphasized organizational structure, roles, and responsibilities of the arms and services and the molding of the various pieces of a field army into an effective team. Proceeding from an apparent assumption of unconstrained resources, the report culminated in a best-case analysis of how to employ the U.S. Army in light of the experience of the AEF. Notably

[24]

absent was any detailed discussion of personnel or industrial mobilization; the report mentioned only briefly the low state of training in the rapidly expanded army. Examined closely, this document offers much more than a record of eminent officers' views on their army; it also opens a window onto their culture and lets us glimpse how it influenced their views on the need for change.

The generals sitting on the 1919 Superior Board were representative of the best of the "Old Army," and none more so than their president, General Dickman. Dickman was graduated from West Point in 1881, with a cavalry commission. The Army he joined was small; it never exceeded 2,200 officers or 27,000 enlisted men until the Spanish-American War. Before that war, the Army was scattered on the periphery of American civilization, largely in company-sized garrisons. The officer corps was a white male hierarchy with prescribed patterns of social behavior and a conservative bent. The seniority-based promotion system proceeded at a glacial pace.[19] Dickman was not promoted to major until 1906, when he was forty-eight years old and twenty-five years out of West Point.[20]

Nevertheless, it was Dickman and his contemporaries who witnessed the beginnings of a transition of the officer corps into a group of modern professionals. The same year Dickman graduated from West Point, General William T. Sherman, commanding general of the Army, established the School of Application for Infantry and Cavalry at Fort Leavenworth, Kansas; the founding of this school marked the shift from purely technical to professional officer education in the U.S. Army.[21] In 1883 Lieutenant Dickman was the honor graduate at Leavenworth. As an instructor, he later added to the credentials that made him a highly respected tactician. Dickman was also an original member of the War Department General Staff, and he drafted the 1905 Field Service Regulations, the bible of Army doctrine.

The vast majority of Dickman's service, however, was in the practical environment of the Army in the field. His early career reads like a campaign history of the Army in the closing years of the nineteenth century: service in the West fighting Native Americans and Mexicans, duty as a staff officer in the Santiago campaign during the Spanish-American War, command of an infantry regiment in action against Filipino insurgents on Panay, and fighting in China during the Boxer Rebellion. By 1917 Dickman was a brigadier general in command of the 85th Division; one year later he was a successful corps commander. After the Armistice he briefly commanded the Third Army as part of the American occupation forces, but five months later he was replaced, in part because of his open criticism of French occupation policies toward German civilians. Still, when he reported to Pershing's headquarters at Chaumont, Dickman was at the pinnacle of his profession. Highly respected as a staff officer and combat commander, he was selected to become one of the few permanent major generals in the Regular Army.

[25]

But how would six months of European combat affect the views of a sixty-one-year-old general with thirty-eight years of commissioned service when he assessed the implications of modern war for his army?

The other generals on the board, although younger than Dickman, had similar backgrounds. All but Hugh Drum were West Point graduates commissioned before the Spanish-American War, and all shared Dickman's extremely limited exposure to modern warfare.[22] As the members of this distinguished body deliberated in Chaumont, they tried to assimilate the lessons of a war that was largely foreign to both their training and their experience. What emerged from their consultations was in many ways a limited accommodation to present needs heavily influenced by the past.

A common thread running through the Superior Board's analysis was the belief that men, not machines, were the ultimate weapons. It followed logically that the infantry was the most important branch. As the board took pains to emphasize, "the infantry of an army must be recognized as the basic arm and all other arms must be organized and made subordinate to its needs, functions, and methods."[23] The American officers also shared with their peers in the British, French, and German armies the major assumptions that only offensive operations were decisive and heavy infantry casualties were inevitable. Although the Americans suffered only a fraction of the losses endured by the other combatants, they too had experienced the carnage of the Great War, with 117,000 casualties in the six weeks of the Meuse-Argonne offensive alone.[24] Nevertheless, an unmistakable air of both innocence and hauteur in the board's findings implied that the U.S. Army was somehow better than the armies it had joined on the western front. The board noted that "the stabilized trench warfare which prevailed in France in 1917 was due in a great measure to the lack of aggressiveness of both sides," stressing that "infantry must be self-reliant. Too much reliance was placed by the infantry on the auxiliary arms and not enough on the means within the infantry itself. This tended to destroy the initiative."[25] General Pershing shared the board's views: "The fact is that our officers and men are far and away superior to the tired Europeans."[26]

The board's continued faith in such skills as marksmanship and the bayonet charge might be explained by the fact that the Americans had been spared the butchery of three years of "big pushes" against impenetrable defenses heavily studded with machine guns and artillery. In September 1918, when the Americans had their chance to seize the initiative in the Meuse-Argonne offensive, they faced a shell of the once formidable German army and were part of a coordinated Allied effort. This limited but highly favorable experience seemed to reinforce the conviction that the U.S. Army's doctrine, based on the importance of the transition from trench combat to offensive open warfare, was basically sound. The major concessions to the European experiences in the Great War were the need to bolster foot soldiers with a higher density of modern weapons, especially machine guns and artillery, and an appreciation that the logistical support of mass armies was complex and critical.[27] Thus, in some areas the board's recommendations suggested that the war had caused at least an evolution, if not a revolution, in the military thinking of its members.

Still, some areas were sacrosanct. The role of the cavalry was one such area. General Pershing, like Dickman, was a cavalryman of unwavering faith. In late August 1918 he asked the War Department to provide the AEF with eight additional cavalry regiments.[28] The Superior Board echoed the sentiments of its commander by expressing disappointment that the American cavalry had not had a chance to demonstrate its capabilities. Again, as with American infantry, the board believed that American cavalrymen were better than European horsemen, who supposedly were hindered by continued reliance on the *arme blanche* (sword or lance) and inferior carbines. American doctrine, "relying on the rifle as the principal weapon," was deemed the correct approach, even though its correctness had never been demonstrated during the war.[29] The board stressed the effective use of cavalry by the Germans on the eastern front and by the Allies in Palestine and northern Italy, overlooking the inappropriateness of cavalry on the western front.

Turning to the postwar mission of defending the United States, particularly along the troublesome Mexican border, the board members found further uses for cavalry. Throughout the war nine cavalry regiments had been posted along that border, and even as the board met, units were pursuing marauding *villistas* in Mexico.[30] In statements that perhaps reflect a longing for the past more than an objective evaluation of the present, the board concluded that "it is improbable that the conditions of Northern France will ever be reproduced on American soil" and "on other fields and under different conditions our cavalry will find useful employment as in the past."[31]

The members of the board shared the assumption that the U.S. Army's fundamental operating principles were sound. Although some relatively minor improvements seemed indicated, the board members believed radical changes were unnecessary. After all, the Army had just decided a war that had stalemated modern European armies for more than three years. Furthermore, criticism of the Army would perhaps be an admission that they, as its leaders, were somehow inept.

As Dickman and his fellow board members labored in Chaumont, a similar exercise had been under way for some time in Washington. Secretary of War Baker and General March believed that the haphazard mobilization in 1917 required a reorganization of the Army. Since the Armistice, a group of officers in the War Plans Division had been working on a project to determine the structure of the postwar Regular Army, based on a peacetime strength of 500,000 officers and enlisted men. Although March had chosen this particular number, Baker and President Wilson concurred and approved a bill with that provision early in 1919.[32]

The Baker-March Bill strengthened the General Staff, emphasized officer education, enhanced industrial mobilization capabilities, and institutionalized organizational changes implemented during the war. Clearly, however, the bill focused on correcting the personnel mobilization problems the War Department had encountered in 1917. The heart of the proposal was the 500,000-man Regular Army. This force, organized into an expansible field army of five corps at half strength, would be responsible for defending the United States and its insular possessions. Reservists, prepared for active service through a system of universal military training, would fill out the Regular Army formations in any emergency.[33]

The bill quickly ran afoul of a legislative branch that reflected the general view of the American public regarding the late European conflict in particular and war in general. The Congress that began hearings on the Army Reorganization Bill in August 1919 was not the compliant group that had acquiesced in the desires of the executive branch during the wartime emergency. The Republicans had captured the majority in the 1918 elections and were bent on returning the country to prewar "normalcy." The Senate, led by Henry Cabot Lodge, was already deeply embroiled in a battle with President Wilson over the ratification of the Versailles treaty and the covenant for the League of Nations that it included, a contest the president finally lost in March 1920.[34] Pushing a major Regular Army bill through Congress would have been difficult for a chief of staff on the best of terms with the legislators; for March, deeply resented by many in Congress, failure was almost inevitable. Legislators' hostility to March, based largely on his perceived high-handedness during the war, was apparent in the comments of Representative Fiorello La Guardia. The World War I Air Service veteran charged that the chief of staff "has no consideration for the desires of Congress . . . [and] has all the despotic will and autocratic characteristics of Ludendorf[f] and the military genius [*sic*] of the Crown Prince." La Guardia concluded, "When I was a soldier I soldiered . . . when I legislate I want to legislate, and I do not want Peyton C. March to tell me what I have to legislate."[35]

Congressional resentment toward General March, a desire to reduce government expenditures, and the absence of any threat to national security were probably enough in themselves to defeat the 500,000-man Regular Army provision of the Baker-March Bill. The death blow, however, was administered when General Pershing, the hero of the AEF, testified: "I am of the opinion that we can place the outside figure [for the peacetime Regular Army] at from 275,000 to 300,000 officers and men."[36]

Pershing's views prevailed, and in June 1920 Congress passed a defense act calling for a regular army of 17,717 officers and 280,000 enlisted men.[37]

Furthermore, the War Department quickly discarded universal military training when opposition to it threatened passage of the entire bill. Instead, the Regular Army would be augmented by the voluntary National Guard and Organized Reserves during any emergency.

Nevertheless, the 1920 National Defense Act contained many progressive measures. In its final form it represented an amalgamation of March's bill, recommendations by officers recently returned from France (most notably Colonel John M. Palmer), and congressional compromises.[38] Under the provisions of the statute, a number of agencies and measures were reformed or modified, generally for the better. The assistant secretary of war was charged with overseeing procurement and industrial mobilization planning in an attempt to avoid the chaos experienced during the war. A more coherent General Staff structure was codified, and only officers qualified through higher military education were assigned to the body. The statute also more fully defined the roles of the National Guard and the Organized Reserves and established an organizational structure for personnel mobilization that replaced the territorial system with a tactical organization of nine corps areas. Each corps area contained one Regular Army division, two National Guard divisions, and the framework of three Organized Reserve divisions.

The act also added agencies to the peacetime military establishment and incorporated the Chemical Warfare Service and Finance Department into the War Department structure because of their demonstrated importance as temporary organizations during the war. Furthermore, the act created posts for chiefs of cavalry, field artillery, and infantry. The duties specified for these branch chiefs were similar to those outlined by Pershing's Superior Board: the chiefs were responsible, within their respective branches, for developing technology, doctrine, and organizations; running service schools; and assigning personnel.

The National Defense Act of 1920 attempted to establish a coherent military policy to correct the massive problems encountered during the American mobilization for World War I. In its final form, the act was a reconciliation of the political realities of the traditional American dislike of standing armies, postwar demobilization, and a hazy realization that the country needed to revamp its defense policies, particularly since any threat to national security seemed remote. It was within this institutional framework that the U.S. Army had to accommodate the new technologies that had demonstrated their military potential during the war. Most prominent were the tank and the airplane.[39]

[2]

The Tank Corps

In the early morning hours of September 15, 1916, the crews of forty-nine British Mark I tanks made their final preparations for battle. They were part of General Sir Douglas Haig's renewed Somme offensive, which had begun with high hopes on July 1 but stalled before the withering fire of German Maxim guns. Casualties were high. On the first day, the British Army lost 57,450 men—the highest toll of any single day in its history. But Haig, ever the optimist, was convinced a positive outcome was possible. He staked his hopes on a belief that the Germans had suffered heavily from the attrition of the past two months and that a determined attack could rupture their weakened lines. Cavalry divisions, waiting in reserve to exploit the expected breakthrough, would pour through the breaches.[1]

Haig also hoped that his anticipated success on the battlefield would relieve some of the pressure coming from London. The heavy casualties caused by his tactics of headlong assault brought mounting criticism from the British Cabinet and the Imperial General Staff. Furthermore, Haig had to force a decision quickly, because the weather was beginning to turn. Haig saw the Somme offensive as the last chance to win the war in 1916; it was time for a final big push.

Haig believed that the surprise effect of the small tank force would give his infantry an edge by destroying any German strong points not neutralized by the artillery. To this end, he ordered the machines spread along his entire line. In so employing the few tanks then available to the British Army, Haig overrode the advice of Colonel Ernest D. Swinton, the chief of the British tank arm, to keep the new weapon a secret until a large force could be equipped and trained.[2] Haig was not of a mind to wait; if tanks could make any contribution to the attack, he would use them.

When the attack began against Flers-Courcelette, only thirty-two of the primitive tanks could move forward with the attacking infantry, with just nine covering the distance to the German lines. The tanks proved valuable by causing panic in the German ranks. Even though the handful of tanks and their accompanying infantry could not exploit the breakthrough, Haig was sufficiently pleased with their contribution to establish a separate head-quarters for the new weapon under the command of Lieutenant Colonel Hugh Elles. Over the ensuing months Elles and his two primary assistants, Captain Giffard Martel and Major J. F. C. Fuller, grappled with the lessons of the Somme offensive as they also tried to develop a coherent tank doctrine, something not available when the first machines were hurried into combat in September.[3]

The British experiences and evolving doctrine shaped American attitudes toward the new weapon. Before the arrival of the American Expeditionary Forces (AEF) in France, the primary source of information from the front was the American Military Mission in Paris. The mission's initial reports were cool toward the tanks because of their lackluster performance with British and French forces after the Somme offensive. When General Pershing arrived in France, he detailed a board of officers to make recommendations on the tank program for the AEF and placed a member of his staff, Colonel LeRoy Eltinge, in charge of tank matters. This board was more enthusiastic than the American Military Mission about tanks and recommended adoption of the British heavy and French light tanks and formation of a separate tank force with its own chief.[4] The board stressed that "the tank is considered a factor which is destined to become an important element in this war" and that "tanks should be used in quantity or not at all."[5]

As organizational plans for the AEF evolved, so, too, did plans for tanks. On September 23 Pershing approved the concept of the Overseas Tank Corps, which was based on the force necessary to support twenty divisions. Hence, the AEF forwarded a request to the War Department for five heavy and twenty light battalions, which required 375 heavy and 1,500 light tanks.[6]

Stating requirements, however, proved much simpler than getting tanks. American attempts to procure tanks made the hapless Springfield rifle program seem like a model of efficiency. In October the chief ordnance officer, AEF, detailed two officers, Majors Drain and Alden, to "collect all information obtainable on the use, design, and production of Tanks."[7] Following the completion of their report on November 10, Major Drain became a member of the new Inter-Allied Tank Commission, a body that attempted to coordinate British, French, and American tank production efforts. One of the commission's first major initiatives was a joint Anglo-American project to produce heavy tanks.

On December 6 the War Department approved a joint venture with the British to produce 1,500 Liberty Mark VIII tanks, so called because they would use American Liberty engines. On January 22, 1918, the American ambassador to England, Walter Hines Page, and the British foreign secretary, Arthur Balfour, met in London and signed an agreement confirming the details of the coproduction arrangement. Each country would provide one-half of the components for the heavy tank.[8] The Americans were responsible for "engines, transmissions, forgings, chains, and other components," while the British would furnish "6pdr guns, ammunition, and armour."[9] These components would be shipped to France for assembly. Deliveries were to begin in July, with the first 1,500 tanks to be completed by October 1918.[10] Although this plan looked promising on paper, its implementation proved much more difficult.

The Mark VIII program competed for Liberty engines with the American aviation program. At this point in the war, the strained industrial base of the United States could not meet the demands of either program, much less both. Despite a repeated litany of revised delivery schedules, no American components ever reached France. The British also had difficulties. The German offensive in March 1918 severely taxed British munitions industries and lowered the priority of the Mark VIII program. By the end of the war, the British had produced only 100 tank component sets. Even if the component production problems had been resolved, there was no place to assemble the tanks, because the French assembly plant was not completed before the Armistice.[11]

American attempts to procure light tanks were similarly hamstrung. Efforts to obtain an agreement with the French to make the light tank in the United States were slow and tedious. Renault, a private concern, made the French light tank and was reluctant to release its proprietary design information. When Renault and AEF representatives eventually worked out a royalties arrangement and design plans, two models of the Renault tank finally went to the United States. On February 2, 1918, the War Department forwarded an estimated delivery schedule that promised 100 American-built Renaults in April, 300 in May, and 600 each following month.[12] As with the Mark VIII estimates, this forecast proved unrealistic. The first two American-built Renault light tanks arrived in France on November 20, 1918—more than a week after the Armistice.[13]

Lack of focus and coordination plagued American tank production as well. Rather than producing the approved War Department designs, Ford Motor, Holt Tractor, General Electric, Endicott-Johnson, and Pioneer Tractor all pursued independent efforts to build tanks.[14] The lack of tanks greatly influenced the organization of the American Tank Corps and caused difficulties for its chief, Colonel Samuel D. Rockenbach.

Colonel Rockenbach arrived at the General Headquarters of the AEF on December 22, 1917, and assumed duties as the chief of the Tank Corps. Rockenbach, an 1889 graduate of the Virginia Military Academy, was a cavalry officer trying to get to a combat unit. Since 1915 he had been assigned to the Quartermaster Corps and had served under General Pershing as the quartermaster officer for the Punitive Expedition in Mexico. During this campaign he had organized the first-ever American logistical system reliant on motor transport. When Pershing became commander of the AEF, he took Rockenbach with him to France, again as his quartermaster. Rockenbach performed superbly, particularly in establishing Base Section 1, which supported the arrival of American forces. In time, Pershing chose this trusted subordinate to head the new Tank Corps.

Rockenbach got an early taste of the immensity of the task facing him as commander of the Tank Corps during his initial reception at the General Headquarters: "The officer of the General Staff in charge of Tank matters pulled open the lowest drawer of his desk, took out a bundle of papers, handed them out, and said, 'Here's all we know about Tanks, go after them.'"[15] The papers Rockenbach received contained the September 1 report by the AEF board, a report on French light and British heavy tanks, and Pershing's September 23 memorandum to the War Department on the Overseas Tank Corps program.

Rockenbach headed an organization that did not exist. While he awaited delivery of his tanks, he began work on the other aspects of establishing a military organization. Rockenbach believed that he was on his own, recording that "all sections of the General Staff and Service Departments had all they could do and could give no help."[16] Nevertheless, Rockenbach had some able assistance.

When Rockenbach assumed his duties in December, several officers were already working with tanks. One of them, Captain George S. Patton Jr., was in the original contingent that had sailed for France with General Pershing. He, like Rockenbach, chafed in his job away from the action as the commander of the troops for Pershing's headquarters.[17] He was an ambitious officer, and the new tank organization appealed to him. On November 6, 1917, he wrote to his father that he had been asked by Colonel Eltinge to transfer to tanks and head the American tank school. He gave his reasons for accepting:

> Here is the golden dream. 1st. I will run the school 2. Then they will organize a battalion. I will command it 3. Then if I make good and the T. [tanks] do and the war lasts I will get the first regiment. 4. With the same "IF" as before they will make a brigade and I will get the star [of a brigadier general].
> On the other hand if I commanded a battalion [of infantry] it might be in reserve in an emergency and some one else get the credit.[18]

On November 10 Patton transferred to tanks. Since the French were doing most of the work with light tanks, Patton toured the French tank school and the Renault works. He also visited with Colonel J. F. C. Fuller, then the chief of staff of the British Tank Corps, and discussed the recent British tank battle at Cambrai.

Upon returning to Chaumont, Patton and his assistant, Lieutenant Elgin Braine, wrote their report. The memorandum, entitled "Light Tanks," was a practical report that dealt with the technical aspects of tanks and their manufacture. It outlined tables of organization, discussed the evolution of British and French tank tactics, and proposed an instructional methodology for American tank troops.[19]

Patton soon had the opportunity to put his plans into action. On December 15 he left the headquarters for Bourg to establish the Tank School.[20] Thus, when Rockenbach became chief, much of the preliminary work for light tanks had already been accomplished by Patton. The same work remained for heavy tanks.

For heavy tanks, Rockenbach relied on the British for advice and assistance. Americans visited British tank units and even participated in maneuvers near Arras. They also inspected the British training centers at Merlimont, France, and Wool, England. Rockenbach was either much impressed with the British operation or, more probably, realized that he would be fully occupied with the effort at Langres, because he decided to send American heavy tank personnel to England for their training.[21] With procurement, organization, and training moving forward, Rockenbach turned his attention to other pressing matters.

The tank force that Rockenbach attempted to bring together had logistical requirements different from any other ground unit in the AEF. Tank tracks were made of steel plates, riveted and pinned into a continuous circuit, and had a very short life span. The standard British heavy Mark IV tank had to have a new set of tracks every twenty miles. Movement to the battlefield from marshaling areas thus required tractor trailers for light tanks and trains for heavy tanks.[22] Additionally, tanks consumed prodigious amounts of fuel; because light tanks could travel only thirty miles and heavy tanks fifty before refueling, more trucks were needed for fuel resupply.[23] Rockenbach had to find trucks, tractors, and trailers to support these unique logistical demands. He chose to rely on existing commercial vehicles to meet the needs of the Tank Corps but had to compete with other units for their allocation.[24]

Rockenbach also had to compete for personnel. Tank Corps soldiers came from both the sustaining base in the United States and the AEF. The AEF requested 50 officers and 100 noncommissioned officers from the War Department, and the Tank Corps was allowed to recruit 600 volunteers from within the AEF for the light tank forces at Langres.[25]

To manage tank matters in the United States, the War Department appointed Colonel Ira C. Welborn to head up the tank service. Additionally,

[34]

the War Department established tank training camps at Camp Colt in Get-tysburg, Pennsylvania, and Camp Polk, near Raleigh, North Carolina.[26] By early 1918 the War Department had formalized personnel authorizations at 14,827 for the deployed forces and 16,600 for the stateside training opera-tions.[27] On March 21 the AEF received approval for five heavy and twenty light tank battalions and for their supporting headquarters, repair and sal-vage, and depot units.[28] Officers and enlisted men slowly began to trickle into the new schools in the United States and at Bourg, but few tanks were available for training.[29]

Lack of tanks, not men, was the greatest problem facing the new Tank Corps. In June the Inter-Allied Tank Committee, consisting of the chiefs of the French, British, Italian, and American Tank Corps, convened at Ver-sailles. One topic on the agenda was the problem of how to equip the Amer-ican forces with tanks. Despite promises from the Ordnance Department to the contrary, it was becoming obvious to Rockenbach that no tanks from American sources would be available until 1919. The French promised to equip two light battalions with Renaults, while the British agreed to provide Mark V heavy tanks to the American tank battalion training in England. The British offer was contingent on the attachment of the American heavy bat-talion to British forces for operations, however.[30] Rockenbach summed up the sad state of affairs on the eve of the commitment of the American Tank Corps to combat:

> *Situation on August 20th, 1918.* The American Tank Corps in France did not have a fighting Tank. It consisted of 600 trained personnel for Light Tanks and 800 trained personnel for Heavy Tanks. 1200 men for Heavy Tanks were training in England and 12 companies of Light Tanks were enroute from the United States.
>
> In the United States we had thirty Light Tank Companies and 15 Heavy Tank Companies. The personnel carefully selected and the companies well trained as Infantry, machine gunners, truck drivers, and motor mechanics. They had never seen a Tank.[31]

The doctrine for the employment of the American Tank Corps was less vexing. Soon after assuming command, Rockenbach dictated a simple, straightforward principle that became the cornerstone of Tank Corps doc-trine: "The function of Tanks is to assist the Infantry by making a path for it through the wire and protecting it from destructive loss from machine gun and rifle fire." Tactics were similarly constrained: "As to tactics for Tanks, Tanks were to conform to the tactics of Infantry. They were an auxiliary arm and must conform."[32]

For the specifics of how to apply this doctrine, the Americans relied on the British. On May 18, 1918, the War Department published Document No. 804, *Infantry and Tank Co-operation and Training*, a verbatim reprint of the

[35]

British pamphlet bearing the same title.[33] This publication stressed the importance of the assault and the primacy of the infantry on the battlefield. Tanks, like all other auxiliary arms, assisted the assaulting infantry. Tanks were deemed capable of providing material and moral support and knocking out enemy positions—or at least getting the occupants to duck for cover.

This approach was fairly conventional and did not differ greatly from General Haig's use of tanks in the Somme offensive. Nevertheless, the lessons of Cambrai were beginning to have some influence. The infantry was enjoined to exploit the opportunities offered by successful tank action. Mention, albeit brief, was made of tanks operating "independently in advance of infantry."[34] Still, the overwhelming emphasis was on the tank as a way to assist the infantry in assaulting enemy trench works. The slow, two- to three-mile-per-hour battlefield speed of the early tanks did not encourage a larger role. The pamphlet also specified the administrative control of tank units. Tanks were General Headquarters assets that would be allocated, usually as brigades, to armies for the duration of a specified operation.

In December 1918 the American Tank Corps finally published its own manual on tanks. *Tanks: Organization and Tactics,* stated that "tanks are essentially an Infantry supporting arm or an auxiliary to the Infantry and only on rare occasions should they act independently."[35] These rare independent missions involved attacking a retreating enemy force or assaulting infantry reserves to prevent the organized opposition to advancing infantry, provided the enemy's main line of resistance had been overcome and his artillery silenced. As with British tank forces, American units were assigned to General Headquarters and organized into brigades for operations. Brigades contained one heavy battalion of forty-five tanks, two light battalions of ninety tanks, and one repair and salvage company.[36] American combat experience would soon show the appropriateness of these limited roles.

American tank forces received their baptism of fire during the September 1918 offensive to reduce the St. Mihiel salient. Rockenbach was the chief of the Tank Corps, First American Army. The 304th Tank Brigade, under the command of Lieutenant Colonel Patton, was attached to IV Corps. The brigade consisted of the 344th and 345th Light Tank Battalions, commanded by Major Sereno E. Brett and Captain Ranulf Compton, respectively, and two attached French tank groups. The attack began on September 12. Patton's brigade had 174 tanks—all light Renaults, except for the 24 heavy Schneider tanks in the French units.[37] German resistance during the four-day operation was light, and losses to direct enemy action were low. Only one American and one French tank were destroyed by enemy fire. The inherent frailty of the tanks themselves caused most of the losses. On the first day alone, twenty-two tanks were lost to "ditching" (getting stuck in shell craters or trenches) and twenty-one to mechanical failure. Still, Patton's brigade had performed commendably, and his tanks had helped the infantry advance.[38] The coming Meuse-Argonne offensive provided an even more severe test.

The Meuse-Argonne offensive was the largest American effort during the war. On September 26 the attack began, supported by 189 tanks, 142 of which were operated by Americans.[39] German resistance was much heavier than that encountered during the St. Mihiel operation.[40] Again, ditching and mechanical failures caused most of the tank losses. By the third day of the offensive, only eighty-three tanks were available, and the entire French contingent had withdrawn because of the exhaustion of its equipment. On the fourth day of action, the 304th Brigade fielded only fifty-five tanks. The attrition continued. Only thirty tanks remained by October 5, and the majority of these were mechanically unreliable. Finally, Rockenbach had to withdraw what remained of the brigade for repairs. The most the Tank Corps could muster to support the remainder of the offensive was a provisional company composed of twenty-four Renaults under Captain Courtney Barnard.[41] When the last great assault began on November 1, only sixteen tanks were available.[42]

The 301st Heavy Tank Battalion, assigned to the British 2nd Tank Brigade, saw even less action than the 304th Tank Brigade. In late September the 301st Heavy Tank Battalion supported the II American Corps in its assault on the Hindenberg line.[43]

These limited actions in the St. Mihiel and Meuse-Argonne offensives constituted the total operational experience of the American Tank Corps. Nevertheless, decisions about the future role of the tank in the U.S. Army were based largely on these operations.

Rockenbach first analyzed the significance of tank forces to the U.S. Army. On October 20, with only Captain Barnard's small contingent still in the battle, Rockenbach had time to finish a brief report, "The Role of Tanks in Modern Warfare." He began by tracing the evolution of the tank as a means to break the deadlock on the western front, a stand-off caused by the ascendant machine gun. He asserted that tanks were a "separate weapon; they are not mechanical cavalry, neither are they artillery or armored infantry." Tanks, said Rockenbach, were an offensive, not a defensive, weapon.[44] They were assault forces, with each class of tank having a distinct role:

> The function of large, medium, and small Tanks in the attack is as follows: where the enemy has intrenched [sic] and is well covered by wire entanglement, the large tanks go with and in front of the leading infantry, clear the way for the infantry and small tanks, reduce strong points, and keep the enemy's infantry in the strong points under cover until the infantry arrives. . . . The small tanks will take care of all those missed by the Heavy Tank. The fast [medium] Tanks will proceed into the enemy's rear, work as much havoc as possible, and return, in short, they are simply raiders.[45]

Rockenbach's comments on the medium tanks as raiders were speculative and based on what he knew about the experimental British medium tank, the Whippet. This tank was supposed to be capable of moving ten to twenty miles per hour, with a radius of action of about 100 miles. Rockenbach also envisioned a role for light and medium tanks in the exploitation of a successful attack, assisting "Cavalry, Motorized Artillery, and Infantry in motor trucks."[46]

Nevertheless, Rockenbach's views had not changed much since he took over the tank corps in December 1917: Tanks were "an additional weapon which has been introduced to aid the infantry in accomplishing its task." Although possessed of a somewhat broader view of how this cardinal principle was to be accomplished than most of his contemporaries, Rockenbach was emphatic that tanks "must be used to *help the infantry to accomplish their task*."[47] Perhaps what Rockenbach was really arguing was that the tank was a sufficiently important weapon to justify the continuance of the Tank Corps as a separate arm.

The views of the postwar Superior Board were more constrained. When the Superior Board turned its attention to the future role of tanks in the U.S. Army, its members were surely informed by the experiences of the Tank Corps. Although frightening in combat, tanks had not performed impressively. The Renault light tanks and Mark V heavy tanks could move barely five miles per hour under the most favorable operating conditions. On the battlefields of the western front, their rate of advance had generally been much slower, and they were often ditched. The tanks frequently ran out of fuel or simply broke down, problems unfamiliar and troublesome to the existing logistical system. The board members concerned themselves with the demonstrated capabilities of the tank, not wasting time to consider its potential: "The tank should be recognized as an infantry supporting and accompanying weapon incapable of independent decisive action."[48] Logically, then, the board recommended relegation of its future development to the chief of infantry. In the opinion of the Superior Board, there was no need for a separate tank corps in the postwar Army.[49]

Still, there was a chance that the Tank Corps would survive, since the Baker-March Bill provided for it. During the congressional hearings on the bill, General March testified that the arm was "technical enough and important enough to keep it as a separate corps."[50] General Rockenbach also lobbied on behalf of his corps. He returned from France in August 1919 and by mid-September had reported to the War Department General Staff on the need for a tank corps. Still, his arguments inextricably tied the tank to the infantry: "*The functions of Tanks* are to make a path thru obstacles for the Infantry and protect it from destructive loss from machine guns."[51] The economy-minded Congressmen picked up on this linkage—they were "unable absolutely to see any reason during peace times for the creation of the overhead that would have to be established to give . . . a separate organization." The testimony of the prestigious General Pershing, however, was probably the key factor in deciding the fate of the Tank Corps. The former AEF commander noted: "The Tank Corps should not be a large organization, only of sufficient numbers, I should say, to carry on investigations and conduct training with the Infantry, and I would place it under the Chief of the Infantry as an adjunct of that arm."[52] The Congressmen heeded the celebrated general's advice, and the National Defense Act of 1920 placed all tank units in the infantry.[53]

The National Defense Act established the institutional arrangements for the Army's future development of the tank. The chief of infantry would decide its doctrine and determine the levels of funding it would receive as one of many infantry weapons. General Rockenbach, reflecting on this decision in his last report as the chief of the Tank Corps, made what would prove to be a remarkably prescient statement: "The successful value of the [tank] arm in the future depends upon the sympathy and support it is given."[54]

[3]

The Air Service

When the United States entered World War I, the airplane, unlike the tank, was an accepted technology within the Army. Indeed, the Army's interest in aeronautics had begun during the Civil War. On June 9, 1861, James Allen and Dr. William H. Helme conducted a balloon demonstration for the Army in Washington. Thereafter, balloons were used intermittently for observation until 1863, when the nascent Federal Balloon Corps was disbanded. Army interest in aeronautics remained dormant until 1892, when a balloon section was incorporated in the Signal Corps. When the Spanish-American War began, the Army deployed its one balloon to Cuba, where it was used with some success for reconnaissance.[1]

Following the war, interest in aeronautics increased. On August 1, 1907, the chief signal officer established the Aeronautical Division within the Signal Corps to "handle all matters relating to military ballooning, air machines, and all kindred subjects."[2] In August 1908 the Army bought a dirigible from Thomas S. Baldwin. This balloon marked an improvement in capability, because the airship could propel itself at nearly twenty miles per hour.[3] The lighter-than-air group within Army aeronautics was an enthusiastic clique and would remain a part of Army aviation until the 1940s.[4] The preeminence of the "balloonatics," however, rapidly dissipated with the emergence of a heavier-than-air technology.

Army involvement in heavier-than-air aeronautics dates from 1898, the year the War Department funded aircraft experiments by Dr. Samuel P. Langley. Langley's earlier success flying unpiloted models of powered craft had impressed the Army and Navy sufficiently to fund his further experiments. On October 7 and December 8, 1903, Langley failed in his attempts to launch his manned machine. Following the second failure, the Board of Ordnance and Fortification terminated its financial support. Nine days after Langley's final setback, Orville and Wilbur Wright made the first successful piloted flight of a powered, heavier-than-air machine. Although the primitive craft traveled only 852 feet in its longest flight on December 17, it began a revolution. Improvements in the Wright brothers' design were rapid, and within the year a new airplane made a sustained flight of almost twenty-five miles. Nevertheless, the War Department showed little interest in the Wright brothers' machine, probably because of their experiences with Langley. In December 1907 the Signal Corps opened competitive bidding for a heavier-than-air flying machine. The Wright brothers' entry prevailed, and on February 10, 1908, they won the contract to provide the Army with its first flying machine.[5]

Between 1908 and the U.S. entry into World War I, the War Department tried to determine the place of the airplane in the military establishment. Progress was steady if unspectacular. On March 3, 1911, Congress made its first appropriation—$125,000—for military aviation. By 1913 congressional interest had increased: The 1914 Army Appropriation Act allowed a maximum of 30 officer aviators, a substantial increase compared with the 1912 strength of only 12 officers.[6] In a more radical vein, Virginia Representative James Hay introduced bills in 1913 to create an aviation corps as part the Army.[7]

Most of the Army aviators who testified on Hay's bill saw no reason for a divorce from the Signal Corps. First Lieutenant Benjamin D. Foulois, for two years the only Army pilot, was indifferent about the location of airplanes in the War Department structure, so long as aviation obtained competent personnel. Captain William Mitchell, First Lieutenant H. H. Arnold, and Second Lieutenant Thomas De W. Milling also supported keeping aviation in the Signal Corps.[8] Only one officer, Captain Paul W. Beck, dissented from this position. He believed that the United States was behind other countries in the development of the "aggressive" potential of the airplane as a bomber, a situation that could be rectified only by creating a separate aviation corps.[9] Captain Mitchell disagreed and was adamant that the most important military roles for the airplane were strategic reconnaissance and artillery spotting. Mitchell also commented on the aggressive use of the airplane: "The offensive value of this thing has not been proved. It is being experimented with—bomb dropping and machines carrying guns are being experimented with—but there is nothing to it so far except in an experimental way."[10] Although Representative Hay did not get a separate aviation corps, his highly amended bill, enacted on July 18, 1914, granted Army aviation its first statutory basis. The act created an aviation section within the Signal Corps and increased personnel allowances to a maximum of 60 officers and 260 enlisted men.[11]

The demonstrated importance of airplanes in the war in Europe increased the War Department's appreciation of their potential. A 1915 War College study recommended an Army organization structured into five tactical divisions. Eight aerosquadrons—one for each of the five divisions, with the other three allocated to Army forces in the Philippines, Hawaii, and Panama —were also recommended.[12] The National Defense Act of 1916 codified most of the views contained in the War College study and further recognized the importance of aviation. Although not specifying a number of aviation units, the act authorized the creation of one aerosquadron per infantry division.[13] Furthermore, the legislation increased aviation section officer authorizations from 60 to 148.[14] Even with this increased emphasis, Army aviation—with only 65 officers, 1,120 enlisted men, and less than 300 outmoded airplanes—was in a pitiful state when the United States declared war in April 1917.[15]

The mobilization problems facing the aviation section were similar in most respects to those confronting the rest of the Army. Personnel had to be recruited, trained, and organized, and equipment had to be procured. But in 1917 the United States lacked an industrial base capable of supporting large-scale airplane production, since no significant commercial market existed. The Army was the chief purchaser, and before the war it had received fewer than 400 airplanes from American manufacturers. Indeed, on the eve of the war, there were only a dozen or so aircraft manufacturers in the United States, none of which were making airplanes suitable for combat.[16] Furthermore, no single agency in the federal government was responsible for rationalizing aviation policy.

In April 1917 three separate agencies were involved in aviation matters bearing directly on the Army. Under the National Defense Act of 1916, the chief signal officer was responsible for the development of Army aviation.[17] But his authority was limited by two other agencies involved in aviation research, the National Advisory Committee for Aeronautics and the National Research Council. In addition, the National Advisory Committee for Aeronautics and the Council on National Defense were both involved in production matters.[18]

Congress had created the National Advisory Committee for Aeronautics in March 1915 to further the development of American aviation. Under its broad charter, it acted as a clearinghouse for inventions and monitored the capabilities of the nascent civilian aviation industry.[19] The National Research Council, created in 1916 by the National Academy of Sciences during the preparedness craze, was an effort to "organize an arsenal of science . . . to promote cooperation among the nation's research institutions and among leading scientists and engineers."[20] Finally, in August 1916, Congress established the Council on National Defense to coordinate industrial mobilization and the allocation of resources.[21] The activities of all of these agencies were fundamental to the establishment of a viable aircraft industry. Unfortunately, it soon became apparent that they lacked the unity of purpose to fulfill that task.

Over the ensuing months various agencies and boards—the Aircraft Production Board, the Joint Army and Navy Technical Board, the equipment division in the office of the chief signal officer, and the Aircraft Board— evolved to try to bring coherence to the aviation program. By May of 1918, despite much expense and effort, the aviation industry had accomplished little, engendering a torrent of public and congressional criticism.[22]

On May 20, 1918, President Wilson created within the War Department the Division of Military Aeronautics and the Bureau of Aircraft Production, which ended the role of the Signal Corps. However, the lack of centralized effort was not resolved. The military-controlled Division of Military Aeronautics oversaw operational requirements; the civilian-led Bureau of Aircraft Production controlled production. Their efforts were not coordinated until August 1918. Finally, the position of director of the air service section, as a second assistant secretary of war, was created to oversee the activities of both organizations, but the potential offered by this realignment was not realized before the Armistice.[23]

Further complicating the American aircraft production effort at its inception were two fundamental issues: how many and what types of airplanes should be produced. The basis of the initial American aircraft program was a cable received on May 24, 1917, from Alexandre Ribot, the French Premier.[24] The implications of the request were enormous. Ribot asked for "the formation of a flying corps of 4500 airplanes—personnel and matériel included—to be sent to the French front during the campaign of 1918." He further recommended that "2,000 airplanes should be constructed each month as well as 4000 engines, by the American factories," adding that "during the first six months of 1918, 16,500 planes (of the latest type) and 30,000 engines will have to be built."[25]

Based on the Ribot cable, the Joint Army and Navy Technical Board prepared a report delineating production requirements. The number of airplanes stipulated was mind-boggling: 4,000 reconnaissance and artillery control, 6,667 fighting, and 1,333 bombing, for a total of 12,000.[26] In July Congress appropriated $640 million to support the program.[27] Nevertheless, as with the tank, the Army soon found that stating requirements and providing funding did not automatically produce airplanes. The American aviation industry, never having produced aircraft in any quantity, let alone of the types of planes envisioned by the Joint Army and Navy Technical Board, needed design information before it could proceed. To this end, the War Department assembled a technical mission.[28]

The Bolling Mission, led by Major Raynal C. Bolling, sailed for Europe in June 1917. Its primary tasks were to select the types of Allied airplanes to be produced in the United States and to make arrangements with Allied manufacturers for production rights and expedite the shipment of specific models to the United States. Ninety-three skilled mechanics and factory experts accompanied the twelve military and civilian technicians and engineers of the Bolling Mission to study Allied aircraft production methods firsthand.[29] The men visited England, France, and Italy and on July 31 decided what types of aircraft the United States would use. They chose for observation and day bombing the British DeHaviland DH-4, for aerial combat the British Bristol and French SPAD, and for night bombing the Italian Caproni.[30] Of these designs, only the DH-4 was ever mass-produced in the United States.

Aside from the administrative problems in directing the aviation program and the inherent weakness of the native industry, a number of other factors hampered American efforts. Designs were slow in reaching the United States, spruce wood for constructing airframes was initially in short supply, and changes and conflicting orders to the industry were disruptive.[31] Another element—the decision to use the Liberty engine in American-produced airplanes—also slowed production. The Liberty engine was designed with the commendable goal of providing a superior engine with the capacity for mass production and use in all American airframes. Unfortunately, the effect of this decision in practice was to "stultify creative design and the development of aircraft as a whole."[32] For example, American efforts to adapt the British Bristol to accommodate the Liberty engine were an abject failure.[33]

Producing bombers was also a problem. Difficulties in the Caproni bomber project were insurmountable, and an American version never entered into combat. Eventually, the chief of Air Service, American Expeditionary Forces (AEF), agreed with the British to produce parts kits in America for their Handley-Page, a bomber regarded as inferior to the Caproni. The kits would be shipped to England for assembly and equip American night bombing squadrons. This effort was also largely a failure. At the end of the war only two American-built Handley-Page night bombing squadrons were training in England, and they never saw frontline service.[34] Even with the seemingly simpler issues involved in fighter production, it soon became apparent that the industry as it existed in the United States would not be able to mass-produce a design that could compete in a war in which "the improvement in pursuit airplanes was so rapid that few types retained their superiority for more than six months."[35] The American aviation industry simply did not have the experience to cope with the challenges of rapid technological evolution.

The American producers, even with approved designs in hand, faced many problems. In August 1917 a sample DH-4 shipped by the Bolling Mission was available for American tests. By October the necessary modifications to convert to the Liberty engine were complete, and on October 18 the Liberty-powered DH-4 was ordered into mass production. The American DH-4 program, although plagued by a series of disruptive glitches, mass-produced airplanes. Still, the process took time, and the first DH-4 did not arrive in France until May 11, 1918. Large-scale deliveries did not begin until July, when the American version of the DH-4 was obsolete by western front standards. Still, the AEF pressed the airplane into service, and on August 2, 1918, the first American squadron completely equipped with DH-4s produced in the United States flew an operational mission in France.[36] This mission may have been a salve to American pride, but it was hardly a comfort to the pilots who had to fly the DH-4 against superior German airplanes. Fortunately, most American tactical squadrons were equipped with more up-to-date French machines.[37]

One of the conclusions of the Bolling Mission was that the United States could not be relied on for aircraft in any quantity until July 1918. Therefore, the availability of foreign aircraft would in large measure determine organizational decisions. Without airplanes, squadrons could not become operational. Accordingly, on August 30, 1917, the French agreed to furnish the American Air Service with 5,000 airplanes and 8,500 engines by June 1, 1918. This delivery schedule proved ambitious for an already strained French aviation industry. American and French authorities had to renegotiate the agreement in May 1918, with the French promising to furnish "aviation material equal both in quality and quantity to that supplied to their own forces and in proportion to the number of [AEF] divisions in France."[38] The subsequent American reliance on the Allies, particularly the French, for airplanes was heavy. During the war, AEF received 4,791 aircraft from the French, 261 from the British, and 19 from the Italians. Of the total 6,287 airplanes delivered to the AEF, only 1,216 came from the United States.[39]

The AEF handled most operational planning for use of the forming American Air Service. When General Pershing sailed for France, Major Townsend F. Dodd accompanied him as the aviation officer, AEF. One of the first officers to greet the Pershing party when it arrived in Paris on June 13, 1917, was Major William "Billy" Mitchell. Mitchell had been in Europe since April observing European aviation. This officer, a newcomer to flying, was destined to play a major role in the AEF Air Service.

Mitchell was from an influential Wisconsin family, and his father had served as a U.S. senator. When the Spanish-American War broke out, the eighteen-year-old Mitchell quit his college studies to join the Army. He soon received a commission in the Signal Corps. In 1901, after service in Cuba and the Philippines, Mitchell accepted a Regular Army commission. Over the next decade, he served in a number of signal postings, highlighted by visits to Europe, Japan, and China. He also took advantage of the growing Army professional education system by attending the Army School of the Line and the Staff College at Fort Leavenworth, Kansas. Mitchell joined the War Department General Staff in 1913; in 1916 he moved to the aviation section in the office of the chief signal officer, as the deputy to Lieutenant

Colonel George O. Squier. That fall Mitchell began taking weekend flying lessons at the Curtiss School in Newport News but did not earn his wings until July 1917.[40] Mitchell and Squier did not get along well, and in January 1917 Mitchell asked for and received a transfer to Europe as a military observer. He departed for Spain on March 17 and after the United States entered the war moved to France. In the weeks before Pershing's arrival, Mitchell was a busy man, visiting French and British aviation agencies and units and even managing to wangle a flight over the front.[41] He also tried to take the lead in AEF aviation planning.

In June Mitchell forwarded two memoranda to Lieutenant Colonel James G. Harbord, the chief of staff of the AEF. In these documents he asserted that aviation should be an independent arm, like the infantry, and that American aviation policy should emulate the strategic aspects advocated by the commander of the British Royal Flying Corps in the Field, Major General Sir Hugh M. Trenchard. To this end, Mitchell proposed an AEF aeronautical organization that would provide for an independent strategic force as well as for aviation with ground units. Harbord forwarded these documents to a board of officers, convened on June 19, to study AEF aviation matters.[42]

The board sanctioned many of Mitchell's ideas. Since Mitchell was the senior aviation officer on the board and one of the few American officers with firsthand knowledge of Allied aviation policy, his opinions carried substantial weight. In its recommendations, the board highlighted its view of the importance of aviation: "It is now a cardinal principle in warfare that a decision in the air must be sought and obtained before a decision on the ground can be reached. . . . The side which can at critical times dominate the enemy in the air has taken the first, if not the vital, step toward victory." The board further recommended the division of the Air Service, AEF, into strategic and tactical aviation, estimating a requirement of thirty bomber groups for the strategic mission and thirty pursuit groups for the tactical role.[43]

The first official organizational plan was completed in early July. On July 10 the AEF forwarded the General Organization Project to the War Department, recommending fifty-nine aviation squadrons to support a ground organization of twenty divisions and five corps. This force would contain thirty-nine observation, fifteen pursuit, and five bombardment squadrons.[44] This program and others put forward before the Armistice were overly ambitious. When hostilities ended, the AEF had only forty-five operational squadrons, of which twelve were equipped with Liberty DH-4s. Within this force were eighteen observation, twenty pursuit, and seven day bombardment squadrons.[45] Production problems meant a lack of airplanes, as reflected in the total number of squadrons anticipated for October 1918 in the final two programs: 109 under the June plan and 53 under the August plan.[46] Neither was attained.

Throughout the war, personnel and training problems also plagued the

[46]

Air Service. Personnel problems had both mobilization and transportation elements because Air Service personnel competed for limited berths on the ships carrying infantrymen to France. The problem became critical after the German offensive in the spring of 1918; for a time, a virtual embargo was placed on the movement of all personnel other than infantry troops from the United States. The Air Service also faced unique training problems, particularly for pilots and aircraft mechanics. People with such skills were rare in a largely unmechanized American society. In spite of these difficulties, the Air Service grew to a strength of 5,692 officers and 74,272 enlisted men by the Armistice. The AEF assumed much of the burden for training and, with help from the Allies, produced 1,674 fully trained pilots and 851 observers.[47]

As the Air Service grew, and as aviation technology made quantum advances in military capability, thoughts on how to employ the air weapon changed radically. At the start of World War I the Army's official doctrine stressed the preeminence of the infantry and the subordination of all other arms and services to its central role. Aviation's functions were confined mainly to "strategical and tactical reconnaissance and the observation of artillery fire." The only potential direct combat mission was "to prevent hostile aerial reconnaissance." Furthermore, although the aviation commander provided immediate control, aviation was under the employment authority of the ground commander to whom it was assigned.[48]

Not surprisingly, Brigadier General George P. Scriven, the chief signal officer and controller of Army aviation, reinforced the importance of the mission to collect and transmit information, noting that "there is no longer a question as to the value of the aeroplane in rapid and long-range reconnaissance work, and of its power to secure and to transmit by radio, visual signal, or direct-flight information of the utmost importance to armies in the field." He also surmised: "It now appears that the actual game of war is played openly with cards laid on the table, and opportunity no longer is given for inference as to concealed movements or for surprises."[49]

Scriven also highlighted the vast improvement in artillery fire control afforded by radio-equipped airplanes. Still, although he clearly grasped the implications of combining two revolutionary technologies, the airplane and the radio, he largely dismissed any consideration of the airplane as a combat weapon. In short, he viewed the airplane from a parochial perspective: "aviation must be reckoned as a vastly important branch of the signal corps of the army."[50] Even as Scriven put these views on paper, aviation doctrine was being reshaped in the cauldron of war on the western front.

Obtaining direct information about European military aviation was difficult because the belligerents refused to accredit War Department military observers. When the United States entered the war, only five U.S. Army aviators were in Europe: Captain Carleton G. Chapman, an assistant military attaché in London; Major William Mitchell, in Spain as a military observer;

and Lieutenants Joseph E. Carberry, Millard F. Harmon Jr., and Davenport Johnson, attending French flying schools. None was able to observe front-line aviation operations.[51] Nevertheless, some information reached the United States and influenced American conceptions about the military uses of aviation. As early as April 1916 Secretary of War Baker testified before the House Committee on Military Affairs that Europeans were "devising a bat-tle aeroplane which is in itself an offensive arm and that places a new phase on the whole thing."[52] In January 1917 Lieutenant Colonel Squier, head of the Signal Corps Aviation Section, and members of Congress discussed vague notions about the importance of "control of the air zone." Represen-tative Julius Kahn wondered whether perhaps "control over the air is just as important as control over the sea."[53] These ambiguous views would become more defined as American aviators gained firsthand knowledge of Euro-pean operations.

Mitchell, heavily influenced by his discussions with General Trenchard, was one of the first Americans to identify a strategic role for aviation: "Air attack of enemy material of all kinds behind his lines" was the way Ameri-can aviation could contribute the most to winning the war. Mitchell had no doubts about the potential of strategic aviation: "If properly applied [strate-gic aviation] will have a greater influence on the ultimate decision of the war than any other one arm."[54] Amplifying on the employment of this class of aviation, Mitchell likened it to "independent cavalry" because it would op-erate behind enemy lines "to carry the war well into the enemy's country."[55]

Other AEF officers were also considering offensive aviation. Major Dodd, the AEF aviation officer, had spent several days in England, where he dis-cussed aviation matters with Colonel William Lassiter, the American mili-tary attaché, and British officials. In a note to the chief of staff, AEF, Dodd wrote that the major demands confronting Allied aviation were gaining air supremacy along the western front and developing an offensive capability. Dodd added that this offensive force "will be able to carry the war two hun-dred or more miles behind the German lines. This force, when first available might properly be considered for use strictly for the attack upon military features, such as arsenals, factories, railways, etc. but should also be suffi-cient to act as a reprisal agent of such destructiveness that the Germans would be forced to stop their raids upon Allied cities."[56] Although Mitchell's and Dodd's thoughts on strategic aviation were important, they were not doctrine and thus not officially approved to be taught within the Army.[57]

One of the first instances of official Army recognition of the role of strate-gic aviation appeared in a report titled "The Role and Tactical and Strategi-cal Employment of Aeronautics in an Army" written by Major Frank Parker, a member of the AEF board convened in June to study aviation matters. Parker's report, attached as an appendix to the board's proceedings, defined two classes of aviation: tactical, "or that acting in the immediate vicinity or directly attached to organizations of troops of all arms," and strategic, "or that acting far from troops of other arms and having an independent mission." Tactical aviation included observation, pursuit, and tactical bombardment aviation squadrons. In addition to the established missions of reconnaissance and artillery spotting, observation aviation also assumed a liaison function. The role of tactical pursuit was to gain and maintain mastery of the air and ground attack. Tactical bombardment was that which operated "within about 25,000 yards of the line or roughly within the extreme zone of long-range artillery." Strategic aviation, in its independent role, operated in the enemy's rear, habitually more than "25,000 yards from friendly troops." Its targets were the elements of the enemy air service and "depots, factories, lines of communications, and personnel." Strategic aviation squadrons included pursuit for destroying enemy aircraft, day bombardment for attacking enemy airfields and long-range reconnaissance, and night bombardment for interdicting enemy lines of communication and deep attack against enemy forces.[58] Major Bolling's August 1917 report to the chief signal officer endorsed this doctrine of tactical and strategic bombardment, albeit in a roundabout manner. Bolling recommended procuring independent night and day bombardment units after meeting the requirement for squadrons to support ground forces.[59] Two of the critical components required to establish an operational air service, doctrine and organizational plans, seemed to be coming together.

By September 1917 the Air Service, AEF, had articulated concepts for the employment of each type of aviation and defined the organizational structure. These concepts, particularly regarding bombing, matured over the coming months.[60] In January 1918 an Anglo-American agreement seemed to clear the way for the Royal Flying Corps to organize, train, and equip thirty AEF night bombing squadrons.[61] The plan hinged, however, on the United States furnishing Handley-Page bomber parts to the British for assembly in England, a program that failed.[62] Without bombers, American strategic aviation plans would remain theoretical. Actual combat experience was confined to a tactical role.

In April 1918 the first American aerosquadrons were deployed in the relatively quiet Toul sector, and Air Service pilots gained experience in the realities of combat flying over the next several months. The first major operation for the Air Service, like the rest of the AEF, did not come until the St. Mihiel offensive in September. During this battle, Colonel Mitchell, chief of Air Service for General Pershing's First Army, commanded the largest aviation force to date in the war. At Mitchell's disposal were a total of 1,481 American, British, and French airplanes. Mitchell also commanded the First Army Air Service during the final Meuse-Argonne offensive. Although their commitment to combat had been brief, the American flyers made a good showing, shooting down 781 enemy airplanes and 73 balloons, dropping

275,000 pounds of explosives during 150 bombing raids, and taking more than 18,000 photographs of enemy positions. Furthermore, they spotted for artillery and provided close air support for the attacking infantry.[63] American aviators had also established a unique niche in the American consciousness, becoming the "knights of the air" in a war that had otherwise been a dehumanizing experience. There was a good deal of truth in Brigadier General Billy Mitchell's later recollection that "the only interest and romance in this war was in the air."[64] But ideas about the postwar role of aviation were diverse.

Although the Superior Board acknowledged aviation's role in the American war effort, it still maintained that aviation's most important function was as a ground support weapon, an auxiliary of the infantry. The board stressed that "this class of aerial work can be made more efficacious and decisive than the distant bombing operations and should receive the greatest attention." Nevertheless, the board recognized the expanded aviation roles and missions developed during the war and recommended the assignment of reconnaissance, observation, and artillery spotting units to divisions and corps; tactical bombing units to corps and army; and strategic bombing and reconnaissance units to the army. The board's final word on aviation, however, reflected its fixation on ground warfare: "Nothing so far brought out in the war shows that Aerial activities can be carried on, independently of ground troops, to such an extent as to materially affect the conduct of the war as a whole."[65]

The Superior Board was not the only AEF effort to examine the role of aviation. Major General Mason Patrick, the chief of Air Service, AEF, also assessed the lessons of the Great War for his arm. In December 1918 Patrick established a staff section, under Colonel Edgar S. Gorrell, to prepare a final report and write a history of the Air Service during the war.[66]

Patrick was also interested in more immediate issues. On May 8, 1919, he convened a board of officers, under the presidency of Brigadier General Benjamin D. Foulois, to make organizational and operational recommendations for the postwar air establishment. The most important recommendation of the board, and one confirmed by Patrick, was that the Air Service remain part of the Army, a position not universally accepted within the Air Service.[67] Foulois, although personally against an independent air organization, realized that many did not share his views. In his January 1919 report, submitted in accordance with the final report directive, he told Patrick that a number of bills that would create a cabinet-level air organization coordinate with the War and Navy Departments were already before Congress. He further warned: "Many of the flying officers of the A.E.F. . . . are strong advocates of a separate Air Service, and unless prompt action is taken the question will be settled in favor of an independent air force."[68] As events would soon prove, Foulois's concerns were fully justified.

[50]

The War Department was also grappling with the question of the postwar status of the Air Service. The Baker-March Bill contained provisions for perpetuating the Air Service, but Secretary Baker wanted to know more about wartime aviation developments. In early 1919 he dispatched a mission, headed by Assistant Secretary of War Benedict C. Crowell, to Europe to investigate British, French, and Italian experiences but told Crowell not to consider an independent air organization. Returning to Washington in mid-July, Crowell recommended a National Air Service, with cabinet-level status, that incorporated all American aviation activities—military, naval, and civilian.[69] Baker was incensed, almost to the point of asking for Crowell's resignation.[70] Shortly thereafter, Representative Charles F. Curry of California and Senator Harry S. New of Indiana submitted bills recommending similar arrangements.[71]

Baker did not release the Crowell Aviation Mission Report until August 13 and then denounced its findings.[72] He then convened a board, under Major General Charles T. Menoher, the War Department director of Air Service since January 2, to consider the proposals for a separate air organization.[73] The Menoher Board predictably recommended against a separate department of aeronautics, concluding that the Air Service should remain within the War Department structure on a basis similar to the infantry, cavalry, and artillery.[74]

The discourse on aviation became increasingly polarized. Those who testified in the congressional hearings on the postwar organization of the Army clearly fell into one of two camps—separatist or antiseparatist. The separatists were adamant in their views that the civilian and military potential of the airplane could be developed only through a centralized department of aeronautics, that military aviation had developed into an independent combat force, and that the War Department was inept and unfair in its control of the Air Service. Their principal spokespersons were Assistant Secretary Crowell; the War Department director of military aeronautics, Brigadier General Mitchell; the chief of the Balloon and Airship Division, Colonel C. deF. Chandler; and Major B. D. Foulois, who had recently been reduced from his general officer rank by the postwar reductions in the Army. Opposing this group were the antiseparatists, who were just as firmly convinced that Army aviation was an adjunct of the ground battle and had to be controlled, in peace and war, by the ground commander. Their chief advocates were Secretary Baker, General March, General Pershing, and General Menoher.

A heated debate ensued before the Senate and House Committees on Military Affairs. On October 17, 1919, Crowell appeared before the Senate Subcommittee on Military Affairs. His testimony carried the authority of his discussions with such notable figures as Winston Churchill, Gen. Hugh Trenchard, Marshal Ferdinand Foch, General Erich Ludendorff, and Field

Marshal Douglas Haig. Crowell stressed that in the future aviation "will have a function quite distinct from the present limitations of its activities as a service auxiliary to the Army and Navy." He also noted that "before the mobilization of armies can be effected in the next war a great conflict will occur in the air. The aggressive nation will be prepared to launch an attack upon the shipping, munition, manufacturing, and storage centers, and even the cities, of its opponent. . . . With Europe only 16 hours removed from this country by air routes, we can not rest in fancied safety of isolation. It is only through the agency of a single responsible organization that we can confidently look to preparedness for such an eventuality." Crowell then discussed the need to establish a strong commercial aviation industry as a constituent part of national defense. But he made a point of telling the subcommittee members that Secretary Baker did not share his views about a separate department of aeronautics.[75]

Mitchell's views were fairly consistent with Crowell's, but he expanded on the future role of military aviation. Mitchell asserted that the air weapon was decisive and had the potential to make navies useless. The main impediment to the further development of military aviation, he argued, was the conservatism of ground officers.[76]

The most strident testimony, however, came from the recent convert to the separatist camp, Major Foulois. He claimed that the War Department was retarding the development of aviation because the General Staff and line officers could not visualize its potential as a fighting weapon. Foulois introduced into the hearing records a thirty-nine-page document, titled "Statement on the Necessity for the Creation of a Department of Aeronautics," that gave a comprehensive history of military aviation in the United States and offered his recommendation for the future of American aviation.[77] In their essence, the separatists' arguments stressed the potential of military aviation as an offensive arm, the lack of vision on the part of the "old school" in the War Department in exploiting that potential, and the importance of a strong commercial aviation industry to the development of military aviation.

The arguments of the antiseparatists were predictably more conservative, with Secretary Baker's testimony setting the general tone. The war, in his view, had shown that "aircraft [are] most useful when [they are] associated intimately with some other branch of service . . . but the major usefulness of aircraft in this war was for observation and bombing." Consequently, Baker believed that "the aerial pilots in the Army ought to be military men, trained in constant association with other men of the other branches with which they are to be associated."[78]

General March agreed with his boss, highlighting the principle of unity of command. For once, General Pershing concurred with March, asserting that "aviation is not an independent arm and can not be for a long time to come, if ever." General Menoher told the legislators that air service was but an auxiliary to the infantry, although perhaps a little more important than the artillery. He added a new dimension to the debate by suggesting that the creation of a new department would surely result in the need for higher appropriations.[79] This appeal for economy probably struck a responsive chord in a Congress determined to reduce expenditures. In the end, no separate department of aeronautics was created.

The separatists nonetheless made some significant gains. Under the National Defense Act of 1920, the Air Service became a combatant arm on a more or less equal footing with the infantry, cavalry, and field artillery. The act also allowed for the permanent assignment and commissioning of officers, detailed to the Air Service from other branches, if they became qualified pilots. Finally, the act specified that flying units should be commanded by flying officers and gave the Air Service authority to develop and supply its own technical equipment.[80]

Anyone who believed that the National Defense Act had settled the aviation issue was sorely mistaken. The Army and Navy were already embroiled in a debate over the roles of their aviation services in coast defense.[81] On June 5, one day after the establishment of the Air Service under the National Defense Act, Congress approved the Appropriations Act for fiscal year 1921. It attempted to settle the Army-Navy debate by specifying that "hereafter the Army Air Service shall control all aerial operations from land bases, and Naval Aviation shall have control of all aerial operations attached to a fleet, including shore stations whose maintenance is necessary for operations connected with the fleet."[82] General Billy Mitchell would soon use the authority contained in this single sentence to reignite the controversy over the role of Army aviation.

[4]

The Army in the Aftermath
of the Great War

The Great War marked the end of the Army's conception of itself as a frontier constabulary. Things had changed fundamentally, although many Army officers had difficulty articulating the change. To the Army's leadership the war offered clear lessons: Modern war required big armies and vast quantities of munitions. To meet these needs, Secretary Baker and General March framed a bill that provided for an unprecedentedly large 500,000-man standing regular army to serve as a cadre for a huge national army. They also recommended a comprehensive reserve component, maintained at a fairly high state of readiness through a system of universal military training. A strong General Staff, manned by officers trained in a revitalized professional education system, would direct the Army. Finally, an assistant secretary of war would supervise industrial mobilization and procurement.

Although the National Defense Act of 1920 was a milestone in the institutional evolution of the Army, the changes in war that its framers recognized and attempted to accommodate were limited. The deficiencies in the National Defense Act largely originated from the cognitive constraints of the act's architects. The officers charged with assessing the lessons of the Great War were by and large "Old Army." Their decades of experience actually served to minimize their comprehension of modern combat. The popular adage "experience is the best teacher" is a useful way of expressing this idea. A more sophisticated view of the important role played by experience is the one central to modern democratic theory: People learn how to think about their society and its institutions—and how to change them—by living in them.[1] To senior Army officers it surely seemed that the American doctrine of open warfare had worked, with relatively few alterations. The American Expeditionary Force (AEF), after all, had turned the tide in a war the Europeans could not decide in more than three years of stalemated slaughter.[2] The Great War had thus verified American strategic and tactical concepts. The areas that had proven deficient—personnel mobilization and industrial production—were those targeted for remedy.

The arguments Secretary Baker used to try to sway the Congress to support his and General March's large army concept flew in the face of American tradition and economic good sense. Congressional attitudes reflected two fundamental American traditions: distrust of large standing armies and an unswerving belief in the preeminence of the citizen soldier. To the legislators, the war record of the AEF proved that this cherished system worked fine.[3] The U.S. National Army had mobilized when it was needed and demobilized when the emergency had passed—just as it always had. Furthermore, the country had just won the "war to end all wars." Representative John F. Miller of Washington asked General March: "What world conditions would make it necessary to have a force of such size?"[4] The physical isolation of the United States and the shield provided by the Navy still seemed to afford it the luxury, by European standards, of maintaining only a small ground force.

Secretary Baker and General March did not respond directly. Instead, they equivocated, arguing that the War Department had at its disposal resources never before available in peacetime. New military training camps, a large cadre of combat veterans, and stockpiles of munitions and equipment stood ready to support reorganization and the inauguration of a universal military training program.[5] Baker's and March's arguments seemed to be based on an assumption that not using the resources at hand would be wasteful. Their arguments backfired. Congress viewed the Army's surpluses as ways to save money—a good excuse to curtail future appropriations for weapons procurement and development.[6] Still, some were suspicious of the Army's motives. A September 1919 *New York Times* editorial speculated that "the truth is that a force of 500,000 is looked upon with favor by every officer who has been demoted and would like to resume his war grade. . . . The taxpayers cannot afford to satisfy this yearning."[7] Congressional approval of a 500,000-man regular army would have been totally out of character and, given the international situation, fiscally extravagant.

That the leaders of the Army were highly focused on personnel mobilization became apparent as they adjusted their plans around an authorization for 17,700 officers and 280,000 enlisted men.[8] The Army's plan was based on nine divisions in nine corps areas in the continental United States. Rather than modify this structure, Army leaders chose to further skeletonize these units. The majority soon became hollow shells to be filled out only upon a general mobilization.[9] Additionally, when Congress forced further personnel cuts by not appropriating funds for the authorized Army strengths, enlisted men were most affected. The size of the officer corps in relation to the enlisted strength was in fact unprecedentedly high in the active force throughout the interwar period.[10] Senior officers tried to justify the in-

[55]

creased officer overhead as necessary to train civilian components.[11] But the demise of universal military training made this argument less compelling. The Army's leadership, aside from being honestly convinced of the central importance of personnel mobilization and training to success in modern war, may have been reluctant to force its fellow officers out of the service. By maintaining the infrastructure of the nine corps area plan, many officer slots could be saved. Furthermore, authorizations for general officers almost tripled over prewar levels to support the reorganized Army.[12]

Whatever the motivations of the War Department, the consequences of its personnel decisions were calamitous. The strength levels of units in the field and the decisions on how to station these units worked against the Army in two ways. First, by significantly increasing its prewar strength, the Army outgrew its housing resources. Housing was especially limited for the officer corps, whose size had almost tripled from its 1913 level. Because officials were aware of housing's significant influence on morale, the Army invested heavily in building new quarters, at the expense of other programs.[13] Second, by spreading skeletonized battalions and regiments throughout the corps areas, the Army severely curtailed opportunities to conduct maneuvers of units larger than a battalion. The Army's standing tactical units—the battalions, regiments, and divisions—had few active personnel and no real operational capabilities. Training, readiness, and morale suffered. One frustrated officer wrote in 1926:

> Can you learn to understand a radio set by observing only an antenna? Can you learn to drive an airplane playing with only half a wing? Can you take only the foreleg of a horse and train it to successfully accomplish the stunts of a well trained animal? No! No! Neither can you take eight squads, and, calling it a battalion, teach your men what a fighting battalion is, its parts, and their functions; nor can you, by such means, achieve skill in utilizing a fighting battalion; nor can you thoroughly teach such a group of men how the various parts of a fighting battalion carry on their individual tasks and, at the same time, cooperate one with another in the necessary coordinated way.[14]

Still, the War Department clung to its tenet that personnel mobilization was the crucial phase in preparing for modern war. This stance hurt efforts to create a coherent system for developing technology.

Most senior officers' attitudes toward technology were a vestige of a prewar army that had relied heavily on animal power. The first even modest use of motor vehicles and airplanes in the field did not occur until the 1916 Punitive Expedition.[15] The anchor to their familiar past was the conviction that man won the war. Even a comparatively enlightened General March saw no reason to challenge these core values, noting that the war "was not won . . . by some new and terrible development of modern science; it was won, as every other war in history, by men, munitions, and morale." Although March conceded the remarkable advances in the machines of war, he was adamant that they were secondary and that man was still the pre-eminent factor in war: "As always heretofore, the Infantry with rifle and bayonet . . . in the final analysis, must bear the brunt of the assault and carry it on to victory."[16] The Superior Board, as already noted, was at least as traditional as General March in its verifications of the primacy of the infantry and the continued importance of cavalry.

In June 1920 General Pershing commented on the board's findings. He noted that many of the lessons of the war required modification in light of conditions on the North American continent, "the theater upon which we are most likely to be engaged." Pershing believed that the division used in France was too large and unwieldy for American conditions but that the necessary cuts should be made "in auxiliaries," while "the infantry must be kept at the greatest number practicable." Pershing's doubts about the potential of technology were most apparent in his comments on maneuver. Throughout his remarks, he emphasized the importance of mobility in the infantry division so that it could make breakthroughs and then maneuver to exploit opportunities. Mobility, however, was judged not by the speed of the machines but by the pace of marching foot soldiers. He also asserted that "it seems obvious that a large proportion of the transport permanently assigned to divisions should be animal drawn."[17]

These remarks, by the senior officer in the Army and a national hero to boot, surely carried authority. In any case, they show the limited accommodations a nineteenth-century horse cavalryman was willing to make toward machines.

Pershing's statements on tanks and airplanes showed that he did not see them as revolutionary weapons. He clearly viewed them as auxiliaries of the more traditional arms. Addressing future tank requirements, Pershing noted: "We might well replace the divisional machine gun reserve by a company of about fifteen tanks." Nor were his ideas about aviation particularly innovative, being limited to a recommendation that the division should have an eight-plane observation flight.[18]

Pershing's coolness toward tanks and aircraft also pervaded his final report, in which he omitted any mention of doctrine or the potential of either weapon.[19] Instead, he cited the aviators' "daring and fighting ability" and their establishment of a "record of courageous deeds that will ever remain a brilliant page in the annals of our Army." Similarly, the men of the Tank Corps "responded gallantly on every possible occasion and showed courage of the highest order."[20] In the rhetoric of a nineteenth-century warrior, these comments on the bravery of the machine handlers were indeed high praise.

Missing were an assessment of the tank or airplane's contribution to the AEF's effort and a discussion of how these new weapons would affect future Army doctrine.

The lessons of the Great War were viewed in two fundamentally different ways. Some officers, including Mitchell, saw potential in the new weapons. Others, such as Pershing and March, were more skeptical. In the aftermath of the war, the skeptical view dominated.

The technological development system put together under the National Defense Act did not correct one of the major deficiencies of the prewar Army—the absence of a central agency to coordinate the increasingly sophisticated components of doctrine, operations, research and development, and production. Although the assistant secretary of war was nominally in charge of industrial mobilization and procurement, with help in functional areas from the General Staff, in reality these important areas were highly decentralized. For one thing, the War Department General Staff authorized by the act consisted only "of the Chief of Staff, four assistants, and eighty-eight other officers not below the rank of captain." This small group had the vast responsibility for war, mobilizing personnel and industry, preparing for military operations, and keeping tabs on "all questions effecting the efficiency of the Army."[21] It would have been hard-pressed to develop weapons and doctrine as well, had it been assigned or assumed the task.

The emphasis on existing Army doctrine—the primacy of well-trained infantrymen—obscured the emerging need for a whole new structure to evaluate, assimilate, and utilize new technologies. Instead, the Army simply added a new level of bureaucracy. To the existing Ordnance Department, Quartermaster Corps, and Signal Corps, each deeply involved in developing Army matériel, the National Defense Act added chiefs of arms for infantry, artillery, and cavalry and a chief of the Air Service. Although created for the commendable purpose of strengthening the voice of the user within the War Department hierarchy, this new arrangement only exacerbated the deficiencies of a system already proven inadequate during the war. One officer, after observing the fragmented system in operation for a number of years, lamented:

> *Our Army is lacking a suitable agency for general research, experimentation, and development.* We have branch boards (Infantry Board, Tank Board, Air Corps Board, Field Artillery Board, and so on), each of which can make studies, within limits. But these minor agencies are severely limited as to what they may do, and they have, individually, scant resources with which to operate. And, most important of all, they are isolated from one another. . . . Criticism that attributes our slow progress to ultra-conservatism is unjust. The fault lies not there but in the lack of a suitable agency. The missing element should be supplied.[22]

[58]

Still, the new chiefs of arms added a dimension to earlier arrangements. All major generals reporting directly to the chief of staff, they had broad charters to supervise their branch service schools, formulate tactical doctrine for their arm, develop organizational plans, prepare instructional and training publications, cooperate with the supply branches in the development of arms and equipment, assign and classify personnel in their branch, and prepare the appropriate mobilization and war plans.[23] In short, they had a say in anything involving their realm. Their focused but comprehensive authority in specific areas made them very powerful men and forceful promoters of the interests of their particular arms. But for these very reasons, they were ill disposed to exploit the new technologies of tanks and airplanes. The chiefs of arms generally concentrated first, last, and always on what was best for their own branches. Advocacy easily turned into parochialism, and intraservice cooperation suffered as a result.

Under the National Defense Act, all tanks were put in the infantry. Consequently, the chief of infantry assumed the central role in the development of tank doctrine and organization. The chief of infantry, however, did not control tank design and production, a critical task that belonged primarily to the chief of ordnance. Authority was thus fragmented. The chief of infantry specified doctrine, organization, and the user's expectations of tank capabilities, while the chief of ordnance developed the actual technology.

The Air Service was better disposed organizationally to support aviation development. The chief of Air Service was in charge of all aspects of the development of the airplane technology. He controlled the airplane in three important functional areas—doctrine, organization, and technology.

The Great War was the stimulus for an evolutionary, rather than a revolutionary, reorganization of the U.S. Army. Preparation by the nation for a European mass war highlighted deficiencies in existing mobilization systems. Combat, albeit very limited, had exposed the Army to a wide panoply of experiences including the possibilities of tanks and airplanes. As a result, the Army's raison d'être changed forever from serving as a frontier constabulary to preparing for total war. Nevertheless, although institutional arrangements and professional conceptions adapted to support this new imperative, the fundamental assumptions of the senior officers controlling the direction of the Army remained largely unchanged from before the war. The experiences in the Great War simply did not transcend the inherited presumptions to incorporate in meaningful ways the awesome possibilities of the tank, airplane, and other new technologies. However, a group of officers who grasped some of the deeper implications of the new weapons emerged. In the aftermath of the war, they struggled for a voice within the military establishment. The effects of institutional arrangements and the increasing tension between the hierarchy and the advocates of change on the development of the tank and the airplane are the focus of the chapters that follow.

[59]

PART II

INERTIA AND
INSURGENCY:
1921–1930

Please advise me as to just what steps are being taken for the development of tanks in the army, and who has charge of this task. My impression is that very little is being done by any department to advance our knowledge of tank construction and use.

—General of the Armies John J. Pershing (1923)

Suitable and adequate preparation of the air arm, and of the personnel required to man the aircraft, manufacture the equipment, and supply such a force, cannot be furnished by the Army or Navy, or by the two combined, as has been the experience in all countries in the recent War.

—Brigadier General William Mitchell, *Our Air Force* (1921)

[5]

Peace and Quiet

On July 2, 1921, the United States ended its technical state of war with Germany by a joint resolution of Congress, having failed to ratify the Treaty of Versailles or join the new League of Nations. In August separate treaties with Germany, Austria, and Hungary formalized the legislative action.[1] The U.S. Senate quickly ratified the documents, thereby rejecting President Woodrow Wilson's vision of American internationalism, since the revised treaties "confirmed her in her privileges but not in her responsibilities under the treaties of Versailles, Saint-Germain, and Trianon."[2] Many saw the Senate's rejection of an international role for the United States as an abrogation of obligation and a key reason for the failure of the League of Nations. Without American participation, the ability of the League to prevent future conflicts was greatly circumscribed.[3]

Although the reason the United States rejected a role of world leadership after the Armistice is debatable, most opinions are written from a post-1945 perspective. Viewing the Treaty of Versailles, and the League of Nations covenant that Wilson bound to its ratification, from the perspective of the senators who had to decide its fate, the commitment to internationalism might seem ominous and sharply in conflict with American traditions.

The most onerous aspect of the treaty was Article 10: "The members of the League undertake to respect and preserve as against external aggression the territorial integrity and existing political independence of all Members of the League." To the "irreconcilables," led by Republican Senate Majority Leader Henry Cabot Lodge, this was a de facto commitment to use military force clearly inconsistent with traditional American foreign relations values and practices.[4] The story of the epic battle over the ratification of the Treaty of Versailles between the president and the Senate ensued. Neither would compromise, and the Senate prevailed.

The Senate had legitimate reason for concern. When Wilson presented the treaty to the Senate on July 10, 1919, the U.S. Army had troops on occupation duty in Germany and others in combat in Soviet Russia.[5] Moreover, many believed that Wilson was willing to take on further burdens. In October 1919 a military commission under the direction of Major General James G. Harbord completed a report that assessed the potential costs if the United States assumed a mandate in Armenia. Harbord estimated that U.S. involvement would require 59,000 soldiers and a five-year cost of more than $750 million.[6] In May 1920, even after the Senate refused to ratify the Treaty of Versailles, the president urged the Congress to take up this burden. He was rejected by a vote of fifty-two to twenty-three in the Senate, with the House concurring.[7]

Wilson's final attempt to force the country to accept an international role came during the 1920 presidential election. Wilson and the Democrats made League membership the focus of the race, and the Republican candidate, Warren G. Harding, won handily. Harding's seven-million-vote margin dissolved any remaining thoughts that the United States would join the League and assume the concomitant international security responsibilities. The American people, disillusioned for a variety of reasons, were tired of the incessant calls from their president for self-sacrifice, particularly when most of the rest of the world seemingly did not share their idealism.[8]

The January 1919 publication of the "secret treaties" negotiated among the Allies made Wilson's promise in the Fourteen Points of "open covenants of peace openly arrived at" appear to be a lie.[9] That the victorious Allies were apparently dividing the spoils of victory instead of ensuring a lasting peace was also disconcerting. This belief was magnified in 1920 with the republication in the United States of John Maynard Keynes's *The Economic Consequences of the Peace*. This blistering polemic cataloged the failures of the Paris Peace Conference and harshly attacked its architects, particularly Wilson.[10] Quite simply, the American people were ready to embrace Harding's campaign slogan of "Back to Normalcy."[11]

Normalcy in the domestic sector meant a return to laissez-faire economics and a reduction in government expenditures. Congress, further asserting its power over the executive branch, assumed a greater role in the budget process when it passed the Budget and Accounting Act in June 1921.[12] After a sharp but brief recession in 1920, the economy boomed. Until the stock market crash in 1929, the decade was one of economic prosperity and expansion.[13]

Normalcy in international relations presumed an avoidance of entangling alliances and a reliance on the rule of law rather than force.[14] To this end the United States sponsored a number of initiatives to encourage disarmament and to reduce the threat of war.

In December 1920 Senator William E. Borah introduced a resolution that called for a conference on naval disarmament. The Harding administration, encouraged by favorable responses from potential delegate nations, proceeded with plans to host a disarmament conference.[15] In November 1921 delegates from the United States, Great Britain, France, Italy, Japan, Belgium, China, Portugal, and the Netherlands convened in Washington. The conference lasted from November 12 to February 6 and resulted in nine separate treaties that limited naval armaments and addressed tensions in the Pacific and China.[16] The Senate ratified each of these treaties, with an attached reservation to only one. In this Four-Power Pacific Pact, which reinforced traditional American policy, the Senate added one caveat: "There is no commitment to armed force, no alliance, no obligation to join in any defense."[17] Furthermore, because of French opposition, the treaties did not limit land armaments.[18]

In 1925 Calvin Coolidge started planning for another naval conference to close loopholes in the 1922 accords.[19] The conference did not convene until 1927; it failed miserably, mainly because France and Italy refused to attend.[20] In January 1930 hopes for further disarmament were rekindled in London. The ensuing treaties resulted in further naval limitations by the United States, Great Britain, and Japan.[21] The unschooled observer reading the daily newspapers must have believed substantial progress was being made in reducing the international arms competition. If, for the more cynical, disarmament conferences were not sufficient cause to declare the coming of the millennium, other indicators suggested that war was less likely than in earlier generations to be an instrument of national policy.

The most spectacular diplomatic success regarding the future of war did not concern itself with the tools of war but with its actual renunciation. In April 1927 Aristide Briand, the French foreign minister, attempted to draw the United States into the French security system by proposing a bilateral Pact of Perpetual Friendship between the two nations. Frank B. Kellogg, the American secretary of state, outmaneuvered Briand by counterproposing a multilateral treaty outlawing war. On August 27, 1928, representatives of fifteen nations signed the treaty at a ceremony at the Quai d'Orsay in Paris.[22] Sixty-two nations eventually subscribed to the provisions of the Pact of Paris, or the Kellogg-Briand Pact.[23]

Many Army officers seemed oblivious to the diplomatic initiatives. Throughout 1921 articles in professional journals advocated the adoption of universal military training, even though the measure had been soundly defeated during the Army reorganization hearings. Leading the campaign were a number of prominent general officers. Major General James G. Harbord, soon to be Pershing's deputy chief of staff in the War Department, cautioned that the era of "Universal Peace" had not dawned and military preparedness was needed. He also argued that the United States, like other major powers, would have to rely on universal military training for the

[65]

mass armies required by any major emergency.[24] Major General Hunter Liggett, commander of the First Army during the final phase of the Meuse-Argonne offensive, believed that compulsory military training was a patriotic duty for American citizens.[25] Major General Robert L. Bullard championed the argument that universal military training was valuable because, aside from providing a body of trained reservists, it created better citizens by instilling in them noble soldierly traits.[26] When the Army finally realized that mandatory military training would be extremely unlikely in peacetime, the arguments shifted to commending and supporting voluntary efforts of the newly established Citizen's Military Training Camps.[27]

Similarly, as disarmament efforts gained momentum, Army officers counseled against the naïveté of the pacifists and called for preparedness. Arguments for military readiness included the uncertainty of the world situation, German violations of the Treaty of Versailles, and the threat of Bolshevism.[28] Some individuals in the Army had more pointed views. General Bullard believed that the United States should not give up its hard-gained military prominence: "We should not lead in disarmament because it would be a deliberate laying aside of our national superiority. Do we wish to abandon it simply to make ourselves equal with others? That would be asinine."[29]

General Pershing was more politically astute than Bullard. Testifying before the House Naval Affairs Committee in February 1921, he stated that he fully supported President-Elect Harding's call for a disarmament conference. Nevertheless, he urged caution: "We should steer clear of drifting into a pacifist state of mind simply because we are discussing this subject. No one wants war, but we do not want to be caught unprepared if war comes."[30] For an economy-minded president and Congress, the Army had to do more than provide platitudes and calls for patriotism if it expected funding for new or expanded programs.

Despite the warnings of military naysayers, the prospects for an enduring peace never seemed more promising than in the 1920s. For Americans, the lessened international tensions only reinforced the sense of security long afforded by physical isolation from the major military powers. The absence of any immediately evident threat to national security, the real prospect that war was becoming increasingly less likely, and a president and Congress bent on economy made the Army budget an attractive target for reduction. The president stressed that his military policies focused on economy; a small, expansible Regular Army; voluntary reserve training; and disarmament.[31] General Pershing, chief of staff since July 1, 1921, made a public show of support for the president's guidelines by stressing the need for "the greatest economy in conducting the military administration."[32] Furthermore, the Harding administration made it clear that it expected compliance and would not tolerate further dissent over its policies.

In June 1922 Secretary of War John W. Weeks issued a public statement that he would not allow any serving Army officer "to go around the country attacking the organization of which he is a part." Weeks made the rules clear: If an officer felt a compelling need to criticize policy, he should resign first. Otherwise, he would be subject to disciplinary action.[33] The service journals quickly fell into line. In October 1922 an editorial in the *Cavalry Journal* completely avoided the repressive aspects of Weeks's statements. Instead, the article called on officers to be "apostles of patriotism" during a period when America was "disturbed by industrial and political dissension to an uncomfortable degree." In short, it was every officer's duty to inform the public about the National Defense Program and arouse popular enthusiasm for its support.[34] Articles by senior officers in favor of universal military training and against disarmament soon disappeared from the service journals. Instead, the focus shifted to how the economy drive was affecting the Army.

The War Department based its operational and mobilization plans on a Regular Army strength of 17,717 officers and 280,000 enlisted men, as provided in the National Defense Act of 1920. But successive budget cuts dramatically reduced the service's real strength. In 1923 the active force consisted of 14,021 officers and 119,222 enlisted men. The aggregate active-duty strength fluctuated throughout the 1920s, never reaching 150,000, roughly one-half the strength authorized in 1920.[35] For an army focused on personnel mobilization as the key to preparedness, the figures were unnerving.

Army officers' public and official statements and articles in the service journals reflected their concerns, but they were careful to construct their arguments to avoid directly contradicting the administration. Views were cleverly framed to give the impression of support for official policy by pleading that the strength authorizations of the National Defense Act of 1920—the basis of American military policy—had to be met. Furthermore, since the executive branch was exempt from reproach, congressional penury became the focal point for criticism.[36]

Budget cuts greatly limited military readiness. In 1924 the corps areas had only three of the planned nine divisions: the First Division in New York, the Third Division on the West Coast, and the Second Division guarding the Texas border. Of these, only the Second Division was more than a hollow shell.[37] Secretary Weeks warned in his 1924 report to the president that the Army could not meet its missions of providing overseas garrisons, maintaining a combat-ready emergency force, and training civilian components with its depleted strength.[38] The paucity of funds also affected training, housing, ammunition procurement, and weapons development.[39] Weeks believed that the Army's plans should be practical rather than theoretical but observed that "practicality does not thrive in inactive units, depleted strengths, imaginary maneuvers, paper plans, ficticious [*sic*] reserve stocks, and theoretical weapons."[40] Such arguments were not well received in the White House.

[67]

Calvin Coolidge became president when Warren Harding died on August 2, 1923. Coolidge's avowed domestic program was to reduce government expenditures and enable a tax reduction, and his foreign policy focused on international disarmament. War Department pleas for a larger Army were contrary to both programs. Indeed, the *New York Times* reported that the president regarded the concerns of the General Staff over Army reductions as "propaganda" and that their pressing for a larger force "annoyed" him.[41] In October 1925 Coolidge amplified these views when he addressed the American Legion at its Omaha convention, stating that the international situation made questionable the "unnecessary expenditure of money to hire men to build fleets and carry muskets." Instead, Coolidge proposed "the turning of such resources into the making of good roads, the building of better homes, the promotion of education and all the others [*sic*] arts of peace which ministry to the advancement of human welfare." The president also stressed the primacy of civil authority over military matters and issued a clear warning to those in the military who did not agree with him: "Any organization of men in the military service bent on inflaming the public mind for the purpose of forcing Government action through the pressure of public opinion is an exceedingly dangerous precedent."[42]

President Coolidge's comments might have been prompted by the remarks of Colonel Billy Mitchell on the crash of the airship *Shenandoah*, discussed later, but they also applied to the General Staff.[43] Secretary of War Dwight F. Davis supported his president. Following the Mitchell court-martial, the *New York Times* reported that Davis "is preparing to read the riot act to certain elements in the army if the Mitchell court-martial conviction fails to make a sufficient impression on officers involved as a disciplinary object lesson." His remarks also made it clear that he was concerned with factionalism throughout the Army, not just in the aviation arm.[44] Regardless, dissent, although muffled, continued.

In October 1927 Major General Charles P. Summerall, chief of staff of the Army, was touring Army posts in the West. He addressed the chamber of commerce in San Diego, California, on October 11, likening the Army to "a mere skeleton of defense . . . living like immigrants or prisoners of war, instead of soldiers of a mighty nation." The question, he continued, was "one of money, and until the United States is willing to support an army of sufficient size, until the Administration is aroused to the real need of adequate defense, nothing can be done, and we shall, as an armed force, continue to perish by fast degrees."[45]

The administration was aroused, but not in the manner General Summerall probably expected. President Coolidge personally recalled the chief of staff to Washington, ostensibly to confer on the Army budget.[46] Although the White House stuck to its budget conference story, it was generally accepted that Summerall's trip had been cut short to discipline him.[47] A *New*

York Times editorial warned military officers that although in the past they had generally been allowed to express themselves in public, so long as they offered suggestions for improvement and filed their speeches or articles with the appropriate War Department agency, the rules had apparently changed. Following the Summerall incident, the *Times* concluded that any criticism of the establishment would have to be internal.[48] Within the Army, avenues for dissent were narrow and fraught with peril.

The administration's efforts to stifle dissent and criticism over what were essentially financial issues understandably had powerful side effects throughout the Army. The military environment, never openly conducive to criticism, became increasingly constrained. Officers could not express their views with impunity and, in many cases, could not even get them printed by their service journals. Articles had to be submitted to the author's superiors for approval, which amounted—at least—to indirect censorship. Even if an article made it past this hurdle, it had to be accepted by the editor of the journal. The *Infantry Journal,* one of the more influential forums in the Army during the 1920s, in 1922 published its position regarding articles on military technology:

> Arrangements have been made whereby the Infantry Board will review certain classes of articles that pertain to Infantry equipment, prior to their publication in the *Infantry Journal.* This applies only to those articles that have a tendency to bring into the Infantryman's mind a suspicion that the equipment he is supplied with, is not the very best that can be had for him. It can readily be seen that the army that does not believe its equipment, weapons especially, is equal to, or superior to that of a possible enemy, will suffer to some degree in morale.[49]

Even after an article appeared, the author had to stand ready to defend his views to superiors. A case in point is a 1930 piece, "Reorganization of Infantry," by Major J. L. Bradley. Bradley, a conscientious instructor at the Infantry School at Fort Benning, Georgia, recommended that the infantry take advantage of new weapons technologies. He wrote that the branch should "modernize and look to the future," that "it must, as far as is practicable, replace men by machines; and it can accomplish this only by motorizing and mechanizing."[50] The article had been evaluated by Bradley's immediate superiors, Colonel George C. Marshall and Lieutenant Colonel Joseph W. Stilwell.[51] Unfortunately for Bradley, Major General Stephen O. Fuqua, the chief of infantry, took exception to the piece. In a letter to Brigadier General Campbell King, the commandant of the Infantry School, Fuqua noted that he had read Bradley's article and that "the ideas expressed therein are not in accord with the thought in this office on the subject and I know are not in accord with your views." Although he assured King that he did not want to repress any infantry officer's right to "free expression," he asked King to watch Bradley to make sure these unsanctioned ideas did not creep into his instruction at the school.[52] Bradley was fortunate that King thought highly of him and so wrote Fuqua. Nevertheless, Bradley was probably only half joking when he wrote a friend, Major Bradford G. Chynoweth, that Fuqua's admonition would "muzzle me for a while" and that "it wouldn't surprise me to be shipped out at any moment."[53]

Major Chynoweth, one of the early advocates of motorization and mechanization within the army, was himself no stranger to run-ins with the infantry hierarchy.[54] In 1930 he was a member of the Infantry Board at Fort Benning. This organization, under the direction of General King, tested infantry doctrine, organization, and equipment. One of the more important items on the board's agenda was the reorganization of the standard infantry battalion. Chynoweth and the other board members knew that General Summerall and General Fuqua endorsed the organizational plans they were studying. It soon became evident that the board's job was to rubber-stamp the battalion organization approved by the chiefs of staff and infantry, not to subject it to rigorous analysis.[55] They were merely to play their role in the bureaucratic process that required every new infantry organization to be reviewed by the board. The board, however, objected to the structure of the battalion and was reluctant to give its approval. King, understanding the political sensitivity of the issue, prepared a favorable report and ordered the board to submit it as its own, not even bothering with the formality of a vote. Chynoweth, who chose not to participate in the charade, instead prepared a minority report and confronted King with the illegality of the board action.[56] Chynoweth's written comments asserted that the Regular Army needed to be modernized, through motorization and mechanization, even if the costs necessary to effect this change required a "corresponding reduction in numerical strength."[57] Given the position of the Army on personnel mobilization, this statement was nothing short of heresy.

Needless to say, King was incensed. In a tense meeting he confronted Chynoweth with what he doubtless viewed as a logical argument:

> He [King] greeted me with cold hostility. He asked "Have you ever had combat experience?" I replied "No Sir." "Then how do you dare to oppose General Summerall who won his great reputation as a warrior?" I replied: "The duty prescribed for the Infantry Board imposed upon me the duty of recommending for the best interests of the Infantry."[58]

Not swayed by Chynoweth's argument, King demanded that he withdraw his objections. Chynoweth refused to comply. King then recommended that Chynoweth apply for transfer, since they both agreed on at least one point: Chynoweth "was not suited to serve on the board under the circumstances."[59] Chynoweth complied and, in a letter to the chief of infantry, asked to be assigned as a student to the Army War College or to duty with tanks at Fort Meade, Maryland. Staying within the bounds of acceptable discourse, Chynoweth justified his request for transfer on compassionate grounds by stating that the south Georgia climate was aggravating his daughter's bronchial condition. He also emphasized that his "personal relations with the President and Director of the Board have been harmonious" but noted that there had been "pronounced differences of opinion."[60] General Fuqua, probably just as irritated as King had been with Chynoweth's intransigence, sent Chynoweth to Fort Sam Houston, Texas.[61]

Based on the examples of Bradley and Chynoweth, it would be simple to conclude that the Army was a repressive institution run by conservative bureaucrats. This judgment, however accurate, is not entirely satisfactory. A more important question needs to be answered: Why did the Army create an environment that so limited the discourse of some of its brightest officers? Perhaps a more useful way to view the Army in the 1920s is as an institution fighting for its concept of what was required to defend the nation.

To the leaders of the Army, the most compelling lesson from World War I was the need to be able to mobilize a mass army. They believed that the active-duty strength authorized in the National Defense Act of 1920 was the minimum force with which to defend national interests and simultaneously serve as a training and mobilization base for the reserves. Presidents Harding and Coolidge, as well as the Congress, were bent on a policy of fiscal economy and international disarmament. It was an era without military threat to the security of the United States. The nation returned to the normalcy of isolationism, and many "viewed the army as virtually obsolete as the nation moved further away from the notion that war would ever again come to America."[62] Consequently, the Army was an attractive target for reduction. The leaders of the Army watched as the Regular Army became a hollow shell of what they believed was essential for national defense. It is not surprising, then, that the generals, given their central anxiety over the size of the Army, were not particularly supportive of ideas that would make further demands on resources already heavily strained. It was in this charged environment that the tank and the airplane competed for acceptance.

[6]

Infantry Tanks

When the infantry absorbed the Tank Corps in June 1920, the Army did not radically shift its views on tanks. The only perceptible changes were in matters of form. Sam Rockenbach, former chief of the Tank Corps, wore the eagles of a colonel; his stars disappeared with his billet as a branch chief. The Tank Corps School at Camp Meade, Maryland, became the Infantry Tank School. Many signs were repainted. Finally, the officers serving with tanks had to decide whether to return to their former branches or to become infantry (tank corps) officers.

Doctrine changed even less because the Tank Corps had always been envisioned as an auxiliary arm of the infantry. Although Rockenbach had argued for a separate tank branch, stating that "to submerge this Tank Corps now into some other arm, such as the infantry, would in my opinion cumber and hamper the infantry, and it would emasculate the Tank Corps," he never articulated a mission or doctrine that would justify an independent tank corps. Instead, his view "that the functions of the tanks are to make a path through obstacles for the infantry and to protect them from destructive losses from machine gun and rifle fire" was an argument that supported the incorporation of the tank, and the responsibility for its development, in the infantry.[1] Quite simply, Rockenbach never addressed the central issue of why the Army needed a separate branch to develop what he himself regarded as an infantry weapon.

In March 1920, only two months before its demise, the branch published its final doctrinal manual, *Tank Combat*, in which the tank was presented as an infantry weapon: "The tank is primarily an aid to the advance of the infantry engaged in a vigorous offensive either in the assault of works or in open warfare situations."[2] The limited capabilities of the existing tanks made it difficult to articulate more ambitious roles for the primitive machines.

The Army's most advanced tanks in 1921 were the thousand-odd domestically produced copies of the Renault light tank and 100 Mark VIII heavy tanks assembled at Rock Island Arsenal from components left over from the abortive Anglo-American wartime heavy tank program.[3] Both were slow and unreliable. Instructors at the Infantry School at Camp Benning, Georgia, taught their students that at most the Mark VIII could reach a speed of around five miles per hour, while the light tank could make six. Furthermore, the officers were cautioned that "the infantry must remember that the tanks cannot always be present, nor is it always desirable to use them." Students were counseled to husband their tank assets because of their inherent fragility: "Tanks expend themselves rapidly in action, due to mechanical wear and tear, and if used when not vitally needed their efforts will be wasted so that there will be no tanks available when the necessity for their use arises." The instructors also used a more traditional line of reasoning in keeping with their self-image as infantrymen. They warned that "when used habitually, tanks may tend to reduce the self-reliance and aggressive spirit of the infantry."[4] Again, there was consistency with earlier Tank Corps doctrine; these employment considerations for the weapon were lifted verbatim from the 1920 *Tank Combat* manual.[5] Therefore, the decision to place the Tank Corps within the infantry seemed logical. This subordination, however, had far-reaching effects. Pulling tanks under the infantry ensured that the weapon would develop in a manner favored by that arm. Henceforth, the chief of infantry would determine the direction of tank doctrine and organization and define the limits of acceptable advocacy.

The War Department was also involved in establishing the relationship between tanks and infantry. In April 1922 the War Department formalized its policy for future tank development in a letter to the chiefs of infantry and ordnance that clearly stated the linkage of the tank to the infantry:

> The primary mission of the tank is to facilitate the uninterrupted advance of the riflemen in the attack. Its size, armament, speed, and all the accessories for making it an offensive force must be approached with above mission as the final objective to be obtained in development.[6]

The directive also specified the intraservice arrangements for the development of tank technology. The chief of ordnance had "great latitude in the development of pilot tanks for test purposes, in close cooperation with the chief of infantry." It further indicated the types of tanks to be developed. In the interest of "simplicity in organization," design efforts were to focus on the development of a light tank and a medium tank, which "should be capable of fulfilling all assigned missions." The War Department based this decision not on any inherent limitations in tank technology but on other factors, such as weight.

[73]

Weight was the critical constraint. Because light tanks under five tons could be transported by the Army's heavy trucks, five tons became a weight ceiling. The fifteen-ton weight limitation for the medium tank followed a similar logic by keeping these vehicles "within the limits of average highway bridges, the capacity of railroads, and the limit of 15 tons placed by the War Department on the medium ponton bridge."

Medium tanks received priority, since the Ordnance Department had already begun designing such a machine. Furthermore, the War Department believed that medium tanks could do everything that a light tank could, with the exception of being transported on trucks. That the Army had almost 1,000 light tanks in its inventory may also have influenced this decision.

The other design parameters for the medium tank focused on its development as an infantry support vehicle. The tank would be armed with machine guns and heavier guns to enable it to engage enemy troops in trenches and hostile tanks. One other important design criterion was specified: although the medium tank had to be capable of a maximum speed of twelve miles per hour, it also had to operate efficiently at the pace of walking infantrymen. Cross-country rather than road speed was the critical consideration. Finally, recognizing the fiscal constraints the Army faced in 1922, the War Department authorized only limited quantities of pilot tanks for testing.[7] Units continued to be equipped with existing World War I–vintage tanks.

Before the announcement of the War Department policy, doctrine had been in a state of flux. Rockenbach had asked his officers at Camp Meade to publish their views on tanks to familiarize the rest of the Army with the machine's capabilities.[8] Consequently, in 1920 and 1921, advocacy articles on tanks appeared in the service periodicals, particularly the *Infantry Journal* and the *Cavalry Journal*. Rockenbach apparently did not censor these efforts, although his own writing was orthodox.[9] Some of his subordinates, however, took issue with the conventional wisdom. George Patton wrote that he believed the Tank Corps should be an independent branch of the Army, like the Air Service.[10] Chynoweth issued a call for the Army to mechanize its infantry, to concentrate on mobility in warfare, and to motorize cross-country transportation.[11]

Chynoweth also attended to the cavalry. His July 1921 article implied that the role of the horse in modern warfare was severely restricted by the introduction of machine guns and tanks. Chynoweth asserted blasphemously that these weapons made the cavalry charge "seem a thing of the past." He further cautioned that Army officers should not think of tanks in terms of the machines they knew in World War I: "blind, dumb, deaf monsters, lumbering across the trenches slowly, if not indeed halted in rear for repairs." Chynoweth predicted that faster and more reliable tanks would surely be developed. He then chastened readers to embrace the machine age; he

[74]

asked cavalrymen to think of the tank as "a great iron horse" and a way to maintain their importance in a modern army.[12]

Freewheeling articles, such as those written by Patton and Chynoweth, disappeared from the journals as the rules for sanctioned discourse tightened. These guidelines were the work of the new chief of infantry, Major General Charles S. Farnsworth. Farnsworth soon moved to establish control over the infantry's new weapon and to discipline the unruly tank officers.

The repression of any criticism of official infantry policy took a number of forms. Direct confrontation with the occasional wayward infantry officer proved effective, as in the case of Captain Dwight D. Eisenhower. Eisenhower had been assigned to the Tank Corps during World War I but never went overseas. In 1920 he and Patton were assigned to Camp Meade, Maryland. Both advocated a role for the tank based on what they viewed as its potential rather than its present limitations.

In late 1920 Eisenhower took up Rockenbach's challenge and published an article in the *Infantry Journal*. Although Eisenhower was careful to note that the tank remained an infantry auxiliary, he lectured his fellow infantrymen on their ignorance of its capabilities and potential. He also asserted that more capable machines could change tank doctrine and essentially advocated what approached an independent mission for tanks.[13] Eisenhower's article did not escape General Farnsworth's attention. The young captain was called before the general, who told him that his "ideas were not only wrong but dangerous and that henceforth I would keep them to myself. Particularly, I was not to publish anything incompatible with solid infantry doctrine." Furthermore, Eisenhower was warned that if he persisted in his unorthodoxy, he "would be hauled before a court-martial." Eisenhower understood the chief of infantry's message and applied for a transfer out of tanks. He believed that his friend George Patton received a similar warning, because he also left tanks.[14]

In reality, Patton likely had another motive for abandoning tanks. George Patton was an ambitious officer and, as one of the most highly placed and successful tank officers, had a bright future in a separate tank corps. In May 1920 he had argued that "the tank corps grafted on infantry, cavalry, artillery, or engineers, will be like the third leg to a duck—worthless for control, for combat impotent."[15] When the Tank Corps disappeared in June 1920, Patton reassessed his career plans, probably realizing that, without a separate tank arm, the highest rank to which he could aspire was colonel. Furthermore, staying in tanks meant a transfer to the infantry. Patton chose to return to the cavalry, where "he could play polo, participate in horse shows, and hunt."[16] He also became a spirited advocate of the value of horse cavalry.

The examples of Eisenhower and Patton, if in fact Patton was warned to comply with official doctrine, are dramatic but uncommon. Unlike Eisenhower, most officers did not require a direct confrontation with the chief infantry to stay in line. Eisenhower may have told the other tank officers, almost all of whom resided at Camp Meade, of his reprimand. Even if he did not, the message to adhere to official doctrine gradually permeated the officer corps. In May 1921 Major A. W. Lane wrote an article for the *Infantry Journal* that described the new Army tables of organization. Attached to his piece was a comment by Major General W. G. Haan, War Department assistant chief of staff. Haan noted that the organizational plans Lane described had been designed by "experienced and well-informed officers and that all the advice so received was carefully studied and given due weight in the final conclusion." Haan also noted that although he did not object to constructive criticism, "in all our criticism we must remember that we cannot saw wood with a hammer."[17] If General Haan's warning was too subtle, General Farnsworth's promise of censorship in the August 1922 edition of the *Infantry Journal* clarified the rules.[18] Articles critical of infantry tank policy disappeared from the service literature. Authors still motivated to publish began to carefully note in their writing the subordination of the tank to the infantry support doctrine.[19] Although much of the proof is based on negative evidence (i.e., the diminished number of radical tank articles), it seems safe to assume that the chief of infantry's policy of intimidation and censorship defined the limits of acceptable tank advocacy and affected what appeared in the service journals.

Authors who wanted to publish outside of the Army periodicals had to receive approval from the War Department adjutant general. In December 1927 Rockenbach, again a brigadier general in his new job as the commander of the District of Washington, submitted an article on tanks to the adjutant general for review. His cover letter says a great deal about the War Department's control over the dissemination of ideas: "I request that the article be reviewed by the proper Staff Section, revised and corrected, and I be informed if there is anything therein that should not be given in lecture to our service or make it inadvisable to publish it."[20]

The adjutant general sent Rockenbach's article to the chief of infantry for comment. Colonel Willey Howell reviewed the article for the chief of infantry, recommending two minor changes before publication. The adjutant general forwarded his approval of the article to Rockenbach, with the suggestion that Howell's changes be incorporated before publication. Major General R. H. Allen, the chief of infantry, wrote Rockenbach that "on the whole, the article is excellent and very clearly expresses our ideas on the subject" but also enclosed a copy of Howell's changes. Rockenbach made the revisions.[21]

The chief of infantry additionally ensured that official infantry doctrine on the tank reached the Army in general. In May 1922 the Fort Leavenworth journal, *Military Review,* printed a summary of an *Infantry Journal* article that contained "the best thought to date" on tank doctrine. The piece clearly focused on the infantry support mission. Although it considered the possible use of tanks in breakthroughs, in rear guard actions, and for fighting other tanks, the discussion centered on how these missions directly assisted the infantry. In an interesting juxtaposition of old and new concepts of warfare, the piece noted that tanks operating in the enemy's rear area could "obstruct roads by killing draft animals or wrecking trucks."[22]

The formal process of writing manuals and service school lesson plans also began. Major Eisenhower prepared one of the first drafts for a training memorandum discussing infantry tanks. Suitably chastened after his meeting with the chief of infantry, Eisenhower obediently stressed that "tanks can never take over the mission of the infantry, no matter to what degree developed. Advancing infantry will continue to be the deciding factor, and the tank should be carefully studied and developed as an important means of aiding this advance."[23] The 1923 version of the *Field Service Regulations* made this vision of the utility of the tank official Army doctrine, stating that "the tank constitutes an armored infantry element" and "its essential mission is to assist in the progression of the infantry by overcoming or neutralizing resistances or breaking down obstacles that check the infantry advance."[24] Service school publications and texts echoed this doctrine.[25]

Determining a suitable tank organization for the Army flowed from the doctrinal decision. Given that the tank existed to support the infantry, it logically followed that tank units should be available to every infantry organization. Accordingly, a light tank company became part of each infantry division, while the remaining tank units formed General Headquarters reserves to give added power to the main infantry effort.[26]

The War Department faced some formidable obstacles in its tank development program throughout the 1920s. To begin with, a national military policy focused on economy and disarmament meant that money was in short supply. Expenditures on new tanks and accessories from 1920 to 1930 totaled only some $1.5 million.[27] Additionally, tanks did not attract much interest from commercial concerns. There was little civilian application for the technology and little prospect for profits given the small tank budget.[28] Finally, the Army faced the same situation with tanks as it did with other surplus war matériel: it would be difficult to explain to Congress why the more than 1,000 tanks in inventory would not suffice for a peacetime training program. All of these considerations affected the April 1922 War Department tank policy. Given these constraints, the Army's decision to produce only limited numbers of prototype models for testing was probably unavoidable.

Unfortunately, the Army created a bureaucratic impediment to tank development that further hampered the already austere program. Because of the power inherent in the chief of infantry's position, it is scarcely surprising that he could fundamentally influence tank doctrine, organization, and the limits of sanctioned behavior. In the area of equipment, however, where the greatest tension developed, he shared responsibility with the chief of ordnance.

The April 1922 tank development policy advanced by the War Department resulted in the following institutional arrangements:

> The using service [the infantry] lays down the *tactical* requirements based on the general principles established by the General Staff. Limited by the above-referred to service requirements, the Ordnance Department then proceeds to make a design after the approval of both the general project and the expenditure of the funds therefore [sic] by the Ordnance Committee, and by the War Department. The Ordnance Committee has on it representatives of the Chiefs of all the using and combat services in addition to the members of the technical sections of the Chief of Ordnance. . . . On the completion of the design, a pilot or experimental model is built, which on completion is sent to Aberdeen Proving Ground for a technical test by the Ordnance Department. After this test the vehicle, after any necessary alterations have been made, is sent to the using service for a complete service, or tactical test. . . . Based on these recommendations [by the user] the Ordnance Department makes modifications in the pilot, or a new pilot vehicle is built to meet requirements of the using service. When these requirements are met the tank is ready for approval as standard by the War Department General Staff, after its approval by the Chiefs of Infantry and Ordnance.[29]

These spheres of responsibility were almost completely separate and jealously guarded by each chief. Furthermore, the Ordnance Department virtually excluded the infantry from participating in the technical aspects of the program. Once the ordnance committee approved a design, the user entered the process only when the pilot tank was delivered to Camp Meade. In the interim, the project was an engineering and manufacturing problem, an Ordnance Department concern not subject to user interference. Additionally, the infantry did not have a permanent agency responsible for tank testing until the creation of the Tank Board in April 1926. Before then, the Tank School appointed a special board as the need to evaluate a project arose.[30] The problems inherent in these tank development arrangements soon became apparent.

The case of the M1921 medium tank is instructive. On September 14, 1923, the office of the chief of infantry forwarded a recommendation to the adjutant general that the M1921 medium tank, with modification, serve as the basis for future tank development efforts. The letter stated that the tank preferred by the Ordnance Department, the M1924, did not meet user requirements. Specific failings included inadequate fighting compartment size; absence of a revolving turret, thereby limiting the field of fire of the main gun to thirty degrees; and a poor weight distribution. The chief of infantry also

[78]

suggested that since the more acceptable M1921 surpassed the fifteen-ton weight limit, this upper limit should be raised to twenty tons.[31] The chief of ordnance responded that the M1921, because it could not cross Army bridging, was unacceptable and that the M1924 was the best tank available within the fifteen-ton limitation. Furthermore, the faults the chief of infantry complained about in the M1924 resulted from having to stay within this weight constraint.[32] Because the weight restriction on the medium tank derived from the capacity of the divisional ponton bridge, the chief of engineers had to offer an opinion. He supported the chief of ordnance, commenting that the fifteen-ton weight capacity for the divisional ponton bridging equipment being developed by the engineers came from a February 1922 letter from the adjutant general.[33] The War Department supported the chief of ordnance, stating that the chief of infantry had concurred in the April 1922 tank policy. The fifteen-ton weight limit stood.[34]

This initial confrontation set the tone for the remainder of the decade. American tank development became a battle for control between the user and the provider. The infantry complained that ordnance ignored tactical requirements in its tank designs. Similarly, ordnance argued that the infantry made unrealistic demands on the design of the tank.

Colonel O. S. Eskridge, the president of the Tank Board, wrote the chief of infantry that many of the defects in the pilot model of the T1E1 light tank could have been avoided if the board had been given a chance to study the design plans. He also believed that there needed to be "a closer cooperation by the designing service with the using service" and recommended that plans for future tanks be submitted to his organization for review before being built.[35] Colonel L. D. Gasser, responding for the office of the chief of infantry, denied the request. He replied that Eskridge's recommendation would "involve the Tank Board in technical detail pertaining to design which is not included in the functions of the board." He further noted that past experience had shown that when the user became involved in the design process, the delivery of pilot tanks was only delayed. Colonel Gasser closed by summarizing the chief of infantry's tank policy as "leaving it entirely to the Ordnance Department to draft the manufacturing plans and specifications as nearly in conformity with the requirements of the using service as sound engineering principles permit."[36]

The hands-off policy of entrusting tank engineering details to the chief of ordnance came back to haunt the chief of infantry. In 1930 the Ordnance Department produced a pilot medium tank with the engine in the front, in direct violation of the chief of infantry's requirement that the engine be in the rear. The chief of infantry did not know of this change until after the fact and was "placed in the embarrassing position of not being completely informed as to the status of development of types of Infantry equipment and arms, a function with which he is specifically charged, under Army Regulations."[37]

The results of the War Department's tank development policy were appalling. By 1930 the Ordnance Department had produced only a dozen or so pilot tanks, none of which met infantry expectations; therefore, none were standardized. The major obstacle was the weight limitation. The Ordnance Department could not manufacture a tank that incorporated all of the design features specified by the infantry within the fifteen-ton limitation. The infantry requirements, mainly that the medium tank have enough armor to stop a .50-caliber armor-piercing bullet, made it impossible for ordnance designers to build a fifteen-ton tank unless engine weight was reduced. Unfortunately, a lighter engine resulted in an underpowered tank that failed to meet performance criteria. And the infantry would not accept any tanks that did not meet its requirements.[38] Consequently, the Army was still equipped with obsolete World War I machines.[39]

Nevertheless, one area of consensus existed between ordnance department and the infantry: tank technology existed to support the infantry. Many in the Army viewed airplane technology from the same perspective. Its subordination, however, would prove more problematic than that of the tank.

[7]

The Failed Revolution and
the Evolution of Air Force

Major General Charles T. Menoher, the chief of the Army Air Service, had his hands full in the year following the passage of the National Defense Act of 1920. He had to oversee the reorganization of his arm in accordance with the act and establish the eleven Air Service schools authorized by the War Department in February 1920.[1] Furthermore, Menoher had to implement the recommendations of the General Reorganization Board, approved by Secretary of War Baker in September 1920, for the peacetime structure of the Air Service.[2] Still, the most vexing task facing Menoher must have been the need to contain the revolutionary struggle being waged by many air officers for an independent department of aeronautics. Perhaps most distressing to Menoher, the ringleader of the insurgents was his own assistant, Brig. Gen. Billy Mitchell.

Menoher had a credibility problem among many of his subordinates. To begin with, he was an artilleryman and had never learned to fly. Still, his ideas about military aviation were not as conventional as those of most of his ground force contemporaries. Menoher had been the commander of the 42d Division during the war and had seen firsthand the importance of air support. This experience convinced him that the Army had to retain air organization.[3] Furthermore, he saw a greater role for offensive aviation than the Reorganization Board had. Although Menoher agreed with the board that Army aviation had two roles, air service and air force, he disagreed with the board's emphasis on the former. In 1921 he requested the formation of an additional two pursuit groups and one bombardment group. He believed that the importance of combat aviation justified the increase.[4]

For Mitchell, however, the issue was not merely numbers and functions but control. The National Defense Act, he and his supporters believed, settled nothing. The subordination of the Air Service to the Army was only a temporary setback in the effort to gain an independent air organization that would guarantee a broader vision of air power.

As early as 1919 Mitchell had articulated his views about the military role of aeronautics, concepts that even then were fundamentally at odds with War Department policy. He wrote that "the principal mission of Aeronautics is to destroy the aeronautical force of the enemy, and, after this, to attack his formations, both tactical and strategical, on the ground or on the water. . . . The secondary employment of Aeronautics pertains to their use as an aux-iliary to troops on the ground for enhancing their effect against hostile troops."[5]

This hierarchy of priorities—air superiority, tactical and strategic attack, and then support of ground forces—served as the fundamental premise for American air power theorists in devising doctrine. The airmen's logic was simple: If the airplane is the most significant weapon in war, then the en-emy's airplanes must be the most important target. Mitchell, however, went further and asserted that the "development of the Air Service will mean the extinction of navies on the surface of the ocean in the future. . . . Its fruition depends on the amount of support given it by Congress and the country."[6]

Mitchell expressed the same views during his testimony on the reorgani-zation of the Army and the creation of a separate department of aeronautics, with one notable exception. He now argued that the airplane could not de-velop as "a decisive element in combat" until it became free of the "older services."[7] Menoher was upset because Mitchell did not cease his congres-sional lobbying efforts after the issue of a separate aviation service was de-cided with the passage of the National Defense Act. Instead, Mitchell placed his views about air power, and the inability of the War Department to stew-ard its proper development, directly before the American public.

In August 1920, less than two months after the passage of the National Defense Act, the *Review of Reviews* published Mitchell's article "Our Army's Air Service." Mitchell wrote: "We are convinced that aviation can only be put on its feet in this country through the unification of all air activities . . . under persons who are actually familiar with flying and the things that go with it."[8] This statement conflicted with War Department policy and im-plied that Menoher, not being a flyer, was not competent to run the Air Ser-vice. Mitchell also renewed his campaign before the Congress, using an ar-gument that aviation rather than the Navy should be the basis of national defense.[9] Ironically, the Navy's own tests on the vulnerability of ships to air attack gave Mitchell the leverage he needed.

In late October 1920 the Navy conducted secret tests to determine the ef-fects of aerial bombs on battleships, using the *U.S.S. Indiana* as a target. Un-fortunately for the Navy, someone leaked the results of the test, including photographs. On December 11, pictures of a battered *Indiana* appeared in the *London Illustrated News*.[10] Mitchell had his opening. In January 1921 he

[82]

testified before the House Committee on Appropriations that "we can either destroy or sink any ship in existence today." Not content with naval heresy, Mitchell attacked War Department policy as well: "Our system of coast defense today is wrong. The only way to really defend a coast is with aircraft and mobile troops and their accessories." He also argued that an air force could defend the country more cheaply than the Navy, since "battleships cost $45,000,000, and we can build a thousand airplanes for the cost of each battleship." For an economy-minded Congress, this was a tempting proposition. The temptation grew when Mitchell offered to demonstrate the effectiveness of airplanes against ships if the Navy could be persuaded to provide a ship for bombing experiments.[11] Shortly thereafter, the War and Navy Departments agreed to conduct aerial bombing tests under Navy control.[12]

In May 1921 Mitchell assumed personal command of the 1st Provisional Air Brigade, the unit formed to conduct the bombing tests. On May 29 one of the brigade's Curtiss Eagle bombers crashed during a severe storm, killing all seven people aboard. The War Department inquiry into the tragedy attributed the crash to the storm.[13] Mitchell, however, laid the blame on the "lack of regular routes, landing facilities, radio service, and weather bulletins for aviation, all of which could be provided by centralized control over aviation."[14] Menoher had had enough and formally requested that Secretary of War Weeks dismiss Mitchell. Weeks, however, was no fool. He was surely aware of the press speculation that the basis of Menoher's ultimatum was a desire to end the "friction between the military and naval services" caused by the proposed bombing tests.[15] Weeks declined Menoher's request and instead embraced the role of conciliator for the headline-seeking newsmen. Eventually Weeks convinced Menoher to retract his demand and the bombing tests proceeded.[16] On July 21 Mitchell's bombers sank the German battleship *Ostfriesland*.[17] From this point the road to an independent Air Force was a straight line.

Mitchell was irrepressible. While the Joint Board prepared its report, Mitchell staged mock bombing raids against New York City, Philadelphia, Wilmington, Baltimore, and, adding insult to injury, the Naval Academy at Annapolis.[18] He realized that his case played better in the court of public opinion than it did in the briefing rooms of the military services.

On August 18 the Joint Board, headed by General Pershing, submitted its report to the secretaries of War and Navy. Although the board predictably highlighted the Navy's vital role in protecting sea lines of communication, and the battleship's preeminence in performing this mission, it nevertheless made some rather remarkable concessions. The board members noted that even with their confined radius of action and susceptibility to weather conditions, airplanes could be "the decisive factor" in coast defense operations.[19] They also admitted that airplanes could "sink or seriously damage any naval vessel at present constructed." In their conclusions, the board

[83]

members showed how deeply their perspectives had been changed when they stated that bombing experiments had "proved that it has become imperative as a matter of national defense to provide for the maximum possible development of aviation in both the Army and Navy." Henceforth, the fleet would need aircraft carriers and improved antiaircraft weapons to protect itself from the aerial threat. Finally, the board recommended that the secret classification of the experiments be rescinded and that their report be made public.[20] The Joint Board did not, however, make the one and only recommendation that would have satisfied Mitchell—the establishment of a separate air force.

Mitchell saw the bombing tests through different lenses. In his August 29 report to Menoher on the activities of the 1st Provisional Air Brigade, Mitchell matter-of-factly noted: "The problem of the destruction of seacraft by Air Forces has been solved, and is finished." He also asserted the implications of this new reality: "It is now necessary to provide an Air organization and a method of defending not only our coast cities, but our interior cities, against the attack of hostile Air Forces." Furthermore, Mitchell believed that his simulated attacks along the eastern seaboard showed the acute vulnerability of American cities to air attack. In Mitchell's opinion, his findings necessitated an immediate, radical revision of national defense policies. An independent air force was at the center of his plan: "A Department of Aeronautics co-equal with the Departments of War and Navy should be created at once. . . . Only then will there result real national protection combined with economy."[21]

Menoher read Mitchell's report, noted his disapproval, and passed it along to Weeks.[22] Before either had a chance to comment on Mitchell's findings, someone leaked the report to the *New York Times,* where it appeared on September 14.[23] Menoher had finally had enough and on September 16 asked to be relieved as the chief of Air Service.[24] Those who speculated that Mitchell would succeed Menoher were disappointed. On September 21 Mason Patrick, the officer on whom Pershing had relied to bring discipline to the Air Service, AEF, when "it had become 'a tangled mess' under Brigadier General Foulois," became the chief of the Air Service.[25] Pershing obviously hoped Patrick could restore order.

The War Department probably received more than it expected when Patrick became the new head of Army aviation. To be sure, he soon gained control over Mitchell. Mitchell confronted Patrick almost immediately, insisting on certain prerogatives as the "senior flying officer in the service," and threatened to resign if Patrick did not meet his conditions. When Patrick called his bluff by offering to accept his resignation, Mitchell withdrew it. Patrick then took flying lessons and became a pilot himself, making Mitchell the second senior flyer in the service. Instantly he achieved a credibility in the aviation fraternity that Menoher never enjoyed.[26] Patrick has

[84]

his own vision of a stronger, more independent air arm. Because he was more tactful and less speculative than Mitchell in how he presented it to the War Department and Congress, he was probably more effective.

Patrick's stewardship of Army aviation lasted until December 1927. During his tenure, a doctrine focused on offensive operations independent of the ground battle and ground officer control emerged. Patrick seemed to have realized that the first step in this process was the enunciation of a mission statement, followed by a low-key campaign to gain its acceptance by the War Department. To this end, Patrick refined Menoher's earlier concepts of *air service* and *air force.* In his 1922 annual report, Patrick noted that the air service role was the function of observation units, which should make up only 20 percent of Army aviation. Pursuit, bombardment, and attack units provided the Army with its offensive capability and should comprise 80 percent of the Air Service. Furthermore, Patrick highlighted the growing importance of aviation to national defense and expressed deep reservations about the adequacy of the current organization.[27] Secretary Weeks responded to Patrick's report, asking him to prepare a study "covering all measures necessary to place the peace establishment of the Air Service upon a basis adequate to meet the approved war time expansion."[28] Patrick had his foot in the door.

Patrick reviewed the approved mobilization plans and found the Air Service structure "incorrect." The one bombardment group authorized in the General Headquarters (GHQ) reserve was inadequate; more pursuit aviation was needed. There should be no aviation in the divisions; the corps observation groups could meet their needs. Indeed, all air force units—pursuit, bombardment, and attack—should be moved to the GHQ reserve. In reporting these findings to Weeks, Patrick asked for permission to submit a revised wartime aviation structure that would serve as the basis for a peacetime organization. He softened the impact of this request by promising that no immediate reorganization need take place, thereby adroitly defusing any General Staff objections. Patrick, in an even more sophisticated ploy, also gave the secretary a way to place the onus for an inadequate air service on the Congress by recommending that any changes to existing war plans or other changes be contingent on legislation "to increase the strength of the Air Service to meet that proposed organization."[29] Weeks told Patrick to proceed.[30]

Patrick's plan, submitted within two weeks of the secretary's go-ahead, made an argument that would serve as the central tenet for American air power theorists: "Very often there is as distinct and definite a mission for the Air Force independent of the ground troops as there is for the Army and Navy independent of each other." In particular, he believed that "bombardment aviation especially will act with ground troops only in very rare instances." Consequently, Patrick was "convinced that the concentration of all

Air Force under one G.H.Q. Reserve Commander is the most effective way of assuring aerial supremacy."[31]

Patrick also forwarded detailed organization plans to support his recommendation. On March 17 Weeks appointed a board under Major General William Lassiter to consider Patrick's proposals.[32]

On April 24 the Lassiter Board issued its formal report. It was a benchmark, even though few of its recommendations were implemented. To begin with, the costs of its specified expansion program were prohibitive for an already strapped Army.[33] Furthermore, the board would not endorse the specifics of Patrick's organizational plan. Still, it was a major Air Service coup in a broad conceptual sense, because the board recognized the categorical distinctions of *air service* and *air force*. More importantly, it legitimized a central principle from which an independent air doctrine could flow by recommending that "an Air Force of bombardment and pursuit aviation and airships should be directly under General Headquarters for assignment to special and strategical missions . . . either in connection with the operation of ground troops or entirely independent of them." The Lassiter Board additionally found "our Air Service to be in a very unfortunate and critical situation" because of the reduction of its personnel strength and the deterioration of its World War I—vintage equipment. The members believed that the Air Service had to have priority in peacetime, since "it is indispensable to be strong in the air at the very outset of a war." The board then noted the critical linkage between military aviation and the nascent American aircraft industry; it went so far as to state that for want of military airplane orders, "our aircraft industry is languishing and may disappear."[34]

The Lassiter Board's report completely changed the framework of the discourse on American aviation policy. Patrick had maneuvered the War Department into acknowledging that the Air Service was inadequate to meet American defense needs. In October the report was released to the public, and the War Department was soon placed in a reactive posture.[35]

In March 1924 the House appointed a select committee, chaired by Representative Florian Lampert of Wisconsin, to investigate the Air Service. During the committee's hearings, War Department aviation policies came under attack. Weeks was personally chastened when the committee pointed out to him that the Lassiter Board had made its report in April 1923, and since one of its key recommendations was for congressional action to redress the "alarming and critical condition" of the Air Service, they wanted to know why the War Department had not forwarded such legislation. Weeks cited interservice disagreements with the Navy, "which have not been ironed out."[36] Clearly, pressure was mounting on the Army to pursue the Lassiter Board findings.

The Lampert Committee hearings had another indirect effect in forcing the War Department to do something about Billy Mitchell. Mitchell made

[86]

frequent appearances before the Lampert Committee, where he castigated War Department aviation policy. In February 1925 he asserted that because the War and Navy Departments were repressing testimony by aviation officers through indirect threats of disciplinary action, the committee could not get the whole truth about the deplorable aviation situation. In contravention of War Department policy, he also urged the adoption of a unified air force.[37] Weeks responded by holding up Mitchell's reappointment as assistant Air Service chief.[38] Mitchell, not intimidated, stepped up his attacks on the War and Navy Departments.[39] Eventually, his assertions became so outrageous that even the press took exception: "It is one thing to accuse our military officials of being too slow or too stupid. But it is quite another to charge them with willingness to hazard the security of the nation for the sake of their own personal comfort."[40]

Mitchell left Weeks little room to maneuver. On March 6 President Coolidge announced that Lieutenant Colonel James E. Fechet would replace Mitchell. The article announcing the appointment also noted Mitchell's feelings: " 'Flying General', Reduced to Colonel, Avows He Will Continue Aviation Fight."[41] Although an editorial stated that Mitchell's departure was "the rule rather than the exception in these temporary promotions," it also correctly noted that Mitchell's notoriety would make the action appear vindictive. Still, the editorial asked the reader to understand that Mitchell's "methods could not be tolerated if discipline was to be maintained. . . . He was too dogmatic, too audacious, too reckless in his conclusions."[42] Weeks surely agreed. Colonel Mitchell left Washington for his "exile" in Texas.

Mitchell's departure from Washington, and the conclusion of the Lampert Committee hearings in early March, provided a respite from the intense aviation debate that had dominated the headlines for weeks. The interlude was brief, and the charges became even more bitter in September, when the Navy airship *Shenandoah* crashed. In San Antonio, Texas, Mitchell issued a statement to the press that alleged that the tragedies were the "direct result of incompetency, criminal negligence, and almost treasonable administration of the national defense."[43] Mitchell seemed to be daring the administration to court-martial him. President Coolidge obliged and personally preferred the charges that "Mitchell had made statements which were insubordinate, contemptuous, disrespectful, and prejudicial to good order and military discipline."[44]

Shortly after he announced Mitchell's court-martial, President Coolidge appointed a board, chaired by Dwight W. Morrow, to examine aviation matters. Coolidge knew that the Lampert Committee's findings would soon be published, and he was likely trying to regain the initiative in determining a national aviation direction.[45] When Mitchell appeared before the board, he disappointed those expecting his usual fireworks. For almost five hours, he read from a prepared statement.[46] True to form, he recommended an inde-

[87]

pendent air organization. General Patrick also endorsed a separate Army Air Corps, analogous in its relationship to the War Department as the Marine Corps was to the Navy. Although he stopped short of recommending an independent aviation service, he stated that the nation needed a "Minister of Defense, but the time is not yet ripe for it."[47]

The Morrow Board released its findings on November 30, 1925, barely edging out the December 14 publication of the Lampert Committee's report. Although both reports recognized aviation's importance to national defense, they differed fundamentally on how aviation should be advanced. The members of the Morrow Board endorsed the administration's economic and disarmament policies, noting that the "fortunate geographical position" of the United States had freed it "from the heavy burden of armament which necessity seems to have imposed upon the nations on the Continent of Europe." The board also asserted that a new weapon, such as the airplane, would not change "our national policy heretofore to oppose competitive armaments." Consequently, the Morrow Board recommended an evolutionary policy, within the confines of the existing structure.[48]

In contrast, the Lampert Committee's conclusions were revolutionary and operated from the premise that "we can have no adequate national defense without an adequate air force." The committee thus prescribed wide-ranging measures to provide such a force.[49]

While the Morrow Board and the Lampert Committee pondered their findings, the Mitchell court-martial began. The War Department, insensitive to the nuances of the highly charged situation, made serious tactical errors. Moving the trial to Washington from San Antonio guaranteed notoriety and constant press attention. Holding the trial in a dilapidated warehouse made it appear that the Army wanted to "dampen the popular excitement aroused by the court-martial."[50] Finally, the composition of the court-martial board guaranteed Mitchell would be viewed as an underdog. Nine of the ten officers who sat in judgment were generals, hardly Colonel Mitchell's peers. All but one of the officers was a member of the so-called West Point fraternity, adding to the sense of unfairness. Congressman Frank Reid, a member of the Lampert Committee and a strong supporter of aviation, was Mitchell's attorney. Mitchell could not have asked for a better stage and supporting cast. As the *New York Times* noted, "the Mitchell trial is a good show, and that's why it's 'S.R.O.' [standing room only] every day."[51]

The trial began October 28 and dragged on for seven weeks. Mitchell, as he had intended from the outset, turned the proceedings into a forum on American aviation policy. Nevertheless, even Mitchell's strongest supporters knew that he was guilty as charged.[52] On December 18 the court-martial panel, with one dissenting vote, found him guilty on all counts and sentenced him to a five-year suspension without pay.[53] On January 26 President Coolidge approved the conviction but reduced the fine to full subsistence and half-pay. Shortly thereafter, Mitchell resigned his Army commission.[54] Although his resignation marked the end of activism for an independent air force, Mitchell's trial had provided the air power insurgents with a martyr.

In the aftermath of the trial, a mythology of central importance to the aviation insurgency evolved.[55] The fog that surrounds the Mitchell legend is difficult to penetrate:

> There were three Billy Mitchells: there was the man they court-martialed . . . who wouldn't rest until he became a martyr; there was Mitchell the air prophet. . . . And then there was the third Mitchell . . . the Billy the public loved, and whom the Air Corps loved. Quite aside from his fine war record and his leaping mind, the Mitchell was the hero who had always had the American public on his side—the dashing, colorful doer-of-deeds who cut red tape, defied the stuffy boss, snapped his fingers in the face of authority, cried, "What, I can't sink your ships?" and sent them to the bottom; exposed the evil interests, paused in the midst of it all to marry the charming girl, and in short, did everything Billy did. After he had gone too far, for a man in uniform, and his superiors had crushed him, the public and the Air Corps still loved him, and Billy . . . went right on fighting.[56]

Yet there was also a fourth Billy Mitchell—the Army colonel who radicalized air officers. Perhaps Billy Mitchell's central contribution to the cause of American air power was not his "vision" but the fact that he fundamentally transformed the limits of sanctioned behavior for Army aviators. Forty years after the trial, a retired Lieutenant General Ira Eaker, a captain at the time of the trial who helped prepare Mitchell's defense, recalled:

> Well, naturally I was sympathetic with General Mitchell. . . . And formed a great admiration for his method, learned a lot from him about how to influence Congress, how to influence the public, how to draw attention to individuals and ideas and concepts. And when it was announced by the President that he would be court-martialed—the young Air Force officers of my age and rank and location, being in the Air Staff—we had a pretty tough decision to make. And as we were told by General Patrick, the Chief of the Army Air Corps, that we must be very careful or we might jeopardize our entire military careers. We realized this as well as he did, but we, in council, after talking it over and deliberating carefully, thoroughly, decided we'd rather stand with Mitchell for a principle and for the future of airpower than to save our necks and skins.[57]

It took some time for the insurgents to realize that they would have to change their methods and go underground. Two officers from General Patrick's staff, Major Henry H. Arnold and Major Herbert A. Dargue, soon found that the ground rules had changed. The two were trying to "keep up the fight" by distributing copies of a circular designed to influence Congressmen to create a separate air corps. Secretary of War Dwight F. Davis was outraged and ordered an inquiry. Arnold and Dargue were discovered and disciplined.[58] Congress, however, needed little prodding to make it move on air policy legislation.

Congress enacted two bills in 1926, the Air Commerce Act and the Air Corps Act, that changed American military aviation. The Air Commerce Act was designed to "foster air commerce" in the United States.[59] One of the many things the Air Commerce Act did was establish a linkage between civilian and military aviation that advanced both.[60]

The Air Corps Act, a compromise between competing positions, was based largely on the recommendations of the Morrow Board. The act authorized an increase in Air Corps officer strength from 900 to 1,514 and expanded its enlisted force from 9,760 to 16,000. These new figures would be met from within the existing overall Army authorizations. The Air Corps was also to maintain 1,800 serviceable airplanes. Congress specified that the Army had to meet the increases in personnel and aircraft through the execution of the "Five-Year Air Corps Program." The legislation also provided for an assistant secretary of war to oversee the Air Corps; three brigadier general assistants to the chief of the Air Corps; the inclusion of an air section in each War Department General Staff division; and the requirement that the chief, two of the three brigadier generals, and 90 percent of each officer grade be flying officers.[61] Finally, the act recognized the importance of aviation research by linking the National Aeronautical Advisory Committee to military aviation.[62]

The Air Commerce Act and the Air Corps Act reflected a growing recognition of the importance of aviation to national defense. They also placed aviation research and development outside of the control of the Army. The National Aeronautical Advisory Committee, rapidly becoming the world's leading aeronautical research establishment, did much of the fundamental research, and the Air Corps, unlike the rest of the Army, did not have to rely on the Ordnance Department for major equipment items. These acts created a symbiotic relationship between the civilian aircraft manufacturers and military aviation since the "only research money was in the military services, in their own testing and engineering programs, and implicitly in the experimental contracts they were authorized to make with manufacturers for the development and delivery of new aircraft."[63] Developments in either benefited both. Additionally, Charles A. Lindbergh's epic flight across the Atlantic Ocean created an enthusiasm for flying in the United States that heightened aviation awareness throughout the country.[64]

The years between 1920 and 1929 truly were the Golden Age of aviation.[65]

The Army Air Corps took advantage of the national interest in flying by staging a number of spectacular flights and setting new records that kept its pilots' exploits before the public eye. Airplane technology also underwent a revolution. The primitive World War I–era cloth and wood biplanes powered by Liberty engines were already artifacts by 1930. Sleek, all metal monocoque monoplanes with powerful engines specifically designed for aeronautical use replaced them.[66] Since civil aviation concentrated on large, multiengined airplanes with commercial utility as cargo or passenger carriers, technology moved in that direction. These improvements in aircraft capability created a push-pull relationship in the minds of air officers: "From the military point of view, if it were possible for a commercial or any other kind of airplane to fly across the Atlantic or from Oakland to Honolulu, an Army bomber could and must do the same thing."[67] As the performance of the airplane improved, Air Corps officers began thinking about how to best harness its potential as a weapon. In the end they developed a doctrine to justify a role independent of the ground forces.

The Air Service Tactical School, opened at Langley Field, Virginia, in 1920, provided much of the textual material used to train air officers. These texts, when used in conjunction with other publications prepared within the air arm, showed how Army airmen viewed their revolutionary role in warfare. The shift in emphasis was fundamental and occurred on three distinct levels. First, the function of aviation changed from air service to air force. Second, the relative importance of the missions within the air force category swung from air superiority to strategic bombardment. Third, with the change in mission priorities, the role of bombardment aviation superseded that of pursuit.

At the close of World War I, airmen generally perceived the principal role of aviation as supporting the ground battle. The Air Service printed and circulated Colonel Gorrell's "Notes on the Characteristics, Limitations, and Employment of the Air Service" and Lieutenant Colonel William Sherman's "Tentative Manual for the Employment of Air Service." Gorrell, explaining the functions of an Air Service, wrote that "the Air Service aids the Infantry, helps adjust Artillery, assists in keeping the staff informed, destroys the enemy air service, by using machine guns and bombs, assists in deciding actions on the ground, and prevents the enemy air service from rendering similar assistance to the hostile forces."[68] Similarly, Sherman noted: "It is . . . the role of the Air Service, as well as that of the other arms, to aid the chief combatant: the infantry."[69] This complete subordination to the ground battle soon underwent revision.

In 1923 General Patrick's office prepared "Fundamental Conceptions of the Air Service," which was subsequently used as a text at the Tactical School.[70] This publication stated:

The primary mission of Military Aviation is to seek out, attack, and destroy the aviation of the enemy; to attack his formations, both tactical and strategical, on the ground and on the water, and to render such assistance to other units of the Army as may be prescribed by competent authority.

As a deduction from the above it is seen that this branch [Air Service] has two distinct functions to perform. On the one hand there is what may properly be called the Air "Force." It is made up of those units which are designed primarily for offensive fighting and operates more or less independently of the ground troops. It attacks and destroys the air forces of the enemy and inflicts direct damage on his ground components; prevents enemy observation of our own troops, attacks his concentration points and lines of communication, and destroys his depots and stores of supplies and munitions. In the second place, there is what may be properly called the Air "Service," which embraces observation airplanes and all lighter than air craft, and which operates as an auxiliary to the other branches of the Army, by procuring information of the terrain in front of the field armies, and of enemy troop movements, and by assisting the artillery, infantry, and other branches of the Army in preparation for battle, and for success therein.[71]

This quotation reveals General Patrick's subtle and politically sophisticated approach in reshaping the War Department's central assumptions about Air Service roles. The publication began with a verbatim quotation from *Training Regulations 10–5, Doctrines, Principles, and Methods of the Army in War,* and a prefatory statement that its principles had guided what followed on Air Service concepts. After this brief nod to convention, "Fundamental Conceptions of the Air Service" became a matter-of-fact narrative on what the Air Service perceived as its role in warfare. The document recognized air service as a mission, but the fact that the air force category should receive "about three-fourths of the total aviation establishment" clearly made it the role of choice.[72] If the air force was the most important category of aviation, then it logically followed that the destruction of the enemy's air force was crucial. Air supremacy, not ground support, was suddenly the most important mission for the Air Service. This mission also made pursuit the prominent category of air force aviation, since its mission was "to establish and maintain supremacy of the air."[73]

"Fundamental Conceptions of the Air Service" also attempted to settle the central issue of control. The air force, it asserted, "operates more or less independently of the ground troops," and its "units are to be permitted to accomplish their missions with as much freedom as possible."[74]

Finally, "Fundamental Conceptions of the Air Service" tried to show that the future held great promise for the military airplane, especially in light of the potential impact of technological advances: "Air craft of today are still in the infancy of their development, and the tactics of aviation must therefore be said to be in a state of flux, and subject to change and development as the design of aircraft is improved."[75]

The other publications used at the Tactical School supported this doctrine of the importance of both the air force role and air supremacy. The 1924 *Bombardment* text recognized two types of missions: tactical missions directly influencing the ground battle and strategic missions executed independently of ground activity. Both missions included bombing enemy aviation facilities.[76] The 1926 *Bombardment* publication generally agreed with its predecessor. Nevertheless, there were signs of friction at the Tactical School over the role of bombardment aviation. Although the text stated that strategical bombardment was important, it carefully noted that "it must not take precedence over the support of ground operations by proper tactical employment." Still, the text implied that the role of the bomber was under review since the weapon possessed "a power of destruction, a range, a flexibility, and a degree of mobility so much in excess of that of any other of its kind." The text then posed the question: "Who can say with certainty that even the most extreme claims of the bombardment enthusiast are untrue?" The text also asserted a position that would grow over the coming years into the central tenet of an evolving creed: "The defenses against aviation are numerous; their powers are real. But no matter how numerous or how powerful they may be they will not prevent bombardment from accomplishing its assigned missions."[77] This stance showed up again in the *Pursuit* publication.

The Pursuit text used at the Tactical School in 1926 reiterated the principles of the 1923 "Fundamental Conceptions" publication, emphasizing the primacy of the aerial supremacy mission. Still, that the bomber advocates had won some ground was obvious when it was admitted that improvements in defensive armament made it increasingly difficult to attack multiseater aircraft and that "attacks by the individual pursuit airplane in daylight operations will be largely limited to harassing fire."[78]

A July 1925 letter by the commandant of the Tactical School, Major Oscar Westover, emphasized the importance of aerial supremacy but it also showed that appreciation of the potential of the bomber was growing. Commenting on "Fundamental Principles for the Employment of Air Service," Westover took exception to the assertion that "the moral effect of bombing industrial centers is much greater than the physical effect." Westover maintained that the "saying [was] completely out of date. While it may have been true during the war, the school holds that it is no longer true. Bombing has developed to the point where it is accurate and destructive."[79]

These two notions—that the bomber would reach its objective and that it was an accurate, destructive, and strategically valuable weapon—soon dominated air doctrine. By 1928 the Air Corps Tactical School was downplaying the aerial supremacy mission. Instead, it embraced the ideas conveyed in the "Doctrine of Employment of an Aerial Force," which focused on a strategic role of attacking vital enemy objectives. The bomber, with its long range and great powers of destruction, became the technology of choice.[80]

Captain Charles W. Walton, a student at Langley in 1929, prepared a paper that provides insight into why the Air Corps so radically changed its doctrine in such a short amount of time. Walton's paper analyzed whether an air force had the capability to operate independently to a degree to justify a new term—*air warfare*. "Within air power," he wrote, "we see the seeds of decisive military action, especially where aviation can operate without restrictions imposed by surface commanders." Walton concluded that independent air warfare was being neglected because of its control by other arms and recommended that an independent air force be established to further its development.[81]

That others at the Tactical School agreed with Walton is apparent in the *Bombardment* text prepared in 1930. This publication operated from the premise that "*Bombardment aviation, under the circumstances anticipated in a major war, is the basic arm of the Air Force.*" Furthermore, it stressed the need for centralized control of bombardment aviation and emphasized that it was a GHQ weapon:

> There will probably be certain vital objectives comparatively limited in number which, if destroyed, will contribute most to the success of combined arms of the Nation. Because bombardment aviation can operate at distances far beyond the front lines of the ground forces and against objectives outside the immediate concern of an army or even a group of armies, and as the amount of bombardment aviation available will be insufficient to strike *all* targets, it follows that to secure the desired results against the *vital* objectives, the control of the operations of bombardment aviation is properly vested in GHQ.[82]

The question of who in the GHQ actually controlled bombardment aviation was addressed somewhat obliquely by determining responsibility for target selection. In an interesting sequence of logic, the text noted that bombardment usually operated in conjunction with other categories of aviation. The grouping thus became an air command, or an air force. Responsibility for the selection of targets for the bombardment component resided with the air force commander. Through this imaginative construct, it became Air Corps doctrine that an air officer should command a largely independent air force attacking vital targets that only the bombardment weapon could reach. Needless to say, the Air Corps realized the implications of this new role, and the bombardment weapon rapidly became the focal point of its doctrinal and technological efforts.[83]

[8]

The War Department

From the War Department's perspective, the 1920s were a decade of frustration. After considerable effort, the Army had gained passage of a defense act that promised to provide the nation a small yet viable defensive force. This policy, which provided six field armies under a general headquarters, attempted to accommodate what the leadership of the Army saw as the principal lesson of World War I: the importance of mobilizing a mass army. Although the desired 500,000-man Regular Army had been almost halved under the National Defense Act, the War Department thought it could adapt to the new constraints. When the authorization for 280,000 regular soldiers was again halved through decreased appropriations, the War Department became alarmed.[1] The secretary of war and chief of staff believed that a regular army with only 140,000 soldiers could not accomplish the peacetime missions of providing for the initial defense of the country and its insular possessions nor train the reserve components needed for the National Army.[2] This concern over personnel severely limited the resources available for other projects.

Despite the realization that the Army's matériel was growing obsolete, the dominant consideration remained the size of the Army. A May 1927 editorial in the *Infantry Journal* echoed a common refrain, noting "the difficulties that have been experienced in maintaining the bare existence of a meager-sized Army, obstacles that have operated to stifle existing projects for improving the Army's efficiency."[3] The origins of this fixation on personnel, even at the expense of technological development, probably resulted from the nineteenth-century backgrounds of the Army's leadership. Although not necessarily antimachine, these officers clung to the preeminence of man on the battlefield.

The December 1921 training regulation manual *Doctrines, Principles, and*

Methods stated that the Army's mission was the destruction of the enemy's armed forces. There lingered, however, a preoccupation with the human dimension of war, with the regulation stressing that "whatever auxiliary methods are employed—strategical, tactical, mechanical, or moral, the final method is the physical encounter with bullet and bayonet—the human element is the decisive one." Such a doctrine obviously made the infantry the focal point of the Army. And it was a heroic force: "The Infantry is never exhausted, it can always advance another step and fire another shot."[4] Indeed, the regulation did not even mention tanks.

The 1923 *Field Service Regulations* formalized the preeminence of infantry. Though the manual noted that the combination of all arms was imperative in warfare, "the mission of the infantry is the general mission of the entire force." The regulations further observed the paramount importance of morale, fighting spirit, and aggressiveness to successful infantry. As always, the "individual fighting man" won battles.[5] This publication remained the basic War Department doctrinal publication until October 1939.[6] Its position that the other arms and services existed only to aid the infantry worked to constrain the doctrinal accommodation of both the tank and the airplane on the battlefield.

The decision to disband the Tank Corps and to place all tanks in the infantry, codified in the National Defense Act of 1920, gave the chief of infantry complete control over the development of tank doctrine and, in conjunction with the Ordnance Department, tank technology. His dominance in the field might well have extended unchallenged into the 1930s but for the secretary of war's chance visit to England.

In 1927 Secretary of War Dwight Davis was in England, where he saw a demonstration of the combined arms—the British Experimental Mechanized Force at Aldershot. Davis was apparently impressed by the British unit, because he ordered General Charles P. Summerall, the chief of staff, to assemble a similar force for the U.S. Army.[7] The War Department G-3 prepared a plan for an experimental mechanized force in December 1927. The unit contained an infantry battalion, two tank battalions and a tank platoon, a field artillery battalion, a cavalry armored car troop, and an assortment of supply and technical units drawn from Army posts in Maryland, Virginia, and Pennsylvania.[8] In July these units assembled at Camp Meade under the command of Colonel Oliver S. Eskridge.[9] Over the next three months, the Experimental Mechanized Force conducted a series of road marches and maneuvers in a limited test of mechanization. The poor performance of the obsolete World War I equipment, particularly the tanks, severely hampered its efforts. Only a few pilot light tank prototypes (T1E1s) offered any promise as modern weapons.[10] In late September, in accordance with the G-3 plan, the Experimental Mechanized Force disbanded.[11]

General Summerall commented on the abbreviated tests in his 1930 annual report. He stated that the tank had developed to the point that it might in the future constitute a separate offensive force, but this strength was not demonstrated during the operations of the Experimental Mechanized Force. He attributed the failure of this initial effort to the obsolete vehicles and blamed the Ordnance Department for failing to develop suitable tanks. Summerall concluded that although another mechanized unit would be constituted at Fort Eustis, Virginia, in late 1930, its success "depended on securing funds for the manufacture of modern equipment."[12] Ironically, Summerall had himself been an obstacle in securing appropriations for mechanization.

While the Experimental Mechanized Force organized and maneuvered, the War Department worked on plans for a more permanent unit. On March 20, 1928, Brigadier General Frank Parker, the War Department G-3, submitted his conclusions on a mechanized force to Summerall. Parker noted that the tank had been constrained since the war, viewed only as an auxiliary to the infantry. He observed that "the slow war-time tank tied to the infantry accomplished little despite heavy losses." Parker envisioned a new role for tanks: A battalion of light, fast tanks would be the core of a combined-arms force that would rely on surprise and speed to restore mobility to the battlefield. A medium tank company, a self-propelled 75-mm artillery battalion, a self-propelled 105-mm artillery battery, an engineer company, a mechanized infantry battalion, and a service detachment would supplement the light tank battalion. Parker further recommended that the unit be assigned to corps or higher level and that its missions include spearheading important attacks, serving as a counterattack unit, providing flank guards, and seizing and temporarily holding "distant key positions."[13] These missions, and the focus on a lightly armed and highly mobile force, bore a strong resemblance to traditional cavalry roles, probably because Parker was a cavalry officer.

Parker also realized that the economic realities facing the Army precluded more than one such mechanized unit in peacetime. This unit would serve as a laboratory for tactics and equipment for the rest of the Army. If Congress could be persuaded to authorize additional personnel and equipment for one such unit, it could be organized in fiscal year 1931, procuring new equipment over a three-year period. Finally, Parker asked the secretary of war to convene a board to further study the issue of mechanization.

Major General R. H. Allen, the chief of infantry, saw Parker's report as a threat to his tank monopoly. Using an analogy replete with meaning far beyond just the establishment of a mechanized force, he stated his opposition: "The tendency in this study to set up another branch of the service is heartily opposed. It is unsound as was the attempt by the Air Corps to separate itself from the rest of the Army." Allen also asserted the fundamental importance of his branch in tank matters: "The tank is a weapon and as such it is an auxiliary to the Infantryman, as is every other arm or weapon."[14]

Nevertheless, Summerall approved Parker's study in principle on April 11. He authorized the appointment of a board of officers, stipulating that their investigation should proceed on the basis that no appeal could be made to Congress for additional personnel. But Summerall made clear in a memorandum to Parker that he was not as enthusiastic about the potential of a mechanized force as Parker or Secretary Davis, noting that at "the present time development of tanks and weapons has not progressed to the point where we would be justified in asking Congress for funds to procure the numbers of modern tanks and weapons necessary for a test as extensive as the one contemplated."[15]

The War Department appointed a board of officers on May 10 to study mechanization. Chaired by Colonel Charles S. Lincoln, members of the board included representatives from the War Department General Staff, the arms, and the services. It began by defining *mechanization* and *motorization*. Mechanization was "the application of mechanics *directly to the combat* soldier on the battle field." Motorization was essentially the replacement of animal transport with motor vehicles. The board also revealed some rather innovative assumptions about the future of war. Noting that the Army needed to join the machine age, as the commercial world already had, it advocated "to the fullest possible degree use [of] machines in place of man-power in order that our man-power can occupy and 'hold' without terrific losses incident to modern fire power." The committee members also predicted that "mechanization will bring radical changes in the tactical doctrine of the next war" and that "any great nation which fails to provide for the utilization of mechanization to the utmost practicable degree must suffer the consequences of neglect in future war."[16]

Mechanization Board members' assumptions on the missions and organizational structure of the Mechanized Force closely paralleled those of General Parker. The members stressed mobility above all and agreed that the heavy tank losses in the war had been caused by the slow speed of the tanks; greater speed, not armor, was the solution. They emphasized Parker's view that a light, fast tank should form the nucleus for any mechanized force and omitted the medium tank company from the recommended unit structure. Finally, board members believed that the unit needed two mechanized infantry battalions, heavily armed with automatic weapons and machine guns, rather than the single battalion in Parker's plan, to "mop up, occupy, and hold" in the wake of the tank battalion's attacks. The total strength of the proposed unit, around 2,000 officers and enlisted men, made it essentially a combined-arms regiment. The board recommended a phased, three-year implementation of the Mechanized Force, beginning in fiscal year 1931.[17]

[98]

The Mechanization Board's most drastic recommendation was not directly related to the concrete issues of constituting a mechanized force. Although the board stopped short of recommending the institution of a "new and separate branch" for mechanization, knowing full well that a separate arm would require the legislative action precluded by Summerall's directive, the board showed that it suspected that the existing bureaucracy was incapable of administering the envisioned program. Specifically, the board recommended that the mechanization project be placed directly under the War Department. The board did "not believe that progress [would] be made if the organization and development of this force [were] placed under any one Chief of Branch as the Branches now exist." Furthermore, the officer in charge of the mechanization program needed to be a general officer with broad powers, able to make decisions—in consultation with the War Department and the affected branches—on "development work and tests; organization and equipment; tactical doctrine; and location and housing."[18] This arrangement was a direct affront to the chief of infantry.

The Mechanization Board completed its report on October 1 and adjourned.[19] On October 31 Secretary Davis approved the report and authorized the establishment of a permanent mechanized force.[20] With the exception of the chief of infantry, all of the branch chiefs supported Davis's decision. Despite infantry objections, the program proceeded.

In late November 1930 the Mechanized Force began training at Fort Eustis, Virginia. Colonel Daniel Van Voorhis commanded the unit, and Major Sereno E. Brett, a veteran tank officer, was the executive officer. The unit did not reach the regimental-sized proportions envisioned by the Mechanization Board; at 600 or so officers and enlisted men, it more closely resembled a battalion. A light tank company, a truck-towed artillery battery, an armored car troop of ten vehicles, and a motorized infantry machine gun company constituted the combat elements of the Mechanized Force. The problem of obsolete equipment, so frustrating during the summer 1928 tests, also plagued the Mechanized Force. The tank company had only four relatively modern tanks; World War I–vintage light tanks made up the rest of the unit's tank strength.[21] These slow, unreliable Renaults severely constrained the operations of the Mechanized Force, whose guiding precept had been speed and mobility. Colonel Van Voorhis noted that "instead of first defining the mission and then building up a force with characteristics which made it capable of executing this mission . . . in our first efforts we got the cart before the horse and made the mission conform to the equipment at hand."[22] Nevertheless, as 1930 drew to a close, this hodgepodge organization began to demonstrate the revolutionary potential of mechanization.

The 1930 establishment of a permanent mechanized force marked a milestone in the Army's tank development efforts. Henceforth, tank technology and doctrine evolved on two separate tracks: as an infantry support system and as the basis for a mechanized unit. In December 1930 Lieutenant Colonel Adna R. Chaffee, a cavalry officer, summed up the essence of the two Army schools of thought on tanks: "first, to assist the infantry of the combat divisions by directly preceding them and neutralizing the organized resistance in the main battle," and second, to "use the light tank as the backbone itself of a force. . . . Along these lines may develop a great part of the highly mobile combat troops of the next war."[23]

In addition to the tank debate, the War Department was also struggling to adapt to the implications of airplane technology. The 1921 *Training Regulations* scarcely mentioned aviation, except to note that it, like all other branches, was an auxiliary to the infantry.[24] The 1923 *Field Service Regulations,* although containing a broader discussion of the Air Service, still inextricably linked the arm to the ground battle. Air Service missions included "combat, observation, and the transmission of information." These missions required heavier-than-air observation, attack, pursuit, and bombardment units. Observation units provided information through reconnaissance, conducted liaison for higher headquarters, and adjusted artillery. Attack aviation assaulted enemy ground troops. Pursuit formations, the "most vital element of the air service," provided "aerial supremacy" by "clear[ing] the air of hostile aircraft as far back as the line of the hostile artillery." Finally, bombardment units attacked ground objectives, especially those "beyond the effective range of artillery."[25]

Although it never met the revolutionary expectations of the airmen, the War Department tried to adapt to the evolving potential of the aerial weapon. The 1923 publication "Fundamental Conceptions of the Air Service" acknowledged that the War Department accepted *air service* and *air force* as "categorical distinctions."[26] Furthermore, the War Department's own Lassiter Board had recognized the importance of the Air Service to national defense.

By 1926 the War Department had made further significant doctrinal concessions. The 1926 *Training Regulations No. 440–15: Fundamental Principles for the Employment of the Air Service,* although paying homage to the primacy of the conventional ground support missions, formally recognized the air service and air force roles along the organizational lines recommended by the Lassiter Board. Furthermore, the regulation stipulated that bombardment, in addition to its "long-range artillery" function, had a strategic, independent mission: "Strategical bombardment operates deep into hostile territory beyond the combat zone against targets which may be far removed from the field of battle, with the object of destroying military supply, main lines of communications, mobilization, concentration, and military industrial centers." Still, the regulation was careful to stipulate that "while strategical bombardment does not involve direct cooperation with ground troops on the field of battle, it should be based on the broad plan of operations of the military forces."[27]

In spite of official support for air power, attempts were made to constrain it. In May 1923 the Hawaiian Department convened a board to examine "the powers and limitations of Coast Artillery and Air Service." Major Lesley J. McNair, himself an artilleryman, headed the board, which determined that the coast artillery provided a better defense against enemy naval forces than aviation, because air power is often "impaired by weather conditions and visibility" and "is vulnerable to hostile aviation and anti-aircraft agencies." McNair concluded that air power "lacks the solidity and dependability of the seacoast gun."[28]

Early in 1925 General Patrick reviewed the McNair Board's findings. He was incensed at the assertion that bombers were highly vulnerable to anti-aircraft fire and that the coast artillery was a better naval defense agency than the Air Service.[29] After all, the Air Service had just spent considerable time and effort proving it could sink battleships. However, critics pointed out that the demonstration was against an immobile ship that took no steps to defend itself. Hence, many officers remained skeptical of the Air Service's claims. Patrick probably realized that the coast artillery, whose existence was jeopardized by the advent of the airplane, was trying to reassert its primacy in coast defense and perhaps even carve out a new niche as an anti-aircraft force. Patrick need not have worried. The McNair Board had little impact because the War Department supported Patrick's assertion "that the development of aviation has rendered 'the continued maintenance of the majority of our Coast Artillery installations uneconomical.' "[30]

That the War Department appreciated the value of the Air Service was never questioned; the central issue was control of military aviation. In 1925 Brigadier General H. A. Drum, the War Department G-3, gave the Army's official position before the Board of Aviation Inquiry: "The establishment of a separate Air Force independent of the Army, no matter what the form of organization, cannot be justified on any sound grounds." Drum, understanding what was at stake, stated that "the difference in fundamental conception between the existing Army Air Service organization, and the separate Air Corps, proposed, is *independence of Army control*." Drum believed that a separate air arm was dangerous because "it favors a special class, to the detriment of the whole of National Defense."[31]

This struggle for control caused harsh, even bitter feelings between air and ground officers. Mitchell's rhetoric was the most inflammatory, but many airmen shared his views. No one but a flyer, they believed, could understand the potential of the aerial weapon, a potential that was being strangled by a conservative, ground-oriented War Department hierarchy.[32] In some ways they were absolutely right. Few ground officers shared their revolutionary zeal for the airplane, but most appreciated the importance of the air arm to the ground battle. They also had difficulty understanding why General Patrick believed that the air arm was being treated "as a step-child."[33]

General Drum's comment that the air branch was in reality treated as "a favored son" surely struck a responsive chord among ground officers. The air arm had grown significantly since the war and was the "most independent Branch of the Army."[34] Furthermore, as the expansion program to meet the provisions of the Air Corps Act of 1926 began, the Army had to deactivate ground units to meet the personnel requirements. Again, for an institution fixated on manpower, this was surely cause for resentment.[35] On a more personal level, the fact that flying officers received 50 percent more pay than their ground comrades was at best irksome.[36] In addition, it became increasingly obvious that Army aviation did not want any help in deciding the direction of American air power. Patrick was emphatic that the shortage of field grade officers in the Air Service should be corrected by internal promotions, not by the transfer of willing majors and lieutenant colonels into the branch. The Air Corps Act stipulations that 90 percent of each grade be qualified as pilots and that all aviation units be commanded by flying officers were not mere competency tests; instead, they provided a legal basis to keep the Air Corps under the control of its current officership. Even if a middle-grade ground officer became an emphatic convert to the cause of aviation, he could not break into the Air Corps fraternity unless he became a qualified pilot. Among air officers it was accepted lore that "it was very, very difficult to teach a person in the grade of major to fly an airplane."[37]

As air and ground officers took increasingly polar positions, each side lost sight of the concerns of the other. Air officers believed that the ever-increasing potential of the aerial weapon made it a strategic system, with an importance far surpassing mere support of the ground battle. Ground officers were just as certain that the increased capability of military aviation meant a collateral gain in the effectiveness of ground forces. They saw the aviator's drive for independence as desertion and a threat to the outcome of the all-important ground battle. Each side was right, in its own way, and neither would compromise on the fundamental issue of independence for the air arm. As a consequence, the air insurgency searched for a way to prove unequivocally that the airplane by itself could play a role of such decisive importance in future wars that independence for the arm would be undeniable. In 1930 the Air Corps Tactical School turned to strategic bombing to prove the importance of the airplane.

The 1920s were years of peace and prosperity for the United States. Given the absence of any threat to national security, the civilian leadership focused on policies of reduced government spending and disarmament. Both directly affected the Army. For officers whose business it was to think about how to defend the Republic, the decade's trends were alarming. The War Department hierarchy had learned one overriding lesson from the Great War—big armies win wars. Consequently, it focused on providing a mass army to meet future threats. Deep cuts in allocated personnel convinced them that Congress did not understand modern warfare. Furthermore, to the leadership of the War Department, the cuts jeopardized the Army as an institution.

With regard to technology, the development of the tank was stifled when the choices came down to buying more tanks or more infantrymen. Furthermore, those who saw a tank role beyond infantry support were either silenced or run off by a parochial chief of infantry. There was little operating space in the Army for tank advocates.

In contrast to the tank, the airplane enjoyed significant advantages. The airplane had obvious civilian applications, and investment in military aviation could further commercial efforts. In 1926 Congress realized this relationship between civil and military aviation and, in an effort to stimulate the flagging civilian aircraft industry, created a linkage between commercial and military aviation. Both would benefit. Furthermore, Billy Mitchell changed the rules of what constituted sanctioned behavior for air officers. Though risks were implicit, flying officers were liberated to do things that a ground officer's concept of loyalty to the service would not allow. Finally, in the Army air arm, the airplane had an institution whose very being depended on its exploitation.

By the end of 1930 most of the institutional arrangements, doctrinal conceptions, and behavioral norms that controlled the development of the tank and the airplane by the U.S. Army were established, if not frozen. These institutional parameters, and the incredible international instabilities of the coming decade, dramatically shaped the roles of both technologies.

PART III

ALTERNATIVES AND AUTONOMY: 1931–1942

I am well aware of the known hostility of the Commanding General, Field Forces to horse cavalry. Nevertheless, in the interests of National Defense in this crisis, I urge upon you [General George C. Marshall] the necessity of an immediate increase in horse Cavalry.

—Major General J. K. Herr, Chief of Cavalry (1942)

The creed of the bomber, the rallying cry on which our entire doctrine evolved, was phrased by Lt. Kenneth M. Walker, then bombardment instructor. It was carefully worded and was approved by the faculty of the school as accepted doctrine. It said—"A well planned and well organized air attack once launched cannot be stopped."

—Brigadier General Haywood S. Hansell (1951)

[9]

From Domestic Depression
to International Crusade

For those who did not live through the turbulent years preceding American participation in World War II, it is difficult to capture the immense changes that occurred between 1931 and 1942. In the space of eleven years Americans experienced incredible contrasts that carried the population from the depths of a national malaise caused by the debilitating depression to the elation of another great crusade for democracy, from zealous isolationism to enthusiastic interventionism, from "hard times" to the "good war."[1]

The Great Depression pervaded every aspect of American consciousness. Confidence in national economic policies and institutions was shattered by the plunge from the "high plateau of permanent prosperity" of the 1920s.[2] Americans watched helplessly as their jobs vanished and their savings dwindled. By 1931 the depression was global and created economic conditions in Europe that supported the rise of fascism. Until the late 1930s American policies and programs focused almost exclusively on domestic issues. Nevertheless, American retrenchment did not stem solely from the economic disaster.

In the early 1930s Americans embraced isolationism as never before, in the process abandoning Wilsonian internationalism. The government found it difficult to concern itself with international affairs when it could not guarantee its own citizens economic security. Furthermore, Americans were increasingly disenchanted with the outside world. In 1931 the web of agreements to outlaw war and limit armaments that had caused such euphoria in the late 1920s and 1930 were shown to be irrelevant when the Japanese, a signatory of the Kellogg-Briand Pact and the Nine-Power Treaty, invaded Manchuria.[3] For a generation of Americans, the Japanese invasion caused a disheartening recognition that legal and moral sanctions alone could not prevent aggression.

American demoralization was also deepened by the widely publicized claims of the Senate Munitions Investigating Committee, chaired by Gerald P. Nye. The Nye Commission asserted that American armament makers and business interests had dragged the United States into World War I because of their insatiable greed for profits. Popular works, such as the book-of-the-month-club selection *Merchants of Death,* inflamed public sentiment by claiming that "the arms maker has risen and grown powerful, until he is one of the most dangerous factors in world affairs—a hindrance to peace, a promoter of war."[4] Consequently, in the early 1930s, the ranks of the American peace movement swelled to more than "twelve million adherents and an audience of between forty-five and sixty million people."[5]

Antagonism toward Europe was particularly acute. With the deepening of the depression, the former Allied powers could not meet their war debt payments to the United States. America responded by passing the Johnson Default Act in 1934, which prohibited future loans to any foreign government in default.[6]

The effects of the domestic crisis caused by the depression, coupled with the disillusionment with internationalism over debts and the alleged nefarious dealings of the "merchants of death," created a national consensus for strict neutrality. When fascist armies marched in Ethiopia and Spain, the United States responded by enacting a series of neutrality acts (1935, 1936, and 1937), which steadily tightened strictures against American assistance to belligerents.[7] A late 1937 opinion poll showed that 73 percent of those asked favored a Constitutional amendment requiring a national referendum on any declaration of war short of an invasion of the republic or its possessions. The Ludlow Resolution, so named for its author, Representative Louis Ludlow of Indiana, failed in the House by the narrow margin of 209–188.[8]

The Czechoslovakian crisis and the Munich Conference in 1938 marked the beginning of the end of American retrenchment. The country, skillfully guided by President Franklin D. Roosevelt, began at least modest steps to rearm and began to take a steadily pro-Allied stance. Public opinion, however, cautioned the president to move slowly and often furtively. Although the American people were appalled and disgusted by German aggression, they had little desire for active involvement. As late as June 1939, a congressional coalition of isolationists, partisan Republicans, and anti-Roosevelt Democrats marshaled enough strength to defeat the president's attempt to loosen the 1937 Neutrality Act's strictures on arms sales to Britain and France.[9]

Only after the September 1939 German invasion of Poland could the president gather a consensus to move the nation toward large-scale military preparedness and active support of the Allies. On September 8 Roosevelt proclaimed a limited state of emergency, and the nation began rearming in earnest.[10] Even then, support was tenuous—a September Gallup Poll showed that only 50 percent of those surveyed favored a repeal of the arms embargo.

But Americans had taken sides: October surveys indicated that "84% were pro-Ally, 2% pro-German, and 14% without opinion."[11]

In November 1939 Congress passed a new neutrality act that allowed "cash-and-carry" arms sales to belligerents. The president pushed the legislation as a "return to the traditional American adherence to international law," whose aim "was keeping the United States out of the war."[12] Nonetheless, the act clearly favored the Allies, since the British Royal Navy controlled the sea lanes.

Thus began Roosevelt's careful shepherding of the nation into the Allied camp. When the Nazis unleashed the blitzkrieg on the low countries and France in May 1940, American support of the Allies became overt. On June 10 Roosevelt stated that his sympathies lay with those nations resisting "fascist aggression" and that henceforth American policy would focus on strengthening American defenses and giving material aid to England and France. This statement, in effect, signaled a policy of "all-out aid short of war."[13] Still, the president realized that there were limits. On June 14 Paul Reynaud, the French premier, pleaded with Roosevelt for a public declaration to provide "all aid short of an expeditionary force" to avert what clearly loomed as a French collapse before the German onslaught.[14] Roosevelt replied that he would try to step up the flow of armaments but that "these statements carry with them no implication of military commitments. . . . Only the Congress can make such commitments."[15]

On June 22 the French signed an armistice agreement with Germany at Compiègne. In the wake of the French disaster, Congress began a rearmament frenzy and also gave the president broad powers to repress domestic dissent when the Alien Registration Act passed on June 28.[16] Aid to Great Britain also increased. On September 3 Roosevelt announced to Congress that he planned to turn over fifty destroyers to the British in exchange for long-term leases on Western Hemisphere naval and air bases.[17] On September 16 Congress passed the Selective Service and Training Act, the first peacetime compulsory military service program.[18] In late December, following his election to an unprecedented third term, Roosevelt appealed directly to the American people in one of his famous fireside chats for the country to become "the great arsenal of democracy" in the fight against Axis world domination. Still, bowing to a strong isolationist sentiment, he also promised that the new policy had as its sole purpose "to keep war away from our country and our people."[19]

The president also took steps to ensure that when the United States did enter the war it would have a coordinated strategic policy. In early 1941 Anglo-American staff conferences in Washington decided on a "Germany-first" policy if the United States entered the war.[20] Efforts to increase aid to a hard-pressed Great Britain intensified with the passage of the Lend-Lease Act on March 11. In June, following the German invasion of Russia, Roosevelt extended the offer of American aid to the Soviet Union as well.[21] Efforts to coordinate British-American policy reached their highest level when President Roosevelt and British Prime Minister Winston Churchill met for secret talks aboard the *U.S.S. Augusta* and the *H.M.S. Prince of Wales* off the coast of Newfoundland. At this meeting, the two heads of state decided the broad lines of postwar policy in a statement of principles called the Atlantic Charter.[22] On December 7, 1941, any need for subterfuge ended when the Japanese bombed Pearl Harbor. The United States was in the war.

Again, the scope of change during these years is remarkable. Every aspect of American life was affected, and the Army was no exception. The effects of the Great Depression on the Army were mixed. At the level of the individual officer and soldier, the era made Army life attractive. Although pay and allowances suffered cuts as Congress reacted to the deepening financial crisis, soldiers, unlike millions of other unemployed Americans, had an income.[23] Consequently, the high desertion and resignation rates experienced during the boom times of the 1920s quickly tapered off.[24] Furthermore, New Deal policies, designed to stimulate the economy, put more than $100 million into Army housing and other Army construction projects.[25]

The Great Depression, however, had an extremely negative impact on the Army at large. As the depression worsened, Congress slashed Army appropriations. How the War Department chose to spend its reduced funds was rooted in the predepression era. In the summer of 1929, President Hoover ordered a survey of the military establishment, "with a view to making extensive reductions in the cost of the Army in all or any of its components or activities, wherever same can be made without manifest injury to adequate National Defense." General Summerall, the chief of staff, gave every indication to the General Staff and the branch and bureau chiefs that he wanted candid responses and asked them to approach the project with open minds.[26]

Summerall posed a series of broad, theoretical questions whose answers would have to rationalize the relationship of the Army to the national defense. What were the causes of war? How did one define *completely adequate preparedness*? What levels of readiness needed to be maintained to cope with internal disorders, preparedness against attack on the American continent, and preparedness against conflict with a major power? What was the status of the Army's procurement, construction, and modernization programs? Could they be slowed without risk? Summerall also asked his subordinates to provide an answer fundamental to the weapons development program: "Explain why time is needed and why it is necessary to conduct research, development, and experiment of new and improved weapons in order that standardized types may be put into production when an emergency comes, regardless of whether or not the military forces are re-armed in peace."[27]

Summerall's inquiry was not limited to the theoretical or broad questions on War Department policy. To meet the president's economy measures, Summerall asked the War Department agencies to tell him how they would go about cutting costs from within their own areas. His suggestions of areas to investigate surely sent shock waves throughout the bureaucracy. None of the sacred cows, nor horses for that matter, were safe from slaughter. Summerall asked whether "coast or fixed defenses" were obsolete and could be replaced by "mobile guns or aviation." Was there "indisputable proof" that horse cavalry was of sufficient value to maintain the branch at its current strength? To what degree could "armored cars and motorization or aviation" replace cavalry? What was the relationship between the Air Corps and other branches? Could aviation replace other arms, and, taking into account the development of commercial aviation since the inauguration of the five-year Air Corps expansion program, could this program be "curtailed or extended over a greater length of time, with extensive reductions in costs"? Should all Regular Army units be concentrated at two or three major posts? Could any of the civilian components be curtailed or abolished? Finally, could the Army be reduced to its 1916 strength without sacrificing national security?[28]

Essentially, Summerall was asking the chiefs to commit bureaucratic suicide. Not surprisingly, each chose to tell the chief of staff why his domain, in particular, should be spared. The War Plans Division of the General Staff assembled the responses and prepared a report that arrived at the expected conclusion that no significant reduction in the military budget could be made without endangering the national defense. Furthermore, the document reaffirmed the sacrosanct World War I paradigm of the preeminence of man in war, the need to mobilize mass armies, and the importance of trained citizen components to the expansion of the National Army. The loudest voice of dissent came from the chief of the Air Corps, who "used the opportunity to re-emphasize the importance and role of the strategic bomber and the need for the Air Corps to be independent from the rest of the Army" and to recommend "that the 1926 five-year program should be scrapped and a larger program inaugurated."[29]

The War Department's conservative response to the chief of staff's directive for a radical reassessment of the existing establishment reflected not only its perceptions of the present but also a blueprint for its future actions. When the depression changed the nature of the exercise from a staff study on how to economize to one of forced retrenchment in the face of budget cuts imposed from above, the War Department remained true to the fundamentals of its 1929 plan. Additionally, the interbranch discord that had surfaced in the 1929 effort turned into intense intraservice rivalry as resources diminished and the chiefs of arms and services scrambled for their piece of the budget.[30]

Throughout the 1930s the Army remained committed to the notion that the strength of the Regular Army was the true gauge of national preparedness. Apparently, the War Department hierarchy did not see that the threat to American security during the Great Depression was from internal economic disaster rather than external military force. As the depression worsened, the Army made critical decisions about where to spend its dwindling budget. The new direction became apparent early in 1930, when the Ordnance Department submitted an estimate of $2,400,000 for fiscal year 1932 for "limited service tests and the purchase of semi-automatic rifles, 3-inch antiaircraft guns, and as many tanks as possible with the remaining money." The War Department slashed this request to less than $1,000,000 and specified that priority should go to the "semi-automatic rifle, and perhaps a few tanks."[31]

In contrast, the War Department vigorously opposed any reductions in personnel, particularly in the officer corps.[32] The testimony by Army leaders before the House Subcommittee on Military Appropriations on the fiscal year 1933 budget almost uniformly stressed that "everything except personnel, training, and the civilian components could be sacrificed."[33] This position was not popular in a nation faced with economic disaster. The *New York Times,* for example, took exception to the pleas of General Douglas MacArthur, the Army chief of staff, before Congress for a larger Army: "The Chief of Staff can hardly indulge the hope that in these times of difficulty in balancing the budget an increase of the army will be authorized."[34]

Again, the exception to War Department policy was the chief of the Air Corps. Major General Benjamin Foulois emphasized the potential of strategic bombing and the need for heavier investment in machines over personnel, noting that "it would be a splendid thing if additional expense could be put in matériel, meaning heavy bombers, rather than into personnel."[35]

The effects of the Army's personnel-first policy in this era of tight budgets extended to its mechanization program. Late in 1932 General MacArthur testified before the House Subcommittee on Military Appropriations on the fiscal year 1934 budget, making clear his position regarding mechanization. The subcommittee chairman, Representative Ross Collins, had castigated MacArthur over the lackluster mechanization program. MacArthur retorted that the main impediment to Army efforts continued to be Congress's refusal to provide funds for modern tanks. Collins responded that even if Congress appropriated more money for the Army, it would not likely result in more tanks but more men.[36] Congress cut appropriations by as much as 20 percent during the depression, but the Army tenaciously guarded its personnel strength—neither officer nor enlisted strength ever declined by more than 5 percent.

This emphasis on personnel did not mean that the War Department no longer recognized the importance of modern weapons. In his 1934 annual report, General MacArthur showed keen insight into the intrinsic relationship among organization, equipment, doctrine, and training: "Almost every important cause for change in tactics, training methods, and detailed organization of military units has its origin in scientific accomplishments in the fields of transportation and communication, weapons, and other technical equipment useful to an army operating in the field." He further noted that "modernization implies the *development and acquisition, in all necessary types, of equipment of maximum efficiency, and the adoption of methods calculated to produce the most effective results from their coordinated use.*"[37] Recognition of the importance of modern equipment did not, however, necessarily translate into funding. In General MacArthur's hierarchy of needs, the size of the Regular Army and National Guard had priority, with training the Officers' Reserve Corps following. New matériel to replace the obsolescent World War I stocks was less important than these personnel requirements. Indeed, MacArthur viewed as his greatest achievement while chief of staff the tactical reorganization of the Regular Army and National Guard units into a "four-army organization" to enhance mobilization in the event of an emergency.[38]

Although MacArthur proposed a modernization program to correct equipment deficiencies, he envisioned a limited effort with four essential components: "continuous experimentation and development" to produce superior pilot models, limited procurement of satisfactory prototypes to equip a test organization, utilization of the proven items to replace existing obsolete equipment when such replacement became necessary, and the "prearrangement in peace for prompt quantity production in emergency." MacArthur placed the onus for funding even this limited scheme on Congress.[39]

Unfortunately, even modest Army modernization efforts suffered during the 1930s because of Army leadership's perceptual limitations. The weapons and systems MacArthur identified as critical to the Army reflected this limitation. As late as 1934, the Army had procured only twelve "modern" tanks, and only one of these met expectations. MacArthur believed that the sixty-seven copies of the satisfactory pilot tank, provided for by the 1935 appropriation, constituted a "real beginning." His vision of what was adequate is even more apparent in the rest of his listing: 3,500 wartime French 75-mm artillery pieces had to be modified because of their limited firing traverse and the fact that their wood and steel wheels limited their mobility; semi-automatic rifles were needed to supplant the model 1903 Springfield as the basic infantry weapon; .50-caliber machine guns, whose armor-piercing ammunition made them effective against both tanks and airplanes, were essential; improved antiaircraft cannon and machine guns were needed; and commercial motor vehicles were necessary to realize the "great possibilities for increasing mobility through substitution of motor vehicles for horse and mule transportation."[40]

Why such a limited plan? MacArthur's own rendition of the persistent Army folkway provides the clearest explanation: "It is easy, of course, to overemphasize the influence of machinery in war. It is man that makes war, not machines, and the human element must always remain the dominant one." Given this conceptual orientation, it is not surprising that when appropriations dwindled during the depression, the Army applied its diminished resources to the area it believed most critical—personnel. This concentration on the human dimension of warfare enabled MacArthur to shift the blame for the inadequacy of the Army's modernization efforts to a penurious Congress and an apathetic American people: "It might possibly, though mistakenly, be inferred that the American people and their representatives have, after mature deliberation, declined to undertake any military preparation in excess of that now obtaining."[41] Despite the deferential language, MacArthur was obviously convinced that the Army's obsolete equipment was not the Army's fault. In reality, the Army made a conscious decision to defer modernization until appropriations increased to such a degree that personnel would not have to be cut in favor of equipment. When appropriations increased, MacArthur believed that the Army could begin correcting its equipment shortfalls.[42] The critical choice belonged to the Army.

Ironically, MacArthur acknowledged the existence of an alternative approach. Discussing the progress of the Air Corps in his 1934 report, the chief of staff noted that "in this one arm we have not fallen behind in quality. . . . In some types of fighting airplanes our latest models are appreciably better than any others known to exist." MacArthur also acknowledged that this progress had occurred despite insufficient funds.[43] He may never have understood the fundamental reason why the Air Corps had advanced equipment while the rest of the Army languished with anachronisms—Air Corps officers were driven by technology, while most of their ground counterparts remained ambivalent to machines, particularly if their development and procurement meant personnel cuts.

The Army's decision not to invest in technology at the expense of personnel resulted in a protracted period in which technological development slowed to a glacial pace in all areas except aviation. The situation was exacerbated by the subsequent decision by General Malin C. Craig, MacArthur's successor as chief of staff, to freeze weapons development. Craig entered office in October 1935, the same year the Italians invaded Ethiopia. The international situation worsened rapidly during the early years of his tenure, with Germany reoccupying the Rhineland in March 1936, the Spanish civil war beginning in July 1936, and Japan renewing its aggression against China in July 1937. In response to these increased tensions, Craig retained the focus on personnel by revitalizing the Army's mobilization plans.

The result was the Protective Mobilization Plan. The plan envisioned a 400,000-man Initial Protective Force, made up of existing Regular Army and National Guard units, to defend the country at the beginning of any emergency. Behind this shield, an additional 600,000 of the 1,000,000-man Protective Mobilization Plan would be mobilized.[44] To equip this force, he froze weapons designs so that the Army could begin procuring standardized equipment for the Initial Protective Force and stockpiling munitions for the remainder of the Protective Mobilization Plan's projected force.[45]

Craig's decision was surely justifiable, given the ominous international situation and the awful state of Army equipment. Unfortunately, his standardization program, when combined with the War Department's central emphasis on personnel, impeded American weapons research and development programs at a time when military technologies were rapidly changing. Consequently, many of the U.S. Army's early World War II weapons were mass productions of designs frozen since the mid-1930s.[46]

A good example of the effects of Craig's policy was the Army's decision to procure a 37-mm antitank gun of German design. The adequacy of this weapon was questionable when it was adopted in 1936 as the M3 antitank gun, but the Army decided to mass-produce it because it was highly preferable to the machine guns then used as antitank weapons.[47] Furthermore, the chief of infantry—the branch chief responsible for antitank developments—favored the light 37-mm gun because he wanted a weapon that "four men could comfortably wheel over the ground." By 1939 the Germans had begun using antitank weapons "ranging from 50 to 80-mm," and the M3 "was obsolete before it was standardized."[48] It was, however, this pitifully weak 37-mm antitank gun that American troops took into combat in North Africa in late 1942, and the 37-mm cannon remained the standard gun on American light tanks until 1944.

The magnitude of the procurement effort prevented completion of even the limited plans to supply the Initial Protective Force before the United States entered the war in December 1941.[49] In addition, Roosevelt's policy of supplying war matériel to the Allies, often over War Department protest, exceeded production capacity.[50] The large-scale production of existing models was emphasized—at the expense of further development—to equip the rapidly expanding U.S. Army and its hard-pressed Allies. Indeed, the procurement task faced by the War Department as the Army grew from a force of 269,023 officers and enlisted men in 1940 to one of 8,267,958 by 1945 necessitated a production program of enormous proportions.[51]

The Army that deployed to Europe in 1942, in accordance with the decision to defeat Germany first, was in reality two separate forces. One was a ground force convinced that man was the final arbiter of conflict. The other was an air force, just as convinced that air power technology was the solution to modern war. These competing conceptions had much to do with how the two forces developed the technologies, doctrines, and organizations of two of their most sophisticated tools, the tank and the airplane, during the final decade before the beginning of the American crusade against fascism.

[10]

Alternatives for Armor

The mechanization policy that governed American tank development until 1940 was established by General Douglas MacArthur on May 1, 1931, when he disbanded the Mechanized Force at Fort Eustis, Virginia. Thereafter, the infantry and the cavalry shared in the development of the tank. To avoid the provisions of the National Defense Act of 1920, which dictated that all tank units be assigned to the infantry, the euphemism "combat car" became the designation for cavalry tanks.[1] MacArthur later explained that he felt compelled to choose between two schools of thought on the future direction of Army mechanization efforts. One advocated the creation of a separate mechanized force, the other the development of mechanization by the "traditional arms and services."[2] MacArthur chose the latter course, and the Army's brief attempt to put together a combined-arms mechanized force ended.

MacArthur's explanation for the breakup of the Mechanized Force conceals much of what was going on behind the scenes at the War Department. A fuller explanation was provided by Major Robert W. Grow, who stated that the unit disbanded because of a number of factors, among them "a fear of the development of an 'elite' corps (the Air Corps situation was in the limelight)" and "the fact that the National Defense Act would not permit the organization of a separate branch or head of branch." Grow also noted that "jealousy of the several arms represented in the Force, difficulties in equipment for the above reasons, and finally, a realization that the missions of the Force were, in reality, cavalry missions" also influenced MacArthur's decision.[3]

Perhaps the most significant reason for the decision was interbranch friction, most notably the objections of the chief of infantry. In March 1931 Major General Stephen O. Fuqua, the chief of infantry, added vigorous protests to those already on record from his predecessor that the Mechanized Force usurped his tank prerogatives. Ultimately, the War Department broke up the Mechanized Force "to compromise the conflicts between branches."[4]

The War Department's decision to decentralize mechanization meant that from 1931 to the formation of the Armored Force in July 1940, the Army's exploitation of the tank proceeded along two separate lines. The chiefs of infantry and cavalry developed tank doctrine, equipment, and organizations with the continued involvement of the chief of ordnance in the technical aspects of design and production. This complex story is probably told most clearly by discussing infantry, cavalry, and armored force developments in turn.

INFANTRY AUXILIARIES

The Army's experiments with mechanization between 1928 and 1932 stimulated discussion among tank advocates, many of whom taught at the Infantry Tank School, about the possibilities of using the weapon in areas other than infantry support. That the War Department publicly sanctioned the tests probably had a lot to do with the relaxation of the normally doctrinaire editorial policies of the service journals. Articles openly critical of the Army's tank development policies and doctrine even appeared in the *Infantry Journal*.[5] Other authors openly called for independent combined-arms units that used the potential of the tank as the basis for revolutionizing doctrine.[6] Instructors at the Infantry Tank School envisioned the tank as a powerful weapon that should be used "in the roles of exploitation, envelopment, deep penetration, and decisive action" and as a weapon "capable of independent action."[7]

Discussions about roles for tanks other than simply supporting the infantry found their way from the classroom into official publications. In November 1931 the War Department released a field manual on tanks.[8] Although the title sheet of the manual stated that it had been "Prepared under Direction of the Chief of Infantry," the manual was written at the Infantry Tank School before the Mechanized Force disbanded and while it was still permissible to think of tanks in other than an infantry role. Major Ralph E. Jones, one of the principal authors of the manual, was a tactics instructor at the school and the author of a number of speculative articles on tanks.[9] In the chapter titled "Tank Principles," the publication began by making the politically mandatory concessions to the traditional tank missions of infantry support. In this role, tanks had two distinct functions—leading tanks and accompanying tanks. Leading tanks supported the attack "by breaking up the strong elements of the hostile defense and penetrating deeply to facilitate the rapid and extensive advance of the attack which follows them." Accompanying tanks provided "close cooperative assistance to the advance of the assaulting waves of attacking troops." The tank manual also postulated on the use of fast tanks, when available; again, bowing to convention, the manual stated that fast tanks were suitable for use in the accompanying or leading roles. The manual implied, however, that the new machines' potential should not be confined to these missions. Instead, the tanks could form the basis for an armored or mechanized force and make possible the execution of decisive missions.[10]

When the Mechanized Force disbanded, the chief of infantry reasserted his control over the tank advocates. To facilitate the integration of tank tactics and infantry missions, the War Department announced the transfer of the Tank School and the Tank Board from Fort Meade to Fort Benning, Georgia—the home of the Infantry School.[11] General Fuqua's testimony before the House Subcommittee on Appropriations in 1932 clearly indicated the conceptual leadership he would provide to future infantry mechanization programs: "Let me make clear that the automatic machine weapons, and the 'land battleships,' called tanks, that our critics predicted would make the infantry archaic, are now merely parts of the Infantry's armament."[12]

During Fuqua's appearance before the subcommittee, Representative Ross Collins asked him what had happened to the Mechanized Force at Fort Eustis. Fuqua, probably without realizing it, summed up the realities of MacArthur's mechanization policy when he stated that the unit had been "decentralized—well, broken into parts." Collins apparently understood more about the interbranch tension over the Mechanized Force than Fuqua realized and responded to Fuqua's explanation with a rhetorical question: "And the reason that the mechanized force at Fort Eustis was broken up was so that the present divisions of the Army would remain intact, and each of them would have a taste of mechanization?"[13]

Although the new mechanization policy theoretically enabled Fuqua to regain control of tank doctrine, it had one major drawback. Infantry fast tanks and cavalry combat cars were the same vehicle. Consequently, Fuqua had to compete with another branch for tanks during a time when Army budget policies made few available. This tension was felt as early as June 1931, with Fuqua complaining that although he supported letting other arms experiment with tanks, he objected seriously to its "being done at the expense of the Infantry."[14]

The major equipment controversy revolved around who would design the Army's fast tanks—the Ordnance Department or J. Walter Christie, an independent inventor. Christie received a contract from the Ordnance Department for seven of his vehicles in June 1931. Four of the machines went to the cavalry, and the remaining three to the tank regiment at Fort Benning.[15] Because Christie would not follow War Department specifications in designing his tanks, however, the Ordnance Department refused to buy any more of his products.[16] The Ordnance Department, believing that the Christie tanks were unreliable and poorly engineered, thus provided the Army with its tanks.[17] But because Ordnance Department tanks were slower, infantrymen who thought that fast tanks could evade antitank gun fire continued to prefer the Christie tank.[18]

When Major General Edward Croft became chief of infantry in the summer of 1933, he brought with him his own ideas on tanks. In August he presented his views to the president of the Infantry Board, who was charged with testing tanks after the demise of the Tank Board. Croft wrote that "it seems to me that light inexpensive tanks, with not too much armor or armament, and stout hearted soldiers manning them, will better serve our infantry purpose than will tanks that are heavy and expensive and calculated to meet every contingency."[19]

In response the board sent Croft a twenty-three-page document explaining why it wanted both medium and light tanks—both to be made by Christie—and insinuated that the Ordnance Department's previous efforts had been disasters. Furthermore, the board believed that only the infantry's active participation in the design process could ensure that the branch would receive the right types of tanks.[20] Croft responded sharply to the president of the Infantry Board: "Whatever mistakes may have been made in the past in the design of tanks . . . I do not consider that it is the mission of the Infantry to take over the work of the Ordnance Department." He also made it clear that during his tenure as chief, the infantry would stick to "our own knitting."[21]

Infantry opinion crystallized on the types of tanks needed. An October 1933 memorandum outlined the need for a light tank and a medium tank to support "the uninterrupted advance of the rifleman in attack."[22] In 1936 the ordnance program started to deliver such tanks to units. The chief of infantry's decision about how to allocate and use the 104 M2 light tanks showed how deeply the currents of economy ran in the Army. The chief of infantry decided to fill the tank companies at Fort Benning and the Hawaiian Department and to distribute the remaining fifty tanks throughout the rest of the Army. Every other tank company would receive a platoon of five tanks. To ensure that these tanks would last, the chief of infantry suggested that "only one platoon of 5 tanks be used daily for training, and that the remaining platoons be maintained in local storage."[23] The president of the Infantry Board correctly noted that this policy would preclude training as companies and battalions. The chief of infantry held off on this restrictive measure but supported a later War Department directive to field commanders to restrict the use of the new machines.[24]

Work also began on a new medium tank. By August 1937 a design study for the medium tank T5 was sent to the Infantry School for evaluation. In early September Major General George A. Lynch, chief of infantry, forwarded further instructions, asking that the Infantry Board give its views on the capabilities and characteristics of the tank. Specifically, why was a medium tank required, and if the infantry adopted a medium tank, did it still need light tanks?[25] These basic questions were posed despite the fact that the Ordnance Department had already designed and constructed a wooden model of the T5.

Brigadier General Asa L. Singleton, president of the Infantry Board, responded that the medium tank would perform the missions that the light tank, because of its vulnerability and light armament, could not. Nevertheless, the infantry still needed light tanks to accompany advancing troops since the medium tank's weight restricted it from crossing certain classes of bridges. Furthermore, the Army had just fielded many light tanks—after considerable effort—and it would be difficult to justify their abandonment.[26]

Development of the T5 proceeded. Early in 1938 General Lynch explained the design rationale for the infantry medium tank, beginning with a statement about its mission: "The infantry tank has just one primary mission: the neutralization of machine guns. . . . It has paid for itself if it succeeds in eliminating this obstacle to the rifleman's advance." In addition, tanks attacked enemy antitank guns. Lynch declared that the tank would have to rely on mobility for protection since it was pointless to try to put enough armor on a tank to afford protection from antitank guns larger than .50 caliber. And he, like others, recognized that adding armor would only lessen crucial mobility.[27]

Lynch also modified the existing doctrinal roles of leading and accompanying tanks. He noted that the conception of leading tanks trying to break through enemy defenses to attack the rear areas had fallen from favor. Instead, Lynch announced that the medium tank would form a "leading wave" to dominate enemy antitank guns and would be followed by a second wave of light tanks accompanied by infantry. The light tanks would suppress enemy machine guns. Consequently, the tanks would be exposed to the same threat but needed different armament to attack their targets. The medium tank thus differed from the light only in the caliber and number of guns. Given Lynch's missions for the machines, differing degrees of armor protection were not needed. Lynch conceded the point, noting that "this is contrary to the thought which has governed the design of tanks heretofore in many armies, i.e., that greater armor protection should be obtained in the medium than the light tank."[28]

In July 1938 Lynch wrote in the *Infantry Journal* that the new medium tank was almost ready for standardization and would probably enter production that summer. He also assessed the reports on tanks from observers of the Spanish civil war. Lynch briefly discussed and then discarded theories that envisioned any role for tanks that conflicted with "our own conclusion . . . that the tank is a powerful *auxiliary*." Lynch also spelled out why the infantry needed a light and a medium tank. Singleton's sketchy rationale of the previous year had become, in the absence of more sophisticated analysis, the branch doctrine. The medium tank provided the ideal assault weapon to assist the progress of the infantry. The light tank guaranteed "tanks that can maintain constant contact with the foot infantry" in the event bridge limitations held back the medium tanks.[29]

The tanks that the Army produced flowed from these infantry support missions. To handle enemy antitank weapons, the 19-ton medium tank had a turret-mounted 37-mm gun. Since the machine had to operate at times in advance of the infantry, it had eight machine guns for self-defense. These lighter weapons could also support the infantry in the close-in battle. The 9.7-ton light tank, designed to stay with the infantry in the assault, had only one .50-caliber and two .30-caliber machine guns.[30]

The War Department endorsed Lynch's concepts in August 1938: The missions for tanks were supporting and accompanying the infantry. The War Department additionally provided an organizational scheme for light and medium tanks. Given the mission of close support of the infantry advance, the department believed that tanks should be organized into light and medium battalions, which was the largest permanent organization envisioned for tanks. If the tactical situation required larger units, existing battalions could be temporarily combined into a tank group.[31]

By early 1939 the infantry had second thoughts about the sufficiency of the armament on its light and medium tanks. Information from the battlefields of Spain highlighted the growing threat posed by antitank guns. To redress this problem, the chief of infantry announced that the .50-caliber machine gun on the light tank would be replaced by a 37-mm cannon to obtain greater "armor-and-concrete piercing ability." At this juncture General Lynch saw no reason to fundamentally reassess the American tank program. Forestalling any movement for heavier tanks, Lynch stated: "Thus far the construction of heavy tanks has not been advocated, because they can be moved into the combat zone only on railroads, and because their radius of action is extremely limited since few highway bridges and no military bridges will bear their weight."[32]

Experimental work on increasing the firepower of the medium tank also began. In February 1939 the chief of infantry asked the Infantry Board to study plans prepared by the chief of ordnance for a medium tank with a fixed 75-mm pack howitzer. The proposed tank would accompany medium tank units to suppress enemy antitank guns and tanks that might impede tanks in their infantry support role.[33] In early March the board responded by stating that such a tank would be capable of defending itself and other tanks against antitank guns and other tanks and that it had potential as an "accompanying gun for foot troops." The report then stated that the board preferred a howitzer over a cannon as the armament of the medium tank because it was shorter and lighter. The major objection voiced over the ordnance designs focused on the mounting of the howitzer. The board wanted the 75-mm howitzer mounted in a turret, noting that a recent military attaché report indicated that the Germans had successfully mounted a 75-mm gun on their medium tank. The Infantry Board report concluded by recommending that the proposed medium tank be tested and, if successful, that future designs incorporate a 75-mm howitzer as the principal armament. It also noted that board members agreed that a medium tank armed with a 37-mm gun would "prove superior to one armed with a pack howitzer."[34]

The Ordnance Department began developing a medium tank with a 75-mm howitzer, designated the medium tank T5, phase III (T5E1). In July 1939 Major John K. Christmas, an ordnance officer involved in the project at Aberdeen Proving Grounds, noted that because the medium tank equipped with a 75-mm howitzer had the mission of "close support of other tanks" its howitzer need only have a range of up to 2,500 yards.[35] Based on these facts, the decision was made by the user, and confirmed by the designer, to make the largest armament of the American medium tank a low-velocity howitzer.

In December 1939 the Infantry Board completed test firings of the 75-mm medium tank weapon, but its report was ambivalent about the improvement in capability offered by the 75-mm howitzer and asked that any decision on its adoption be deferred. The rationale for this recommendation resulted from what the infantry envisioned as the mission of the medium tank. The priorities of these targets from the infantry's perspective were (1) antitank weapons and "small point targets," (2) "machine-gun nests [and] ground-troops in trenches," and (3) "hostile tanks and armored vehicles." The infantry wanted a turret-mounted cannon of between "fifty and sixty millimeters" with "muzzle velocity sufficient to penetrate the armor of tanks equal to the modern medium tanks at close and medium ranges." The infantry believed that the 75-mm howitzer or a gun of comparable caliber was too big because of the space required to accommodate the weapon and its ammunition. To develop a new tank cannon would delay a more powerful medium tank, and so tests of the modified medium tank continued. The infantry wanted this tank to contain a hull-mounted 75-mm howitzer and a turret-mounted 37-mm gun and machine gun, as well as the capability to fire high-explosive, armor-piercing, and canister ammunition from the 75-mm howitzer.[36]

When the Nazis invaded France in June 1940 the infantry reassessed its tank requirements, but the lessons drawn from the blitzkrieg did not lead to any doctrinal redirection. In fact, the chief of infantry believed that the developments called for a heavy infantry tank that could "live on the battlefield and inflict the greatest possible harm upon hostile personnel and material." The issue became the survivability of the infantry tank in the face of heavier antitank weapons and artillery. The targets, "hostile pill boxes . . . as well as troops both in the open and in trenches," required large, rapid-fire guns. The chief of infantry suggested two heavy tank concepts, called type A and type B. The type A heavy tank was a modified M2 medium tank with up to three inches of armor, a hull-mounted cannon of between 60 and 75 mm with sufficient muzzle velocity to destroy enemy tanks, a turret-mounted 37- to 50-mm cannon, and enough machine guns to provide all-around defense. The type B tank was an extraordinarily heavy tank, with a maximum weight of eighty tons and a maximum length of eighty-five feet. Other characteristics included three inches of armor, a main hull-mounted cannon of between 75 and 105 mm for use against "materiel and troops in trenches," a hull-mounted mortar, a turret-mounted 37- to 57-mm cannon, and the usual panoply of defensive machine guns.[37]

The war in Europe also led to a reexamination of the medium tank program. On June 5, 1940, the chief of infantry told the chief of ordnance that he was concerned about the ability of the M2A1 medium tank to perform "its mission as a supporting tank for Infantry." He recommended that the armor on the experimental T5 tank be increased and that the earlier hull-mounted 75-mm and turret-mounted 37-mm design be the armament of the tank. The infantry, realizing that these changes would modify the performance characteristics of the medium tank, approved in advance an increase in weight to twenty-eight tons. Speed was reduced to approximately twenty miles per hour.[38]

On June 10 the Ordnance Subcommittee on Automotive Equipment approved an increase in weight for the M2 medium tank to twenty-five tons to accommodate more armor, which reduced its speed to twenty-five miles per hour, and specified the hull-mounted 75-mm cannon as its principal armament. The upper weight limit meant less armor than requested by the infantry, but adding armor would require a major redesign of the suspension and transmission. The committee recommended that future medium tank designs incorporate the extra armor and turret-mounted 75-mm cannons. It further emphasized that these changes should be made "as soon as can be done without delay in production."[39]

Major General C. M. Wesson, the chief of ordnance, approved the medium tank changes on June 19. As an interim measure, the M2 tank's armor was upgraded and a 75-mm howitzer with a muzzle velocity of 1,650 feet per second was mounted on its hull. Future design efforts concentrated on a turret-mounted 75-mm gun with a muzzle velocity of 1,850 feet per second.[40] The infantry, however, did not want to sacrifice any machine guns to obtain a hull-mounted cannon and asked that a machine gun be mounted in the 37-mm gun turret to compensate for the one lost with the placement of the 75-mm howitzer.[41]

Infantry's twenty-year dominance in tank development ended when the War Department consolidated all Army tank activities in a new armored corps. Every chief of infantry since Major General Allen had approached tank doctrine and design with a singleness of purpose—exploitation of the technology to make it the best infantry support weapon possible. When the infantry's tank monopoly ended in July 1940, Lynch believed that his branch had lost a valuable weapon.

CAVALRY COMBAT CARS

The cavalry perspective on tank technology was quite different from that of the infantry. The role of the cavalry in the U.S. Army had been under fire since World War I. Of the seventeen regiments in the Army, only one, the 2d Cavalry, had deployed to Europe. This regiment saw little action and spent most of the war running remount stations for transportation purposes. One squadron of the regiment, hastily improvised for the Meuse-Argonne offensive, saw limited combat duty.[42] The majority of the U.S. cavalry remained in the United States and guarded the long border with Mexico.[43] In a region of the country with few roads and restrictive terrain, the cavalry regiments proved quite effective. The postwar Superior Board and General Pershing both verified the continued importance of cavalry, particularly on the North American continent.

In the wake of the National Defense Act of 1920, the cavalry fought like the rest of the Army to maintain its strength. Unlike the other branches, however, the cavalry had no wartime experiences to parade as justification for its relevance in modern war. Consequently, the chief of cavalry clung to the mission of defending the Mexican border.

Concomitantly, the cavalry began a long fight to justify the horse in war. In the early 1920s this task was fairly simple, since tank, airplane, and automobile technologies were in their infancy and had clear weaknesses. In 1921 Major General Willard A. Holbrook, the chief of cavalry, highlighted the primitiveness of these machines when he pled for exemption from the impending personnel cuts. Holbrook stressed the mobility and reliability of the horse in marginal regions where roads were neither "numerous nor good." He also stressed the fact that the cavalry had a continuing peacetime mission along the Mexican border for which it was uniquely suited: "Only the most mobile arm can secure results against the incursions of mounted troops, who strike swiftly and who lead their pursuers into terrain guaranteeing escape except from mounted troops."[44]

The cavalry had more visceral arguments to fall back on as well. In an army fixated on the power of man over machine, the horse had a strong following. The mystique of the glory and the masculinity of war, both challenged by the slaughter in the trenches, found a sanctuary in this branch, which believed its very existence depended on thwarting the machine. George Patton, now comfortably home in the cavalry after his brief stint with tanks, had a unique flair for capturing the machismo of the nineteenth-century warrior spirit that pervaded the Army in general and the cavalry in particular: "The bayonet charge and the saber charge are the highest physical demonstration of moral victory. The fierce frenzy of hate and determination flashing from the bloodshot eyes squinting behind the glittering steel is what wins."[45]

The horse also played a central role in the social culture of the Army. During the interwar era "there was an upsurge of interest in fox hunting, polo, steeplechasing, and in the competition of horse shows."[46] The *Cavalry Journal* devoted a section in every issue exclusively to polo. This romance with the horse was not confined to the cavalry, however. Virtually every Army post had its hunt club, and most officers rode.[47] Unfortunately for the cavalry, the social significance of the horse did not guarantee its future military utility.

Many cavalry officers realized that machines had dire implications for the horse's relevance in war. Consequently, thought within the branch about the future of cavalry began to polarize. One faction maintained that the horse had a place in modern war, and the other believed that cavalry missions had a vital role in war but that machines had to replace the horses.

The horse advocates tried to modernize the cavalry and viewed technology only as a means to enhance the capabilities of the horse—the inveterate horse cavalrymen focused on the capabilities rather than the deficiencies of the horse. Major General Herbert B. Crosby, the chief of cavalry, confidently told the 1928 class at the Army War College that the horse was at home in swamps, forests, and mountains and could even swim rivers; machines could not. Crosby also noted that "tanks, tankettes, armored cars, armored airplanes, smoke projectors, gas, and all modern means of warfare in use or still to be adopted cannot take the place of the men and the horse."[48]

Other cavalry officers lacked enthusiasm for the horse. Brigadier General George Van Horn Moseley, commander of the 1st Cavalry Division at Fort Bliss, Texas, believed that the cavalry division needed to be modernized. Moseley wrote Crosby in December 1927 that his division had too many animals and needed more motor transportation, particularly in the logistical elements. Furthermore, he wanted more armored cars. To drive his point home, Moseley wrote: "When the cowboy down here is herding cattle in a Ford we must realize that the world has undergone a change."[49]

President Hoover's 1929 survey of the military establishment exacerbated existing tensions over the future of the cavalry. A number of the areas General Summerall specifically targeted for analysis boded ill for the future of the cavalry. Could the strength of the branch be cut? To what degree could cavalry be replaced by "armored cars and motorization or aviation"? Could "all or any portion of the horses and mules used by the Army be replaced by motor vehicles"?[50]

General Crosby understood the implications of these questions and prepared a comprehensive reply. Major George S. Patton, one of the officers on Crosby's staff, researched and wrote much of the report. As one might expect, Crosby held that the cavalry was too valuable to be cut. In fact, Crosby used the opportunity afforded by the survey to plead that the Regular Army needed more cavalry. He pointed out that the constant mounted guerrilla warfare along the Mexican border posed the greatest threat to the United States and that the cavalry was the best arm to "dispose of Mexican horsemen." Cavalry could easily negotiate terrain impassable by machines; it was economical when compared with the other combat arms since horses cost less than tanks or airplanes. To Crosby, the thought of replacing cavalry with another arm "scarcely deserved consideration." Patton was even more emphatic, writing that "the effectiveness of cavalry is in no way reduced by the advent of mechanical units," and "the individual mobility of cavalry and its universal adaptability are unaltered and undisturbed by the advent of new arms."[51]

To support his conclusions, Crosby included an exhibit with quotations from notable military figures who commented on the importance of cavalry. Among the laudatory comments by the legendary leaders of World War I—Pershing, Haig, Allenby, Petain, Foch, Hindenburg, and Ludendorff—Crosby strategically placed statements by two officers on the War Department General Staff. Crosby recalled that Major General Frank Parker, the G-3 who had prepared the 1928 mechanization study, had once said: "In all the history of war cavalry was never more important than it is today." Finally, Crosby turned the chief of staff's own words against him, noting that as late as August 1927 General Summerall had related that "there has been a great deal of misinformation broadcasted relative to the cavalry. It is a fact that cavalry is of far more importance than it has ever been."[52]

Although Crosby held a strong line in defending his branch, he also seemed to admit grudgingly that things might change in the future. Commenting on the American experiments with mechanization, Crosby believed that "in time a mechanized force will be a necessary component of a modern army." Nevertheless, he stressed that the time had not yet arrived and that the creation of *"any new arm* would seem to be premature." To Crosby the dogmatic alternative posed by partisans on each side of the issue—"cavalry *or* machine"—was not the answer. Instead, he urged that armored cars and tanks be included in cavalry organizations since the machines' "speed and radius of action" would complement the horse's flexibility.[53] Crosby's admission that machines could supplement horses was probably about as far as a chief of cavalry could go and still retain the sup-

[126]

port of the branch as a whole. His taking this cautious middle ground, however, set an important precedent since Crosby had conceded that some cavalry missions could be performed by machines.

Opinion within the cavalry on mechanization continued to polarize. The Army's experiments prompted an intense debate in the *Cavalry Journal* over the future of the horse, with two July 1930 articles presenting opposing views.

Lieutenant Colonel K. B. Edmunds defined the position of officers in favor of mechanization. Commenting on the Mechanized Force, Edmunds wrote: "The tendency of existing arms is to adapt the new arm to our present tactics. What we rather must do is to change our tactics to fit the characteristics of the mechanized force." Edmunds also stressed that recent technological developments had vastly increased the speed, reliability, and range of the tank. He believed that this new machine, and the Mechanized Force experimenting with its capabilities, should be embraced by the cavalry as a way to increase its capabilities to perform its missions, missions that the horse could no longer accomplish in the face of machine guns and barbed wire. Nonetheless, Edmunds was a realist and understood the forces arrayed against mechanization, noting that "our Cavalry is instinctively hostile to any machine which may supplant the horse, and inclined to disparage its effect. We are retreating to mountain trails and thick woods, hoping that no fast tank can follow."[54]

Major Patton championed the importance of the horse. He argued, buttressed by the authority of his wartime tank command experience, that machines, particularly tanks, had severe limitations. Patton stated that the horse had to remain the focus of the cavalry, since only the horse could perform the traditional cavalry missions. Emphasizing the all-terrain capability of the horse, he further predicted that too heavy a reliance on machines would condemn "the army which relies principally on them to disaster and defeat." Patton argued that although the new devices might appear decisive, it was folly to "pin our whole faith in their efficacy" because each new weapon would surely lead to a counter.[55]

War Department planning for a permanent mechanized force proceeded amidst the increasingly strident cavalry debate over mechanization. The designation of Colonel Daniel Van Voorhis, a cavalryman, as the commander of the 1930 mechanized force was surely no accident. Two forward-thinking cavalry officers occupied key positions in the War Department. Lieutenant Colonel Adna R. Chaffee, one of the principal authors of the 1928 Mechanization Study, headed the War Department's G-3 Troop Training Section.[56] Major General George Van Horn Moseley, the modernization-minded commander of the 1st Cavalry Division, was in the powerful position of deputy chief of staff of the Army.[57]

Chaffee was one of the leaders of the faction that sought to protect the cavalry's missions rather than its horses. He had also participated in the War Department meeting that selected Van Voorhis to head the Mechanized Force.[58] In December 1930, just as the Mechanized Force began its maneuvers, Chaffee completed another study on mechanization in which he envisioned the Mechanized Force as an organization that would capitalize on the increased potential of a new generation of light tank technology. Although Chaffee conceded that the infantry needed medium tanks, he asserted that the new light tanks' speed of "25 miles per hour on the road, 19 miles per hour cross country" should not be tied to "infantry advancing at 2 miles per hour." Instead, Chaffee argued that fast tanks should serve as the backbone of the "highly mobile combat troops of the next war." He then admitted that the Mechanized Force had been constituted to test this concept. Chaffee, however, did not burn any bridges. He emphasized that this force would supplement the horse cavalry since animals could operate on any terrain.[59] Despite this politically necessary concession, Chaffee defined how the tank would develop in the U.S. Army in the future: as an infantry support weapon and as a machine to provide the cavalry with mobility.

General Moseley's role in deciding the issue of mechanization was less direct. Although the May 1931 decisions to break up the Mechanized Force and to give both the infantry and the cavalry responsibility for exploiting the tank were attributed almost exclusively to General MacArthur, the specifics of the plan probably derived from Moseley.[60] MacArthur surely played the major role in disbanding the Mechanized Force because of his reluctance to use the shrinking budget for anything other than personnel and a desire to end the interbranch squabbling over the unit. Major Patton, from his seat in the chief of cavalry's office, believed that Moseley was one of the "powers that be" who pushed mechanization in the cavalry.[61] Furthermore, it seemed to be common knowledge in the chief of cavalry's office that Moseley had personally dictated the May 1, 1931, memorandum that specified the Army's new mechanization policy.[62]

The May 1931 mechanization memorandum reflected Moseley's modernization bent and surely alarmed the horse advocates. The memorandum, which discussed the relationship between mission and equipment, concluded that in the past Army organizations had been erroneously determined by the type of equipment available rather than the mission of the unit. This discussion led to the next major issue—the role of modern tanks in the Army. The directive noted that the slow tanks of the past provided only tactical mobility and limited their use to close support of the infantry. New tanks, however, had vastly greater potential and could provide "strategic mobility." Finally, since the mission of the cavalry had traditionally been strategic mobility and reconnaissance, its organizations needed to be modernized with tanks. The directive then turned to a more explicit argument: "Modern firearms have eliminated the horse as a weapon, and as a means of transportation he has generally become, next to the dismounted man, the slowest means of transportation."[63]

The document then enumerated the missions of the cavalry and observed that they had not changed from strategic and tactical reconnaissance, fighting for control of theater reconnaissance, seizing important objectives, pursuing or delaying enemy forces, exploiting a breakthrough, and making up part of a combined-arms strategic reserve. Although the missions remained, technological advances dictated that equipment had to change to realize the goals under "modern conditions." Therefore, the Mechanized Force would be reorganized as a reinforced cavalry regiment to take advantage of the potential offered by mechanization. Finally, the directive specified the two directions in which cavalry organizations would proceed in the future. For special tactical missions or operations in terrain where machines could not go, "the horse and mule may remain only where they cannot be replaced by the motor." The other option was "a second type of cavalry (mechanized) in which the horse and mule shall have disappeared entirely."[64]

The War Department released this new mechanization policy to the press on May 18. Every cavalry officer soon knew that the future of the horse in the U.S. Army was in jeopardy. All of the past arguments that had been used to justify its continued value had been reversed: Since the new light tanks had great range and speed, they could provide strategic mobility. Furthermore, the directive defused the long-used argument about the value of the horse in restrictive terrain by allowing that the role was limited and only a supplement to machines. Finally, the War Department clearly implied that the horse would remain in the cavalry only until more capable machines could be developed.[65]

By October 1931 the War Department had worked out the details in constituting a mechanized cavalry regiment. The plan reflected the handiwork of someone—possibly General Moseley—with a deep understanding of how the Army bureaucracy functioned. In any event, the arrangements ensured a minimum of interference from the chief of cavalry, an important consideration given that the regiment's charter focused on "the development of the technique and basic tactical principles applicable to cavalry in which the horse is replaced by machines."[66] The station for the regiment, Fort Knox, Kentucky, promised a comfortable separation from both Washington and the Cavalry School at Fort Riley, Kansas. Regarding the vital issue of control, the War Department made the Fifth Corps Area commander responsible for carrying out the War Department's Mechanized Cavalry Regiment program. The War Department also limited the chief of cavalry's role in the project to one of making recommendations and conducting inspections of the unit. The War Department, however, headed off any rush to interfere with the regiment's operations by specifying that any inspections of the unit would be conducted only at its specific direction.

The Mechanized Cavalry Regiment was slow to organize. The selected portions of the Fort Eustis Mechanized Force did not leave for Fort Knox until November 1931. In the interim, the War Department finalized its plans for the scope of the mechanization program. The October plan stated that once the regiment had been developed, "other elements may be organized and supporting troops developed and attached for operations therewith."[67] In January 1932 the War Department formed the 7th Cavalry Brigade (Mechanized). The unit would consist of a headquarters and headquarters troop, two cavalry regiments, and "attendant auxiliary units." Initially, it was a brigade in name only, because the 1st Cavalry Regiment was the only unit at Fort Knox. The headquarters would activate at a later date, and the additional cavalry regiment, the 4th Cavalry, kept its horses and was assigned to Fort Meade, South Dakota. Still, the brigade plan was an important step in the mechanization program. It expanded the scope of the mechanization effort to brigade size, and the quartermaster general could begin the process of constructing housing and other facilities at Fort Knox to support a brigade.[68]

Getting even one regiment to Fort Knox proved difficult. For almost a year, the mechanization program languished because of events beyond War Department control. The 1st Cavalry Regiment at Fort D. A. Russell in Marfa, Texas, had been designated as the horse outfit that would deactivate to provide the personnel for the Mechanized Cavalry Regiment. Texas Congressmen, sensitive to the economic implications of losing an Army post during the depression, vehemently opposed the transfer. Not until December 1932 did the 1st Cavalry Regiment finally depart Texas.[69]

While the Mechanized Calvary Regiment went through its birthing pains, the chief of cavalry tried to adapt to the new realities dictated by the War Department. In March 1932 Major General Guy V. Henry, chief of cavalry since May 1930, wrote an article in the *Infantry Journal* that explained the War Department program. He noted that the establishment of one regiment was the first step in the program. Eventually, since the War Department wanted to expand the unit to a brigade of two regiments, at least one more horse regiment would have to be deactivated. He then tried to straddle the fence by assuring the readership that horse and mechanized cavalry both had a place in the future cavalry and would complement each other. Henry concluded by stating optimistically: "Our cavalry officers are sincerely interested in mechanization. With proper financial and official support they may be relied upon to develop efficient mechanized and horse cavalries suitable to our needs."[70]

General Henry also let the cavalry officers know that he supported the War Department mechanization program. In December 1932 Brigadier General A. G. Lott, the commandant of the Cavalry School, forwarded a letter to the chief of cavalry from Colonel Selwyn D. Smith, commander of the 2d

Cavalry Regiment.[71] Smith had reviewed an experimental organization for a new horse cavalry regiment and believed the increased capabilities of the new organization, "while retaining all basic cavalry characteristics, will be able successfully to combat mechanization and prevent the latter from assuming the principle [*sic*] cavalry strategical functions."[72]

Henry seized upon Smith's statement and fired a letter back to Lott that let him know the ground rules at the Cavalry School. He began by castigating Smith: "Attention is invited to this quotation because it conveys the thought that the Cavalry school is seeking to *prevent* the development of mechanization." He further noted: "This belief was held by certain individuals in the War Department and was a strong contributory reason why the Mechanized Cavalry was not sent to Fort Riley for station. . . . The role of the Cavalry school is to develop our own cavalry, horsed and mechanized, to their highest point of efficiency."[73]

While General Henry set about making sure that the cavalry would not openly oppose mechanization, General Moseley tried to protect the nascent mechanized cavalry regiment. In February 1933 he wrote Colonel Van Voorhis that for the project to succeed, they all had to stay focused on the independent cavalry missions for which the regiment was best suited. He also told Van Voorhis that he had disapproved a request by the War Department G-3 to let the regiment participate in the coming summer maneuvers at Fort Benning. Moseley was as shrewd as ever, writing: "I do not intend to see our first regiment (mechanized) killed off in a close-in tactical problem for which they are not equipped or organized."[74]

By early 1933 the cavalry community had at least tacitly accepted the inevitability of the War Department mechanization policies. When Henry completed his tour as chief of cavalry in April 1934, he was selected to become a permanent brigadier general. His next posting—as commander of the 7th Cavalry Brigade—added legitimacy to the mechanization program.[75] Major General Leon B. Kromer replaced Henry and continued his predecessor's even-handed mechanization policy, vowing that he would push the advancement of both horse and mechanized cavalry.[76]

That General Kromer supported mechanization became patently clear in December 1934, when he submitted a plan to the General Staff that envisioned a program far beyond the scope of a brigade at Fort Knox. Kromer requested that the mechanization plan for the cavalry proceed on the basis of having a mechanized regiment in each cavalry division, a corps armored car squadron, and a mechanized brigade. In his initial plan Kromer dealt with personnel increases and priorities, requesting an increase in cavalry strength of 1,731 enlisted men. Kromer's first priority was the completion of the 1st Cavalry Regiment. Next, Kromer wanted to establish a mechanized regiment for the 1st Cavalry Division and then finish the expansion of the 7th Cavalry Brigade. Providing the other two divisional mechanized regiments and the corps armored car squadron filled out Kromer's list of objectives.[77]

In February 1935 Kromer estimated the costs for the equipment needed for his expanded mechanization program. For $4,793,674 the necessary combat cars (light tanks) and armored cars could be purchased. Again, Kromer specified his priorities. He began with a request for $1,062,000 to equip the 1st Cavalry Regiment, the 7th Brigade Headquarters, and "fully existing mechanization in the 1st Cavalry Division." Kromer then wanted to spend $2,443,674 to mechanize the 4th Cavalry Regiment. The remainder of Kromer's equipment agenda included an armored car troop at the Cavalry School for service with the 2d Cavalry Division ($295,550), an armored car troop for the 3d Cavalry Division ($295,550), a combat car troop for the 1st Cavalry Division ($348,450), and a combat car troop for the 2d Cavalry Division ($348,450). Finally, Kromer asked the War Department G-3 if the 4th Cavalry Regiment, once mechanized, would be transferred to Fort Knox, Kentucky, or remain at Fort Meade, South Dakota.[78]

On February 11 Brigadier General John H. Hughes, the War Department G-3, asked Kromer to justify his proposed equipment increases, particularly when the Army as a whole was short of mechanized equipment.[79] Kromer replied that the addition of a mechanized regiment to the cavalry division would provide it with a highly mobile "shock unit" for combat missions that could "quickly be detached for use in independent action or with other units."[80]

On April 4 Kromer requested a substantial increase in the combat car authorizations for the 1st Cavalry Regiment. He believed that changing the number of combat cars in the regiment from thirty-six to fifty-six would bolster the "shock power of the regiment by 33-1/3 per cent and the fire power to even a greater degree."[81] This request was made one day before the release of the War Department's revised mechanization policy, one that added the 1st Battalion, 68th Field Artillery (Mechanized), to the 7th Cavalry Brigade.[82]

Kromer's request for more tanks in the 1st Cavalry Regiment, on top of the new artillery battalion for the 7th Cavalry Brigade, prompted Hughes to question where the cavalry mechanization program was headed. On April 17 he sent a memorandum to the chief of staff expressing his concern that the 7th Cavalry Brigade seemed to be turning into another mechanized force. Hughes pointed out that the chief of cavalry's conception of the role of mechanized cavalry exceeded that specified in the missions delineated in General MacArthur's May 1931 directive. Hughes noted that the mechanized cavalry alone needed the capability to perform the first five missions since these tasks were "purely Cavalry missions" that required mobility, not firepower. The exploitation mission could be performed by mechanized cavalry without greater firepower under most conditions. If a situation called for more capability beyond that of the cavalry, the cavalry could be augmented with other arms. Finally, Hughes stated that the 1931 directive never envisioned mechanized cavalry acting alone as a reserve force but rather as part of a larger combined-arms unit. Hughes concluded that "its future development should be along the lines of Mechanized Cavalry rather than that of a Mechanized Force of which the Cavalry is an essential element."[83]

Kromer took issue with Hughes's analysis, stating that the combat car increases he desired would better enable the 1st Cavalry Regiment to perform its prescribed missions. He stressed that the cavalry had to be able to fight to perform its missions. Therefore, "the more power it can carry consistent with mobility, the more effectively can it perform the tasks assigned." Furthermore, Kromer asserted that the whole purpose of the 7th Cavalry Brigade was to determine the "powers and limitations of mechanized cavalry," not to constrain its development.[84]

This exchange between General Hughes, the War Department G-3, and General Kromer, the chief of cavalry, marked a critical juncture in the development of mechanized cavalry. From this point forward, two fundamental assumptions served as a basis for the development of the 7th Cavalry Brigade. First, although Kromer emphasized the need for firepower, he only asked for the combat car, which he received. The War Department approved his request for fifty-six combat cars in the mechanized cavalry regiment tables of organization and equipment. These light tanks had as their heaviest armament a turret-mounted .50-caliber machine gun.[85] The cavalry did not request any of the medium tanks being developed by the infantry, because these slower tanks, although possessing more firepower than combat cars, lacked the latter's mobility. Second, by acknowledging that the cavalry mechanization program was for cavalry missions, Kromer bought into Hughes's argument that mechanized cavalry would not become a separate mechanized force.

In early 1936 General Kromer moved to activate the second regiment for the 7th Cavalry Brigade. He told Colonel A. M. Miller Jr., his executive officer, that, if need be, the personnel for another mechanized regiment could be provided by cutting horse unit strength.[86] Furthermore, Kromer took the position that the new regiment needed to be stationed at Fort Knox so that the 7th Cavalry Brigade could be trained and developed as a complete brigade. Mechanizing the 4th Cavalry Regiment and leaving it in South Dakota precluded brigade-level operations and would retard the development of "the tactics and technique of the new arm."[87]

Moving the 4th Cavalry to Fort Knox disappeared as an option when the regiment ran into the same political snag that had jeopardized the move of the 1st Cavalry to Fort Knox in 1932. South Dakotan Congressmen did not want to lose the cavalrymen's paychecks. Nonetheless, Kromer was serious about activating another mechanized regiment and considered deactivating one of the horse regiments at the Cavalry School at Fort Riley.[88] This option proved to be the only tenable one and in September 1936 the 13th Cavalry Regiment gave up its horses and moved to Fort Knox.[89]

In December Kromer made another decision that shaped the development of mechanized cavalry. Following the 1936 Second Army Maneuvers, Brigadier General Van Voorhis, now commander of the 7th Cavalry Brigade, recommended an increase in the rifle strength or infantry of the regiments. Van Voorhis believed that the one rifle platoon currently in the regiments was not adequate to serve as a "holding element." Colonel Miller responded to the G-3 that the "chief characteristic of mechanized Cavalry [was] mobility" and a larger holding element was not warranted. Miller, aware that Van Voorhis's request could easily be construed as an attempt by the cavalry to add infantry units to the mechanized brigade, moved to forestall any interbranch jealousy. He routed his memorandum to the G-3 through the chief of infantry, who surely noticed the statement that if the brigade ever needed more rifle strength, it would be provided by cavalry units.[90] This action ensured that the brigade would continue to develop along purely cavalry lines and would be suited only for missions requiring mobility, not staying power.

Constraining the missions of the mechanized cavalry did not mean that Kromer did not envision a bigger organization. Officers on Kromer's staff recommended expanding the brigade into a mechanized cavalry division.[91] Kromer seemed to be thinking along similar lines. In a December 1936 letter to Van Voorhis, Kromer broached the topic of expanding mechanization, referring to German, Italian and English developments. He also noted: "The German Cavalry was offered the Panzer Corps in 1933 but turned it down, and as a result has been greatly reduced." Kromer also hinted that tension between the cavalry and infantry over mechanization was increasing. He wrote that the infantry was teaching that its light tank units could be used as exploiting forces, which "indicates the intention to take over the Cavalry mission of exploitation." Kromer concluded by asking Van Voorhis to respond with his thoughts on the future direction of mechanization.[92]

Van Voorhis replied that mechanization would "occur regardless of the cavalry's desire to retain horse regiments." He stressed that the intelligent course was for the cavalry to gain control of the program and profit by the expansion. Van Voorhis believed that the next step in the mechanization program was the establishment of a mechanized cavalry division and recommended that the 7th Cavalry Brigade serve as the basis for the first such unit.[93]

It certainly seemed as though the cavalry had begun to lose its antipathy toward machines. Between late 1936 and early 1938 cavalry mechanization expanded on both practical and theoretical planes. In April the headquarters troop for the 7th Cavalry Brigade was organized. In June an Air Corps observation squadron was attached to the brigade.[94] The brigade received its M1 combat cars, and brigade-level training finally became a reality. On a conceptual level the discourse on mechanization seemed to open up, with discussions about the operations of the mechanized brigade, the need for branch solidarity, and proposals for mechanized divisions appearing in service journals.[95]

Limitations in this evolutionary approach to the inclusion of armored fighting vehicles in the Army persisted, however. The officers of the 7th Cavalry Brigade, albeit advocates of mechanization, clearly considered themselves cavalrymen, and their deeply embedded presumptions shaped the direction in which the brigade developed. Their views were particularly evident when a German officer, Lieutenant Colonel Adolf von Schell, visited Fort Knox in July 1937. The candid Colonel von Schell noted that the combat car's .50-caliber machine gun was an inadequate antitank weapon. When Van Voorhis responded that the cavalry did not expect to fight the heavy tanks supporting infantry, von Schell told him that avoiding these tanks would be impossible. The German officer stated that the majority of his army's tanks would be of the heavier class and that the ratio would probably be only one light to four heavy tanks. He also noted that the light tank was limited to a reconnaissance role: finding "soft spots for the attack of heavier tanks."[96] Von Schell then further elaborated on German tank doctrine:

> [It was designed] to hurl thousands of tanks against the enemy position to overcome the hostile resistance. After this mass of tanks has disposed of the main elements . . . German infantry will then follow through, protected at close quarters by a small number of additional tanks which will mop up any chance machine gun nests or strong points which may have escaped the initial mass tank assault.[97]

Von Schell was unable to modify the American view of mechanization because of the conceptual limits that shaped cavalry officers' view of the tank's role, not because of any strictures imposed by the chief of cavalry. The climate during General Kromer's watch certainly favored mechanization. He demonstrated that he would advance modernization within the branch, even at the expense of horse units, and published his views in the *Cavalry Journal*. Commenting on the 1936 Second Army maneuvers, he stressed that "the future of cavalry is inextricably interwoven with mobility, regardless of the source."[98] As chief of cavalry, General Kromer had a mixed constituency, so he did not dash all of the horse advocates' hopes. In 1937 he testified before the House Subcommittee on Appropriations that there was a role for the horse in the Army: The horse, he said, remained the best means of conducting reconnaissance on difficult terrain. He also implied that the horse

now filled a tactical function, while the strategic role had passed to the machine.[99]

Kromer's tenure as chief of cavalry was marked by an open-minded approach to mechanization. His principal concern was that the cavalry not
surrender its control over its appropriate mechanization missions to either
the infantry or an independent mechanized arm. He believed neither that
mechanization was a threat to the cavalry nor that the horse had been totally
supplanted. Rather, he tried to adapt to change and give each a role in the
cavalry.

In March 1938 Kromer retired and was replaced by Major General John K.
Herr. General Herr was one of the Army's most noted horsemen and had
been a member of the legendary 1923 Army polo team that had defeated a
heavily favored British team at Meadowbrook, Long Island.[100] On the eve of
becoming chief of cavalry, Herr published an introductory article in the *Cavalry Journal*. In this piece he gave the members of the branch a foretaste of
his philosophy: "We must remember that, after all, the spiritual transcends
the material."[101]

Herr approached his new position with a single goal in mind—to preserve the horse cavalry. The climate of openness created by Henry and
Kromer abruptly ended. In its place, Herr generated an environment in
which only horse advocates had a voice. This new attitude soon became apparent in the articles that appeared in the *Cavalry Journal*. Brigadier General
Hamilton S. Hawkins, a former commander of the 1st Cavalry Division,
started a regular feature, "General Hawkins' Notes," that focused almost
exclusively on the value of the horse in modern warfare. He resurrected all
of the old arguments about the limitations of the machine in restrictive terrain. Hawkins also portrayed the mechanization advocates as misguided,
accusing them of "a sheep-like rush toward mechanization and motorization without clear thinking or any apparent ability to visualize what takes
place on the field of maneuver or the battlefield." In Hawkins view, this had
"led to a foolish and unjustified discarding of horses."[102]

On October 10, 1938, Herr attended a conference with the G-3 in which he
enunciated what became his consistent position on mechanization. When
the question of forming a mechanized division was raised, Herr stated that
he was all for it, but "he was unwilling to give up a single horse or man from
the horse cavalry in order to organize any mechanized units." He went on
to compare the mechanized cavalry with the air force, since both robbed his
branch of needed cavalrymen.[103]

One week later, Herr sent a memorandum to the chief of staff that made
his position on mechanization and the horse crystal clear, emphasizing that
mechanization "has not yet reached a position in which it can be relied upon
to displace horse cavalry." He further asserted that mechanization was "for
a considerable period of time . . . bound to play an important but minor role

[136]

while the horse cavalry plays the major role so far as our country is concerned." Herr went on to explain that the mood of the public, Congress, and even Army officers had mistakenly turned against the horse. Herr believed that this was a serious error and that the cavalry should constitute 15 to 25 percent of the active Army. He concluded with the admonition that "we must not be misled to our own detriment to assume that the untried machine can displace the proved and tried horse."[104]

In November Herr made it branch policy that any further increases in mechanized cavalry were contingent on a corresponding gain in horse cavalry strength. Lieutenant Colonel Willis D. Crittenberger, a member of Herr's staff who had also served with the 7th Cavalry Brigade, urged Herr to reconsider his hard-line stance and argued that a move to increase mechanized cavalry would be approved by the chief of staff. Crittenberger even believed that a mechanized cavalry division was a definite possibility and that the branch should go after anything it could get.[105] Herr ignored Crittenberger's warning, and the 7th Cavalry remained a brigade, the only mechanized brigade in the Army until 1940.

Herr also made his position known to the branch at large. In January 1939 he wrote an article for the *Cavalry Journal* in which he emphasized the need for more horse cavalry in the Army. He then enjoined his fellow cavalrymen to spread the word to the American people about the "efficiency and worth" of horse cavalry and encouraged them to share in his "abiding faith in the future of modern Cavalry."[106]

In March the *Cavalry Journal* reprinted extracts from Herr's testimony before the House Subcommittee on Appropriations. Herr had stressed to the Congressmen the need for cavalry, citing examples of its importance from the Civil War. Although he admitted that mechanized cavalry was important, he obviously valued the horse more. Herr believed that the Army needed a cavalry corps of three horse cavalry divisions and one mechanized cavalry division. The discussion eventually arrived at the main issue: Would General Herr justify the continued need for horse cavalry in a modern world? Herr was ready for such a question and cited examples of how only the horse could perform true cavalry missions. He asserted that the value of the horse had been proven during World War I, when cavalry was properly used in open-warfare situations. He also emphasized that the "airplane and motor cannot displace the cavalry by executing its historic missions." Herr cautioned the Congressmen not to be deceived by European conditions. He implied that the armies that had abandoned the horse had done so because of a shortage of animals and forage. Nations fortunate enough to have sufficient resources maintained "great masses of horse cavalry." As examples, Herr cited Poland and Russia and further noted that the United States shared their good fortune in that it had 12,000,000 horses and 4,500,000 mules. Herr believed that another reason for the large Polish and

Russian cavalry forces was that their "wider reaches of country" forced them to a strategy centered on a war of movement. Herr then stressed the similarities to the American situation. As late as the recent war in Spain, Herr told the Congressmen, the horse had again proven its value and that it could not be displaced by machines. He concluded by citing his "abiding faith" that the U.S. cavalry would acquit itself well in any future war.[107]

Herr's position received an important boost from General Malin Craig. Craig, himself a former chief of cavalry, clarified his views on mechanization in his 1939 annual report. Craig expressed concern that mechanized tactics had become too independent and dispersed. He believed that the doctrine of the mechanized cavalry brigade needed to be refocused on a role of support rather than separate action.[108]

The *Cavalry Journal* picked up on the theme of the importance of horse cavalry and in its July–August issue reprinted two articles on the Polish cavalry. The first, "Training of Modern Cavalry for War," covering Polish cavalry doctrine and training methods, confidently stated that the Polish horsemen were ready for modern war and that they could cope with machines. Indeed, the Polish troopers had been given intensive marksmanship training to enable them to stop tanks by firing "at a range of 40 to 50 meters against the chinks in the armor of the tanks."[109] The second piece, "Cavalry in Poland," noted that Poland was the only European nation that retained a large horse cavalry—but with good reason. Poland's wealth in animals, its lack of a large industrial base, and the difficulty of the terrain made reliance on the horse a logical choice for the Polish army.[110] The arguments sounded remarkably like those Herr used to defend American horse cavalry.

In September 1939 the Polish cavalry seemingly let Herr down. Its complete failure against the Nazi blitzkrieg of tanks and airplanes forced Herr to defend the horse even more strenuously. He also began to realize that he would have to at least partially accommodate mechanization. This shift was evident during a September 19 lecture at the Army War College. Herr noted that German horse cavalry had "proven highly valuable in seizing and occupying the positions the mechanized forces had overrun." Herr also seemed to have a greater, albeit belayed, appreciation of mechanization. He noted that the 7th Cavalry Brigade was highly adept at mechanized tactics and stood ready to expand. Nevertheless, this expansion depended on the cavalry being given "the money and personnel to do it."[111]

As soon became evident, any expansion in the 7th Cavalry Brigade meant a cut in horse cavalry personnel. On September 21 Colonel H. J. M. Smith, one of Herr's staff officers, sent Herr a memorandum on a conference he had attended with the War Department G-1. The purpose of the meeting was to decide how to allocate any additional officers the Army might receive from a recent increase of 17,000 enlisted men. One of the issues raised during the session was the officer strength of the 7th Cavalry Brigade. Smith noted that the brigade's peacetime tables of organization authorized 104 cavalry officers and that it only had 57; he related his recommendation to the G-1 that the brigade's 47-officer deficit be a priority. Herr seemed to go along with Smith until the G-1 decided that the addition to the 7th Cavalry "could only be furnished at [the] expense of [the] rest of the Cavalry." The request to augment the 7th Cavalry Brigade was withdrawn.[112]

The Germans' success in Poland stirred cavalry officers, who had heretofore been silenced, to openly advocate mechanization. Brigadier General Adna R. Chaffee, now the commander of the 7th Cavalry Brigade, addressed the Army War College shortly after Herr. He had drawn different lessons than the chief of cavalry had from the German performance: "There is no longer any shadow of a doubt as to the efficiency of well trained and boldly led mechanized forces in any war of movement and that they cannot be combated by infantry and horse cavalry alone."[113] In light of the German success, Chaffee urged an immediate expansion of the 7th Cavalry Brigade into a mechanized cavalry division. He also put himself in direct opposition to the chiefs of cavalry and infantry by recommending that the personnel for the division "be supplied at the expense of our present quota of horse cavalry and possibly some infantry." For equipment, Chaffee urged an increase in appropriations and the reallocation of any light tanks made "surplus to the infantry, through its trend towards the medium tank."[114]

Chaffee viewed mechanization differently than the Germans—he wanted a mobile division built around light tanks and armored cars. The division would have three echelons: reconnaissance, combat, and service. In a side-by-side comparison with the proposed mechanized cavalry division and the German panzer division, Chaffee conceded that the American division was not as strong as the German in "either tanks or in the holding and supporting elements." But Chaffee dismissed this difference by emphasizing that his proposal ensured greater mobility and that it was "organized along traditional American concepts."[115]

Chaffee also rationalized the disparity in tank strength between the American and German division in both numbers and types. He noted that although the tank brigade of the German division contained 448 tanks, 148 of these were for command and reconnaissance and not combat. Furthermore, only 60 of the remaining machines could be termed medium or heavy tanks. He then applied American assumptions about tank nomenclature to the supposed roles of the German tanks. He argued that since their medium tanks were surely slower than their light tanks, they would be used to "protect the artillery and to operate in support of the infantry component of the division." Chaffee then deducted the 148 command and 60 medium tanks of the German brigade and noted that this left 240 light battle tanks, making the 170 light tanks in the American division "somewhat lighter" by comparison. Chaffee noted that even this disparity in like types was not significant because American tanks were of better quality. Nonetheless, Chaffee believed that if it became necessary to modify the American division along the lines of the German division, it would simply be a matter of attaching "a motorized infantry regiment, and possibly a battalion of medium tanks."[116]

The chasm between horse and mechanized cavalry advocates widened as each faction drew its lessons from the war in Poland. General Hawkins asserted that the experience was irrelevant to the role of horse cavalry since the Poles "were simply overwhelmed by superior forces." Furthermore, Hawkins warned that when the Germans turned their attention toward the west, "the Allies would rue the day when they suppressed their cavalry."[117] The contrary views of mechanization advocates also made their way into the *Cavalry Journal,* although the most caustic chose to remain anonymous. In the same issue in which Hawkins defended the past, "Earnest Grouch" wrote "Time to Wake Up." He concluded:

> The prime mover of the German attack may be said to have been the gasoline motor in the air and on the ground; the basis of the Polish defense was the man, propelled only by his legs or by a horse. . . . The army whose destructive, striking effort was based on mechanization, aviation, and motorized infantry swept the enemy from the battlefield.[118]

The War Department encouraged Herr to increase mechanization. In February 1940 Brigadier General Frank M. Andrews, the War Department G-3, informed Herr that the War Department intended to activate a number of mechanized units at the Cavalry School. Andrews also related that the personnel to staff these new units would probably come from the cavalry.[119] Herr was incensed and replied that he would *"reluctantly"* consent to the request but that he had reached his limit. Herr made his position perfectly clear: "Any further attempt to encroach on my horse cavalry will meet with bitter opposition. . . . Under no circumstances will I agree to any further depletion of my horse cavalry. To do so would be a betrayal of the national defense."[120]

General Herr proved that he was a man of his word by campaigning against any reduction in horse cavalry strength. In April he wrote General George C. Marshall, the chief of staff, that he was opposed to transferring men from the 14th Cavalry to augment the 7th Cavalry Brigade.[121] But the War Department published the orders to move the horse soldiers to Fort Knox over Herr's objections. Herr was not deterred and fought the transfer. In May Colonel K. S. Bradford, Herr's executive officer, triumphantly wrote the commander of the 14th Cavalry Regiment that General Herr had "thwarted the inactivation of two of your troops even after the order was published."[122]

The War Department had had enough of the intransigence of the paro-chial branch chiefs. The department ordered the motorized 6th Infantry Regiment, the 7th Cavalry Brigade, and a "Provisional Tank Brigade" to participate in the Third Army maneuvers. In the first phase of the exercise, which took place in April near Fort Benning, Georgia, the Army experi-mented with various combinations of the two brigades and the infantry reg-iment. Between May 5 and 25 the maneuvers continued near Camp Beaure-gard, Louisiana. During this second phase, both of the brigades and the motorized regiment combined to form a "provisional Mechanized Force"—the first American mechanized unit larger than a brigade. As this single American "armored division" maneuvered in Louisiana, German panzer divisions and corps were slashing their way across Western Europe.[123]

Following the maneuvers, General Andrews, the War Department G-3, met with selected members of the ad hoc armored division, including Gen-erals Chaffee and Magruder and Magruder's executive officer, Colonel Al-van C. Gillem. Few from outside the mechanized group had been asked to the meeting, a notable exception being Colonel George Patton, an observer during the exercises. It seemed that Patton had observed more than the ma-neuvers: He had seen the conglomerate mechanized force humiliate Major General Kenyon A. Joyce's 1st Cavalry Division and had apparently de-cided that it was time for a career change.[124] Although General Lynch, the chief of infantry, and General Herr were in Louisiana, Andrews did not in-vite them to the meeting.[125]

Andrews's purpose for calling the meeting was to determine the best course for the future development of American mechanization. The atten-dees, veterans of years of infantry and cavalry control over mechanization, were unanimous in their opinion that mechanization had to be taken away from the branch chiefs. They also agreed that the new organization should use the "relatively large number of light tanks on hand, but thereafter the production of medium tanks should be stressed."[126]

General Andrews returned to Washington and discussed the Louisiana events with General Marshall. The result was a memorandum announcing a conference with the chief of staff to discuss War Department mechaniza-tion policies and consideration of a change from the existing policy that placed mechanization under the control of the chiefs of infantry and cavalry. Andrews proposed the establishment of an armored corps "charged with the organization, training, and development of mechanization." Additional-ly, all infantry tank regiments and the 7th Cavalry Brigade would be trans-ferred to the armored corps. Andrews concluded his memorandum by ask-ing for comments and recommendations.[127]

General Lynch was quick to respond to Andrews's infringement of his tank prerogatives. On June 2 he wrote a memorandum to Andrews that, ironically, must have reinforced Andrews's belief that a radical change in mechanization policy was needed. Lynch began by stating that he presumed that the formation of an armored corps was due to the success of the German panzer divisions in breaking through the Sedan front in northeastern France. Lynch then revealed his conceptual limits. He told Andrews that earlier reports that the panzer divisions were responsible for the breakthrough were erroneous. To prove his point, Lynch provided an extract from the June 3 issue of *Time* magazine, which stated that "the German technique of achieving a break-through such as that at Sedan a fortnight ago is *not by means of* armored (Panzer) divisions" but "by engineers and infantry, proceeded by air bombing and *accompanied by heavy (over 20 tons) tanks detailed to the infantry.*" The article continued, noting: "Panzer units are in effect *armored cavalry. After the break-through,* they move out ahead of the infantry to outflank the enemy and to reach and harass his rear. They influence the direction of the enemy's retirement, but all important is *pressure by the masses of infantry.*" Citing *Time* as the authority, Lynch argued that events in Europe showed that the existing War Department mechanization policy was sound. Furthermore, Lynch was concerned that putting all tanks in the armored corps would surely result in the needs of the infantry being overlooked: "If a reorganization is effected by which the attacking infantry is deprived of the support of tanks, then the blood of countless soldiers will be wasted in onslaught on material objectives which should be attacked by armored weapons."[128] Lynch continued by asserting that the logic behind the argument for a separate armored corps was no different than that for a separate air corps. Both needed to remain as they were to ensure maximum support of the ground battle and, by implication, the infantry. Lynch saw only the need for more infantry tank units to support the "assault missions of our foot infantry."[129]

General Herr's response to Andrews was similar to Lynch's. He asserted that current Army mechanization policy was sound and that the expansion of mechanization had been retarded "by a lack of funds, not the absence of a separate corps." He contended that German operations in Poland and France showed that panzer divisions were used for traditional cavalry missions, particularly the exploitation of a breakthrough. Herr argued that the 7th Cavalry Brigade was already organized for such missions. Events in Europe showed the need for an immediate expansion of the brigade into a division and the formation of additional mechanized cavalry divisions—not the creation of a separate armored corps.[130] Herr, perhaps not trusting Andrews to convey his views, sent a separate memorandum to the chief of staff that outlined the cavalry position on the G-3's proposal for an armored corps.[131]

Herr's next move showed the depths of the schism between his office and the 7th Cavalry Brigade. On June 7 he wrote Chaffee and Brigadier General

C. L. Scott to advise them that the chief of cavalry might be asked to "suggest a definite organization for an armoured division."[132] Herr asked Chaffee and Scott to provide their recommendations for an American equivalent to the German panzer division. On June 8 Herr received a note from a member of his staff. One can only imagine Herr's anger and sense of betrayal as he read that Chaffee and Scott were both en route to Washington to form a board on mechanization.[133]

Events moved rapidly. On June 10 Andrews chaired a meeting on "armored equipment and organization in the Army."[134] The conference was largely a formality, because General Marshall had already made the decision to create the Armored Corps. Nevertheless, the branch chiefs had a chance to air their objections to the Armored Corps one more time. Needless to say, they held out for the status quo.[135]

Chaffee's board hammered out the real plans for the Armored Force.[136] A June 17 memorandum from Scott to Andrews showed the conceptual basis for the major organizational unit: "The mechanized division should be a fast-moving, hard-hitting, maneuverable unit for employment on independent missions." Scott noted that the board did not intend to "follow blindly" the German organization since American equipment was different. Another central assumption guided their planning: "Unless we are organizing to go to Europe, the terrain, the road nets, bridges, and many other features on the theater of operations where we may be employed will be entirely different."[137]

The division Scott recommended was similar to the mechanized cavalry division Chaffee had proposed in 1939, with the addition of a medium tank regiment and an infantry regiment. The division would have a headquarters and four echelons: reconnaissance, assault, support and holding, and service. The assault echelon would have two light and one medium tank regiments, whereas the support and holding echelon would contain a single infantry regiment and an artillery regiment.[138] The missions the board envisioned for the mechanized division were very similar to the ones General MacArthur had stated in 1931, and had a distinctively cavalry-like tone:

a. Employment in battle in conjunction with other arms.
b. Offensive action as a powerful spear-head directed at important strategic objectives and hostile nerve centers.
c. Exploitation of a break through.
d. Seizing and holding points of strategic and tactical importance until troops in rear can be pushed forward to exploit its success.
e. Pursuit and delaying action.
f. Covering and assisting the advance of less mobile and unarmored units.
g. Reconnaissance, long distance and tactical.
h. Use as a mobile reserve.[139]

[143]

On June 20 General Andrews sent copies of a draft memorandum for the chief of staff to the chiefs of infantry and cavalry for comment. Any lingering illusions about their roles in the new armored corps vanished. Andrews recommended the formation an armored corps of two armored divisions under the direction of a field force commander.[140]

Herr tried to maintain at least a modicum of influence by recommending that a number of the units in the armored division be designated cavalry units. He probably agreed with Lieutenant Colonel Crittenberger, one of his staff officers, that not calling any of the units in the division "cavalry" was "a step towards the establishment of a separate Armored Corps."[141]

Lynch resented an inference in the G-3 paper that the infantry had not kept up with tank developments. Directing his comments to the chief of staff, he argued that designating a field force commander was tantamount to creating a new branch chief for armor, a move that was unnecessary in his view. Lynch asserted that he needed only a bigger budget to take care of "infantry tank materiel, organization, and general doctrine."[142]

On July 1 General Marshall approved the creation of an armored force "for the purposes of a service test."[143] The Armored Force initially consisted of the Headquarters, I Armored Corps (Fort Knox); the 1st Armored Division (Fort Knox); the 2d Armored Division (Fort Benning); and a General Headquarters (GHQ) Reserve medium tank unit, the 70th Armored Regiment (Fort Meade, Maryland). To constitute these new units, the G-3 directed the consolidation of all of the Army's infantry tank and cavalry combat car units under the Armored Force. General Chaffee was named chief of the Armored Force and commander of the I Armored Corps. He was given virtually complete control over the development of doctrine, organization, and equipment for the Armored Force.[144]

On July 10 the adjutant general made the Armored Force official.[145] The chief of infantry retained a degree of influence over the development of doctrine for the GHQ tank battalions, but the chief of cavalry was out of the tank business.[146] Major Robert W. Grow, an officer on Herr's staff, later noted: "The Armored Force had been created, not because a new Arm was necessary but because the Cavalry did not grasp it."[147]

The Armored Force was a radical institutional innovation for a conservative War Department, but its creation did not result in a fundamental reassessment of the tank's role in the U.S. Army. Officers who rose to lead the new organization were, in general, conventional officers whose views on tanks were tempered by years of branch indoctrination. These officers brought with them their own deeply embedded assumptions that had a deterministic effect on the institutional shape and technology of the Armored Force.

Furthermore, there was little time for prolonged debate. In the aftermath of the fall of France, expansion became the imperative. In the winter of

1940–41, the active Army grew from 172,000 to nearly 1,500,000 officers and enlisted men.[148] Inducting, equipping, training, and incorporating into units the citizen soldiers who swelled the Army's ranks were demanding tasks for the traditional branches. For a new organization such as the Armored Force, these challenges were even more burdensome.[149] Fundamental decisions about doctrine, organization, and equipment had to be made early to provide a foundation for growth.

The key decisions that shaped the direction of the Armored Force were doctrinal, because doctrine formed the basis for determining the roles and missions, organizations, and equipments of the constituent units of the Armored Force. In the Armored Force's crucial first year, the formulation of doctrine was firmly under the control of General Chaffee. Indeed, most of the formative decisions had already been made during the meetings of the mechanization board in June. Chaffee had been in a position of power as the head of the board and guided the deliberations from an assumption that "the organization, doctrine, and employment of the two reconnaissance battalions and the four light armored regiments should be strictly mechanized Cavalry."[150] The cavalry-based missions that the board had settled on for the mechanized division became the missions of the armored divisions.

Still, there were conspicuous accommodations of the past. Chaffee's foremost concern was the combined-arms armored division, but he was also responsible for GHQ tank units.

The GHQ tank units were memorials to the War Department's reluctance to completely discard its conventional tank wisdom for a new concept. The mission of these units was to provide additional combat power to "infantry, cavalry, and armored divisions for specific operations."[151] The basic functional unit was a group headquarters and several battalions, equipped mainly with either medium or heavy tanks.

From the beginning, the GHQ tank units were envisioned as infantry support forces. Cavalry officers in the Armored Force were more than willing to make this concession, and "even the most ardent Cavalry officers admitted that the tactical doctrine and organization of the GHQ Reserve Tank Battalions under the Armored Force should be Infantry (Tank) in character."[152] This admission almost resulted in reincorporation of the GHQ tank units into the infantry structure. General Lynch had logic on his side—if these units were infantry support forces, then they should be under his control. The chief of the Armored Force would be an adviser in the "cooperative development of equipment." Chaffee appealed to the chief of staff that such a step would result in considerable confusion and duplication of effort. To assuage the demands of both Lynch and Chaffee, the War Department stated that the chiefs of the Armored Force and infantry would cooperate in the development of "the tactical doctrine on the employment of GHQ tank elements as infantry supporting units."[153]

[145]

The collaborative efforts between the chiefs of the Armored Force and infantry yielded a doctrine for the GHQ tank units that was vintage infantry.[154] The GHQ tanks were offensive weapons whose mission was to aid the advance of the supported troops. The imprint of the infantry concept was most clear in the discussion of how to provide this support. Tanks would attack in two echelons, with the first destroying the hostile antitank guns and the second accompanying the attacking units.[155] This was the same concept General Lynch had articulated in 1938.[156] The War Department was serious about this infantry support role and began forming additional GHQ tank battalions simultaneously with the organization of the two armored divisions. Furthermore, the perceived importance of these units did not diminish. By early 1943 the Army had activated sixty-three separate tank battalions and sixteen armored divisions with forty-eight tank battalions.[157]

Notwithstanding the accommodation of infantry concerns, the central focus of the Armored Force was the development of the armored division. Indeed, Chaffee may have been gracious about satisfying the infantry so as to guarantee him complete latitude in designing the armored division. Although he had long conceded that tanks had an important role in the "close support of assaulting infantry," he believed that this mission was "separate and distinct in thought, conception, method, and equipment from the role of mechanized cavalry or mechanized forces."[158]

Chaffee also made some shrewd personnel arrangements to prevent the plodding infantry tank mentality from infecting the armored divisions. To ensure the dominance of the mechanized cavalry doctrinal concept, he assigned cavalryman General Scott to command the 2d Armored Division at Fort Benning. General Magruder, the infantry tank officer, was brought to Fort Knox—where Chaffee could keep an eye on him—to command the 1st Armored Division, which had as its organizational base the 7th Cavalry Brigade. Chaffee went even further in placing the cavalry stamp on the 2d Armored Division by specifying that "since the personnel of the 2d Armored Division was [sic] to be furnished from infantry tank units, it was essential that the above units 'be commanded and leavened initially by mechanized Cavalry officers.'"[159]

Chaffee's doctrinal concept for the armored division emphasized mobility and independent operations. The role of the division was first specified in the August 1940 "Training Memorandum No. 4." The mission of the armored division was, in essence, that of the augmented mechanized cavalry division Chaffee had offered to the War College in September 1939: "to conduct highly mobile offensive warfare through a self-contained unit composed of the requisite arms and service."[160]

Chaffee's views about the armored division's role were further sanctioned when they were incorporated into the War Department's May 1941 *FM 100-5, Field Service Regulations: Operations,* which specified the armored division as "the basic large armored unit of the combined arms . . . a self-contained unit, capable to a considerable extent of independent action . . . a powerfully armed and armored, highly mobile force." The manual further noted: "The armored division is organized primarily to perform missions that require great mobility and firepower. It is given decisive missions." Although the armored division was "capable of engaging in all forms of combat . . . its *primary role is in offensive operations* against *hostile rear areas.*"[161] The War Department made a major conceptual concession to Chaffee's emphasis on mobility and decisive action by stipulating that the responsibility for creating the initial breakthrough against enemy forces belonged "with other large units of the combined arms."[162]

The decision that the armored division would exploit breakthroughs rather than create them determined its air support requirements. Unlike the German concept, which envisioned dive bombers assisting the panzer forces in making breakthroughs, the American armored doctrine presumed highly mobile operations against light resistance.[163] Hence, the first requirement was for observation aircraft to "reconnoiter the area essential to armored operations."[164] Combat aviation would counter any resistance that might impede the rapidity of the pursuit or exploitation missions.[165]

From Armored Force doctrine flowed organizational decisions. Chaffee instituted five echelons in the division: command, reconnaissance, striking, support, and service. The striking echelon, with its two light armored regiments and one medium armored regiment, was the heart of the division, and its essential characteristic was mobility, even if this meant outrunning its artillery support.[166] Through "bold maneuvers executed at high speed" the striking force would exploit breakthroughs created by other units. The support echelon, with its single infantry regiment, would "occupy and hold objectives seized by the striking force."[167]

The focus on mobility determined the types of tanks the Armored Force wanted for the division. In the summer of 1940 deciding which tanks were needed was crucial—the Armored Force had only 400-odd obsolete tanks in its inventory.[168] Selecting tank designs was the necessary first step in the production process. For its light tanks, the Armored Force chose the M2A4 and an improved version, the M3, each with a 37-mm gun as the main armament. Armament needed only to be heavy enough to cope with enemy infantry and the occasional strong point.[169] By the summer of 1941 light tank production had begun to meet Armored Force requirements.[170]

Medium tank design efforts were tempered by the same doctrinal imperative for mobility. Therefore, medium tanks were designed with speed and mechanical reliability as the foremost requirements. The medium tank regiment was envisioned as a supporting unit for the two light tank regiments. It would destroy enemy resistance too strong for the light tanks and be the main weapon in a counterattack.[171] This concept of the armored role prevailed despite ominous reports from France that the Germans had tanks with 75-mm guns. Furthermore, the chief of infantry had already decided that the M2 medium, with its thin armor and 37-mm gun, was inadequate.[172]

When Chaffee assumed responsibility for the user side of tank research and development he endorsed the medium tank plans that General Lynch and the chief of ordnance had arrived at earlier. This plan entailed the production of the M3 medium tank, armed with a hull-mounted 75-mm low-velocity howitzer (1,930 feet per second) and a 37-mm turret-mounted gun as an interim vehicle. This machine was later replaced by the M4 medium tank, armed with a turret-mounted low-velocity (2,030 feet per second) 75-mm gun. The main stumbling block with the M4 was the manufacture of a turret that would accommodate a 75-mm cannon. Neither ordnance nor industry had yet developed the capability to manufacture a turret with 360-degree traverse large enough to house a 75-mm cannon.[173] Until these problems were worked out, the M3 had to fill the Army's medium tank requirements. Even the first production models of the simpler M3 were not available until April 1941.[174]

Major General Chaffee, terminally ill with cancer, relinquished command of the Armored Force to Major General Jacob L. Devers in August 1941. The Armored Force was a memorial to his vision of modern armored warfare. During his brief one-year tenure, Chaffee had established Armored Force doctrine, organization, and equipment needs. Subsequent adjustments were adaptive modifications rather than radical redesigns of basic concepts.[175]

The few changes in the Armored Force resulted from deficiencies observed during the great GHQ maneuvers of 1941. These maneuvers began in June, with a corps-versus-corps war game in Tennessee. Major General Patton's 2d Armored Division stole the show by using the light tanks of its striking echelon in highly mobile operations. The phenomenal success of the 2d Armored Division's slashing cavalry tactics seemingly verified Chaffee's concepts. However, part of the reason for this success lay in the almost nonexistent antitank capabilities of the forces opposing Patton.[176]

In September the maneuvers continued in Louisiana with the Second Army pitted against the Third Army. The Second Army controlled the I Armored Corps, which was made up of the 1st and 2d Armored Divisions. The Third Army met this armored onslaught with three newly formed GHQ antitank groups. One of the major insights from this exercise was that the performance of the GHQ antitank units seemed to offer a solution to the vexing problem of stopping tanks.[177]

The final phase of the GHQ maneuvers took place in November in the Carolinas. In this phase, the IV Corps, which included the I Armored Corps, fought the First Army. The First Army commanded the three GHQ antitank groups from the September exercises and three more created for the third phase.[178] During the Carolinas maneuvers, "the outstanding question was the struggle between tank and antitank, fairly well tested . . . by the use of 865 tanks and armored cars, against 764 mobile antitank guns and 3,557 other pieces of artillery."[179] The greatly increased antitank strength confronting the I Armored Corps stymied the striking echelons of the armored divisions. Whenever the tank regiments attacked without infantry and artillery support, they suffered heavy losses to the antitank guns.[180]

This experience had two ramifications for Army tank doctrine. First, the Armored Force revised the structure of the armored division, with the new structure stressing combined-arms operations. The division now contained two armored regiments and one infantry regiment, each regiment containing three battalions. Additionally, the artillery regiment was reorganized into three separate battalions controlled by a division artillery command headquarters. The major addition to the new organization was inclusion of two combat command headquarters, which integrated the tank and infantry units into combined-arms task forces. Additionally, an adjustment was made to the potent antitank threat met in the Carolinas: the ratio of light to medium tank units changed from 2:1 to 1:2.[181]

The second key lesson drawn from the Carolinas maneuvers was that the antitank gun was the best antidote to the tank. In many ways the importance of the antitank gun was not so much proven during the maneuvers as it was verified. The concept had a strong supporter in the War Department, Lieutenant General Lesley J. McNair, chief of staff of the GHQ. McNair had made it clear that one of the major objectives of the maneuvers was "to see . . . if and how we can crush a modern tank offensive."[182]

McNair's advocacy of the gun as the solution to the tank began when he was the commandant of the Command and General Staff School at Fort Leavenworth, Kansas. In July 1940 he had commented on a study by General Lynch, the chief of infantry, on the best means to defend against tanks. Lynch had written to the War Department G-3 about his concerns that the Army might draw the wrong lessons from the inability of the French to stop the German blitzkrieg. He believed that the French failure had shown conclusively that the French, heavily reliant on antitank guns, had met with disaster when these guns proved inadequate to stop the German breakthroughs. Lynch was concerned that the U.S. Army was following the French antimechanization trend and wrongly placing its faith in the antitank gun, a course of action that would "fail wholly to apply the proper remedy and waste our resources in the development of ineffective means." Lynch contended that the most efficient means was to oppose "mechanization by mechanization" and that "the best antitank defense lies in the defeat of hostile armored forces by our own armored units."[183]

McNair did not agree with Lynch. Instead, he contended that the tank had been designed to "secure immunity from small arms fire" and that "its natural and proper victim is unprotected personnel and materiel." McNair believed that to use tanks against other tanks would be wasteful of a valuable resource, particularly when there was a more efficient solution to the problem. McNair asserted, in an analogy replete with his inherited artillery assumptions, that the antitank gun was the best alternative for mechanized defense: "When the armored vehicle faces the antitank gun, the combat is essentially a fire action between a moving gun platform in plain view and a small, carefully concealed, stationary gun platform. The struggle is analogous to that between ships and shore guns, and there is no question that the shore guns are superior—so much so that ships do not accept such a contest. The Chief of Infantry in effect asserts that ships are superior to shore guns." McNair then reached a conclusion that crystallized as American antitank doctrine: "If the gun outmatches the tank, then not only is the gun superior to the tank in antitank defense, but employing armored units against other armored units positively should be avoided whenever possible. The gun, supported properly by foot troops, should defeat hostile armored units by fire and free the friendly armored units for action against objectives which are vulnerable to them."[184]

Because McNair was one of Marshall's most trusted subordinates and a powerful man, his views carried a great deal of authority. After Patton's 2d Armored Division demonstrated in Tennessee that the U.S. Army's ability to stop determined tank attacks was no better than that of the Poles or the French, McNair's views prevailed. In August he directed the formation of three GHQ antitank units. These units had troubled the Armored Force in Louisiana, but by the Carolinas maneuvers they were able to prevail over the unsupported tanks. Unfortunately, none of the GHQ maneuvers in 1941 tested what the U.S. Army would confront in the coming war—tank units fighting other tank units. McNair's scenario limited the scope of the maneuvers to a tank-versus-antitank test.[185]

By March 1942 the War Department had a separate tank destroyer command at Camp Hood, Texas. The doctrine that the tank destroyer command developed for tank destroyer units was aggressively proclaimed in its motto: "seek, strike, and destroy."[186] These units had two roles. During offensive operations, they protected friendly forces from enemy armored counterattacks "and thus allow full exploitation of their success."[187] During defensive combat, a portion of the tank destroyers were deployed in depth to protect against enemy armored attack. The majority, however, were held in a mobile reserve to react to the main enemy attack.[188]

The need for extreme mobility and an effective antitank gun were implicit in tank destroyer doctrine, and the doctrine determined equipment design. Tank destroyers were hence lightly armored and equipped with relatively high-velocity guns.[189]

McNair's decision to adopt tank destroyers as the American solution to tank defense did not go unchallenged. Colonel K. B. Edmunds, assistant commandant under McNair at the Command and General Staff College, favored the tank-versus-tank approach and had so advised McNair during the July 1940 debate with the chief of infantry over antimechanized doctrine.[190] In June 1941 Edmunds wrote an insightful article about the Army's factional perspective on stopping tanks and the possible pitfalls of such an approach:

> An engineer presented with the problem will think of obstacles and mines. An artilleryman will think of the fire of cannon. An infantryman or cavalryman will first consider movement, maneuver, shock, because that is the way he was brought up to think.
>
> But as a result of the different mentalities that have been brought to bear on our question, our present doctrine contains all of these ideas. It is a compromise and open to the weaknesses of all compromises.[191]

Like Colonel Edmunds, Major General Devers, the new chief of the Armored Force, disagreed with McNair on the validity of the tank destroyer concept. Devers believed that the solution to stopping enemy tanks was heavier guns on the opposing tanks. In December 1941 he wrote to McNair that tanks were the underlying reason for success on every front in the war. Devers cautioned McNair that he should not be "misled by the [GHQ] maneuvers" in which antitank guns had seemed effective. Devers asserted that tanks, "supported by Air and Infantry," would "always win" because they combined mobility with firepower; the armored force needed heavy tanks "with larger calibered weapons [to] support and protect the advance of the smaller calibered but more mobile weapons."[192]

McNair did not share Devers's views about the lessons from the war. In May 1942 he responded to a request by Devers to merge the tank destroyer command with the Armored Force. McNair emphasized that he did not want to change the recently established institutional arrangements since they would affect equipment production. Furthermore, he was convinced that tank destroyer "progress is satisfactory or is definitely on the way to become so." McNair also told Devers that tank destroyer units had a different mission than that of the Armored Force, writing: "Tank destroyers should free the Armored Force as much as possible so that it can strike the hostile force as a whole in a decisive fashion, while the hostile armored force is taken care of as much as possible by the destroyers." McNair's final word on the subject was that the existing tank and tank destroyer doctrinal arrangements would stand, since "we have not yet had war experience which can be taken as a definite guide."[193]

Devers was not convinced by McNair's arguments. In July he wrote that "this is an air-gun-tank war." He further noted that although he agreed with McNair that "tank versus tank is an expensive and undesirable procedure

... I am sure that it is not going to be totally avoidable in future battles." The crux of Devers's argument was that the U.S. Army's tank destroyers, with their open turrets and essentially defensive missions, had limited utility on a highly lethal battlefield. The tank, with its heavier armor, could survive, and he thus preferred to mount higher-velocity guns on tanks. Finally, Devers believed that tank destroyer units would be treated as "stepchildren" and would "always have a hard time getting along."[194]

Although McNair drafted a written response to Devers, he decided instead to telephone the chief of the Armored Force.[195] His written comments, which probably served as the basis for his unrecorded conversation with Devers, revealed rigid views about tank destroyers and the reports coming from the North African battlefields. McNair used the example of the devastating adaptation of the 88-mm antiaircraft gun in an antitank role by the Germans as evidence that "unarmored guns can exist on the modern battlefield." This conclusion formed the basis for McNair's justification of the lightly armored American tank destroyer: "The tank destroyer should be one of our principal means of avoiding tank versus tank action and of preserving our armored mass for the main attack."[196]

McNair, commanding general of the Army ground forces since the March 1942 War Department reorganization, was responsible for both the Armored Force and the Tank Destroyer Command.[197] His decisions regarding the best way to defeat enemy tanks prevailed.

By late 1942 the Army had settled on the doctrines, organizations, and equipments to support its theories about the most efficient way to fight a modern armored war. The result was in many ways a hybrid of the inherited biases of the officers who made the decisions. Armored Force doctrine originated with General Chaffee and reflected his cavalry background. The GHQ tank battalions represented, in many ways, the Army's reluctance to remove any weapon from the infantryman's arsenal. The tank destroyer was the artilleryman's solution to the problem posed by a mobile, armored target.

In November 1942 the Army faced the first practical test of its hastily improvised arrangements for armored warfare. On the battlefields of North Africa, America's mobilized citizen soldiers would attempt to validate the War Department's decisions about tanks in the harsh cauldron of combat.

[11]

Autonomous Air Power

The Army Air Corps entered the 1930s with the outlines of a concept for the employment of military aviation that promised a decisive role in warfare—strategic bombardment. For a generation of insurgent air officers who believed that the War Department had repressed the potential of the airplane, strategic bombardment had a seductive appeal. The most important issue for these officers was control of military aviation. As long as the Army Air Corps remained an auxiliary of the ground battle or part of an integrated Army-Navy coast defense effort, a cogent argument for independence from the War Department could not be made. If it could be shown that the aerial weapon had advanced sufficiently to be a decisive offensive force in and of itself, however, a compelling argument existed for the control and development of the technology by air officers.

The theory of strategic bombardment enunciated in the February 1931 Air Corps Tactical School *Bombardment Aviation* text provided all of the conceptual pieces for a doctrine that gave the Air Corps a strategic, offensive capability beyond the control of ground officers. The text made four fundamental assertions that directed the future development of the doctrine: (1) targets vital to the enemy could be reached only by bombardment aviation; (2) to be effective, bombardment aviation had to be under centralized control; (3) an air force commander would select the targets to be attacked; and (4) bombardment aviation could not be deterred from reaching and destroying its objectives. From these premises, if accepted, flowed an ineluctable conclusion: *"Bombardment aviation . . . is the basic arm of the Air Force."*[1]

In 1931 a number of seemingly unrelated events merged to enable the Air Corps to turn the theory of strategic bombing into a reality. First, an agreement was made between General Douglas MacArthur, Army chief of staff, and Admiral William V. Pratt, chief of Naval Operations, in January regarding coast defense. In the decade since Congress had established spheres of responsibility for the employment of Army and Navy aviation for coastal defense, the two services had sparred intermittently over their respective rights. The Army had a tendency to extend its sea reconnaissance farther from shore than the Navy believed was its proper jurisdiction. The Navy had begun looking to land-based airplanes for missions for which its carrier-based craft were not suited.[2] The MacArthur-Pratt agreement was designed to settle these disputes. Henceforth, Naval air forces would be "based on the fleet and move with it as an important element in performing the essential missions of the forces afloat." The Army Air Corps would "be land based and employed as an element of the Army in carrying out its missions of defending the coasts, both in the homeland and in overseas possessions."[3] This agreement provided a War Department–sanctioned justification for developing long-range aircraft to fulfill the coastal defense mission. It also gave the Air Corps an approved defensive use for bombers that was acceptable in an era in which the isolationist mood in the country would have made procurement of these airplanes for offensive purposes difficult.[4]

Also in 1931 the American aviation industry demonstrated that it was possible for a bomber to conduct long-range missions with heavy bomb loads. In response to the Air Corps's design proposal for an "advanced type heavy bomber," six aircraft manufacturers submitted experimental models.[5] A comparison of the capabilities of the 1930 standard Air Corps bomber, the Keystone B-3A, and the 1932 performance test results of the Martin bomber entry, showed the qualitative leap aviation had made in just a few years. The B-3A, a fabric-covered biplane with fixed landing gear, represented the limits of what could be expected from aircraft design. It had a maximum speed of 102 miles per hour, a ceiling of 12,700 feet, and a maximum bomb load of 2,496 pounds. In stark contrast, the sleek, all-metal Martin airplane had mid-wing monoplane construction, monocoque fuselage, and retractable landing gear. The airplane's performance matched its visual appeal: a maximum speed of 207 miles per hour, a ceiling of 21,000 feet, and a maximum bomb load of 4,380 pounds. What was most encouraging about the Martin plane, later designated the B-10, was the promise it represented for future heavy bomber designs.[6] Almost overnight the limitations on large airplane speed, altitude, and carrying capacity had been exploded. Range soon followed.

A further technological advance in 1931 had significant implications for what became a uniquely American approach to strategic bombardment. In October 1931 Air Corps officers observed Navy tests of Carl L. Norden's bombsight. Quite simply, Norden had created an efficient solution to high-altitude precision bombing. In April 1933, through an agreement with the Navy, the Army began procuring Norden's device to replace its own D-4 and C-4 bombsights.[7]

The last of the constellation of 1931 events occurred in the summer when the Air Corps moved its Tactical School from Langley, Virginia, to Maxwell Field, Alabama.[8] The leadership of the school understood that "radical and rapid changes in materiel, such as airplane performance, armament, and other equipment" and "the absence or inaccessibility of representative historical data upon which to base our conclusions" had resulted in an air doctrine that was largely theoretical and in a constant state of flux.[9]

Early in 1932 Lieutenant Colonel John F. Curry, the commandant, suggested to the chief of the Air Corps that the Tactical School become a "clearing-house into which tactical ideas can flow, where they can be tried, and where the doctrine can go out to the service to be put into practice and be evaluated." Curry's vision of the Tactical School's role was realized; it became the hub of air power advocacy and indoctrination. Furthermore, some of the best minds in the Air Corps worked at Maxwell to turn the radical strategic bombing theory into an institutional doctrine. The leadership of the Tactical School understood its importance as a center for both doctrine and indoctrination: "It occupies a position of utmost importance in the development of the Air Corps because of its permanent effect upon our own officers and those of other branches."[10]

Views on bombardment crystallized early among the instructors at the school. During the 1932–33 academic year, First Lieutenant Harold L. George, chief of the bombardment section at the tactical school, lectured on bombardment aviation at the Marine Corps school in Quantico, Virginia. George began by explaining the immense "power of destruction" inherent in a bombardment formation. Using an analogy that his audience understood, he noted that a normal bombardment formation carried "over 6 tons of high explosive, or as much as is contained in about 7,000 3 inch H.E. [high explosive] shells or 3,000 105 M.M. H.E. shells." He then discussed the appropriate targets for bombardment. His view was that this awesome force should be used on strategic targets, "industrial centers where ammunition, armament, and other war supplies are produced; great quantities of reserve stores which represent the national resources; and important political centers."[11]

George continued by discussing the recent improvements in aviation technology that would make strategic bombardment feasible. He noted that the Air Corps was fielding new bombers of markedly improved speed, ceiling, bomb capacity, and range. These airplanes could accurately bomb from their service ceiling because of a new bombsight whose accuracy rivaled "any sight or range finder for big guns." George also elaborated on a critical assumption undergirding the entire argument for strategic bombardment— that the bombers could penetrate enemy air space and survive pursuit aviation defenses while en route to distant targets and survive antiaircraft fire during the actual bombing. He explained that each bomber was armed with six machine guns, for a total of fifty-four in a typical nine-bomber formation—"rather a formidable target for hostile pursuit to attack!" Furthermore, the bombers would have the element of surprise on their side. As for anti-aircraft artillery, George believed that its effectiveness would "have to increase by leaps and bounds before it need be given serious consideration by air force commanders." Finally, George drew all of the pieces of his argument together by noting that these formidable capabilities should cause a reassessment of "the employment of Air Force, not as an auxiliary but as a separate and distinct agent of national defense, a force capable of acting independently from ground troops."[12]

George's statements represented a growing consensus among the faculty at Maxwell. By late 1932 the Tactical School had developed its strategic bombing concepts to a degree that they could be offered to the chief of the Air Corps as approved doctrine. In September First Lieutenant Kenneth N. Walker, one of the school's bombardment instructors, was tasked to review a draft Air Corps field manual sent from the office of the chief of the Air Corps. His changes to the bombardment section showed how far thought on the specifics of strategic bombardment had progressed.

Walker began by noting that the manual was deficient since it did not recognize that "bombardment aviation is the basic arm of the Air Force." He continued by stating two fundamental tactical principles that would guide the future direction of American bombardment doctrine. First, "precision targets, which require accurate bombing will normally be engaged during daylight hours." Second, "one of the principles of Bombardment employment is that it should be used only against the vital material targets and that it never engages in harrassing [sic] operations."[13]

Walker's assertions completed the American concept of how bombardment aviation should be employed. The skeleton of the doctrine was present: Bombardment was the most important branch of the air force; it should be used only against vital targets beyond the influence of ground forces; centralized control was paramount; daylight precision bombing at high altitudes was the preferred method of target engagement; bombardment formations had sufficient defensive firepower to ward off pursuit attack; antiaircraft fire was not a significant deterrent to bomber attack; and well-planned, vigorously executed bombardment missions could not be stopped. By 1933 each of these basic tenets was incorporated into the bombardment course at the Tactical School.[14]

Although the majority of the Tactical School faculty embraced the primacy of bombardment aviation, there were naysayers. The most vocal of the objectors was Captain Claire L. Chennault, a pursuit aviation instructor at the school from 1931 to 1936.[15] Chennault maintained that pursuit, not bombardment, was the most important class of military aviation, a direct challenge to the bombardment instructors' contentions. Chennault seemingly acknowledged the powers of bombardment aviation: "It is certain that the ability of a nation to wage war can be impaired if not wholly destroyed by an enemy who is able to employ, without opposition, a vast number of bombardment airplanes against factories, lines of communication, mobilization centers, centers of wealth and population, and harbors.... A nation deprived of the means for waging war will not maintain the desire to fight very long."[16]

The key phrase was "able to employ, without opposition, a vast number of bombardment airplanes."[17] Chennault contended that air defense warning systems, using a vastly improved radio technology to link far-flung listening posts and pursuit aircraft, could deny bombers the element of surprise. The bombers would be detected and intercepted by pursuit aircraft. Furthermore, advances in armament enabled the intercepting force to attack a bomber formation with great effectiveness.[18] Chennault thus concluded that a crucial component of the bombardment theory—that bombardment could not be stopped by pursuit—was flawed.

Chennault's arguments placed him in direct opposition to the majority position at the Tactical School. What made his stance particularly irksome to bomber advocates was his refusal to offer a solution to the pursuit threat to bombardment.

The 1933 *Pursuit Aviation* text was emphatic in its insistence that pursuit aviation should not be used to protect other classes of aviation. Using pursuit in this "close protection" role "was undesirable because it sacrificed surprise, position, initiative, and aggressiveness in combat."[19] In December 1934 Chennault elaborated on this stance by stating that long-range pursuit escort of bombers was "not practical, especially when an air force must be developed in accordance with a national policy of defensive warfare only."[20] This statement was probably galling to the bombardment instructors, who were patently aware that the doctrine they were developing was not defensive. The question of which group would control the direction of Air Corps doctrine was crucial in the early 1930s, but with the nation firmly in the grasp of the Great Depression, air officers knew that appropriations would be scarce and that the doctrine that prevailed would probably receive what little funding was available.

The development of a long-range bomber became the focus of Air Corps procurement efforts in 1933. In that year, the Boeing and Martin aircraft companies responded to the matériel division requests for informal design proposals for multiengine bombers. In June 1934 the manufacturers were contracted to provide "technical data, mock-up, wind tunnel models, and static test of various airplane elements," and in August the Air Corps released Circular Proposal 35-26 for multiengine bombers.[21]

While the Air Corps was attempting to develop the aircraft that would give it long-range bombardment capability, the War Department was reconsidering the role of its air arm in the overall scheme of national defense. In June 1933 the War Department requested that the Air Corps submit recommendations on how General Headquarters (GHQ) aviation would support war plans under MacArthur's revised Four Army Plan. The General Staff also specified that these air plans would be based on a strength of 1,800 serviceable airplanes. Brigadier General Oscar Westover, the assistant chief of the Air Corps, directed the effort. The plan Westover submitted to the General Staff vastly exceeded his charter. Instead of tying air strength to any single war plan, Westover's plan, which required 4,459 airplanes, told how to defend the United States from air attack.[22]

To the General Staff, the air plan appeared to be another attempt to increase the Air Corps at the expense of the rest of the Army. General MacArthur convened a board in August 1933 to reassess the Westover plan. Major General Hugh Drum, MacArthur's deputy, headed the board, and the Air Corps was represented by its chief, Major Benjamin General Foulois. The board used the Red-Orange plan for war against a British-Japanese coalition as the worst-case basis for its analysis of required airplane strength.[23]

The Drum Board submitted its report in October. To support the Red-Orange plan, the board believed that the Air Corps required 2,072 airplanes but could get by with 1,800.[24] Although this conclusion appeared to merely reassert the status quo, in reality it provided a rationale for expansion, because in June 1933 the Air Corps had only 1,555 airplanes.[25] The Drum Board recommended meeting the 1,800-airplane authorization, and, realizing that a percentage would always be in overhaul maintenance, suggested that 2,025 aircraft would be needed to keep 1,800 available. The board also recommended a war reserve that brought the total requirement to 2,320 airplanes. Nevertheless, the Drum Board stipulated that Air Corps strength not go beyond a total figure of 1,800 airplanes "if additional aircraft could be procured only at the expense of the other arms and services."[26]

Although the Drum Board did not recognize an independent mission for the Air Corps, it called for the institution of "a GHQ Air Force to meet effectively the requirements of any or all of our war plans."[27] This agency would control combat aviation units supporting the coast defense and ground forces. The War Department understood the implications of this recommendation; MacArthur noted that the GHQ Air Force "would, both in organization and mission, occupy an independent status under its own Air Corps commander, subject only to the authority of the military head of the Army."[28]

The Drum Board's recommendations, approved by Secretary of War George H. Dern in January 1934, were soon overtaken by external events. The War Department intended to incorporate the Air Corps increases into its modernization program, but limited resources meant that expansion would take time.[29] Congress, however, passed bills for Air Corps expansion far beyond the War Department plans.[30]

President Roosevelt helped move aviation matters to the forefront of national attention in early 1934. He was searching for an alternative to the air mail contracting system that he believed was not only fraudulent but also resulted in a monopoly among a few large commercial airlines. On February 9 Second Assistant Postmaster General Harllee Branch and General Foulois discussed the possibility of temporarily using the Air Corps to fly the mail. Foulois believed the Air Corps could handle the job and would be ready to begin delivering mail by February 19. Based on Foulois's commitment, the president canceled the commercial carriers' contracts.[31]

Unfortunately, the Air Corps pilots had neither the equipment nor the training to cope with the air mail mission. By June 1, when the Air Corps returned its last mail route to a commercial contractor, twelve pilots had died in sixty-six crashes.[32] In the wake of these highly publicized disasters, the War Department and the president both hurried to preempt the expected congressional probes. The War Department convened a board under former Secretary of War Newton Baker while Roosevelt appointed a Federal Aviation Commission, headed by Clark Howell.[33]

The majority of the Baker Board's membership, which included General Foulois, recommended a solution similar to that of the earlier Drum Board—a reorganization of the Air Corps into a GHQ Air Force, corps and army observation units, and detachments for overseas garrisons. Furthermore, the committee recommended that 2,320 airplanes be provided but that personnel increases and any expansion not be done "at the expense of the rest of the Military Establishment." Not all members of the Baker Board agreed, and one member, James H. Doolittle, filed a minority report, stressing: "I am convinced that the required air force can be more rapidly organized, equipped, and trained if it is completely separated from the Army and developed as an entirely separate arm."[34]

The War Department believed that the measures recommended in the majority opinion of the Baker Board were sufficient. On September 11 Brigadier General C. E. Kilbourne, chief of the War Plans Division, sent a memorandum with the Army's official position on the Air Corps to the various agencies in the War Department. The paper summarized, with War Department elaborations, the Baker Board's findings. Kilbourne further noted that the chief of staff required that any officer called to testify before Howell's Federal Aviation Commission be familiar with the War Department position. If called in an official capacity, officers would "conform to these principles." Those called not as War Department representatives but as individuals were warned that while they could "express personal opinions at variance with the principles announced in this document . . . after expressing such opinions, [they should] inform the Commission that such testimony represents personal opinion only."[35]

The War Department had little to fear from Howell's Commission, because the sections concerning the Air Corps were largely a restatement of the Drum and Baker Boards' recommendations. The closest the commission came to a criticism of current procedures was a guarded reference to the inadequacies of interservice cooperation. The commission endorsed increased Air Corps autonomy, albeit under Army control, noting that "the employment of air force as an independent striking unit should continue under constant study."[36]

A limited concession to autonomous air power, the recommendation surely disappointed a number of the most committed bombardment advocates who had appeared before the Howell Commission. Each had either taught, or was presently teaching, at the Air Corps Tactical School. Each began his statements with the qualifier that he was stating personal views. That they were not in accord with War Department policy was obvious, since most berated the Baker Board recommendations as inadequate.

The air officers' testimonies shared several common themes: the United States was vulnerable to air attack, and the only defense to such an invasion was a strong air force. Furthermore, such an air force could not be improvised after the commencement of hostilities but had to be maintained in a constant state of readiness. Finally, an adequate air force could be developed only by an independent agency coequal with the Army and Navy. The testimony of Captain Robert M. Webster was representative:

> Our most rigid and conventional institution has been the army. . . . It has vigorously opposed every innovation in warfare, every contribution of science; it has held on to the pike when the muzzle loader was available; it held on to the muzzle loader when the breech loader was a fact. . . . In the Air Force we have the only agency with direct access to the fundamental objectives in war . . . with a spirit that is immunized from the effects of army doctrine by a growing consciousness of its own independent power in war. . . . A casual survey of the evidence now available, must be convincing, that the creation of a separate and independent Air Force is the rational, simple, and inevitable solution to this problem.[37]

Although the Air Corps did not gain the independence sought by Captain Webster and his fellow air officers, it gained an unprecedented measure of autonomy. On March 1, 1935, the War Department established the GHQ Air Force, responsible for all of the combat aviation in the continental United States. Only observation aircraft remained under the control of the nine corps area commanders. Major General Frank M. Andrews commanded the new organization and from his headquarters at Langley Field, Virginia, directed the organization, training, and operations of three air wings: one at Langley and the others at Barksdale Field, Louisiana, and March Field, California. In peacetime, Andrews reported directly to the chief of staff; in war he was responsible to the commander of the field forces. This situation resulted in dual control of air matters in the War Department, because the

[160]

chief of the Air Corps still retained most administrative responsibilities, including personnel training and procurement.[38] The long-sought-after centralization of air force aviation under air officers was largely achieved.

While the boards and commissions debated the organization of the Air Corps, the instructors at the Tactical School further refined bombardment doctrine. Major Donald Wilson prepared a number of lectures for the 1933–34 air force course that reflected a much more sophisticated approach to employing strategic bombardment.

Wilson asserted that modern nations were highly dependent on industrial production to wage war. Furthermore, the means of production in the most advanced nations depended greatly on raw materials, transportation, and power to maintain output. Wilson believed that this situation created an "industrial web" of interdependent components. It was not necessary to destroy the entire industry of an enemy nation but rather the critical nodes. From these assumptions flowed a crucial concept: "Modern industrial nations are susceptible to defeat by interruption of this web, which is built to permit the dependence of one section upon many or all other sections, and further that this interruption is the primary objective for an air force."[39]

Wilson's theory was attractive to air power advocates, because immense political power was implicit in Wilson's logic. It offered a compelling rationale not only for an independent air force but for preeminence: "Since armies and navies cannot attack the roots of a nation's power, it is maintained that the air force should be the principal arm in future warfare."[40]

In January 1935 Major Wilson drafted the tactical school comment on a proposed Air Corps doctrine prepared by the General Staff 's War Plans Division. Wilson's concepts about the proper use of air force were explicit: "The principal and all important mission of air power, when its equipment permits, is the attack of those vital objectives in a nation's economic structure which will tend to paralyze that nation's ability to wage war." Wilson believed that such a decisive use of air power would "contribute directly to the attainment of the ultimate objective of war, namely, the disintegration of the hostile will to resist." Wilson continued, stating matter-of-factly that in a "war between major powers, an air force phase, which may be decisive, will be initiated prior to the contact of ground armies." Additionally, the air force plan, once decided on, must have "unwavering adherence" to be effective. Finally, in an ironic twist, the Tactical School also noted that the importance of aviation justified the diversion of ground troops to guard air bases.[41]

Quite simply, the Tactical School proposed that air power by itself could be the decisive factor in war if its control was left to those who knew how to employ the weapon—air officers. Furthermore, the study admitted that this doctrine was offensive and was to be directed against modern industrial nations once a suitable airplane made the theories feasible. Bomber technology was driving the development of a doctrine to exploit its potential, regardless of whether this doctrine was appropriate to stated American defense policies, but two crucial elements were still missing. First, the vital objectives in a nation's economic structure that could paralyze its ability to wage war had to be identified. Second, an airplane capable of executing the doctrine was needed.

Key elements in the industrial web were identified through research at the Tactical School. Captain R. M. Webster decided that New York City was a good example of a city "highly dependent upon the mechanisms of modern civilization." Accordingly, he wrote to the commander of the 2d Corps Area at Governor's Island, New York, asking for assistance. He noted that he was conducting research to determine the "sensitive points in that city to air attack" to evaluate "the probable effects induced by their destruction." Webster specified that he was particularly interested in the relation of New York City to the national economic structure as well as the city's water, food, electric power, illuminating gas, and transportation systems.[42]

Major F. V. Hemenway, an officer assigned to Governor's Island, responded that the data were available but could be viewed only at the headquarters due to their nature. If Webster could not visit, Hemenway suggested he write to a number of New York state agencies for assistance.[43] Webster took the advice and began a letter-writing campaign that included the National Board of Fire Underwriters, the New York City Board of Water Supply, the Director of the Bureau of the Census, the Museum of Sciences and Industry, and the Consolidated Gas Company. Most of the addressees provided Webster with the information he requested, and he soon amassed an impressive amount of data. From such efforts the Tactical School determined the targets most vulnerable to bombardment attack.[44]

Technology supporting the evolving doctrine was also forthcoming. In August 1935 the Douglas, Martin, and Boeing aircraft companies each sent bomber prototypes to Wright Field in Dayton, Ohio, to compete for the Air Corps multiengine bomber contract. The Martin entry was a larger version of the firm's B-10, while the Douglas airplane was a derivative of its commercial DC-2 design. Each had two engines and were evolutions of existing aviation technology.[45]

The Boeing entry, the four-engined model 299, was revolutionary. It had flown nonstop the 2,100 miles between the Boeing plant in Seattle, Washington, and Wright Field, at an impressive average speed of 232 miles per hour.[46] The operational capabilities promised by the model 299 were impressive: a top speed of 251 miles per hour; a cruising range of 2,600 miles, with an increase to 3,150 miles feasible; a normal bomb load capacity of 2,500 pounds; and a service ceiling of 27,600 feet.[47]

The Boeing airplane caused General Foulois, chief of the Air Corps, to rethink the entire Air Corps procurement program for fiscal year 1936. On October 1 Foulois requested that the approved requirements of 438 airplanes of all types be revised downward to a total of 333 so that 65 Boeing bombers could be purchased.[48]

Within the month, however, the airplane procurement plan again had to be revised. On October 30 the Boeing prototype bomber crashed, not because of any defect in the airplane but because the crew had neglected to unlock the rudder and elevator controls during preflight checks.[49] Unfortunately, the crash occurred before the necessary regulatory evaluations of the airplane had been completed, precluding "an award being made to the Boeing Aircraft Company under competitive conditions for 65 of these bombers."[50]

Still, Westover believed that the Boeing plane was a "remarkable aeronautical development" and that thirteen of the bombers should be procured "under Section 10 (k) of the Air Corps Act for experimental service test." Westover went on to recommend that in addition to the thirteen Boeing planes, eighty Douglas prototypes be purchased if they proved superior to the Martin entry.[51] Colonel William T. Carpenter, Supply Division, G-4, advised the chief of staff to approve Westover's new Air Corps plan.[52]

On November 21 the chief of staff approved the request, and thirteen Boeing airplanes were ordered.[53] The contract for the Boeing bomber, designated the Y1B-17 pending service test, was closed on January 17, 1936. Delivery began the following January, and by August 1937 all thirteen of the B-17 bombers had been accepted by the Air Corps.[54]

Over the next three years, the Air Corps asked for more B-17s and bombers of even greater range, but the War Department resisted. Its position stemmed from two considerations. First, the department believed that the twin-engined B-18 (the standardized Douglas prototype) was adequate for national defense purposes, particularly since substantially more B-18s than B-17s could be purchased with the limited budget.[55] Second, the War Department argued that bombers with greater ranges than that of the B-17 were out of step with American policy, since they could "bomb points in Europe and South America and return without refueling." Consequently, such an airplane was inappropriate "in the armament of a nation which has a National Policy of good will and a Military policy of protection, not aggression."[56]

The Air Corps arguments were articulated well by General Andrews. At a September 1936 conference concerning the continued funding of the Project D airplane, Andrews stated that the Army needed "airplanes of long endurance" to "stop hostile air expeditions at their sources," to maintain continuous reconnaissance to guard against sea invasion, and to bomb enemy aircraft carriers at distances from national coasts that would prevent them from launching their aircraft. Andrews argued that the Air Corps should have the most advanced equipment available. Since "a future international situation may set up a need for planes of greater power," the War Department authorized research and development of a generation of bombers beyond the B-17 but offered little more.[57]

General Andrews undoubtedly envisioned roles for long-range bombers, including the B-17, beyond those he mentioned in the conference. The missions he discussed were those sanctioned for the GHQ Air Force by the October 1935 War Department training regulations—that is, air operations that were "beyond the sphere of influence of ground forces," in the "immediate support of ground forces," or involved "in coastal frontier defense and in other joint Army and Navy operations."[58]

Even in the unlikely event that Andrews wanted more bombers at least as capable as the B-17 to perform only the War Department–authorized missions, some air officers at the Tactical School believed strongly in the old adage "the best defense is a good offense." In a 1936 lecture on the principles of war, Major Harold George blithely dismissed American military policies in the face of the new bomber technology:

> I like to compare the strategy of an air force with the measures used by the Medical Department in ridding the Canal Zone of mosquitoes. That department did not put fly swatters in the hands of the population and then go back to its hospitals. Not by any means. The Medical Department went to the places where those mosquitoes lived and breeded and there they exterminated them,—not by defensive action but with offensive action.[59]

This offensive doctrine called for an airplane of great range, whose "ultimate radius of action . . . is that which will enable us to strike the nerve centers of any potential enemies from our own territory."[60] The B-17 was a major step in this direction. Here, for the first time, was an airplane capable of transforming the bomber advocates' theory into reality.

Aside from its range and bomb load, the B-17 had capabilities that seemingly made it virtually invincible. Its demonstrated speed of 250 miles per hour was faster than the standard Air Corps pursuit airplane, the P-26, whose maximum speed was 234 miles per hour.[61] Increased speed also enabled bomber advocates to dismiss antiaircraft fire as a threat. The 1935 *Bombardment* text proclaimed confidently: "Higher speeds will also give the bombardment airplane a higher degree of immunity from antiaircraft fire than it already enjoys."[62] Furthermore, it appeared that bomber speed would only increase as bomber design advanced, further widening the gap between the bomber and pursuit aircraft. The reigning wisdom among American aviation engineers, particularly in the matériel division of the Air Corps, was that "increased aerodynamic efficiency could be achieved with increased size." The apparent solution to increased speed, range, and carrying capacity was to design airplanes with larger airframes and powered by multiple engines of great horsepower.[63]

In addition to the B-17's impressive performance characteristics, it was the Air Corps's first bomber large enough to mount guns larger than .30 caliber. The capability to carry heavier armament meant that the B-17 had a much greater chance of defending itself.[64] Many Air Corps officers thus came to believe that when bombers were flown in tight formations the synergy of their massed weapons would create a wall of fire through which no pursuit plane could pass. For the bomber advocates, the B-17 settled the issue of the ascendancy of the bomber over the pursuit airplane. They were convinced that the "present and potential single engine pursuit planes" were "ineffective" against the new bomber since they were slower and had less range and weaker armament.[65] Quite simply, the Air Corps was convinced the B-17 was an unstoppable weapon. Brigadier General Henry H. Arnold, commander of the 1st Wing, GHQ Air Force, asserted that "with the wide variety of targets available to long range bombardment, it is out of the question to expect that pursuit can be so placed as to intercept all air raids."[66]

The conviction that long-range bombers could not be deterred, reinforced by the technological breakthrough of the B-17, was the catalyst that made American air doctrine dogma.[67] The invincibility of the bomber was a powerful assumption on a number of levels. First, if the United States could develop such a formidable bombardment capability, it had to be assumed that potential enemies could do so as well. Therefore, since their bombers would be invulnerable to defensive means, they could be stopped only by counter–air force operations. This mission, which required strategic long-range bombers in a defensive role, did not tie their procurement to the contentious coast defense. Second, the mission against an enemy's air force, if presumed to be the most important role for aviation, gave the Air Corps additional arguments for autonomy. How could such a valuable weapon possibly be tied to the support of ground forces? The Air Corps understood clearly the implications of such arguments: "The United States must provide bombardment aviation at least the equal in numbers, range and speed performances, and striking power, to that of any other nation or possible coalition."[68]

From these crucial assumptions the Tactical School made the final refinements to Air Corps doctrine. The doctrine had two fundamental premises. First, "modern nations cannot wage war if their industries are destroyed." Second, "aircraft can penetrate any known air defenses and destroy any known targets with bombs." These premises led to the conclusion that "air warfare is . . . a method of destroying the enemy's ability to wage war. It is primarily a means of striking a major blow toward winning a war, rather than a direct auxiliary to surface warfare."[69]

The conviction that the bomber was all important and all but unstoppable had a telling effect on how the Air Corps viewed other classes of aviation. By 1937, when the rout of the pursuit advocates was complete, their most vocal champion, Claire Chennault, retired. Forty years later General Laurence Kuter, a former bombardment instructor, recalled the victory of the bomber advocates: "We just overpowered Claire; we just whipped him."[70]

Kuter further explained that the bomber advocates defeated Chennault and the pursuit boosters by edging them out in a number of crucial areas, including "attention by the chief's office, for appropriations, for personnel assignment, appropriations primarily. We got money for B-17s; he didn't get anything." Kuter also noted that Chennault was myopic about pursuit: "He wouldn't talk about a fighter to accompany a B-17, a supporting defensive fighter, because that put the fighter in a secondary role." Finally, Kuter noted the chasm between the competing camps in the Air Corps: "We wouldn't talk about it [pursuit] either because that implied some of the limited funds might have to go to a supporting fighter of some sort. We didn't believe we needed it in the first place, and where there was doubt, we believed that the limited amount of money was barely enough to get a bomber program started."[71]

The crucial assumption that enemy pursuit would be ineffective against American bombardment was repeated in the Air Corps doctrine about its own pursuit tactics. The 1939 *Pursuit* text noted that although the role of pursuit remained the attack of enemy bombers, the mission was questionable. Since pursuit had lost its speed advantage and had limited range, its attacks on heavily armed enemy bombardment formations "must be confined to harassing by long-range fire or by bombing if so equipped."[72]

The conviction that air power was potentially decisive also shaped the doctrine for support of the ground battle. The Tactical School rationalized that since air forces were so powerful the best service the Air Corps could provide to the ground commander was the defeat of enemy air power. Thus, the "neutralization of the hostile air attacking force" became the principal Air Corps contribution to the ground battle. Furthermore, the old contention that aviation was viewed by ground officers as "long-range artillery" was now used to the aviators' advantage by asserting that "air attacks are not made against objectives within the effective range of friendly artillery, or against deployed troops, except in cases of great emergency." Finally, Tactical School instructors emphasized that bombardment was simply too valuable to use in any type of ground support role.[73]

Attack aviation doctrine was radically altered by this view that counter-air force operations were primary, since attack aviation had as its principal role "the attack of hostile ground forces . . . in close cooperation with ground forces in battle."[74] By 1935 targets for attack aviation were enemy air bases and parked airplanes; coast defense; antiaircraft defenses; and "the destruction, or the interruption of movement of personnel and materiel through the attack of factories, logistical establishments, lines of communication, and concentrated bodies of troops."[75]

[166]

The Tactical School's marginalization of the ground support mission extended to the integration of tanks and airplanes into a combat team. In October 1938 Colonel John H. Pirie, acting commandant of the school, wrote to the chief of the Air Corps that he believed that airplanes, when compared with tanks, were fragile and susceptible to ground fire and that using them in a close support role jeopardized a valuable weapon system. Furthermore, air power was most effective when employed "beyond the local ground combat zone." Therefore, using airplanes to "clear the path of the more rugged tank . . . clearly appears to be tactically unsound . . . except in the gravest emergency."[76]

The deteriorating European situation provided the impetus to expand the Air Corps into a force capable of executing the doctrines espoused at the Tactical School. When in September 1938 British Prime Minister Neville Chamberlain acceded to Adolf Hitler's demands to dismember Czechoslovakia, George Fielding Elliot, a respected military commentator, suggested that Chamberlain had capitulated because of Germany's immense advantage over England in air strength. Elliot concluded: "It is blackmail which rules Europe today, and nothing else: blackmail made possible only by the existence of air power."[77]

Joseph P. Kennedy, the American ambassador in London, shared Fielding's opinions about the power of the Luftwaffe. On September 22 he informed the secretary of state of his recent conversation with Charles Lindbergh, who had just returned from a review of European air forces. Lindbergh's opinions were alarming. He asserted that "Germany's air strength is greater than all other European countries combined and that her margin of leadership is constantly being increased. . . . If she wishes to do so, Germany now has the means of destroying London, Paris, and Prague." He further observed that only the United States could hope to compete with Germany in the aviation field.[78]

On October 13 William C. Bullitt, the American ambassador to France, told President Roosevelt that Hitler had been able to dictate his terms at Munich because of his vastly superior air strength. He echoed Lindbergh's conviction that only the American aviation industry could compete with Germany's. Bullitt also told the president that the French believed that they and the British would have to rely on American production to counter the threat posed by the Luftwaffe.[79]

Roosevelt soon settled on how America would respond to German military power. On November 14 he assembled key civilian and military advisers and sketched the outlines of a new national defense policy based on his belief that American defenses had to be bolstered in light of the situation in Europe. The country had to be "prepared to resist assault on the Western Hemisphere 'from the North to the South Pole.' "[80] The key to the plan, the president argued, was a massive expansion of American air power. Although he wanted an Army air corps of 20,000 planes and an annual production capacity of 24,000, he realized that Congress would not support such numbers and instead directed the War Department to develop a program based on 10,000 planes.[81]

Roosevelt's pronouncement produced mixed views in his military subordinates. General Arnold believed "that the Air Corps had achieved its Magna Carta."[82] He was fully receptive to the president's conclusion that a strong air corps, not a large ground force, was the best way to deter aggression in the American hemisphere.[83] Arnold also concluded that "the president had not only made permissible but had required the development of the long-range heavy bomber."[84] He left the White House with the seed of an idea for a balanced American air force branch planted firmly in his mind.

General Marshall, who had openly opposed the president's fixation on air power during the conference, preferred to strengthen the entire Army, not just one component.[85] Furthermore, he and Arnold both agreed that "a lot of airplanes by themselves ... were not air power."[86] Consequently, the War Department, applying its best military judgment, planned a balanced program.

The War Department did not grasp that what the president wanted was airplanes. Marshall later realized that the president "was principally thinking at that time of getting airships for England and France," but when in December the military officers returned to Roosevelt with their conventional program, the president was incensed. The military leadership interpreted his anger as an inability to understand the complexities of modern armies, but they misread Roosevelt's intentions. They recommended a professional approach that would develop an army capable of defending the hemisphere. Roosevelt simply wanted airplanes.[87] When his military chiefs made their recommendations, he retorted that the "services were offering him everything except planes" and that "he could not 'influence Hitler with barracks, runways, and schools for mechanics.'"[88] The military chiefs failed to recognize that Roosevelt's "emphasis on sheer numbers of planes and his irritation at arguments for the supporting apparatus that would make them effective attested to an interest similar to Hitler's in an air force whose appearance would be more important than its use."[89]

In spite of the president's wishes, the military chiefs prevailed and Roosevelt "felt compelled to accept a balanced force."[90] The War Department modified the 10,000-airplane program: by January 1939, the totals had been adjusted to 6,000 aircraft.[91]

For the Air Corps, the president's sudden emphasis on air power was an institutional windfall. In September 1939 the appointment of General Marshall as chief of staff further enhanced the air arm's position. Marshall understood the importance of aviation in a political as well as an operational sense.

In May 1940 President Roosevelt told Congress that he wanted a program that could produce 50,000 aircraft a year and "provide us with 50,000 military and naval planes."[92] Shortly thereafter, on June 26, Marshall approved the first aviation objective of organizing fifty-four combat groups by April 1942.[93] The size and complexity of the expansion program resulted in a reappraisal of the air arm's position within the War Department. General Arnold became the deputy chief of staff for air in November, a position above both the office of the chief of Air Corps and the GHQ Air Force. Robert A. Lovett was appointed as the special assistant to the secretary of war in December to manage air affairs. In April Lovett filled the reestablished position of assistant secretary of war.[94]

These new arrangements were not satisfactory, because the office of the chief of the Air Corps and the GHQ Air Force still shared the management of air matters. Henry L. Stimson, the secretary of war, directed in March 1941 the placement of the air arm "under one responsible head." He also told the War Department "to develop an organization staffed and equipped to provide the ground forces with essential aircraft units for joint operations, while at the same time expanding and decentralizing our staff work to permit Air Force autonomy in the degree needed."[95] In June 1941 the Army Air Forces was created, with General Arnold as its chief, assisted by an air staff.

On July 9, 1941, President Roosevelt directed the secretary of war and the secretary of the Navy to begin "exploring at once the over-all production requirements required to defeat our potential enemies."[96] By September the "Joint Board Estimate of United States Over-all Requirements," a document designed to support the ABC-1 and Rainbow-5 war plans that assumed an Anglo-American coalition, had been prepared.[97] The plan was based on defeating Germany first.[98] The Joint Board's report included an air section prepared by the new Air War Plans Division (AWPD). This document, called AWPD-1, would form the basis for the organization of the American air effort in the coming war.

Four officers prepared the important sections of AWPD-1: Colonel Harold L. George, Lieutenant Colonel Kenneth N. Walker, Major Laurence S. Kuter, and Major Haywood S. Hansell.[99] All were staunch bomber advocates and former instructors at the Tactical School. The plan they prepared reflected the essence of the radical air power doctrine that focused on the preeminence of the long-range strategic bomber:

> The effectiveness of an Air Force in contributing to the *defeat* of an enemy is measured by the efficiency of the bombardment component in destroying vital enemy objectives. Day bombing, in which the target may be most readily seen, will result in the highest bombing accuracy.[100]

AWPD-1 proceeded to explain how Germany could be defeated by air power. The plan recognized three major tasks for the Army air forces:

a. Destroy the industrial war making capacity of Germany.
b. Restrict Axis air operations.
c. Permit and support a final invasion of Germany.[101]

The air planners outlined 154 targets that would "virtually destroy the sources of military strength of the German state."[102] These targets were grouped into six prioritized target categories that would ensure the disruption of the German industrial fabric: fifty to disrupt electric power, forty-seven to disrupt the transportation system, twenty-seven to destroy 80 percent of the synthetic petroleum production, eighteen to destroy airplane assembly plants, six to destroy 90 percent of aluminum production, and six to destroy magnesium production.[103]

The air planning team realized that its entire plan hinged on the question of whether it was feasible to deeply penetrate German territory and conduct precision bombing without prohibitive losses. They themselves raised this issue and outlined the threat posed to their plan by German air defenses. German fighter opposition had made "daylight bomber operation excessively expensive" until "the appearance of the British Sterling bomber and the American [B-17] Flying Fortress." The defensive fire power of these more capable bombers would enable them to cope with the fighter problem. German antiaircraft artillery, although capable, would not prevent success. These assumptions led the planners to the conclusion that "by employing large numbers of aircraft with high speed, good defensive fire power, and high altitude, *it is feasible to make deep penetrations into Germany in daylight.*"[104]

AWPD-1 conceded that the failure of the German daylight bombing offensive over England had been caused by the superiority of British pursuit airplanes. The planning group believed that the Germans had had to meet the "British pursuit on unequal terms." The solution posed to redress the German "technical deficiency" was to increase the armament and armor on bombers. The planning group recognized that this approach might not work, since it was "not impossible that the present relative superiority of the interceptor over the bomber may be maintained." In that event, they recommended the development of escort fighters "designed to enable bombardment formations to fight through to the objective."[105]

The planners, even after revealing a crucial weakness in one of their key assumptions—that bomber formations could rely on their own defensive armament to fight their way through to their objectives—did not give high priority to any alternative plan. Although they concluded that pursuit could pose a significant threat to bombardment and recognized a "possible need" for escort fighters, the project received little attention. AWPD-1 recommended a research and development effort, not a crash program. A squadron of thirteen escort fighters would be established to test the concept. Furthermore, only "if the need for this weapon is determined" would production plans be altered.[106]

AWPD-1 was the quintessential expression of American strategic bombing theory. The plan was alluring because the airmen seemed to promise that "precision bombing will win the war."[107] Indeed, AWPD-1 specifically stated that "if the air offensive is successful, a land offensive may not be necessary."[108] Furthermore, the air offensive could be initiated in April 1942, well in advance of any possible major ground operations. The air officers asked only *that this project be given priority over all other national production requirements.*[109] And it needed a high priority. The plan called for an Army Air Force of 251 combat groups equipped with more than 63,000 operational aircraft and staffed by 2 million officers and enlisted men.[110]

AWPD-1 was approved by Secretary of War Stimson on September 25. His endorsement was significant on two levels. First, it recognized that the air effort would require immense resources. Second, and perhaps more important for the air power advocates, it provided license for the air arm to try to prove that it could be a decisive, independent force. Regardless of whether ground officers believed the air power advocates' claims, they had pragmatic reasons to at least try to implement the plan, because "there was certainly much to be gained if it worked. If it did not, the Army and Navy would be called upon to do what they had been planning on doing anyway."[111]

For air officers, AWPD-1 had enormous significance. It was the enunciation of an air power manifesto that had been twenty years in the making. Clearly, the future institutional form of the air arm depended on its contribution to winning the impending war, but the Air Forces had also staked out an irreversible position: unescorted, high-altitude, daylight precision bombing would have a decisive impact on the outcome of the war.

General Arnold understood the implications of AWPD-1. Realizing he would be hard-pressed to stay abreast of the expansion program, and when war came, the deployment of the air arm, he moved to forestall any further calls for independence. In late August General Marshall learned that the American Legion planned to introduce a "storm of resolutions" for a "unified air service or independent striking arm" at its national convention.[112] Marshall apparently asked Arnold to help defuse this movement. In September 1941 Arnold sent letters to Norman M. Lyon, chairman of the National Aeronautics Commission, American Legion, and Warren Atherton, chairman of National Defense, American Legion. In these letters, Arnold explained his position: "Our expansion is being effected in accordance with ou[r] plans and program but not without the greatest effort on the part of all of our Air Force officers. . . . Additional work, and no one can gainsay but that there will be a tremendous amount of it in connection with the transformation from an Air Force organization to a separate Air Force, may be just enough to 'break the camel's back.' "[113] On September 2 Arnold informed Marshall that he had written Lyon and Atherton and had explained to them "why a separate Air Force is undesirable [at this time]."[114]

Arnold's stance that the Air Forces should remain within the War Department did not mean that he did not try to gain greater autonomy over air operations. He and his subordinates did not find the arrangements for control of the air arm satisfactory. The air staff members chafed under their continued subordination to the War Department General Staff. Furthermore, the chief of the Army Air Forces only "coordinated" the operations of the office of the chief of the Air Corps and the former GHQ Air Force, now renamed the Air Force Combat Command.[115]

The War Department reorganization in March 1942, discussed in the next chapter, corrected most of these deficiencies. The Army Air Forces was made an autonomous force, coequal with the Army Ground Forces and the Services of Supply. Furthermore, the War Department General Staff was restructured so that 50 percent of its members were air officers.[116]

As the War Department grappled with its organizational problems, the planning and production to deploy American air power against Germany accelerated. Ominous lessons from the air war in Europe also began to surface. In the closing months of 1941 the British had determined that daylight bombing was suicidal and that existing technologies employed under combat conditions precluded precision bombing.[117] A September 1941 report by the Royal Air Force (RAF) noted that performance of American-supplied B-17s in "daylight Continental bombing missions thus far are not encouraging." German fighters had shot down two B-17s, while "as yet the B-17's gunners have failed either to shoot down or damage a single enemy plane."[118] Furthermore, German antiaircraft weapons were reported to be accurate up to 30,000 feet.[119] Eventually, the British abandoned daylight precision bombing for a new strategy centered on area bombing of German cities at night.[120]

The American bomber enthusiasts were not deterred by either the British experiences or the earlier German failure during the Battle of Britain. In a January 1942 memorandum for General Marshall, Laurence Kuter faced the issue squarely by posing the question: "How can the AAF [Army Air Forces] (Victory Program) succeed in softening up the enemy when the RAF and GAF [German Air Force] have been unable to do the same thing?" Kuter explained that the issue was one of training:

> Attrition in airplanes in the Bomber Command of the RAF is over 50% per month and at the same time they are accomplishing no material results. The inevitable consequence of this vicious cycle which is initiated by entering combat without the training required to effect material accomplishment and at the same time having to withstand extraordinary attrition has resulted in

the unpalatable fact that the bombardment combat crews of the RAF are no longer trying.[121]

General Arnold was as confident as Kuter but more diplomatic. He wrote in a March 1942 letter to Air Chief Marshall Sir Charles F. A. Portal, British chief of air staff, that he believed that with the "greater defensive fire power of our bombers, and a carefully developed technique of formation flying with mutually supporting fire, that our bombers may be able to penetrate in daylight beyond the radius of fighters."[122] American airmen were convinced that their doctrine and technology, in the hands of trained bomber crews, could succeed where others had failed. They soon had the chance to prove their contentions.

On February 20, 1942, Brigadier General Ira Eaker and six other air officers arrived in England. Two days later Eaker assumed command of the newly established VIII Bomber Command. Over the coming months he and his staff laid the foundations for the envisioned American bomber offensive against the Continent.[123] It was a difficult task. Plans for the invasion of North Africa and diversions of air groups to the Pacific theater sapped the strength of the force being assembled for what the air officers viewed as the main effort against Germany.[124] In mid-June the Eighth Air Force became operational under the command of Major General Carl "Tooey" Spaatz. In early August Eaker wrote Arnold that the initial B-17 group appeared ready for its first mission. In his letter, he also expressed the crucial assumptions developed by American air power advocates between the two world wars:

The tempo is stepping up as we approach the zero hour. Tooey's and my theory that day bombardment is feasible is about to be tested where men's lives are put at stake.

It will interest you to know that several months ago when the date of our entering operations seemed far away, a great many people told us that day bombing could be done by well trained crews and airplanes despite the stiffness of fighter opposition. As the hour approaches for the test, with the chips down, a lot of these people have grown luke warm or actually deserted our camp. Tooey and I however, remain steadfast in the belief that it can and must be done. Everything depends on it. Here are the reasons, well known to you why we must bomb by daylight:

We can hit point targets in day bombing. A smaller force can therefore destroy vital objectives.

The British bomb by night and the German defences sleep by day; when we are at them in the day time, they will be alerted 24 hours a day and get no rest.

The operational losses will be greatly reduced; It is much better to combat the normal weather in this theater in daylight than at night.

Navigation will be greatly improved; crews with much less training and experience can do an acceptable job.

Our aircraft, super-charged and unflamed dampened, are not well suited for night bombardment.

Tight formations can be flown and pursuit protection can accompany.

We can see the enemy fighters and knock them down; we shall not be slinking through the forest evading the enemy, but shall be boldly looking for him; asking for combat in order to reduce his air power, knowing that our production and replacement capacity is superior to his.

By chance, or by keen foresight on your part, you have two zealots in Tooey and myself who believe whole-heartedly that the foregoing reasons are compelling and that daylight bombing can be done without irreplaceable losses.[125]

Spaatz also wrote Arnold and was more to the point: "The question of the ability of a formation of B-17's to take care of itself against fighter attack must be decided."[126]

Their confidence seemed justified. On August 17 twelve B-17s of the 97th Bombardment Group flew the first American mission against the Rouen-Sotteville marshaling yard in occupied France. The force suffered no losses, and Sergeant Kent R. West, a B-17 gunner, bagged a German fighter. On August 19 twenty-two B-17s hit the Abbeville/Drucat airfield, again without loss. The next day eleven bombers attacked the Longeau marshaling yard, with all planes returning to base.[127] Spaatz, as assured as Eaker, wrote Arnold on August 21 that these first three missions proved the soundness of American training and equipment. He further noted that "our daylight bombing of precision objectives will be decisive provided we receive an adequate force in time."[128] Three days later, after only one week of operations, Spaatz concluded that "daylight bombing with extreme accuracy can be carried out at high altitudes by our B-17 airplanes." Furthermore, Spaatz was convinced "that such operations can be extended, as soon as the necessary size force has been built up, into the heart of Germany without fighter protection over the whole range of operation."[129]

Arnold used Eaker's and Spaatz's reports as ammunition to obtain more resources for the Eighth Air Force. Early in September he wrote Harry Hopkins that the Eighth Air Force's operations had shown the validity of American bomber doctrine and the B-17's worth in battle. Therefore, it was time to concentrate the air resources for a decisive effort against the "German war machine."[130]

Arnold also wrote to Spaatz that AWPD-1 was being revised. He noted that the underlying premises for the new plan remained the same, with Germany the principal enemy. He asked Spaatz to keep up the pressure for more resources and to continue to send him reports on the bombing effort, which he was using to show that precision bombing was the correct strategy. Arnold also stressed the importance of the Eighth Air Force's success to supporting a "lick Germany first" policy and in arguing that the air offensive should be extended against Germany itself: "The accuracy of your *precision bombing* to date and the remarkable record with respect to losses that you have established has done much to convince everyone that our former theories are now facts."[131]

General Arnold was exuberant. By late October it seemed that two decades of struggle to build American air power were finally paying off. Arnold wrote to Hopkins about "miraculous results," noting that the Eighth Air Force had conducted 16 missions, with 336 bombers reaching their targets. Only 9 bombers had been lost, and 498 enemy airplanes had been engaged, 63 of which had been destroyed, 97 probably destroyed, and 107 damaged.[132]

The airmen's claims about the invincibility of the B-17 and the soundness of their doctrine were, Arnold believed, being proven. This initial success probably further confirmed in his mind the validity of the advice he had received from Eaker earlier in the month. Eaker believed that as soon as the Eighth Air Force bomber strength had increased, an air assault against Germany proper was possible. On October 20 he wrote: "I am absolutely convinced that the following answers are sound and I am certain Tooey agrees with me. Three hundred heavy bombers can attack any target in Germany by daylight with less than four percent losses. . . . The daylight bombing of Germany with planes of the B-17 and B-24 types is feasible, practicable and economical."[133]

In the next year, Arnold provided Eaker with enough planes and air crews to test their shared assumptions.

[12]

A Crisis in the War Department

On September 1, 1939, the same day Hitler unleashed his blitzkrieg against Poland, George C. Marshall became chief of staff of the Army—an army that was in no way prepared for a modern war. To begin with, as Marshall later recalled, the active Army was small and dispersed and "consisted of approximately 174,000 enlisted men scattered over 130 posts, camps, and stations." Furthermore, "within the United States we had no field army," and "there existed the mere framework of about 3,1/2 square divisions approximately 50 percent complete as to personnel and scattered among a number of Army posts. . . . There were virtually no corps troops, almost no Army troops or GHQ special troop units . . . necessary for the functioning of the larger tactical units," and "the Air Corps consisted of but 62 tactical squadrons." Training was "impracticable," because of shortages of personnel, equipment, and funds. The equipment the Army did have, "modern at the conclusion of the World War, was . . . in a large measure obsolescent." Marshall believed that the "continuing paring of appropriations had reduced the Army virtually to the status of a third-rate power." Not surprisingly, he concluded: "As an Army we were ineffective." On September 8 President Roosevelt issued a limited emergency proclamation and authorized an increase of 17,000 men in the Regular Army.[1] Each branch chief lobbied for his own fair share of the bounty to fill the depleted ranks of his arm.[2]

In the first year of Marshall's tenure, personnel and money ceased to be the factors inhibiting the Army's readiness—after the fall of France, the president and Congress began lavishing resources on the military services. Marshall's challenge became one of managing the sudden deluge to create an army capable of defeating a modern opponent. It soon became clear to the new chief of staff that the institution he headed was not well suited to making the radical changes necessary to cope with modern war. The War Department was decentralized and unwieldy: "At least sixty-one officers had the right of direct access to the Chief of Staff and . . . he had under him thirty major and 350 smaller commands."[3] Marshall found that he was immersed in petty details, a situation that detracted from the major issues he needed to focus on.

Perhaps the greatest obstacle Marshall faced was the inertia of the War Department bureaucracy. In the two decades since the passage of the National Defense Act, the institution had "lost track of its purpose of existence . . . [and] had become a huge, bureaucratic, red-tape-ridden operating agency."[4] Quite simply, the War Department had evolved into an agency whose focus was preserving itself. During the Great Depression, sustaining the institution had been exceedingly difficult. In an era of scarce resources, meticulous planning and intraservice compromise had been necessary. Even though times had changed, the War Department continued to function in a punctilious, bureaucratic fashion. What Marshall wanted was "speed and vigor"; what he got was "deliberate planning."[5]

When France fell to the blitzkrieg, it was obvious that mechanization had become a crucial element in modern war. Nonetheless, when the War Department G-3 had moved to put together an armored force, he had been consistently opposed by the parochial chiefs of infantry and cavalry. These officers had argued that the National Defense Act and General MacArthur's ten-year-old mechanization policy made them responsible for the Army's tanks.[6] When in November 1940 it became apparent to the G-3 that the armored force would develop faster as a separate arm, he began the necessary staff coordination to make it so. General Herr, the chief of cavalry, wrote that such a move would constitute "two specific violations of the provisions of the National Defense Act."[7] Technically, Herr was correct and the G-3 was blocked.

In response to the Allied disaster in Europe, Marshall activated the General Headquarters (GHQ) and made Major General Lesley J. McNair its chief of staff.[8] McNair was given broad powers to train and organize the masses of citizen soldiers responding to the call from their draft boards. Within the year, McNair was given even more power when Marshall transferred officers from the War Plans Division, General Staff, to the GHQ. To McNair's training mission, this move added the authority to undertake operational planning.[9] Marshall explained that the move allowed the GHQ "to perform its normal theater of operations functions."[10] A more likely reason for the shift of responsibilities is that Marshall had found in McNair a man who could get things done.[11]

More radical measures were under way to increase War Department efficiency. In August 1941 Lieutenant Colonel William K. Harrison, assigned to the War Plans Division and a member of a committee studying ways to im-

[177]

prove the operations of the GHQ, drafted a plan to reorganize the War Department. The committee had come to realize that the War Department required wholesale reorganization because its problems could not be fixed by merely adjusting existing arrangements. Harrison's plan envisioned service, air force, and ground force commands to oversee the "preparation and maintenance of the field forces for combat" and an "Operations or Command Section . . . to assist the Chief of Staff in exercising his command functions over overseas departments and bases, defense commands, task forces, and theaters of operations." Under Harrison's plan, the War Department General Staff would have been limited to "an abstract, advisory plane."[12] Harrison's supervisor, Brigadier General Leonard T. Gerow, did not endorse the plan, and it never left the War Plans Division.

Harrison's study was discussed during committee meetings, however, where Army Air Forces member Brigadier General Spaatz embraced it. For the air arm, it provided a superior arrangement, because it meant freedom from the existing subordination to the General Staff and the GHQ. Air officers were already trying to redress this issue by pushing a revision of *Army Regulation 95-5: Army Air Forces,* the regulation that constrained their autonomy. When the War Plans Division refused to go along with the Harrison proposal, General Arnold sent General Marshall a similar plan to reorganize the War Department.[13]

Marshall knew that something had to be done about the War Department. Earlier he had told Gerow that it was "the poorest command post in the Army and we must do something about it." McNair told Marshall that reorganization was the best option, and Arnold's plan, endorsed in principle by Gerow, gave Marshall something to work with.[14] Arnold recommended "that the Chief of Staff function as the Commander of the military forces of the War Department, that he be provided a small General Staff, and that he exercise his control within the continental United States through the Ground, Service, and Air Force Commanders." He further advised "that Theater Commanders and Department Commanders report directly to the Chief of Staff."[15]

Arnold's plan—that the chiefs of arms and services be swept from their powerful positions and that the power of the General Staff be severely curtailed—was radical. In addition, the air forces would be made equal to the ground forces. In the fall of 1941, however, drastic measures were needed. Accordingly, Marshall endorsed Arnold's concept and directed the War Plans Division to further develop the plan.[16]

Marshall did not make any immediate move to reorganize, although he was convinced that the institution needed to be overhauled. Arnold's plan would surely have been vigorously resisted by the reigning hierarchy, most of whom had friends in Congress. Since a new structure would require legislation, Marshall knew that timing was critical.[17]

When the Japanese attacked Pearl Harbor on December 7 the War Department's inadequacies became even more obvious. Particularly alarming was the failure of the War Plans Division to follow up properly on a November 27 message to Lieutenant General Walter J. Short, commanding general of the Hawaiian department. The War Plans Division had sent Short a message warning him that "hostile action [was] possible at any moment" and directing him to take a number of defensive measures. Short was to "report measures taken." The War Department G-2 also sent Short a message that warned of impending hostilities and "subversive activities." Short cabled back to the War Department that his "department was alerted to prevent sabotage" and only referenced the War Plans Division message.[18] Nobody in the War Department acted on what was clearly an inadequate response by Short to the War Plans Division's warning.[19]

In mid-December President Roosevelt directed Secretary of the Navy Frank Knox to appoint a commission to investigate the attack on Pearl Harbor. Supreme Court Associate Justice Owen J. Roberts, a man who had gained fame as the special prosecutor in the Teapot Dome and Elk Hill trial, was named to head the investigation. The military members were Admiral William H. Standley, Rear Admiral Joseph M. Reeves, Major General Frank B. McCoy, and Brigadier General Joseph T. McNarney. The Roberts Commission worked from December 22, 1941, to January 23, 1942. General Short and Admiral Husband E. Kimmel, the commanders responsible for defending Hawaii, were charged with "dereliction of duty."[20] The commission concluded that one of the factors in the humiliating disaster was "the failure of the War Department to reply to the message relating to the antisabotage measures instituted by the commanding general, Hawaiian Department."[21]

While the Roberts Commission aired the Army's dirty linen, the president put even more pressure on the War Department. On January 3 Roosevelt directed the secretary of war to reassess munitions requirements for 1942 and 1943. Roosevelt emphasized matériel, writing that "the victory over our enemies will be achieved in the last analysis not only by the bravery, skill, and determination of our men, but by our overwhelming mastery in the munitions of war." He also noted that "the united nations are already extended to the utmost in the manufacture of munitions and their factories fall far short of the needs of their own armies. . . . We must not only provide munitions for our own fighting forces but vast quantities to be used against the enemy in every appropriate theater of war, wherever that may be."[22]

The quantities the president had in mind were vast. In 1942 he wanted 45,000 airplanes produced, including 11,300 bombers. For 1943 he raised the quota to 100,000 airplanes, including 30,000 more bombers. The tank numbers were equally staggering: the figure in 1942 was 45,000 and in 1943 75,000.[23]

The existing War Department structure, one that had had problems coping with the comparatively modest prewar expansion programs, could probably not have met the enormous demands of Roosevelt's decree. The situation was similar to the one General Peyton March had faced in World War I, when the War Department bureaucracy had shown that it could not contend with the demands of a massive mobilization. Like March, Marshall also had to wait for a declaration of war to act. In World War I March had obtained permission from President Wilson to use the powers of the Overman Act to revamp the War Department. On December 18, 1941, the same option became available to Marshall when Congress passed the First War Powers Act. Colonel Harrison had continued working on a reorganization plan, with the assistance of Major Laurence Kuter from the office of the chief of staff. Marshall was poised to quickly set in motion the plans that would "make the most drastic and fundamental change which the War Department had experienced since the establishment of the General Staff by Elihu Root in 1903."[24]

In late January Marshall added General Joseph T. McNarney to the reorganization team. McNarney was a shrewd choice. As an air officer who had worked in the War Plans Division, he could represent the two groups sponsoring the reorganization. He was known as an able officer who "would not give his best friend a break."[25] Marshall was clearly betting that McNarney would be the "tough hatchetman with a rhinoceros hide and the nerve to push through the reorganization in the rugged infighting that was almost certain to follow." On January 25 Marshall told McNarney to design an organization that would let the chief of staff concentrate on strategy.[26]

McNarney, Harrison, and Kuter finalized the plan and on January 31 presented recommendations similar to Arnold's for streamlining the General Staff and creating three commands for ground, air, and service.[27] McNarney, however, wanted to cut even deeper. He advised the elimination of the GHQ, the Air Force Combat Command, and the chiefs of the combat arms since they were "unnecessary or obsolete headquarters." Finally, McNarney asked that Marshall create "an 'executive committee responsible only to the Chief of Staff' to put the reorganization into effect without giving 'interested parties' a chance to record nonconcurrences and cause 'interminable delay.' "[28]

On February 5 Major General John Herr, the chief of cavalry, called on Marshall, which probably reinforced his conviction for the need to reorganize the War Department. It may also have made him think that McNarney's recommendation to eliminate the chiefs of arms was sound.

Herr wanted to discuss a recent directive by the G-3 that nine horse-mechanized cavalry regiments be completely mechanized.[29] Herr was a strong proponent of the horse-mechanized regiment concept, which relied on mechanized elements for distant reconnaissance and *porté* horse units for tactical chores and to cover difficult terrain. In what he regarded as an innovative accommodation of machine-age warfare, the *porté* horse units were provided with "strategic" mobility—that is, they were carted around the battlefield in large trailers.[30] Herr believed that there was "general hostility against the horse on the part of the War Department General Staff" and that this aversion to horse cavalry "arose from two classes of people—one, those little brats who had graduated from Leavenworth and who knew nothing about anything, and the other on the part of those Coast Artillerymen and men of like ilk who had never had a dynamic thought." He was convinced that "cavalry, in fact, is little understood in our own Army. The officers have no breadth of understanding, they know little except about their own branches. In fact, it is a provincial army." Herr then castigated those in the Army whom he viewed as antihorse, particularly General McNair: "Most of these officers know nothing about the horse and don't want to know anything about it. This fellow, McNair, hates the horse and believes that a truck could go anywhere that a horse could go." Herr ended the meeting by thanking the chief of staff for his patience and again telling him that he had made a bad decision in letting the G-3 deactivate any more horse units.[31]

One week after his meeting with Herr, Marshall told McNarney to form the reorganization committee.[32] McNarney thus designed a plan "to streamline the General Staff and subordinate elements of the Army in order to facilitate speedy and most effective control of mobilization and operations." At its heart, the plan was an attempt to address, structurally, the two great challenges facing the Army: "mobilization and preparation of the forces for war" and "operations in the field." McNarney's plan created "three separate and autonomous commands, the Army Air Forces, the Army Ground Forces and the Services of Supply" to address the mobilization and preparation of forces function. The chief of staff, working through the War Plans Division of the War Department General Staff, would thus be freed to focus his attention on war operations. Marshall's decisions would be "implemented by the Air Forces and Ground Forces who provide the trained forces, [and] by the Service of Supply which provides supplies . . . and moves them to the theaters of operations." Finally, "commanders of the various theaters of operations and task forces" would "actually control combat operations in their respective areas of responsibility."[33]

On February 28 President Roosevelt signed Executive Order 9082, which made the new arrangements effective March 9, 1942.[34] Thus, in 1942, just as in 1918, the institution that had nurtured the Army in peace but was incapable of leading it in war was scrapped by presidential fiat.

The reorganization did much more than merely streamline the War Department. Marshall swept away the bureaucratic impediments to decisive, rapid action by greatly reducing the General Staff's power and eliminating the chiefs of combat arms. The chiefs of the services remained but were brought under the control of a powerful new commanding general of Services of Supply. The reorganization occurred during one of the darkest hours in American history, when daily newspaper headlines carried news of one defeat after the other. Since such a massive restructuring carried with it heavy risks, even to the Army's already limited effectiveness, Marshall must have believed that extreme measures were indicated.

The new arrangements had been made largely to enable rapid action in personnel and industrial mobilization, but the War Department did little to change the doctrine that governed how the draftees would fight. Nor could it change the technology. Where doctrine and technology were concerned the War Department surveyed what was available and replicated it. For example, field manuals on every conceivable subject were produced to indoctrinate the masses of civilian soldiers rallying to the colors, but these publications largely expounded the assumptions developed in the 1930s.

Much of the Army's doctrinal thinking was conditioned by the decentralization after World War I and the conflict between ground and air officers. The chiefs were charged with developing the doctrine for their particular arms, and the War Department did little to integrate the doctrine into a cohesive system. Lieutenant Colonel Bradford Chynoweth, himself a member of the General Staff, had written about the essence of the problem: "The General Staff has quite frequently failed to make the basic unifying decisions which would serve to coordinate the arms. . . . Each arm and service has been made to feel that it is expected to battle all other arms for its existence."[35] Hence, Army doctrine was more a collection of branch parts than an integrated system.

The German conceptions of the blitzkrieg were not secret. They were available to the U.S. Army through reports by military observers and attachés, and German panzer officers, proud of their creation, published their views extensively. A number of these articles found their way into American service publications. From these reports and articles one could discern a number of recurring themes. First and foremost, the power of the blitzkrieg was derived from the synergy of tanks and highly mobile ground auxiliaries combined with combat aviation. Aviation's role was not limited to tactical ground support; German officers expected the Luftwaffe to contribute in other ways to the strategic effort by conducting counter–air force operations, interdicting enemy military operations, and bombing industrial targets. A second theme was that blitzkrieg tactics required the powerful combined-arms force to make its own breakthroughs at the critical time and place and then to exploit the opportunities it had created. Finally, German officers stressed that their tanks had to be designed to fight other tanks.[36]

As 1942 drew to an end, the tank and airplane doctrines and technologies

[182]

developed by U.S. Army officers, however flawed, were about to meet the test of combat. The Eighth Air Force believed that its early missions against occupied Europe had verified its concepts and was preparing for an air offensive against Germany. American ground forces were preparing to test their armored divisions against the Wehrmacht's panzers. How the American concepts of air and armored warfare held up in the crucible of war is the subject of the remaining chapters.

PART IV

DYING FOR CHANGE:
1942–1945

Lack of a principal gun with sufficient penetrating ability to knock out the
German opponent has cost us more tanks and skilled men to man more
tanks than any failure of our crews, not to mention the heartbreak and
sense of defeat I and other men have felt. To see twenty-five or even many
more of our rounds fired and ricochet off the enemy attackers. To be finally hit, *once*, and we climb from and leave a burning, blackened, and
now a useless pile of scrap iron. It would have yet been a tank had it
mounted a gun.

—Corporal Francis E. Vierling, Tank Commander (1945)

In our new planes, with our new crews, we bombed
The ranges by the desert or the shore,
Fired at towed targets, waited for our scores—
And turned into replacements and woke up
One morning, over England, operational.
It wasn't different: but if we died
It was not an accident but a mistake
(But an easy one for anyone to make).
We read our mail and counted up our missions—
In bombers named for girls, we burned
The cities we had learned about in school—
Till our lives wore out; our bodies lay among
The people we had killed and never seen.
When we lasted long enough they gave us medals;
When we died they said, "Our casualties were low."
They said, "Here are the maps"; we burned the cities.

—Randall Jarrell, *Losses*

[13]

The Arsenal of Attrition

Shortly after the March 1942 War Department reorganization General McNarney stated that its purpose had been "to decentralize, giving officers in charge of activities greater powers of decision and responsibility in matters under their control." The General Staff streamlined its operations and abandoned the time-consuming rituals of excessively formal staff paperwork. The emphasis shifted to finding answers and taking action rather than satisfying bureaucratic protocols. General Marshall was freed from the day-to-day oversight of the institution and concentrated on strategic issues.[1]

Decentralization, however, did not prevail. Beyond the broad policy apparatus, which the General Staff agencies (G-1, G-2, G-3, and G-4) managed, the Army became extraordinarily centralized. The operations division became General Marshall's command post and assumed broad authority to plan and direct operations, but the new air, ground, and service commands had unprecedented powers in preparing, equipping, and deploying Army units to the theaters of operations.[2]

In 1942 the institutional imperative became the mobilization of both personnel and industry. And the results were incredible, as shown in tables 1 and 2.

The scope of the program was monumental—as was the pressure on the War Department to meet its goals. The senior leadership of the Army surely remembered the haphazard mobilization for the Great War, when poorly trained units had been rushed overseas. American industry never provided the tanks and airplanes needed by the American Expeditionary Forces, and the Army was forced to rely mainly on the Allies for these war machines.[3] World War II, however, did not afford the War Department such alternatives. The tenuous position of the Allies, and President Roosevelt's January

Table 1. Army active-duty strength, 1940–1945

Year	Officers	Enlisted	Total
1940	18,326	250,697	269,023
1941	99,536	1,362,779	1,462,315
1942	206,422	2,869,186	3,075,608
1943	579,576	6,414,896	6,994,472
1944	776,980	7,217,770	7,994,750
1945	891,663	7,376,295	8,267,958

SOURCE: *Historical Statistics of the United States,* 1141.

Table 2. American tank and airplane production, 1940–1945

Year	Tanks[a]	Airplanes[b]
1940	331	3,807
1941	4,052	19,433
1942	24,997	47,836
1943	29,497	85,898
1944	17,565	96,318
1945	11,968	46,001
Total	88,410	299,293

SOURCES: Thomson and Mayo, 263; and Craven and Cate, 6:352, 354.
[a]Includes procurement from July 1, 1939, to December 31, 1940.
[b]Within these overall aircraft production figures, heavy and very heavy bomber production totaled 12,667 B-17s, 16,188 B-24s, and 3,760 B-29s.

1942 directive, made it clear that the United States would not only provide its own weapons but also a large portion of those needed by the Allies.

Another major difference between World War I and World War II was the importance of the tank and the airplane. During the interwar years the U.S. Army had clarified its vision of how these powerful weapons should be employed in war. Because it envisioned the tank as a mobile weapon of exploitation, tank designers focused on providing a machine that was both fast and reliable. Thus, American light and medium tanks, with their thin skins and low-velocity guns, were precisely what American armored doctrine required from the tank technology. Similarly, the B-17 "Flying Fortress" and the B-24 "Liberator" were the ideal weapons to execute the American concept of unescorted, high-altitude, daylight precision bombing. These heavy bombers, flying in close-knit formations, would have the firepower to overwhelm enemy air defenses and to fight their way to and from crucial industrial targets deep inside Germany. Clearly, the success of both armored and strategic bombing doctrine was inextricably linked to the performance of these weapons.

[14]

Armored Bludgeon

American armored doctrine and equipment were first tested in combat in North Africa. One of the first illusions to evaporate in the heat of battle was the effectiveness of the light tank.

On November 26, 1942, Lieutenant Freeland A. Daubin and his platoon of M3 light tanks from Company A, 1st Battalion, 1st Armored Regiment, 1st Armored Division, fought the first engagement of the war between American and German tanks. Daubin and his crew entered the battle with a "great and abiding faith in the prowess of the 37mm 'cannon'" with which their tank was armed.[1] When a German Panzerkampfwagen (Pzkw) IV came into range, Daubin confidently ordered his crew to begin firing. His confidence soon turned to panic:

> The 37mm gun of the little American M3 light tank popped and snapped like an angry cap pistol. . . . The Jerry seemed annoyed by these attentions. Questing about with his incredibly long, bell-snouted, "souped-up" 75mm Kw K40 rifle, the German commander spotted his heckler. Deciding to do the sporting thing and lessen the extreme range, he leisurely commenced closing the 140 yard gap between himself and the light tank, but keeping his thicker, sloping frontal plates turned squarely to the hail of 37mm fire.
>
> The crew of the M3 redoubled the serving of their piece. The loader crammed the little projectiles into the breech and the commander (who was also the gunner) squirted them at the foe. . . . The German shed sparks like a power-driven grindstone. In a frenzy of desperation and fading faith in their highly-touted weapon, the M3 crew pumped more than eighteen rounds at the Jerry while it came in. Through the scope sight the tracer could be seen to hit, then glance straight up. Popcorn balls thrown by Little Bo Peep would have been just as effective.[2]

[189]

One hit from the German's high-velocity 75-mm gun ended the contest.[3] As Daubin lay bleeding on the floor of a wadi, he watched the Germans destroy five more M3s. Fortunately, Major William R. Tuck, commander of Company B, was able to maneuver his light tanks to the flanks and rear of the enemy force. Firing at close range, the 37-mm guns knocked out seven enemy tanks before the Germans withdrew.[4] Tuck's tactical innovation—maneuvering to engage the less heavily armored sides and rear of a German tank—was one that American tankers came to rely on heavily.

As the campaign proceeded in North Africa, General Devers, commanding general of the armored force, arrived from Fort Knox. Devers headed a mission "to examine the problems of Armored Force units in the European Theater of Operations." Overseas from December 14, 1942, until January 25, 1943, Devers found few flaws in armored force equipment and claimed that "the M-4 (General Sherman) [was] the best tank on the battlefield."[5]

The ordnance annex to his report probably fueled Devers's enthusiasm. British Generals R. L. McCreery and C. W. Norman were noted to have said that the "American M3 [medium] tanks had stopped the Germans at the El Alamein line and that the M4 tanks defeated the Germans in the break through." The report cited interviews with British soldiers that led to the blanket conclusion that the M4 tank with its 75-mm gun "could easily defeat any German tank." The British tank crews also stressed that they preferred to use the M4 in a "hull-down," or defensive, position. Thus, the M4s were concealed and largely protected from return fire. The report further noted that the 75-mm armor-piercing (AP) ammunition "was found capable of penetrating all German tanks at ranges as great as 2,500 yards."[6]

British soldiers also commented that the M4, with its high explosive (HE) shell, destroyed antitank guns at ranges up to 3,500 yards.[7] Range was particularly important in North Africa, because the German 88-mm anti-aircraft gun, also used in an antitank role, was the most feared tank killer on the battlefield. The fragmentation of the HE round killed the German crews servicing the 88s, because they had virtually no armor protection. The British tanks, which fired only AP rounds designed to penetrate armor, were not effective against personnel. Consequently, British tank crews had not been able to silence the 88s before the advent of the M4.[8] This report must have been particularly encouraging to the Americans personnel were a target—because the M4 had been designed to handle. Finally, the ordnance team reported that it had interviewed a number of Americans. Incredibly, Lieutenant Daubin's battalion commander, Lieutenant Colonel John K. Waters, had "praised the 37mm gun and stated that it gave good results in battle destroying the German Mark 3 and Mark 4 tanks at about 300 yards." Either the ordnance officers were hearing what they wanted to hear or Colonel Waters was not aware of how his battalion felt about its M3 tanks.[9]

Devers was also pleased with Armored Force tactics. He noted that the

British Eighth Army had used "the same tactical principles and doctrines taught by the Armored Force" with great success, but Devers did not find everything to his liking. He noted that the "present war is definitely one of guns" and that successful offensive operations were those that integrated "air, tanks, and artillery," while a viable defense required "air, concealed antitank guns, and artillery." Devers then reasserted his earlier arguments against tank destroyers, stating that "the separate tank destroyer is not a practical concept on the battlefield." In Devers's opinion, "the weapon to beat a tank is a better tank. Sooner or later the issue between ground forces is settled in an armored battle—tank against tank."[10]

Shortly after the Devers mission departed the combat zone, American armored forces experienced blitzkrieg firsthand. On February 14 General Curt von Arnim attacked Faïd Pass and overran the haphazard American defenses. The 1st Armored Division's Combat Command C counterattacked and was soundly defeated by the veteran Germans. As von Arnim continued his advance, the Americans retreated in disarray. On February 19 Field Marshal Erwin Rommel attacked American positions at Kasserine Pass, and the next day the panzers broke through. Fortunately for the Allies, the Germans lacked sufficient resources to exploit their offensive successes. The Allies poured in men and matériel to bolster their defenses and checked the German advance.[11]

For the Americans, their first experiences against a determined and professional German offensive were unnerving and humiliating: "American armor was employed piecemeal, not massed. . . . American tankers had been outwitted by veteran Germans. The Army Air Force had been ineffectively coordinated. . . . Worst of all, American troops had fled in panic before the enemy." Eisenhower, believing they "had proven to be indecisive in crisis," relieved the II Corps commander, Major General Lloyd R. Fredendall, and the 1st Armored Division commander, Major General Orlando Ward.[12]

The Americans attributed the defeat at Kasserine to "green troops" and poor leadership. The War Department believed that "failures or tactical reverses . . . resulted from misapplication of . . . principles, or from lack of judgment and flexibility in their application."[13] The Army applied the traditional correctives of training, discipline, and leadership—all of which were abundantly supplied when General Patton replaced Fredendall as the II Corps commander. Unfortunately, obvious breakdowns in the human dimension obscured doctrinal and technological deficiencies.

General McNair, commanding general of the Army ground forces, received a copy of Devers's report and on February 19 wrote a letter to Major General A. D. Bruce, commander of the Tank Destroyer Center at Camp Hood, Texas. McNair stated that he had discussed with Secretary of War Stimson "that Devers seemed not to care much about tank destroyers." McNair then reassured Bruce that Stimson was still on their side: "The Secretary bounced right back with the statement that he was one of the original backers of the tank destroyers, and that he would have to have Devers in for a talk on the question." McNair also believed that American combat experiences verified his position and wrote to Bruce that he was "confident that the track we are on—in both tank destroyers and antiaircraft—is both sound and not in jeopardy." He was also convinced that "developments in Africa only serve to demonstrate the soundness of this conception." Indeed, he believed that "if they had piled in tank destroyers instead of armored units, the 1st Armored Division would be still intact."[14]

By September 1943 the lessons from North Africa had been applied to the American armored forces. The adaptations were evolutionary: The structure of the armored division changed to a more balanced organization whose combat elements included three tank battalions, three armored infantry battalions, and three armored field artillery battalions. These units were combined or "task organized" for operations and controlled by three combat command headquarters (A, B, and Reserve). The thick German antitank defenses, consisting of guns and mines, had discredited the notion of unsupported tank attacks and established the need for more infantry. The number of light tanks in the divisions was significantly reduced. All three tank battalions had three medium tank companies and only one light tank company, which was primarily used for reconnaissance.[15]

Armored doctrine remained largely unchanged. On September 29, 1943, the Army ground forces issued a field manual that reaffirmed the exploitation role of the armored division. Infantry divisions were to make holes in enemy lines so that "the armored division may pass through the gap created and exploit the success." Exploitation was defined as "an attack to destroy enemy installations or formations, to seize critical terrain." Furthermore, the manual again clarified that "the primary role of the tank is to destroy enemy personnel and automatic weapons." The armament of American tanks supported this mission: "The main purpose of the tank cannon is to permit the tank to overcome enemy resistance and reach vital rear areas, where the tank machine guns may be used most advantageously." The publication also stated that "antimechanized protection," if required, would be provided by attaching tank destroyer battalions.[16]

In May 1943 General Devers departed the armored force to command the European theater of operations.[17] Major General Alvan C. Gillem, an infantryman, replaced Devers, which probably explains the increased emphasis on medium tanks and infantry support in the armored division.[18] Gillem brought his own assumptions about armored warfare. In September he reversed his earlier decision to arm all future M4 tanks with more powerful 76-mm guns. In keeping with vintage infantry tank doctrine, he believed that the 75-mm cannon had a better high explosive shell than the 76-mm cannon. Therefore, the 75-mm cannon–equipped M4 was a better weapon against the targets that tanks were doctrinally designed to defeat. Gillem believed that only one-third of the Shermans should have the better antitank gun.[19]

McNair supported Gillem's decision to use the 75-mm cannon, and when Devers cabled from Europe to request that the development of the T26 tank, armed with a 90-mm gun, be given highest priority to counter German tank developments, McNair's response was predictable: "I see no reason to alter our previous stand . . . essentially that we should defeat Germany by use of the M-4 series of medium tanks. There has been no factual developments [*sic*] overseas, so far as I know to challenge the superiority of the M-4."[20]

McNair was firmly committed to the tank destroyer concept. He believed that the Americans had experienced nothing in combat against the Germans that justified heavier tanks, with their attendant mobility and overseas shipping problems. American forces had encountered German Pzkw V Panthers and Pzkw VI Tigers in Italy and had been able to stop them with seemingly little difficulty.[21] Since he controlled the promulgation of American armored and tank destroyer doctrine, his opinions were in effect law, and he was not alone in his conclusions.

McNair's position on tank and antitank missions was shared by many ground officers. In April 1944 General Patton sent McNair a copy of his "Letter of Instruction No.2," in which Patton gave his views—in accord with McNair's—on armored tactics. Patton stressed that "the primary mission of armored units is the attacking of infantry and artillery. The enemy's rear is the happy hunting ground for armor."[22]

Although the doctrinal debate was relatively tame, the Ordnance Department and the Army Ground Forces squabbled intensely over tank technology. This friction closely resembled the prewar disputes between the chief of ordnance and the chief of infantry. The Ordnance Department wanted to standardize heavier armored and armed tanks to remain competitive with new German designs. The Army Ground Forces did not interfere in ordnance development programs but blocked standardization in most cases. The Army Ground Forces believed that if the Germans developed a significantly more powerful tank, the appropriate technological response was not to abandon the proven M4 design but to develop more powerful tank destroyers. Consequently, the most powerful tank available to American troops when they landed at Normandy was the M4 with a 76-mm gun.

Even after the invasion the M4 initially seemed adequate to deal with German armor because long-range engagements were rare in the thick hedgerow country. Nevertheless, the difficulty of defeating German armor was becoming a concern. Soon after D day, the First Army conducted test firings against a captured Panther. The results were alarming. Only the 90-mm antitank gun and the 105-mm howitzer could penetrate the front glacis of the German tank—and even these guns were effective only at close ranges.[23]

Particularly disconcerting was the ineffectiveness of the new 76-mm gun mounted on the M4 medium tank. General Omar N. Bradley, commander of the Twelfth Army Group, noted that "this new weapon often scuffed rather than penetrated the enemy's armor." In July 1944 General Dwight Eisenhower was dismayed when Bradley told him of the failings of the 76-mm gun: "You mean our 76 won't knock these Panthers out? Why, I thought it was going to be the wonder gun of the war." When Bradley responded that it was better than the 75-mm gun but still not good enough, Eisenhower was irate: "Why is it that I am always the last to hear about this stuff? Ordnance told me this 76 would take care of anything the German had. Now I find you can't knock out a damn thing with it."[24]

Unfortunately, little could be done to correct the inadequacy of American tanks in the summer of 1944. Following the breakout and the drive against Germany, the deficiencies of the Sherman and the inappropriateness of tank destroyer doctrine became increasingly obvious. The M4 Sherman, even with its 76-mm gun and the new hypervelocity armor-piercing (HVAP) ammunition, could not take on Panthers or Tigers head-to-head—nor could any other American gun at ranges outside the engagement envelope of German tanks (see table 3).

American tankers had to employ the tactics learned in the North African desert of maneuvering to attack the more vulnerable sides and rear of the German tanks. The costs were high. One battalion of the 2d Armored Divi-

Table 3. American and German gun penetration against armor at 30 degrees obliquity at 500 to 2,000 yards (in millimeters)

Model/armor/gun	500 yards	1,000 yards	1,500 yards	2,000 yards
American				
M4/81 mm/75 mm	68	60	52	47
M4/81 mm/76 mm	150	132	112	97
M26/110 mm/90 mm	129	122	114	106
M10 TD/59 mm/3 inches	157	135	116	98
M18 TD/25 mm/76 mm	150	132	112	97
M36 TD/51 mm/90 mm	129	122	114	106
German				
Pzkw IVJ/80 mm/75 mm	154	123	99	80
Pzkw V/120 mm/75 mm	197	150	119	100
Pzkw VI Tiger I/100 mm/88 mm	112	105	94	86
Pzkw VI Tiger II/185 mm/88 mm	202	164	136	113

SOURCES: Baily, 110, 147–56; Green, Thomson, and Roots, 372–73; Hunnicut, 562–67; Mayo, 334–36; and Ross, 330–33. Armor on all tanks is the thickest available on the latest models. Penetration data are for the most effective ammunition. The American M26 is included even though it was not fielded until mid-April 1945. On V-E day there were 310 M26s in Europe, of which 200 had been issued to troops. The 88-mm L71 gun on the Pzkw VI Tiger II could punch through the front of an M4 Sherman at 3,500 yards.

sion lost 51 percent of its men and 70 percent of its tanks in two weeks of action.[25] American soldiers began to lose faith in their tanks—with good reason. Sergeant Thomas P. Welborn explained the risks in trying to overwhelm a German Panther:

> On 5 August in the vicinity of St. Sever Calvados, France, [I] witnessed a German Mark V tank knock out three M4 and three M5 tanks during and after being hit by at least fifteen rounds of 75mm APC from a distance of approximately 700 yards. All of these shells had ricochetted, with the exception of a sixteenth round which finally put the Mark V tank out of action.[26]

The closer the Allies got to Germany, the more determined the German resistance became. In mid-November the 1st Battalion, 67th Armored Regiment, 2d Armored Division, was on the Roer River plain near Puffendorf, Germany, preparing to attack toward Gereonsweiler. Suddenly, between twenty and thirty German tanks, including Tigers and Panthers, opened fire. As the Shermans tried to maneuver for flank shots, they became mired in the muddy ground and were picked off. In only two days the 2d Armored Division suffered 363 casualties and lost 57 tanks. Most of these losses occurred at Puffendorf. It had been an uneven exchange; the 1st Battalion, 67th Armored Regiment, claimed only two German tanks destroyed by Shermans and two by M36 tank destroyers.[27] Corporal James A. Miller expressed the overwhelming sense of fear and frustration the American tank crews felt:

> One morning in Puffendorf, Germany, about daylight I saw several German tanks coming across the field toward us; we all opened fire on them, but we had just about as well have fired our shots straight up in the air for all the [g]ood we could do. Every round would bounce off and wouldn't do a bit of damage. I fired at one 800 yards away, he had his side toward me. I hit him from the lap of the turret to the bottom and from the front of the tank to the back directly in the side but he never halted. I fired one hundred and eighty four rounds at them and I hit at least five of them several times. In my opinion if we had a gun with plenty of muzzle velocity we would have wiped them out. We out-gunned them but our guns were worthless.[28]

Americans were also finding that German tanks had better "flotation" in the muddy terrain of the Roer Plain and the Hürtgen Forest. German tanks had wide tracks that enabled them to maneuver in the boggy terrain. The Shermans, with their narrow tracks designed for speed on good surfaces, no longer had a maneuverability edge over the panzers. Additionally, the Germans had long since figured out American flanking tactics and positioned their tanks so that only the virtually impenetrable front was exposed to any avenue of approach.[29]

The U.S. Army felt the full power of a determined German panzer attack when on December 16 Hitler launched his assault in the Ardennes, spearheaded by 1,500 tanks and assault guns.[30] Any lingering faith in the M4 vanished in the face of the determined German attack. American tankers, writing home to their families and friends, told how their tanks could not stand up to German panzers. They were right—between June and December 1944 the Twelfth Army Group had lost more than 2,000 medium tanks.

In January 1945 American newspapers were asking for answers. Hanson Baldwin, the distinguished *New York Times* correspondent, wrote some of the most critical editorials and urged a congressional inquiry.[31] The Army leadership closed ranks, and a flurry of articles appeared in February lauding the quality of American equipment generally and the M4 tank specifically. Major General Levin H. Campbell Jr., the chief of ordnance, released a letter that General Eisenhower had written to him to defuse further criticism. In it, Eisenhower wrote that "the mobility of our ordnance enabled us to exploit our first successes in the drive across France, into Belgium and Germany."[32] Campbell also cited two other popular American generals, Devers and Patton, "who made their reputations in tanks." While General Devers indicated that he was satisfied with American equipment, General Patton was more effusive in his praise: "We've got the finest tanks in the world! We just love to see the German Royal Tiger [Tiger II] come up on the field."[33] General Campbell concluded that "our commanders . . . still prefer the 'more mobile' lighter and earlier M-4 model for general tactical action."[34]

Still, the press would not leave the tank issue. Even when the War Department announced the deployment of the new M26, correspondents nagged Eisenhower. On March 18 he wrote to Brigadier General I. D. White, commander of the 2d Armored Division, and Major General Maurice Rose, commander of the 3d Armored Division, that he kept finding newspaper stories in which reporters purportedly quoted noncommissioned officers as saying that American tanks were inferior to German panzers. Eisenhower doubted the truth of these accounts and cited his own conversations with armored soldiers as evidence:

> Our men, in general, realize that the Sherman is not capable of standing up in a ding-dong, head-on fight with a Panther. Neither in gun power nor in armor is the present Sherman justified in undertaking such a contest. On the other hand, most of them realize that we have got a job of shipping tanks overseas and therefore do not want unwieldy monsters; that our tank has great reliability, good mobility, and that the gun in it has been vastly improved. Most of them feel also that they have developed tactics that allow them to employ their superior numbers to defeat the Panther tank as long as they are not surprised and can discover the Panther before it has gotten in three or four good

shots. I think that most of them know also that we have improved models coming out which even in head-on action are not helpless in front of the Panther and the Tiger.[35]

Eisenhower concluded by asking for White's and Rose's personal opinions on the quality of American tanks and for their assessment of the potential of the new M26 tank to cope with the Panther. He also asked for a sampling of their soldiers' views on the two issues.[36]

White and Rose were quick to respond to Eisenhower's request. Within two days, White and his staff queried more than 150 officers and enlisted men and prepared a 76-page packet for Eisenhower. White's comments on his division's equipment were balanced. He believed that the M4A3E8 with a 76-mm gun was an improvement over earlier models, particularly with HVAP ammunition. Unfortunately, HVAP ammunition remained in short supply, and his tanks had less than four rounds each. Nevertheless, lest Eisenhower conclude wrongly that the HVAP shortage was his central concern, White stressed that "the 76mm gun, even with HVAP ammunition, is not effective at the required ranges at which we must be able to effectively engage enemy armor." He was concerned that the M26, without HVAP ammunition (none of which had been fielded), would be as disappointing as the M36 tank destroyer, which mounted the same 90-mm gun. White believed that "the most important point, and upon which there is universal agreement, is our lack of a tank gun and anti-tank gun with which we can effectively engage enemy armor at the required range. . . . The correction of this deficiency has made progress, but the problem has not as yet been satisfactorily solved."[37]

White's subordinate officers were more openly critical of their tanks. All believed that the M4 placed a poor second behind the German Panthers and Tigers. Brigadier General J. H. Collier, commander of Combat Command A, wrote that "all personnel in the 66th Armored Regiment" believed that German tanks and antitank weapons had better flotation and mobility than the American models. Furthermore, German gunners had crucial advantages in any engagement since they had better sights, higher-velocity guns, and smokeless powder.[38] Additionally, the "better sloped armor and better silhouette" of the German panzers made them much less vulnerable than American tanks. Collier's despair over the equipment his men had to fight with must have emboldened him, because he contested some of Eisenhower's principal rationalizations:

> The fact that our equipment must be shipped over long distances does not, in the opinion of our tankers, justify our inferiority. The M4 has proven inferior to the German Mark VI in Africa before the invasion of Sicily, 10 July 1943.

It is my opinion that press reports of statements by high ranking officers to the effect that we have the best equipment in the world do much to discourage the soldier who is using equipment that he knows to be inferior to that of the enemy.[39]

The other officers in the division echoed White's and Collier's frustrations with their tanks. For example, Lieutenant Colonel Wilson M. Hawkins, commander of the 3d Battalion, 67th Armor, stated bluntly: "If such a choice were possible, I would prefer to fight in the present German Mark V or VI tank against the present U.S. medium tank and tank destroyer with the 90mm gun."[40] Colonel S. R. Hinds, commander of Combat Command B, although concurring with the M4's technical deficiencies, also attacked doctrine: "In spite of the often quoted tactical rule that one should not fight a tank versus tank battle, I have found it necessary, almost invariably, in order to accomplish the mission."[41]

The comments from the 2d Armored Division's citizen soldiers were even more damning than those of their officers. Sergeant Chester J. Marczak left little doubt about how he felt:

The German's high-velocity guns and souped-up ammunition can penetrate our thickest armor. At a range where it would be suicide for us to shoot, they shoot. What we need is more armor, higher velocity, not necessarily a bigger gun, souped-up ammunition, and a means whereby we can maneuver faster, making sharper turns. I've seen many times when the air force was called out to wipe out scattered tanks rather than letting our tanks get slaughtered. All of us know that the German tanks are far superior to anything that we have in combat. They are able to maneuver on a space the length of their tank. How can we outflank them when all they have to do is pivot and keep their frontal armor toward us? Their frontal armor is practically invulnerable to our 75's, except at exceptionally close range—and they never let us get that close. We've got a good tank—for parades and training purposes—but for combat they are just potential coffins. I know! I've left them burning after the first few rounds of German shells penetrated our thickest armor.[42]

Sergeant Joseph O. Posecoi agreed with Marczak and asked a probing question: "If our tanks aren't out-armored and out-gunned, why does every outfit that has ever been up against a German Mark V tank use 100 to 150 sand bags for added protection?"[43] Almost every one of the more than 150 respondents recounted his own bitter experience of watching well-aimed rounds bounce off German tanks and of seeing friends die trying to maneuver for a side or rear shot to compensate for the inadequacies of their tank guns.

The soldiers also told how they had been able to contend with the superior German panzers. Sergeant Nick Moceri said it well: "The only reason

[198]

we've gone as far as we have is summed up in 'Quantity and Co-operation of Arms.' "[44] Sergeant Harold E. Fulton was even more explicit: "Our best tank weapon, and the boy that has saved us so many times, is the P-47 [fighter airplane]."[45]

Rose's March 21 response to Eisenhower, although only five pages long, echoed White's views on American tanks. Rose wrote: "It is my personal conviction that the present M4A3 tank is inferior to the German Mark V." He told Eisenhower that the soldiers compensated for their "inferior equipment by the efficient use of artillery, air support, and maneuver." Nevertheless, the burden was clearly on the tank crews, "the individual tanker and gunner, who maneuvers his tank and holds his fire until he is in position most favorable to him." Rose also told Eisenhower that he had personally seen "projectiles fired by our 75 and 76mm guns bouncing off the front plate of Mark V tanks at ranges of about 600 yards." This undesirable head-on approach was often unavoidable "due to the canalizing of the avenue of approach of both the German and our tank, which did not permit maneuver."[46]

Rose's subordinates also denounced their tanks. The opinion of Staff Sergeant Robert M. Early, a tank commander with nine months' combat experience, was clear: "I haven't any confidence in an M4. Jerry armament will knock out an M4 as far as they can see it." Corporal Albert E. Wilkinson, an M4 gunner, agreed: "We can't compare with the Jerry tank. We haven't the armor nor gun."[47] Finally, Lieutenant Colonel Matthew W. Kane, commander of the 1st Battalion, 32d Armored Regiment, expounded on the price his unit had paid for being equipped with the M4 tank:

> This battalion has lost 84 tanks through enemy action in nine months of combat. In a tank versus tank action, our M4 tank is woefully lacking in armor and armament when pitted against the super velocity 75mm or 88mm gun of the German tank. Greater maneuverability and speed have failed to compensate for this deficiency, and our tank losses in the Belgian Bulge were relatively high, even when we were in defensive positions. Crews recognized the deficiencies in our tanks, and know that success on the battlefield is attributable to our superiority in numbers of tanks, and resolve to sustain heavy casualties in men and tanks in order to gain objectives.[48]

Eisenhower, taken aback by White's and Rose's opinions, replied immediately: "I feel that your conclusions . . . should go at once to the War Department, and I am sending them on to General Marshall without delay."[49]

Unfortunately, at the end of March 1945, little could be done to redress the technological inferiority of American tanks. The Ordnance Department had already pulled out all of the stops to get the M26 to Europe. Again, its efforts would be too little and too late to have any effect. Nevertheless, that the views of General White and General Rose were apparently so unexpected by General Eisenhower is compelling evidence for why American tanks and the doctrine for their use were inadequate. General Eisenhower, the commander whose authority gave him the most power to demand corrective action, was long unaware of any serious problems.

The obvious question is why, as late as the closing weeks of the war, did Eisenhower remain ignorant of the substantial technological inferiority of American tanks? Surely part of the reason was that he was shielded from the truth. His premier tank officers, General Devers and General Patton, had praised existing American equipment. The Army's chief of ordnance, General Campbell, had promised even more and better tanks. Poor counsel, although a contributory factor, was probably not the central reason Eisenhower was uninformed.

Perhaps a more plausible explanation for Eisenhower's continued neglect of the tank problem is that it never became a crisis in and of itself. In the hierarchy of disasters that Eisenhower had to contend with, tank failings were simply overshadowed. In Tunisia, when the 1st Armored Division was outgunned by the new Pzkw IVs, Eisenhower's attention was riveted on the catastrophe at Kasserine Pass. Poorly trained, disheartened troops and faulty leadership were the problems that demanded action. The introduction of the Pzkw VI Tiger I, with its 88-mm gun, was largely overlooked. Americans had not opposed any of the nineteen Tigers the Germans had in North Africa, and the British reportedly had not been overly impressed by the new tank.[50]

After North Africa, Eisenhower focused on preparing for the invasion of France. In the breakout from the beachhead, the euphoria of the rapid advance toward Germany probably suppressed any anxiety over tanks. Under Patton's determined direction, American armored doctrine had been immensely effective. During the Battle of the Bulge, when the qualitative disparity between American and German tank weapons became patently obvious at the level of the tanker, it remained invisible to Eisenhower. Faced with the destruction of an Army, tanks were a marginal issue. Only when the press paraded the irate comments of his soldiers before him did Eisenhower turn his attention to tanks. By then, it was too late for significant matériel correction.

In the aftermath of victory, General Marshall tried to explain the American tank failures. In his rationalizations, the heritage of two decades of Army assumptions about tank doctrine and technology became clear:

> Another noteworthy example of German superiority was in the heavy tank. From the summer of 1943 to the spring of 1945 the German Tiger and Panther tanks outmatched our Sherman tanks in direct combat. This stemmed largely from different concepts of armored warfare held by us and the Germans, and the radical difference in our approach to the battlefield. Our tanks had to be

shipped thousands of miles overseas and landed on hostile shores amphibiously. They had to cross innumerable rivers on temporary bridges, since when we attacked we sought to destroy the permanent bridges behind the enemy lines from the air. Those that our planes missed were destroyed by the enemy when he retreated. Therefore our tanks could not well be of the heavy type. We designed our armor as a weapon of exploitation. In other words, we desired to use our tanks in long-range thrusts deep into the enemy's rear where they could chew up his supply installations and communications. This required great endurance—low consumption of gasoline and ability to move great distances without breakdown.

But while that was the most profitable use of the tank, it became unavoidable in stagnant prepared-line fighting to escape tank-to-tank battles. In this combat, our medium tank was at a disadvantage, when forced into a head-on engagement with the German heavies.[51]

For want of adequate tanks, the U.S. Army had applied an overwhelming armored bludgeon of inferior machines, complemented by enormous air and artillery resources, against a qualitatively superior German panzer technology. Quite simply, the deficiencies of the tank component did not create a crisis for the whole, and the U.S. Army pushed into Germany.

[15]

Air Force Triumphant

The early successes of the Eighth Air Force—particularly the October 9 attack on Lille, France—gave its commander, General Hap Arnold, leverage in the intense interservice battle for resources. In a memorandum for Roosevelt confidant Harry Hopkins, Arnold claimed that the Lille mission proved "the contention by the Army Air Forces . . . that B-17s in strong formations can be employed effectively and successfully without fighter support." The crews of the Flying Fortresses claimed that 107 Luftwaffe fighters were "destroyed, probably destroyed, or damaged." The 107 planes represented nearly one-fourth of the single-engine fighter strength of the Luftwaffe thought to be in Western Europe, and only four American bombers had gone down. Thus, the airmen confidently predicted that the continuation of this "rate of attrition could only result in the destruction, or complete incapacitation, of the Luftwaffe's front line fighter strength." Furthermore, Lille pointed the way to victory—the air campaign against the continent had to "be continued and enlarged to the fullest possible extent."[1]

General Arnold, however, was still concerned. He wrote General Spaatz that he remained convinced that "unless we are careful, we will find our air effort in Europe dispersed." He also warned of the danger that "we will find the air being used more as a support for the ground arms than it should be . . . when if there ever was a time to use it strategically, that time is now."[2]

Arnold did everything he could to keep public attention focused on the operations of the Eighth Air Force. John Steinbeck, author of *The Grapes of Wrath*, wrote *Bombs Away: The Story of a Bomber Team*, for the Army Air Forces. Steinbeck's prose dramatically conveyed the airmen's message: "The thundering ships took off one behind the other. At 5,000 feet they made their formation. The men sat quietly at their stations, their eyes fixed. And the deep growl of the engines shook the air, shook the world, shook the future."[3]

Arnold also ensured that the Eighth Air Force had skilled public relations coverage. In November he assigned Lieutenant Reagan McCrary to General Eaker's organization. Arnold had high hopes for McCrary: "He thoroughly understands all media of reaching and directing public opinion. He also has a deep understanding of the capabilities of air power, particularly as concerns the heavy bomber in its mission in the European theater. I feel sure that he can be helpful to you and the Army Air Forces."[4]

Despite the best efforts of the Army Air Forces, the buildup of the strategic bombing force was agonizingly slow. Airplane production fell behind schedule, and the invasion of North Africa diverted resources from the Eighth Air Force.[5] Furthermore, there was increasing pressure for the Americans to join the Royal Air Force (RAF) in its night bombing campaign. This latter issue came to a head in mid-January 1943.

On January 14 President Roosevelt and Prime Minister Churchill met in Anfa, near Casablanca, French Morocco, to plan the Allied strategy for 1943. One of the points they addressed was the future of the American daylight bombing campaign. Although Roosevelt was committed to strategic bombing, he apparently did not much care how it was accomplished. Churchill, on the other hand, believed that the RAF's night bombing campaign was the most promising strategy. General Eisenhower summoned Eaker to the conference to state the case for daylight bombing.[6]

When Eaker arrived on January 15, General Arnold told him that Churchill was pressing Roosevelt to give up daylight bombing and needed to understand the virtues of American bombing doctrine.[7] Eaker built his case around a series of questions Arnold had posed.[8] Why have there been so few missions? Why have you bombed Lille and other French targets? Why have there been so many abortive sorties—bombers that did not reach their targets? Why have U.S. bombers not bombed Germany? How do you select your targets? Eaker's planned answers focused on resources and missions. Although the Eighth Air Force wanted to attack Germany, it had been constrained by its small size, due mainly to diversions to support the invasion of North Africa. Additionally, the command had been told to concentrate its attacks on the German submarine pens on the Brest peninsula.[9]

Regarding the central issue of daylight bombing's efficacy, Eaker rested his case on seven fundamental presumptions:

1. We can do a better job; day bombing is more accurate; small targets like individual factories can be found, seen, and hit.
2. It is more economical; a smaller force can destroy a given target; we suffer smaller losses.
3. It prevents German defenses from resting by day; it is a marvelous complement of the RAF night effort; it keeps German defenses alerted around the clock 24 hours of the day.

4. It prevents airdrome and air space congestion. The RAF works by night, we by day, the resulting reduction in air space, ground, and communications confusion is at least 50%.
5. We are trained for day bombing; our crews will do a better job by day. There would be a long training delay to train them for night bombing; it is a different specialty requiring a different technique.
6. Our planes and equipment are designed, built, and equipped for the day bombing task. They can defend themselves from enemy fighters. Day bombing permits the destruction of enemy day fighters; it reduces the German Air Force—one of the prime objectives.
7. Our ability to bomb by day permits some excellent cooperation with RAF bombers; we see and set on fire by daylight small targets which the RAF cannot see at night, but they can bomb on our fires, started late in the afternoon. This plan has already been worked out with Air Marshall Harris.[10]

On January 20 Churchill and Eaker shared a private luncheon in which Eaker stated his arguments on the importance of daylight bombing.[11] The prime minister replied that although the United States had been in the war for a year, "absolutely nothing, not a single bomb had been dropped on Germany" by the Americans. However, Churchill believed that Eaker had "pleaded his cause with skill and tenacity." Eaker promised better results in the near future, and Churchill relented and decided to back Eaker.[12]

The final obstacle to American strategic bombing doctrine had been overcome. Churchill's acquiescence cleared the way for the combined chiefs of staff to issue the Casablanca Directive for the air offensive against Germany. The objective of the offensive was vintage Air Corps Tactical School doctrine: "the progressive destruction and dislocation of the German military, industrial, and economic system, and the undermining of the morale of the German people to a point where their capacity for armed resistance is fatally weakened."[13]

General Spaatz, the man who later commanded the American strategic bombing forces, recalled that with the Casablanca Directive, "strategic bombing had the green light."[14] In addition, the Army Air Forces were given the nod to justify two decades of claims that their arm, operating independently of the ground forces, could be decisive. In January 1943 this doctrine was contingent on one fundamental assumption—that the firepower of an unescorted heavy bomber formation would preclude "unacceptable losses" during missions.[15]

The pressure on the Eighth Air Force to prove the decisiveness of strategic bombing was intense. Arnold and Eaker had created conditions in which the small American bomber force had enormous political and public visibility. Nevertheless, their faith in their doctrine appeared to be justified. The Eighth Air Force's losses before the Casablanca Conference had been well within the acceptable range. Furthermore, the bomber formations had re-portedly wreaked havoc against the Luftwaffe. All of the assumptions un-dergirding their doctrine seemed to be validated under combat conditions.

Still, the skeptics could point to the fact that on most of their missions, the American bombers had been escorted by fighters.[16] The first unescorted mission against Germany settled the issue for the American bomber advo-cates. On January 27 the 306th Group bombed the U-boat yards at Wil-helmshaven, Germany. Of the ninety-one planes dispatched, fifty-three at-tacked. Only three bombers were lost.[17] Additionally, bomber crews claimed that they had destroyed twenty-two German fighters.[18] On January 30 Eaker wrote Major General George E. Stratemeyer, chief of the air staff: "The one thing our heavy bombers have done during the past few months, and don't let anybody ever tell you anything to the contrary—we have knocked the ears off the German day fighters."[19]

The attack on Wilhelmshaven was the final mission in January 1943. A tally of the attrition during the month was decidedly in the Eighth Air Force's favor. Of the 338 bombers dispatched, 241 had bombed their targets, for an attack rate of 71 percent, a decided improvement over the 1942 aver-age of only 51.2 percent. Furthermore, only 18 bombers had been lost (5.3 percent of the force dispatched), while the bombers claimed 115 enemy fighters.[20]

In February the Luftwaffe offered stiffer resistance and the Americans paid an increasingly heavy price for their unescorted missions.[21] On Febru-ary 4 eighty-six bombers left from bases in England to attack Emden, Ger-many. Only thirty-nine bombers attacked, and five were lost. Over the next two weeks, the Eighth concentrated on targets in occupied France. Even there, the losses were heavy. On February 16 eight of the sixty-five bombers that attacked the U-boat base at St. Nazaire were lost.[22]

General Arnold was upset not only about the losses but also that the Eighth had flown so few missions over Germany. He expressed his displea-sure to General Stratemeyer: "Our records indicate that there are 173 B-17s and 34 B-24s in the 8th Air Force as of February 24, 1943, giving a total of 207 4-engine bombers. This is quite a sizeable force and one that should not be allowed to remain idle on the ground."[23] The day Arnold sent his note to Stratemeyer, the Eighth mounted its second mission against Wilhelmshaven. It was a costly effort: of the sixty-three bombers attacking, seven were lost.

Eaker had long maintained that he needed at least 300 bombers to "effec-tively attack any German target and return without excessive or uneco-nomical loss."[24] At the end of February, Eaker faced a critical situation be-cause the operational strength of his heavy bomber force had declined from 155 airplanes in January to 146 in February. Eaker was perhaps even more alarmed by another telling statistic: Available bomber crew strength had de-clined from 85 in January to 74 in February.[25] Eaker knew that the crew losses had more than operational implications. He wrote to General Andrews about the "very serious depression in morale of our bomber forces, due to the failure to build them up to what they know to be requisite proportions if they are to continue to exist and do a worthwhile job."[26]

Arnold used the 300-plane argument himself. In a late March letter to General Andrews, he wrote that "300 bombers was the absolute minimum that must be in the air" to keep losses from being prohibitive during deep penetrations into Germany. He had also informed the joint chiefs that to put 300 bombers over Germany repeatedly would require a total force of 1,200 airplanes in the theater.

Arnold told Andrews that he was pleased with the targeting work of Colonel C. P. Cabell and his group of operations analysts. They had identified a target that caught Arnold's attention—the ball bearing industry. Arnold noted that this system of targets was particularly attractive to him for two reasons. First, destroying the Nazi's ball bearing capacity "would virtually paralyze all German industry." Second, Arnold believed that the ball bearing industry could be destroyed in 1943 by the Eighth Air Force if its buildup continued as planned. If the analysts were right, the implications were enormous. The ball bearing industry might be the critical node in the industrial web of Germany. Knocking it out could "result in air action that will prove the decisive factor in the European conflict." All that remained was to build the Eighth to sufficient strength to do the job.[27]

General Arnold began to lobby the White House. On March 27, in a memorandum to Harry Hopkins, Arnold stated that heavy bomber production had reached a point at which the forces in England, whose strength had withered from diversions to North Africa, could be reestablished and expanded. He also told Hopkins that "the time has come to use *airpower*" and that "all that is needed is the green light from the Commander in Chief to accumulate an adequate air striking force in England."[28]

Over the next several months, the Army Air Forces struggled to enlarge the Eighth Air Force, while simultaneously trying to replace its losses from missions against occupied France and Germany. The buildup was slow and the attrition heavy. By July 1943 the Eighth Air Force had 315 crews for 589 heavy bombers and had lost 109 crews and 128 bombers.[29]

As the strength of the Eighth Air Force grew, so too did Arnold's impatience for results. In late April he wrote to Andrews: "I am rapidly coming to the conclusion that our bombing outfit in the 8th Air Force is assuming a state of routine repetition of performance and perhaps finding many excuses and alibis for not going on missions, which with more aggressive leaders might be accomplished." Arnold, as if his message was not already clear, added: "Maybe we need new blood all along the line from the Bomber Commander down through his whole staff."[30]

Eaker responded to the pressure. On May 13 he wrote Arnold that the new replacement crews and airplanes would enable him to increase the tempo of his operations.[31] Five days later he again wrote Arnold, telling him that the Eighth had bombed Kiel with superior results and that the bomber crews were "gaining in confidence and morale with each succeeding mission." He also noted an ominous change in Luftwaffe fighter capabilities and tactics:

> The German Air Force now has two squadrons of FW 190's equipped with 37 mm. cannon. Yesterday, they stood off at 1500 yds., outside our effective range, and knocked down three of our bombers with this long range cannon fire. At Kiel, and again yesterday, a considerable number of large bombs, 250–300 lbs. were dropped on our formations by pursuit aircraft. At Antwerp, 23 FW 190's in a fairly tight formation, dive-bombed our formation with large bombs.[32]

General Spaatz, writing to Arnold from North Africa, also noted the change in German fighter operations. He was more direct than Eaker: "It is reasonable to believe that the German will eventually solve the problem of meeting the B-17."[33]

The Army Air Forces' initial response to this new threat was to place more machine guns and armor on a B-17 and use it as an escort "fighter-destroyer."[34] Hopefully, this airplane, designated the YB-40, could protect the bomber formations until the range of escort fighters could be extended.[35]

Arnold continued to press Eaker to get more bombers in the air and sent a number of cables to that effect.[36] On June 10 Gen. Barney M. Giles, chief of the air staff, told Arnold that he had seen no change in Eaker's tactics. Furthermore, Giles could see no reason for Eaker's delay in putting up the all-important 300-bomber formations.[37] The next day Giles wrote to Eaker that Arnold was concerned about the small number of bombers the Eighth was getting into combat.[38]

Eaker's difficulty in increasing bomber strength in the fight largely involved maintenance and repair. Assistant Secretary Lovett, visiting Eaker in England, told Arnold: "During my 2 1/2 weeks visit with the operating groups, battle damage of aircraft ran as high as 80 per cent of the planes employed." Lovett also stressed the need for long-range escort fighters.[39]

In June Arnold stepped up the pressure on Eaker to provide favorable publicity about his operations. On June 28 he wrote to Eaker that he was concerned that "both the Navy and the Army have had outstanding heroes receive public acclaim and have had them decorated by the President." The Air Forces had not had a real hero since Doolittle received the Medal of Honor for his raid on Tokyo. Arnold added that with "all the operations that you have had in England there must be some outstanding hero."[40]

Arnold also wanted publicity for the force as a whole. On June 29 he asked Eaker to send photographs of bombing raids so that the Army Air

Forces could improve its public relations campaign. Arnold told Eaker: "We want the people to understand and have faith in *our way of making war*. That faith can grow in strength only as we *show* them what we are doing, and how well we are doing it."[41]

Assistant Secretary Lovett had a different concern with the press. He noted that the press had begun to speculate about whether the Eighth Air Force could continue to sustain high losses during its operations over Germany. Lovett told Eaker that he would "try to do some 'anticipatory propaganda' in the nature of preventive medicine."[42]

Eaker was under great stress and on June 29 asked Arnold if he still had his confidence. That he was tired of the incessant prodding from Arnold and his staff was clear: "I do not feel . . . that my past service . . . indicates that I am a horse which needs to be ridden with spurs." Eaker emphasized that he needed Arnold's support since the Germans were "marshalling their strongest and best defenses to cope" with the bombing campaign. He predicted "a bloody battle," with victory going eventually to the force that could replace its losses—in short, a battle of attrition. Eaker also noted that the bombers could expect no help from the heavily gunned and bombless YB-40—it was a failure.[43]

On July 7 Arnold replied that he had full confidence in Eaker and was happy with the Eighth Air Force's work. Furthermore, he told Eaker that although he was worried about the increasing loss rate, it was not because he did not think "that your men can take it." Rather, he had been concerned that "we could not produce the number of crews required to maintain your strength." Arnold noted that he believed that the training base could now sustain the bombing campaign and that Eaker should press on.[44]

As the summer of 1943 wore on, the Eighth Air Force's losses increased. But the bomber formations defended themselves well enough to keep losses within the acceptable range and claimed a heavy toll on German fighters. Additionally, sufficient replacement crews and airplanes arrived to enable 300-plane missions to be flown routinely by mid-July. Finally, General Arnold promised that "high priority" was being given to the development of long-range fighter escorts, "to break up this German attack from long range firing, the overhead bombing, and other forms of attack outside of reach of the 50 caliber guns installed on bombers." He told Eaker: "These airplanes should be able to accompany your bombardment as far as Berlin. . . . I visualize sending four or five hundred heavy bombers well into the interior of Germany, escorted by six to eight hundred long range fighters. . . . When we get this going we would welcome the German pursuit to come up and fight."[45] Unfortunately, the fighters to support Arnold's vision were not available to prevent the disasters the Eighth Air Force met over Germany from August to October 1943.

On August 17, 376 American bombers left from their fields in England for two targets in Germany: the ball bearing factories at Schweinfurt and the airplane factories in Regensburg. The First Bombardment Wing, commanded by Brigadier General Robert B. Williams, attacked Schweinfurt with 183 bombers. The Germans shot down 36. Colonel Curtis E. LeMay led 127 B-17s of the 4th Bombardment Wing in the attack against Regensburg and lost 24.[46] In exchange for the 60 B-17s, the Americans claimed 472 German fighters.[47] In fact, German losses were considerably less: 47 fighters downed, of which only 21 were lost to bombers.[48]

The leadership seemed confident that although the losses on August 14 were heavy, the importance of the targets justified them. Assistant Secretary Lovett's words to Eaker were typical: "We know that you have taken heavy losses but I, for one, can not get too disheartened about it when you consider that a 15% loss on Schweinfurt is actually only the equivalent of three days operations at 5%." Nevertheless, Lovett hoped that crew morale had not been shaken by the battle. He wrote that he "assumed that the crews understand the mathematics of the business. . . . Heavy losses on one raid is offset by other factors so that the average over a month remains surprisingly constant." Still, he realized that long-range fighter protection would be "a more realistic comfort to them."[49]

In the coming weeks, it became apparent that the Germans had made radical changes in "the mathematics of the business." On September 6 the Germans brought down 45 of the 262 bombers attacking Stuttgart.[50] The leaders of the Army Air Forces, although realizing they faced a serious new threat from the Luftwaffe, clung to their doctrine. On September 17 Brigadier General Haywood Hansell, the former Air Corps Tactical School instructor, was quoted in the Command Informational Intelligence Series. He noted that the enemy was using rockets and heavy-caliber cannons to attack bomber formations from outside the range of the B-17's defensive firepower. Nevertheless, he believed the Germans "haven't got a solution now that will stop our offensive, provided it is pushed as vigorously and rapidly as possible."[51]

General Arnold shared Hansell's sense of urgency. On September 25 he called for a maximum effort against targets in Germany, "now that German air power appears to be at a critical stage." Arnold also noted that if more planes were sent on missions, the percentage of loss would be the lower when compared with a smaller force. Finally, he got to the heart of the matter: "We are under constant pressure to explain why we do not use massive flights of aircraft now that we have planes and pilots in sufficient quantity to put over 500 planes in the air. What is the answer?"[52]

Eaker responded to Arnold's demands. On October 4 the Eighth Air Force began a ten-day series of raids that proved conclusively that the doctrine of daylight bombing without fighter escort was bankrupt. Eaker and the others were forced to accept the reality that the heavy bomber could not adequately defend itself, no matter how large the formation. It was a hard-learned lesson. From October 4 to 14, the Eighth Air Force was slaughtered in the skies over occupied Europe and Germany and lost 164 bombers.[53]

The final blow had been the sixty bombers—26 percent of the attacking force—lost during the October Schweinfurt mission.[54] The Army Air Forces finally recognized the crisis: the Luftwaffe had achieved a technological edge in aerial weaponry that could never be met by the B-17 or the B-24. Quite simply, the German airplanes had a range advantage with their cannons and rockets that allowed them to engage the bomber formations from outside the effective range of the American .50-caliber machine guns. Furthermore, the Germans had developed an efficient radar and ground control system that ensured that any bomber penetration would be detected and met with stiff opposition.[55]

Eaker maintained a courageous facade. The day after the disastrous Schweinfurt raid he wrote Arnold that he thought that the Luftwaffe attacks were "last final struggles of a monster in his death throes" and that "there [was] not the slightest question but that we now have our teeth in the Hun Air Force's neck." Eaker also recognized the obvious. He told Arnold that on October 14 the Germans, using mostly twin-engined fighters to launch the rockets, had conducted their first large-scale coordinated rocket attack on the bomber formations. He then proclaimed that these slow airplanes would be "duck soup for our fighters, and we shall have them knocked down before long."[56] Despite the aggressive language, Eaker had in a roundabout way stated that he desperately needed escort fighters for his bombers to wrest the advantage back from the Luftwaffe. Until he got them, the American daylight bombing campaign against Germany would remain at a standstill.[57]

General Arnold, however, was apparently not overly concerned by the Eighth Air Force's losses. In a press conference following the Schweinfurt mission, he told reporters that he was willing "to lose 25 per cent. of a flight . . . if an important objective can be destroyed."[58]

That the German ball bearing industry was such an "important objective" was questionable. The postwar Strategic Bombing Survey noted that the Germans adapted to the loss of ball bearings caused by the Schweinfurt missions and were "thus able to make good their boast, '*Es ist kein Geraet zurueck geblieben weil Waelzlager fehlten*' (no equipment has been held up because of a shortage of bearings)."[59] Furthermore, key Army Air Forces planners knew before the costly October Schweinfurt mission that the Germans could obtain ball bearings from foreign sources if their domestic industry was destroyed. When General Kuter learned on September 11 that the Germans could procure ball bearings from Sweden, he provided this information to Colonel Guido Perrera, director of the Army Air Forces committee of operations analysts, the group that had selected the ball bearing industry for destruction, and Major General Bennett E. Meyers, a member of General Arnold's staff.[60]

Despite Arnold's continued pressure to hit German targets, Eaker stood firm. On December 13 he wrote that he was aware of "the feeling there [in Washington] of great irritation that we have not attacked the fighter factories recently." At first, Eaker blamed the weather, but he admitted that even if the weather cleared, he was not optimistic: "These deep penetrations and the impossibility of fighter escort will cost us 80–120 bombers. . . . We must, therefore, be reasonably certain of their destruction before we launch any expedition entailing such cost."[61] And the human costs were high. In late December 1943 the Army Air Forces provided General Marshall an analysis of the Eighth Air Force's losses between July and November. The Eighth had experienced 5,784 casualties and further high crew losses were predicted:

> On the basis of 25 missions to be performed during a tour of duty and a loss rate of 3.8% per combat mission, a total of 36 out of every 100 crew members starting on a tour of duty would complete the prescribed tour and be eligible for return to this country. The balance, or 64 crew members, would be lost during performance of tour.[62]

In December Arnold replaced Eaker with General Carl Spaatz, and in 1944 the Eighth Air Force stepped up its operations against Germany. The combination of fighter escorts and an almost endless supply of bombers and crews allowed the Army Air Forces to continue what had become a bloody battle of attrition for command of the air over Europe.[63] Because of this overwhelming quantitative superiority, losses returned to an acceptable range. As Eaker had predicted, the side that could make good its losses won.[64] The Army Air Forces had triumphed.

[16]

Coequal Land Power and Air Power

The evolution of the tank and the airplane in the U.S. Army resulted in technologies and doctrines for their use that were fraught with inherent operational vulnerabilities. Another dimension of the interwar experience of America's ground and air forces was the absence of cooperation between the two institutions to develop doctrines and procedures that would enable them to operate jointly. The results of this inability to fight together became tragically clear in July 1944.

General Omar Bradley faced a difficult situation in mid-July 1944. It had been almost six weeks since D day, and the advance of his First Army was far behind the timetable set in the OVERLORD plan.[1] The fighting in the French hedgerows had been brutal: By July 19 the First Army had suffered some 40,000 casualties in its fight from the Carentan plain to St. Lô.[2] Furthermore, the press was beginning to criticize the sluggish Allied offensive.[3]

General Bradley worked on a plan to break the stalemate—Operation COBRA. COBRA, on the surface, was relatively straightforward. The VII Corps, under the command of Major General J. Lawton Collins, would make the main effort. Three infantry divisions, the 4th, the 9th, and the 30th, would attack to create and hold open a breach in the German lines. The 2d Armored Division, the 3d Armored Division, and the 1st Infantry Division (motorized) would pour through this gap and conduct an exploitation.[4] Up to this point, the plan was conventional and in accord with accepted Army doctrine. Bradley, however, introduced a new twist. He wanted more firepower than the artillery and tactical air support normally available to the ground commander could provide. He wanted the awesome destructive power of the strategic bomber.

Bradley turned to Major General Elwood R. "Pete" Quesada, commander of the IX Tactical Air Command, for help in designing the plan. Quesada's fighter bombers had already shown their immense worth in supporting the First Army and had gone beyond existing doctrinal precepts to provide air power to Bradley's forces. Quesada had even placed some of his air support parties in Sherman tanks so they could work directly with the armored units that would exploit COBRA. Before Quesada's innovation, air liaison officers in the European theater were found only at corps and higher headquarters.[5]

Bradley believed that Quesada "was an imaginative man unencumbered by the prejudices and theories of so many of his seniors on the employment of tactical air."[6] Although Bradley's assessment of Quesada's seniors may have been harsh, Quesada's vision of how to employ air power differed from that of many of his fellow generals in the Army Air Forces. Brigadier General Laurence Kuter was one of the most ardent and effective advocates of the prevailing Army Air Forces view that air power had to be centralized under the control of an air officer. Indeed, he had done much of the behind-the-scenes work to gain this control.

Kuter had been the deputy commander of the Anglo-American Northwest African Tactical Air Forces, under British Air Marshal Sir Arthur Coningham.[7] In mid-May 1943 he wrote General Arnold that the campaign in North Africa had proven that "a modern battle is not fought or won by ground force or by a naval force alone. Any modern successful battle consists of a battle in the air which must be won before the surface battle is begun."[8]

Kuter stressed that the potential of air power could not be realized until it was firmly under the expert control of air officers. Accordingly, he recommended to Arnold that all War Department publications be rewritten "to delete all references to the supporting role of aviation and to stress the coordinate role of air, land, and sea forces."[9]

Another observer of operations in North Africa, Assistant Secretary of War John J. McCloy, had a different view. He wrote to Lieutenant General Ben Lear: "It is my firm belief that the Air Forces are not interested in this type of work [close air support], think it is unsound, and are very much concerned lest it result in control of Air units by ground forces."[10]

Kuter returned to the United States and on May 22 held a press conference to discuss air lessons from the North African campaign. His conception of the role of tactical air power was clear: "The function of the tactical air force is one of working in partnership with other components of air power, with the strategical bombing force which uses the longest range bombers on relatively long-term targets." He also cautioned: "It is easy to say that it gives air support to the army, but the word 'support' has now so many old-fashioned and wrong implications in the public mind that it is much better not to use it," since the term brought "to mind a picture of bombing to extend the range of artillery." Kuter then observed that this "narrow conception of air support is firmly imbedded [*sic*] . . . particularly in the mind of the inexperienced soldier who is having his first taste of enemy bombing or strafing. . . . Although it is the method by which the Germans advanced through France . . . it is surely the method that was found to be totally obsolete and leading more toward defeat than victory in operations against a well-trained army and a well-trained Air Force in Africa."[11]

Kuter maintained that tactical air power had three missions: "Counter Air Force, first and always"; "isolation of ground units"; and "battle area bombing."[12] When the War Department published *FM 100-20: Command and Employment of Air Power* on July 21, Kuter's views became Army doctrine. The new manual was published "without the concurrence of General McNair . . . and viewed with dismay by the Ground Forces—as the Army Air Forces' 'Declaration of Independence.' "[13] The ground officers were right. The first paragraph of *FM 100-20*, set in capital letters, said it all: "RELATIONSHIP OF FORCES.—LAND POWER AND AIR POWER ARE CO-EQUAL AND INTERDEPENDENT FORCES; NEITHER IS AN AUXILIARY OF THE OTHER."[14]

Kuter knew a great victory had been achieved. On the eve of the publication of *FM 100-20*, he wrote to Air Marshal Coningham, telling him that the manual made the air forces and ground forces coequal and that "more people were defeated in Tunisia than Germans and Italians."[15] General Arnold, also enthusiastic, moved to ensure that the new doctrine received wide dissemination by ordering that every officer in the Air Forces be given a copy of the manual "to read and study."[16]

The institutional implications of *FM 100-20* for the Army Air Forces were obvious—the twenty-five-year intraservice battle over who would control air power and how it could best be employed was largely won. The manual stated, again in all capital letters, that

THE INHERENT FLEXIBILITY OF AIR POWER, IS ITS GREATEST ASSET. THIS FLEXIBILITY MAKES IT POSSIBLE TO EMPLOY THE WHOLE WEIGHT OF THE AVAILABLE AIR POWER AGAINST SELECTED AREAS IN TURN; SUCH CONCENTRATED USE OF THE AIR STRIKING FORCE IS A BATTLE WINNING FACTOR OF THE FIRST IMPORTANCE. CONTROL OF AVAILABLE AIR POWER MUST BE CENTRALIZED AND COMMAND MUST BE EXERCISED THROUGH THE AIR FORCE COMMANDER IF THIS INHERENT FLEXIBILITY AND ABILITY TO DELIVER A DECISIVE BLOW ARE TO BE FULLY EXPLOITED. THEREFORE, THE COMMAND OF AIR AND GROUND FORCES IN A THEATER OF OPERATIONS WILL BE VESTED IN THE SUPERIOR COMMANDER CHARGED WITH THE ACTUAL CONDUCT OF OPERATIONS IN THE THEATER, WHO WILL EXERCISE COMMAND OF AIR FORCES THROUGH THE AIR FORCE COMMANDER AND COMMAND OF GROUND FORCES THROUGH THE GROUND FORCE COMMANDER. THE SUPERIOR COMMANDER WILL NOT ATTACH ARMY AIR FORCES TO UNITS OF THE GROUND FORCES UNDER HIS COMMAND EXCEPT WHEN SUCH GROUND FORCE UNITS ARE OPERATING INDEPENDENTLY OR ARE ISOLATED BY DISTANCE OR LACK OF COMMUNICATION.[17]

Aside from who would command air power, the manual had other significant ramifications for ground officers, because it stated explicitly what they could expect from the air forces. Operations of the strategic air forces, whose goal was "the defeat of the enemy nation," were dealt with first. Only in situations "when the action is vital and decisive" would they be diverted to tactical air force missions. The tactical air forces were also remote from the ground battle. *FM 100-20* categorized air superiority, isolation of the battle-field, and battlefield support of ground units as the three phases of operations. In this hierarchy, battlefield support had third priority. Furthermore, even within this third priority, missions against enemy units or "contact zone missions" were downplayed as expensive and consequently critical only when they were "profitable."[18]

In the months that followed the issuance of *FM 100-20*, little emphasis or direction was given to close air support by the Army Air Forces. As late as May 1944 a report from a conference at the Headquarters, Third Air Force, noted that "much attention has been placed during this war on the development of equipment and tactics for fighter and heavy bombardment aviation, but that the problem of close air-ground cooperation has been given less consideration." The report went on to caution: "The approaching invasion of Europe will undoubtedly demand an extensive close support of the ground forces by all types of aviation except heavy bombardment." The report also stated that in the absence of central direction, "new and different tactics [were] being developed for the support of ground troops in each active theatre separately."[19] Major General Westside T. Larson, commander of the Third Air Force, wrote to General Arnold on May 22 and "urgently recommended" that the Headquarters, Army Air Forces, provide the "centralized coordination" needed in "the development of appropriate weapons, equipment, tactics and technique, and organization of air units employed in air-ground cooperation."[20]

The Army Air Forces had little time to act on Larson's recommendations before the Allied armies landed in Normandy on June 6. General Quesada, in the absence of any written close air support doctrine, created his own. He had also helped General Bradley plan the air support for the June 22 attack on the Cherbourg peninsula. Even though the ground forces had requested "the total effort of both the Eighth and Ninth Air Forces" to support the attack, Air Marshal Coningham decided that the "desired effort could be accomplished by the Tactical Air Forces and would be limited there-to."[21]

The First Army had mixed opinions about the results of the Cherbourg air attack. Ground officers noted that the effect on the "enemy's will to resist" was less than expected and that the Germans still fought hard. Nevertheless, the bombing of individual strong points had been effective.[22] Given a choice, however, ground officers indicated that they preferred fighter bombers over medium bombers because of "the close coordination of ground and air due to very high frequency radio (VHF) communications."[23]

Bradley believed that even though the "bombing at Cherbourg was not notably effective," better results could probably be expected with heavy bombers.[24] For COBRA, he planned to use air power to lay a rectangular "carpet" of bombs, 7,000 yards wide and 2,500 yards deep, over the enemy positions in front of the VII Corps.[25] On July 19 the First Army was in position just north of the road connecting St. Lô and Périers, a small town to the northwest. Bradley believed the conditions were right to initiate COBRA.

General Bradley flew to the Allied Expeditionary Air Forces (AEAF) headquarters at Stanmore, England, to confer with air planners. There he and Quesada met with "a platoon of senior air commanders" that included Air Chief Marshall Sir Arthur Tedder, Eisenhower's deputy; Air Chief Marshall Sir Trafford Leigh-Mallory, AEAF; General Carl Spaatz, U.S. Strategic Air Forces in Europe; Major General James Doolittle, Eighth Air Force; and Major General Lewis Brereton, Ninth Air Force. Aside from these commanders, Professor Solly Zuckerman, one of the principal Allied bombing analysts, and Brigadier General F. H. Smith Jr., the director of operations, AEAF, also participated in the meeting.[26]

Bradley explained COBRA and then asked that light fragmentation bombs be used to avoid any cratering that might slow down the VII Corps's advance. He further recommended a bomb line 800 yards from his troops and that the attacking airplanes follow a route parallel to this line to lessen the chance of hitting friendly forces. The air officers agreed to plan their bomb loads to preclude cratering and asked Bradley to allow 3,000 yards between the target and his forces. Bradley was reluctant to pull his troops back from positions they had bought so dearly but eventually compromised and accepted a 1,500-yard safety margin.[27]

There remained one contentious issue—the route the airplanes would fly. Bradley insisted the air attack be made parallel to his lines, using the St. Lô–Périers road as a guide. The air officers were just as adamant that they fly perpendicular to the friendly positions and maintained that the bombing would be more accurate using this approach. Additionally, they could deliver their bombs much more quickly, preventing congestion over the target, and their plan would lessen exposure to German flak.

Bradley and Quesada left the meeting thinking they had prevailed on the bombing approach issue. Perhaps the fact that the bombers had flown a parallel course during the Cherbourg operation conditioned them to this assumption. The air officers continued their preparations, believing they had made their views understood to Bradley. To them, the attack route was a technical issue. They canvassed their bombardiers, who verified the notion that the perpendicular approach was superior. They were well within their authority under *FM 100-20*, as coequals of Bradley, to make such a decision.[28]

The start time, or H hour, for COBRA was delayed by bad weather until 1300 hours, July 24. Air Chief Marshal Sir Trafford Leigh-Mallory joined

Bradley at his command post. Leigh-Mallory's decision that the mission would be postponed because of poor visibility in the operational area was too late. The Eighth Air Force units had already taken off and could not be recalled from England. Nor could the forces in France stop the bombers—they did not have the Eighth Air Force's radio frequencies. Nearly 1,600 heavy bombers headed for the target on a course perpendicular to Bradley's lines. Although the majority of these bombers were diverted from the target area because of poor visibility, some bombed and most of those had satisfactory results. Unfortunately, a number missed the target, largely due to human errors. The costs were tragic: The 30th Division suffered 25 deaths, 131 soldiers were wounded, and three bombers were lost to flak.[29]

The VII Corps was in disarray from both the bombing and the uncertainty over whether to continue with COBRA. General Bradley was incensed when he learned that the bombers had come in over his soldiers instead of parallel to the St. Lô–Périers road. Leigh-Mallory told Bradley that the route had been flown intentionally. Furthermore, a course change for the bombers would force a several-day postponement of the offensive. Bradley, under pressure to continue the offensive, and worried that he would lose surprise, consented to another perpendicular attack on July 25.[30]

On July 25, 1,507 heavy bombers, 380 medium bombers, and 559 fighter bombers flew over the American lines along the St. Lô–Périers road. As the first formations completed their runs, dust and smoke from the bomb explosions obscured the target area. Again, as on the previous day, air crews made errors. Bombs from thirty-five heavy bombers and forty-two medium bombers fell on the ground troops. The losses were appalling: 111 dead and 490 wounded. The Air Forces lost six bombers. Among the dead was an observer from the Army Ground Forces, Lieutenant General Lesley J. McNair.[31]

In the aftermath of the COBRA tragedy, Bradley staunchly maintained that he had been misled by the air planners. Quesada supported Bradley's claim. The air officers asserted, just as vigorously, that they thought Bradley had approved their plans.[32] What neither side seemed to understand was that the mistakes that occurred during COBRA were, if not inevitable, highly likely, because existing doctrine gave lowest priority to the close support of ground operations. Indeed, the existing doctrine precluded the use of the heavy bomber in a tactical role except when such action would be "vital and decisive."[33]

COBRA was such a mission, but unfortunately neither the ground nor the air officers had given much thought to using bombers in this role. Consequently, the necessary control measures—radio communications between bombers and ground forces, clearly visible targets, and agreed-upon approach routes—were never developed or practiced. Finally, given the intense interwar struggle for control of the aerial weapon between the air advocates and a conservative War Department hierarchy, it would have been surprising if such a doctrine had been developed.

Conclusion

The sober realities of combat revealed the serious flaws in the technological assumptions underpinning the U.S. Army's tank and airplane doctrines. American tanks had to fight superior German tanks, and unescorted heavy bomber formations could not defend themselves against enemy fighter attacks without incurring unacceptable losses. Both doctrines had to be adapted to the realities of war, and the decisiveness expected by American planners from the tank and the heavy bomber was never fully realized. Instead, each machine simply became another weapon in America's arsenal of attrition. Unfortunately, the Army's tank and bomber crews paid the price for the doctrinal failures.

Why did the Army make its decisions about tanks and airplanes? Why were American armor and air doctrines mutually exclusive, even in the face of an apparently successful model, the German blitzkrieg, that emphasized cooperation between air and ground forces? Answers to these questions are elusive. Clearly, many external factors influenced the Army's development of tanks and airplanes. Both weapons evolved during the interwar period, when the Army was struggling to adapt to the changing nature of war in a period of constrained budgets and rapid technological change. Nevertheless, the airplane enjoyed a number of advantages over the tank. The airplane had more clearly demonstrated its potential during World War I than the tank had. It was also a "dual-use" technology that had an important civilian dimension that the tank did not. In the years following World War I industrial and research organizations achieved further developments in aviation—developments that relied heavily on requirements from the Army's air arm. Quite simply, the tank technology lacked this commercial utility, because it "could not be used in civilian life. . . . Therefore, armored warfare was technologically feasible but not technologically necessary."[1] Finally, largely because of its commercial utility, the airplane had a substantial congressional constituency that pushed for its advance.

The domestic and international conditions between the wars also influenced the development of tanks and airplanes. In the aftermath of World War I, there was no immediate threat to U.S. national security. American defense policy focused on disarmament and isolation. Consequently, military preparedness received little emphasis from an economy-minded Congress. Given this absence of civilian interest in the Army, Edward Katzenbach's conclusion about the cavalry, perhaps the most traditional branch in the Army, rings true:

> When there was no interest in the military, as in the United States, there was no pressure to change, and the professional was given tacit leave to romanticize an untenable situation. Thus the U.S. Horse Cavalry remained a sort of monument to public irresponsibility in this, the most mechanized nation on earth.[2]

Ironically, this absence of civilian interest in anything related to the military during the interwar period also influenced the development of American strategic bombing doctrine. In contrast to the ground army, in which civilian ambivalence supported conservatism, in the air arm this disinterest and the absence of oversight created a permissive environment within which an offensive doctrine, focused on bombing industrial targets and clearly at odds with the isolationist policies of the United States, could be developed.

During the Great Depression the United States faced a domestic economic crisis. To meet domestic needs Congress trimmed already-slim military budgets. In the late 1930s, when the international situation presented a threat to national interests, the War Department began to receive more adequate budgets. Even then the airplane maintained its advantage over the tank. When military policies focused on hemispheric defense, heavy bombers could augment the Navy in defending the nation and its possessions from enemy attack. Finally, when the United States entered the war, the Eighth Air Force was the only way to take the war directly to the German homeland.

These interwar conditions explain what on the surface seems to be a compelling justification for any failures by the War Department. Major General John S. Wood, a wartime armored division commander, stated the argument eloquently:

> Back to normalcy was the post-war slogan, and back to normalcy the post-war Army went, struggling to keep alive a flickering flame and faltering spirit of national preparedness, struggling to maintain and modernize its arms and

equipment, and struggling for its very life to obtain the funds necessary for its meager existence. Back it went to promotions few and far between, to small posts and small units, and to the apathy that follows periods of high endeavor.[3]

Though the essence of Wood's argument was that the Army did the best it could under austere conditions, the evidence indicates otherwise. When the United States entered World War II, budgetary constraints were no longer an issue, but Army leaders apparently saw no reason to analyze tank and airplane technologies and doctrines. Instead, existing designs were rushed into mass production to support already-sanctioned doctrines.

Internal arrangements—culture, prevailing paradigms, and bureaucratic politics—exercised the most pervasive influence on how the War Department responded to the potential of tanks and airplanes and exacerbated the effects of external factors.[4] Ironically, the Army had faced these same weaknesses before World War I. Major General Johnson Hagood, a member of the War Department General Staff before World War I, argued in 1927: "Our unpreparedness did not come from lack of money, lack of soldiers, or lack of supplies. It came from lack of brains, or perhaps it would be fairer to say, lack of genius." Hagood also noted the difficulty in addressing the Army's deficiencies: "Why, seeing these things did I not do something to correct them? The answer is that I did not see them, or seeing them did not understand. Hindsight is better than foresight."[5]

Hagood was unable to gauge events accurately because of the culture surrounding his career. The challenge he faced before World War I was similar to the one his successors encountered during the interwar period: immersion in the day-to-day realities of an Army making the difficult cultural and institutional transitions from frontier constabulary to modern army, from absolute faith in man and animal to reliance on machines and science.

The prevailing internal dynamics of the post–World War I Army were perpetuated in the National Defense Act of 1920. This legislation, reflecting the perspectives of the Army's ranking officers, abolished the wartime Tank Corps, thus submerging the tank within the infantry until 1931, when the cavalry was allowed to experiment with mechanization. The act also created the Air Service as a branch within the War Department hierarchy. Quite simply, the act engendered a constituency for the airplane within the Army—one vitally interested in its advancement—and abolished the structure that might have nurtured the tank. The future of U.S. Army aviation was in the hands of advocates; the potential of the tank was controlled by traditionalists, largely satisfied with the existing doctrines and technologies.[6]

The decisions in the Defense Act were not, in the context of the times in which they were made, particularly surprising. The airplane had demonstrated its immense potential in World War I; the tank had not. The airplane had vocal champions during the congressional hearings on Army reorganization after the war, many of whom pressed for a separate aviation service equivalent to the Army and Navy; most of the proponents for the continuance of the Tank Corps believed, as did officers in other branches, that it was an adjunct of the infantry. Therefore, the decision to place the Infantry in charge of tank development was not particularly contentious. It went largely unchallenged.

Still, little should be presumed about the impact the presence of an independent tank arm might have had within the U.S. Army. The British example is instructive here. Even though an independent Royal Tank Corps existed in the British Army, it still had to contend with the entrenched infantry, cavalry, and artillery branches for constrained resources and acceptance. Consequently, the tank arm remained immersed in the British Army, of which it was clearly a component. Given the ascendance of these same branches in the U.S. Army, the highly decentralized nature of the War Department that sanctioned the prerogatives of the branches, the intense competition for resources within the Army, and the absence of a civilian dimension for the tank, innovation with armor would probably not have been radically different if the Tank Corps had survived World War I as a separate branch. Like the other branches, it would likely have focused on its own parochial interests. Given these dynamics within the U.S. Army, it is doubtful that an independent Tank Corps would have been a catalyst for the combined-arms cooperation at the heart of German effectiveness.

Nevertheless, the National Defense Act of 1920 established the institutional parameters within which the tank would develop in the U.S. Army. From the promulgation of the act until the creation of the Armored Force in July 1940, the tank was viewed as an auxiliary of the infantry or as a way to modernize the cavalry. The biases inherent in these traditional branches shaped American tank doctrines and designs. Infantry tank designs focused on providing a weapon to aid foot soldiers in the assault against enemy machine guns and strong points; cavalry combat cars provided an "iron horse" to conduct traditional cavalry missions.

The powerful chiefs of infantry and cavalry repressed officers who advocated a broader role for tanks. Additionally, the last chief of cavalry, Major General John Herr, viewed mechanization as a threat to the continuance of horse cavalry and actively thwarted the expansion of the 7th Cavalry Brigade (Mechanized). The limit of Herr's acquiescence in technology was the formation of horse-mechanized corps reconnaissance regiments. This admixture of horse and machine was reflective of Herr's underlying approach to technology: "As always, Cavalry's motto must remain: When better roller skates are made, Cavalry horses will wear them."[7] Retention of the horse remained his absolute goal.

When the War Department created the Armored Force in response to the

German blitzkrieg, the officers who controlled the organization brought their biases with them. Major General Adna Chaffee designed the armored division to conduct traditional cavalry missions. Concurrently, the General Headquarters (GHQ) tank battalions remained in the Army, perpetuating the traditional tank role of supporting infantry. The debate within the Armored Force focused largely on organizational arrangements—the proper mix of light tanks, medium tanks, infantry, and artillery—not the appropriateness of the existing tanks or the doctrine for their employment. Further complicating doctrinal and technological decisions about tanks was Lieutenant General Lesley McNair's dogmatic support of the tank destroyer as an antitank panacea. He was a powerful man, and tank destroyers proliferated in the Army.

The creation of the Air Service provided an institution vitally concerned with the airplane's exploitation. Air officers, led at first by Brigadier General Billy Mitchell, believed that World War I proved the potential of independent air power and that only airmen could realize the full implications of military aviation. The fight to gain independence for the air arm politicized the technology and radicalized its proponents. These insurgents struggled tenaciously to wrest control of the aerial weapon from the War Department hierarchy, whom they believed repressed the potential of air power.

In the early 1930s a doctrine that would ostensibly prove the decisiveness of air power began to evolve—unescorted, high-altitude, daylight precision bombing of the industrial infrastructure of an enemy nation. Crucial to this concept was the assumption that heavy bomber formations could defend themselves during long-range penetrations to attack the enemy's centers of production. The B-17 seemed to offer the technology to realize this goal.

By World War II the bomber advocates, having gained control of the air arm, had simply overwhelmed any air officers critical of their doctrine. Since prevailing military authority believed that the success of bombardment was not contingent on long-range escort fighters, the development of this type of airplane received low priority. Additionally, since the bomber proponents viewed air power as a decisive, independent force, they paid little attention to the support of ground forces. They feared that this role could restrict their hard-won autonomy, because ground officers would almost certainly control such a mission.

Consequently, the Army Air Forces entered World War II with an institutional imperative to prove the decisiveness of strategic bombing. If it failed, there could be no justification for the long-cherished goal of an independent air force. Therefore, the Army Air Forces focused on building the Eighth Air Force, and General Henry Arnold placed enormous pressure on Lieutenant General Ira Eaker to make the air campaign against Germany succeed.

The structure of the War Department itself, codified in the National Defense Act of 1920, as well as the attitudes of the officers who controlled the institution, also influenced the development of tanks and airplanes. During the interwar years the War Department became a cumbersome, decentralized bureaucracy. The powerful branch chiefs were allowed to develop doctrines and technologies for their arms with little direction from above or integration with the other branches. They proved largely incapable of critical self-analysis, consistently interpreting reports from the Spanish civil war, the invasion of Poland, the fall of France, and the Battle of Britain in ways that supported their predilections. To the chief of infantry the lesson was clear—tanks were most effective as infantry support weapons. The chief of cavalry concluded that the horse was still a vital factor in war. The head of the Armored Force saw German blitzkrieg tactics as validation of mechanized cavalry concepts. And air officers saw aerial successes as validation of their views and elected to see failures as incorrect applications of fundamental air power principles. The War Department provided little leadership, critical or otherwise, to sort out these matters; the nominal head of the institution was not in control of the component parts. Thus, innovation in the interwar Army was constrained by unquestioned faith in ruling paradigms—paradigms that shaped perceptions of external experiences.

The Army school system, rather than serving as an agent for change, focused almost completely on accepted doctrine. In the absence of practical opportunities in the field, officers learned the intricacies of maneuvering and supporting large units through exercises, mainly in Army schools. The Command and General Staff School trained officers for duty at division, corps, and army level and "dealt exclusively with professional military subjects."[8] The Army War College prepared its students for command and staff at and above the army level and for service on the War Department General Staff. Finally, the Army Industrial College opened in 1924 to school officers in wartime procurement and industrial mobilization. Collectively, the schools focused on developing officers who could supervise the mobilization, fighting, and supplying of a mass army along World War I lines. As one scholar of the Army War College noted, the institution

> failed to produce a Clausewitz, Mahan, Liddell Hart, or Quincy Wright. It contributed only marginally to any body of theory on the phenomenon of war. But that had not been its aim. Its aim had been utilitarian—to produce competent, if not necessarily brilliant, leadership that could prepare the Army for war and fight a war successfully if it came.[9]

The same purpose applied generally to all of the Army's schools during the interwar era—the production of "able military practitioners," not "military theoreticians."[10] Nevertheless, the schools were a reflection of the institution they served, one dominated by senior officers who "looked with satisfaction on the achievements of World War I, and were cautious and conservative in their outlook."[11] Although the Command and General Staff School at Fort Leavenworth, was generally viewed as the "source of Army doctrine and procedure," it was clearly a captive of the Army's sanctioned doctrine.[12] Instruction remained riveted on conservative doctrines, largely ignoring emerging, competitive perspectives such as mechanization and air power.

The curriculum of the 1938–39 regular course is a good example of the conservatism reigning at Leavenworth. It contained 198 hours of instruction on the World War I–vintage four-regiment, "square" infantry division. The study of mechanized units and tanks merited only 29 hours and aviation a mere 13 hours of the students' time—small wonder many air officers believed "it was silly to send air officers to the Command and General Staff School for 2 years to learn the minutia of ground officers' duties."[13] In April 1939 the War Department sent Brigadier General Lesley J. McNair to Leavenworth to modernize the course of instruction. McNair accomplished little. Before he could significantly change the regular course at Leavenworth, the War Department curtailed it, as well as the courses at the War and Industrial Colleges. The Army needed officers in units, not classrooms, as war approached.[14]

The Command and General Staff School at Fort Leavenworth also reflected the cultural mores of an Army imbued with the upper middle class traditions of the gentleman soldier.[15] Although the notion of the "indefinable social prestige which the man on horseback, the cavalier, the hidalgo, the gentleman" possessed was perhaps most evident within the cavalry branch, the social routine at Fort Leavenworth, like that of many Army posts, revolved around horse shows, polo matches, and the hunt.[16] The course of study at the Command and General Staff School reflected and reinforced the cultural importance of the horse; as late as 1939, officers still participated in thirty-one hours of equitation.[17] Air Corps officers could substitute flying for equitation, but on the days they did not fly they had to join their classmates in learning the "proper adjustment of the saddle and bridle and to riding at all gaits with a comfortable seat."[18] Most students had little problem with the requirement. A survey of the class of 1939 showed that more than half of the respondents favored equitation in the curriculum, an indication of the importance of horsemanship in officer culture.[19]

Army culture had another pervasive influence over the officer corps. Throughout the interwar era, the values of an American society caught up in "the business liberalism of the 1920's and the reform liberalism of the 1930's" was bothersome to Regular Army officers. That the country was seemingly "abandoning its moral anchor and venturing out into a chaotic sea of pragmatism and relativism" was anathema to a conservative officer corps wedded to a belief in the moral superiority of the military life. The result of this conflict of values was "the isolation forced upon the military by the hostility of a liberal society" and "a renewed emphasis upon military values, and a renewed awareness of the gulf between military values and those values prevalent in American society."[20] One officer wrote in 1936 that "if a man cannot find satisfaction in living a purely military life, he should get out of the army. . . . The soldier and the civilian belong to separate classes of society."[21]

Of all the military values, one ranked the highest: loyalty. Loyalty was the "cardinal military virtue" stressed during the interwar years, a trait clearly at odds with the prevailing societal value of individualism. Loyalty placed bounds on initiative, since it required "loyal identification with, and understanding of, the desires of the superior." At the heart of this emphasis on loyalty was "a feeling that as the officer corps came to think alike, to adhere to the same body of doctrine, subjective cohesion would replace objective restraints."[22]

The Army was also largely isolated in American society, because its ethos stressed loyalty to the organization. Denied a voice in any debate over national policy, the Army turned inward. There was little tolerance within the Army for dissent. The system repressed those who agitated for change, and early advocates of a larger role for tanks quickly abandoned their cause. There were no Harts, Fullers, de Gaulles, or Guderians in the U.S. Army. The air arm was different, though. Air officers transferred their loyalty from the Army to the concept of an independent air force. The means to effect this ideal was the development of air power as a decisive, war-winning instrument independent of ground combat. In pursuit of this goal, the air arm developed its own institutional orthodoxy, to which it demanded loyalty. Bomber advocates dominated the air arm and marginalized air officers who did not share their views.

When the United States entered the war, the War Department had to be turned upside down to make it function. The new institutional arrangements that created the Army ground forces and air forces resulted in an army that was prepared to fight two separate wars—one on the ground and one in the air. Much of the basis for this internal dichotomy was the result of another factor that had determined the War Department's approach to technology and doctrine. During the interwar years the War Department and its branches, except the air arm, were in the firm grasp of a succession of ground officers bent on protecting the Army's personnel strength. When tight budgets seemingly forced a decision between men and machines, the War Department inevitably opted to cut its modernization programs to preserve its personnel. When war came, and the Army's tanks proved inferior to those of the Germans, the failure was not critical to the success of ground operations. Hence, the rapid development and fielding of a replacement for the M4 tank was not a priority. There were enough Sherman tanks to aid the infantry and armored divisions in overwhelming the Germans, although the cost to American tank crews was unnecessarily high.

Air officers viewed machines differently. They embraced technology as the crucial factor in warfare. Using machines to attack the enemy's means of producing machines was their way of war. In the quest to realize their vision, the air officers invented a doctrine that hinged on the ability of their bomber technology to meet their expectations. When, in the autumn of 1943, the Germans proved that heavy bomber formations could not survive without fighter escorts, the Army Air Forces faced a technological crisis. When the institution responded by providing escort fighters, losses were reduced to an acceptable level and the doctrine, albeit modified, was saved.

One result of the unresolved intraservice dispute over how to wage war was the U.S. Army's failure to develop a coherent doctrine to combine ground and air forces to achieve the synergy demonstrated by the Germans. A postwar review of operations in the European theater asserted that the Army's failure to develop air-ground doctrine meant that means of cooperation had to be invented extemporaneously in the field.[23] In the combat theaters, ground and air commanders were forced to create ad hoc procedures for tactical air power because their superiors provided no centralized direction. Indeed, by the end of the war, American armored doctrine had come to resemble the German blitzkrieg in that it stressed the importance of coordinating ground and air tactical operations. The final after-action report of General Omar Bradley's 12th Army Group emphasized that "the air-armor team is a most powerful combination in the breakthrough and in exploitation. . . . The use of this coordinated force, in combat, should be habitual."[24] Thus, although air support of ground operations played an important role in the Allied drive into Germany and procedures were continually improved, the initiative came from below. In the combat zones, where Americans were dying, intraservice agendas were discarded and field expedients were devised to overcome institutional inertia.

At the end of the war a general board convened to assess the performance of the U.S. forces in the European theater. Its conclusions about American armored forces were telling. Although the board's various reports declared that the doctrine in existing field manuals was essentially correct for the missions and employment of the armored division and the separate tank battalions, the board recognized that changes were necessary. Its recommendations generally reflected the lessons learned about the importance of close cooperation between tanks and infantry, stressing the integration of tanks and infantry, both in armored divisions and infantry divisions.[25] Furthermore, the board recognized that tactical air power was a necessary, and often critical, component of successful ground operations.[26]

The General Board, however, judged existing tanks inadequate to execute American armored doctrine. Fundamental to the board's analysis of American armored vehicle performance was the premise that "the European campaign demonstrated that tanks fight tanks." The board thus recommended

that the Army adopt as the *"minimum* standard for future [tank gun] development . . . [f]or exploitation tanks of an armored division, a 'gun capable of
penetrating the sides and rear of any enemy armored vehicle and the front
of any but the heaviest assault tank,' at normal tank fighting ranges." Even
reconnaissance (light) tanks required a gun able to penetrate the "sides and
rear of any enemy armored vehicle."[27] The board also specified the protection required for future infantry support tanks: "Frontal armor and armor
over ammunition stowage must be capable of withstanding all foreign tank
and anti-tank weapons at normal combat ranges."[28]

The acknowledgment that "tanks fight tanks" led ineluctably to the conclusion that tank destroyers were unnecessary. Armored division commanders believed that given "the trend to tanks with high velocity weapons
capable of destroying other tanks," there was no requirement for tank destroyer units in the armored division.[29] Infantry division commanders confirmed this view: "If a tank is given to the Infantry with a proper anti-tank
gun, the division commanders favor the replacement of the tank destroyer
with a tank."[30]

The American strategic bombing effort was also assessed. The U.S. Strategic Bombing Survey, after conducting exhaustive analyses of the air war
against Germany, concluded that the use of air power in the war in Europe,
although important, "might have been employed differently or better in
some respects." Although "it brought the economy which sustained the enemy's armed forces to a virtual collapse . . . the full effects of this collapse
had not reached the enemy's front lines when they were overrun by Allied
forces."[31]

This inability of the Army Air Forces to independently end the war was
due in large measure to "battle conditions," the resilience of German industry, and the fact that formation flying resulted in bomb patterns in which
"only a portion [of the bombs] could fall on small precision targets." The
survey surmised that during bombing operations over Germany, "only
about 20% of the bombs aimed at precision targets fell within this target area
[within 1,000 feet of the aiming point]."[32]

In the blinding flash of the nuclear detonation in Hiroshima, Japan, the
criticisms of the bombing campaign in Europe became largely irrelevant.
With the advent of the atomic bomb, air power seemed to become the decisive force envisioned by a generation of American bomber advocates. The
destructive capability of air power no longer hinged on precision bombing
or large formations of bombers fighting their way to enemy industrial centers. Instead, a single aircraft could deliver an overwhelming blow against
virtually any target, as the *Enola Gay* had done at Hiroshima. The Strategic
Bombing Survey asserted that "the atomic bomb . . . raises the destructive
power of a single bomber by a factor of somewhere between 50 and 250
times, depending upon the nature and size of the target." The survey also

postulated that "given an adequate supply of atomic bombs, the B-29s based in the Marianas had sufficient strength to have effectively destroyed in a single day every Japanese city with a population in excess of 30,000 people."[33]

Air officers quickly grasped the implications of this revolution in destructive power. In the aftermath of the bombing of Hiroshima, Army Chief of Staff General George Marshall sent a message to General Carl Spaatz, commanding general of U.S. Army Strategic Air Forces in the Pacific, asking him to refrain from commenting on the implications of the bomb. Marshall told Spaatz that he was "being widely quoted in [news]papers . . . regarding results of such a bomb on landings on Normandy, to the effect that our present Army is not necessary for the further prosecution of the war in the Pacific and tha[t] an invasion will be unnecessary."[34] Spaatz apologized to Marshall for any possible embarrassment he may have caused but added that he had told the press that "if such a bomb had been available early in the European War it might have shortened the war by about six months."[35]

Ironically, the atomic bomb fundamentally reframed the debate between air and ground officers: one of the points Marshall had specifically asked Spaatz to stop raising was "that the future of Armies has been decidedly curtailed."[36] The Strategic Bombing Survey, although not seeing an end to the need for armies, predicted that "the context in which they are employed [has changed] to such a degree that radically changed equipment, training, and tactics will be required."[37] In the future, the ground army would struggle to justify its existence in the context of a nuclear world largely dominated in the American defense structure by an independent U.S. Air Force. As the historian Russell Weigley has observed, "the Army in the late 1940's seemed almost irrelevant. . . . To the extent Americans saw the Communist threat as a military threat, their answer to it was simply the American atomic monopoly. . . . The United States would win such a war with air-atomic power."[38]

The story of the Army's development of the tank and the airplane between the wars has implications beyond either the technologies or the times. Although internal arrangements were the most important factor in how the Army developed these weapons, a central paradox lurks in this conclusion. The tank was developed in an environment in which its advocates were suppressed and the technology itself was subordinated to the traditional arms. In contrast, the aims of the air power advocates were fulfilled largely because of the nurturing climate within the air arm. Nevertheless, neither weapon met its supporters' prewar expectations. In the case of the tank, innovation was stifled by traditional biases. The development of the airplane, relatively free of any constraints imposed by tradition, was guided by a generation of insurgents who viewed strategic bombing as a means to achieve their freedom from the Army. Their zealousness blinded them to the flaws inherent in the technology and the doctrine they designed around it.

Conclusion

In the final analysis, the U.S. Army that entered World War II was a re-flection of the biases and institutional arrangements that existed in the War Department throughout the interwar era. Branch parochialism, a largely powerless War Department General Staff, tension between air and ground officers, a conservative culture, and disparate views about technology all conspired to inhibit innovation and intraservice cooperation. Although the War Department's focus on personnel enabled it to create and deploy a mass army in World War II, it constrained weapons research and development throughout the interwar period.

How valid, then, is the traditional interpretation of the Army's unpre-paredness for World War II? Were congressional penury and public malaise responsible for the Army's deficiencies? What the Army would have done if it had been more generously funded can only be answered by speculation. Nevertheless, given the internal dynamics of the Army during the interwar period, more resources would probably have resulted in more of the same. The ground Army, focused on personnel mobilization, would almost surely have used any additional resources to fill the 280,000-man structure autho-rized by the National Defense Act of 1920. If it had achieved that number it probably would have pressed for more. The air arm, bent on achieving au-tonomy, just as certainly would have invested any increased funds in strate-gics that would have facilitated its long-cherished goal of independence. In short, the ground Army would have bought more personnel, and the air Army would have bought more bombers.

The Army, in short, was responsible for its own unpreparedness. Tight budgets and an isolationist-minded Congress and public were powerful constraints, but the Army would not have been ready even with adequate resources.

Notes

INTRODUCTION

1. C. V. Wedgwood, *William the Silent* (London: Cape 1967), 35; quoted in Guenter Lewy, *America in Vietnam* (Oxford, England: Oxford University Press, 1978), 420.

2. Mark Skinner Watson, *Chief of Staff: Prewar Plans and Preparations,* U.S. Army in World War II (1950; Washington, D.C., 1985), 17.

3. Martin Blumenson, "Kasserine Pass, 30 January–22 February 1943," in *America's First Battles, 1776–1965,* ed. Charles E. Heller and William A. Stofft (Lawrence: University Press of Kansas, 1986), 226.

4. Allan R. Millett and Williamson Murray, *Innovation in the Interwar Period,* Contract no. MDA903-89-K-0194 Final Report (Washington, D.C.: Office of Net Assessment, 1994), i–viii. See also Gordon R. Sullivan and Anthony M. Corrales, *The Army in the Information Age* (Carlisle Barracks: U.S. Army War College, Strategic Studies Institute, 1995), 15–21.

5. Robert A. Doughty, *The Seeds of Disaster: The Development of French Army Doctrine, 1919–1939* (Hamden, Conn.: Archon Books, 1985), 190.

6. Williamson Murray, "Armored Warfare: The British, French, and German Experiences," in *Military Innovation in the Interwar Period,* ed. Williamson Murray and Allan R. Millett (Cambridge, England: Cambridge University Press, 1996), 12–13.

7. Doughty, 182.

8. Larry H. Addington, *The Blitzkrieg Era and the German General Staff, 1865–1941* (New Brunswick, N.J.: Rutgers University Press, 1971), 31.

9. Doughty, 4.

10. Eugenia C. Kiesling, *Arming against Hitler: France and the Limits of Military Planning* (Lawrence: University Press of Kansas, 1996), 143, 140.

11. Donald J. Harvey, "French Concepts of Military Strategy, 1919–1939" (Ph.D. diss., Columbia University, 1953), 137; quoted in Barry R. Posen, *The Sources of Military Doctrine: France, Britain, and Germany between the World Wars* (Ithaca, N.Y.: Cornell University Press), 131.

12. Murray, "Armored Warfare," 32.

13. Kiesling, 150, 151, 171.

14. Charles de Gaulle, *Vers l'armée de métier* (1934), published in English as *The Army of the Future* (1941; Westport, Conn.: Greenwood, 1976).

15. Doughty, 38, 11–12, 161.

16. Murray, "Armored Warfare," 34.

17. André Beaufre, *The Fall of France* (New York: Knopf, 1968), 43, quoted ibid.

18. Posen, 134.

19. Allan R. Millett, "Patterns of Military Innovation in the Interwar Period," in Murray and Millett, 364.

20. Posen, 224.

21. Murray, "Armored Warfare," 9–12.

22. Ibid., 11.

23. Harold R. Winton, *To Change an Army: General Sir John Burnett-Stuart and British Armored Doctrine, 1927–1938* (Lawrence: University Press of Kansas, 1988), 232.

24. Murray, "Armored Warfare," 23.

25. Ibid., 20, 25.

26. Ibid., 24; and Winton, 225.

27. Winton, 27.

28. Murray, "Armored Warfare," 26.

29. A. A. Montgomery-Massingberd, "The Autobiography of a Gunner," 53, in Montgomery-Massingberd Papers; quoted in Winton, 97.

30. Winton, 116–20.

31. Ibid., 225.

32. Ibid., 204, 231.

33. Frederick E. Morgan, *Peace and War: A Soldier's Life* (London: Hodder & Stoughton, 1961), 134; quoted in Winton, 220.

34. Murray, "Armored Warfare," 11.

35. Winton, 220.

36. Williamson Murray, "Strategic Bombing: The British, American, and German Experiences," in Murray and Millett, 104.

37. Richard R. Muller, "Close Air Support: The German, British, and American Experiences, 1918–1941," in Murray and Millett, 170.

38. Wing Commander R. H. M. S. Saundby, "Lecture: Small Wars, with Particular Reference to Air Control in Semi-Civilized Countries," RAF Staff College, 19th Course, 1936; quoted in Muller, 172.

39. Muller, 172, 164, 163.

40. Malcolm S. Smith, *British Air Strategy between the Wars* (Oxford, England: Clarendon Press, 1984), 76; quoted in Muller, 167.

41. Murray, "Strategic Bombing," 104.

42. Ibid., 117.

43. Ibid., 102.

44. *Hansard*, vol. 292, July 30, 1934, column 2339, quoted in Murray, 105.

45. Posen, 146.

46. Murray, "Strategic Bombing," 119–20.

47. Posen, 173.

48. Charles Webster and Noble Frankland, *The Strategic Air Offensive against Germany, 1939–1945*, 4 vols. (London: HMSO, 1961), 1:76; quoted in Posen, 173.

49. Murray, "Strategic Bombing," 103.

50. Addington, 28–29; and James S. Corum, *The Luftwaffe: Creating the Operational Air War, 1918–1940* (Lawrence: University Press of Kansas, 1997), 49–50.

51. Murray, "Armored Warfare," 36.

52. James S. Corum, *The Roots of Blitzkrieg: Hans von Seeckt and German Military Reform* (Lawrence: University Press of Kansas, 1992), 38–39, 199; and Murray, "Armored Warfare," 37.

53. Murray, "Armored Warfare," 37, 38. Emphasis in original.

54. Addington, 25–26.

55. Ibid., 25–27.

56. Ibid., 30.

57. Hans von Seeckt, *Thoughts of a Soldier*, trans. Gilbert Waterhouse (London: Ernest Benn, 1930), 17; quoted in Corum, *Roots of Blitzkrieg*, 31.

58. Corum, *Roots of Blitzkrieg*, 31.

59. Addington, 29–30.

60. Corum, *Roots of Blitzkrieg*, 198.

61. Murray, "Armored Warfare," 39–40.

62. Corum, *Roots of Blitzkrieg*, 190–97.

63. Murray, "Armored Warfare," 39, 42.

64. Addington, 35.

65. Posen, 208–13.

66. Murray, "Armored Warfare," 41–42.

67. Ibid., 209–11; Addington, 36. See also Murray, "Armored Warfare," 41. Murray notes: "This is not meant to suggest that Guderian had no role, but rather to underline his considerable overestimation and exaggeration of his importance in his memoirs *Panzer Leader.* In fact, the reader should be warned that of all the memoirs by senior German generals (and there are many) Guderian's number among the most dishonest *and* misleading."

68. Addington, 36–38; and Corum, *Roots of Blitzkrieg*, 199–200.

69. Addington, 37.

70. Murray, "Armored Warfare," 42.

71. Murray, "Armored Warfare," 47.

72. Ibid., 42–43.

73. Corum, *Roots of Blitzkrieg*, 198.

74. Murray, "Armored Warfare," 42, 43.

75. Williamson Murray, *Strategy for Defeat: The Luftwaffe, 1939–1945* (Maxwell Air Force Base: Air University Press, 1983), 19.

76. Corum, *Luftwaffe*, 284.

77. Ibid., 75–76.

78. Addington, 42–43.

79. Ibid., 43, 44.

80. Williamson Murray, "The Luftwaffe Experience, 1939–1941," in *Case Studies in the Development of Close Air Support*, ed. Benjamin Franklin Cooling (Washington, D.C.: Office of Air Force History, 1990), 104.

81. Murray, *Strategy for Defeat*, 15–16; Corum, *Luftwaffe*, 274–75.

82. Murray, "Strategic Bombing," 111, 132, 133, 135.

83. Muller, "Close Air Support," in Murray and Millett, 175, 176.

84. Lt. Col. Edward C. Johnson, *Marine Corp Aviation: The Early Years, 1921–1940* (Washington, D.C., 1977), 35; quoted in Muller, "Close Air Support," 176.

85. Barry Watts and Williamson Murray, "Military Innovation in Peacetime," in Murray and Millett, 394.

86. Geoffrey Till, "Adopting the Aircraft Carrier: The British, American, and Japanese Case Studies," in Murray and Millett, 211.

87. Edward L. Katzenbach Jr., "Tradition and Technological Change," in *American De-*

fense Policy, 5th ed., ed. John F. Reichart and Steven R. Sturm (Baltimore: Johns Hopkins University Press, 1982), 639, 649. This is a reprint with minor revisions of Edward L. Katzenbach Jr., "The Horse Cavalry in the Twentieth Century," *Public Policy* 7 (1958): 120–49.

88. Posen, 173–75.

89. Stephen Peter Rosen, *Winning the Next War: Innovation and the Modern Military* (Ithaca, N.Y.: Cornell University Press, 1991), 4–5.

90. Ibid., 251, 255.

91. Brian Bond and Martin Alexander, "Liddell Hart and De Gaulle: The Doctrines of Limited Liability and Mobile Defense," in *Makers of Modern Strategy: From Machiavelli to the Nuclear Age*, ed. Peter Paret (Princeton, N.J.: Princeton University Press, 1986), 623.

92. Carl H. Builder, *The Masks of War: American Military Strategy and Analysis* (Baltimore: Johns Hopkins University Press, 1989), 3, 27.

93. Morton H. Halperin, *Bureaucratic Politics and Foreign Policy* (Washington, D.C.: Brookings Institution, 1974); James Q. Wilson, *Bureaucracy: What Government Agencies Do and Why They Do It* (New York: Basic Books, 1989); and Michael H. Armacost, *The Politics of Weapons Innovation: The Thor-Jupiter Controversy* (New York: Columbia University Press, 1969).

94. Thomas S. Kuhn, *The Structure of Scientific Revolutions*, 2d ed. (Chicago: University of Chicago Press, 1970).

95. Murray and Millett, *Military Innovation in the Interwar Period*, 3.

96. Barry Watts and Williamson Murray, "Military Innovation in Peacetime," in Murray and Millett, 381.

CHAPTER 1

1. Quoted in T. Harry Williams, *The History of American Wars from 1745 to 1918* (Baton Rouge: Louisiana State University Press, 1985), 375.

2. Quoted in Charles Seymour, *The Intimate Papers of Colonel House*, 2 vols. (Boston: Houghton Mifflin, 1926), 2:472.

3. Russell F. Weigley, *History of the United States Army*, 2d ed. (Bloomington: Indiana University Press, 1984), 265–342; and C. Joseph Bernardo and Eugene H. Bacon, *American Military Policy: Its Development since 1775* (Harrisburg, Pa.: Military Service Publishing Co., 1955), 274–313.

4. Williams, 380.

5. Weigley, 357–58; and Peter Young and Michael Calvert, *A Dictionary of Battles, 1816–1976* (New York: Mayflower Books, 1977), 321–22.

6. Correlli Barnett, *The Swordbearers: Supreme Command in the First World War* (New York: William Morrow, 1964), 215.

7. Edward M. Coffman, *The War to End All Wars: The American Military Experience in World War I* (1968; Madison: University of Wisconsin Press, 1986), 8.

8. Coffman, 156–57; and Weigley, 358.

9. A. Hunter Dupree, *Science in the Federal Government: A History of Policies and Activities to 1940* (Cambridge: Harvard University Press, Belknap Press), 303; Coffman, 38–39; and Daniel J. Kevles, *The Physicists: The History of a Scientific Community in Modern America* (New York: Alfred A. Knopf, 1978), 103, 132.

10. Thomas P. Hughes, *American Genesis: A Century of Invention and Technological Enthusiasm* (New York: Viking, 1989), 96–137.

11. Coffman, 35–42.

12. Edward M. Coffman, *The Hilt of the Sword: The Career of Peyton C. March* (Madison: University of Wisconsin Press, 1966), 54, 134–51; Weigley, 378–80; and Williams, 404.

13. Williams, 398.

14. Barnett, 336–61; and Young and Calvert, 334.

15. Barnett, 356.

16. Coffman, *Hilt of the Sword*, 171.

17. "Report of Superior Board on Organization and Tactics," July 1, 1919; Records of the Chiefs of Arms, Office of the Chief of Cavalry, Correspondence, 1921–1942 (OCC), Box 13, Record Group 177 (RG 177), National Archives (NA), Washington, D.C., 1–4. Hereafter cited as "Report of Superior Board." The board included Major General J. T. Dickman (senior member), Major General J. L. Hines, Major General William Lassiter, Brigadier General Hugh A. Drum, Brigadier General W. B. Burtt, Colonel George R. Spaulding, and Colonel Parker Hitt.

18. Ibid., 5. Emphasis in original.

19. Ulysses Lee, *The Employment of Negro Troops: U.S. Army in World War II* (Washington, D.C., 1966), 3–20; Morris J. MacGregor, *Integration of the Armed Forces*, Defense Studies Series (Washington, D.C., 1981), 3–7; Mattie E. Treadwell, *The Women's Army Corps: U.S. Army in World War II* (Washington, D.C., 1954), 3–5; Samuel P. Huntington, *The Soldier and the State: The Theory and Politics of Civil Military Relations* (Cambridge: Harvard University Press, Belknap Press, 1957), 257–66, 297; and Weigley, 290–91.

20. Roger J. Spiller, Joseph G. Dawson III, and T. Harry Williams, eds., *Dictionary of American Military Biography*, 3 vols. (Westport, Conn.: Greenwood, 1984), 1:263–64.

21. Huntington, 237–40; and Timothy K. Nenninger, *The Leavenworth Schools and the Old Army: Education, Professionalism, and the Officer Corps of the United States Army, 1881–1918* (Westport, Conn.: Greenwood, 1978), 21–33.

22. Michael J. Krisman, ed., *Register of Graduates and Former Cadets of the United States Military Academy, 1802–1973* (West Point, N.Y.: Association of Graduates, U.S. Military Academy, 1973), 90, 296, 302; and Spiller, Dawson, and Williams, 1:279–82, 472–75.

23. "Report of Superior Board," 18, 20.

24. Young and Calvert, 335–36.

25. "Report of Superior Board," 20.

26. John J. Pershing, *My Experiences in the World War* (New York: Stokes, 1931), 2:189–90; quoted in Weigley, 389.

27. Weigley, 393; and "Report of Superior Board," 18–62, 132–84.

28. Weigley, 392.

29. "Report of Superior Board," 64–65, 77–78.

30. U.S. War Department, *War Department Annual Reports, 1919* (Washington, D.C., 1920), 480. Hereafter all (1919–1939) cited as *War Department Annual Report*, followed by the year.

31. "Report of Superior Board," 77–78.

32. Coffman, *Hilt of the Sword*, 175–76.

33. Peyton C. March, *The Nation at War* (Garden City, N.Y.: Doubleday, Doran, 1932), 331–33; and *War Department Annual Report, 1919*, 60–61.

34. Coffman, *Hilt of the Sword*, 191; and Robert H. Ferrell, *Woodrow Wilson and World War I, 1917–1921*, New American Nation Series (New York: Harper & Row, 1985), 156–77.

35. Congressional Record, 66th Cong., 1st sess., vol. 58, pt. 1, 876, quoted in Coffman, *Hilt of the Sword*, 192.

36. Congress, Senate, Committee on Military Affairs, *Reorganization of the Army: Hearings before the Subcommittee of the Committee on Military Affairs*, 2 vols., 66th Cong., 1st sess., 1919, 2:1578.

37. *War Department Annual Report, 1920*, 11–14.

38. Coffman, *Hilt of the Sword*, 206–9. For an analysis of Colonel Palmer's pivotal role in the preparation of the Defense Act, see I. B. Holley Jr., *General John M. Palmer, Citizen Soldiers, and the Army of a Democracy* (Westport, Conn.: Greenwood, 1982), 402–79.

39. U.S. War Department, *Acts and Resolutions Relating to the War Department Passed during the Sixty-sixth Congress, Second Session, December 1, 1919, to June 14, 1920* (Washington, D.C., 1920), 424–36; and *War Department Annual Report, 1920*, 11–14.

CHAPTER 2

1. Tim Travers, *The Killing Ground: The British Army, the Western Front, and the Emergence of Modern Warfare, 1900–1918* (London: Allen & Unwin, 1987), 166–67, 179–81; John Keegan, *The Illustrated Face of Battle* (New York: Viking Penguin, 1988), 183; and Young and Calvert, 338.

2. Travers, 74; Chris Ellis and Peter Chamberlain, *The Great Tanks* (London: Hamlyn Publishing Group, 1975), 17; and Timothy K. Nenninger, "The Development of American Armor, 1917–1940" (M.A. thesis, University of Wisconsin, 1968), 13–14.

3. Nenninger, "Development of American Armor," 13–15; and Kenneth Macksey, *Tank versus Tank: The Illustrated Story of Armored Battlefield Conflict in the Twentieth Century* (Topsfield, Mass.: Salem House, 1988), 16–17.

4. Nenninger, "Development of American Armor," 16–17, 18–19.

5. S. D. Rockenbach, "The Tank Corps: A Talk to the General Staff, 24 Sept. 1919," typed manuscript (TMs), p. 3, U.S. Army Military History Institute (USAMHI), Carlisle Barracks, Pa. Hereafter cited as Rockenbach, "The Tank Corps."

6. American Expeditionary Forces, Office of Chief of Tank Corps, "Operations of Tank Corps A.E.F. at St. Mihiel, in the Meuse-Argonne Operation, and with the British E.F.," by S. D. Rockenbach, December 27, 1918, 2, USAMHI. Hereafter cited as "Operations of Tank Corps A.E.F."

7. Ibid.

8. U.S. Army, *The United States Army in the World War, 1917–1919*, 17 vols. (Washington, D.C., 1948), 14:221–22; and Ellis and Chamberlain, 24–26.

9. Ellis and Chamberlain, 25.

10. Ellis and Chamberlain, 24–26; and "Operations of Tank Corps A.E.F.," 2–4.

11. *United States Army in the World War*, 14:221–22; "Operations of Tank Corps A.E.F.," 4; and Ellis and Chamberlain, 26–27.

12. "Operations of Tank Corps A.E.F.," 2–5.

13. Ibid., 3–5; *United States Army in the World War*, 14:221–22.

14. Nenninger, "Development of American Armor," 26; and Ralph E. Jones, George H. Rarey, and Robert J. Icks, *The Fighting Tanks since 1916* (Washington, D.C.: National Service Publishing Co., 1933), 153–55.

15. Rockenbach, "The Tank Corps," 3.

16. Ibid.

17. Martin Blumenson, *The Patton Papers*, 2 vols. (Boston: Houghton Mifflin, 1972), 1:390, 398, 432–33.

18. Ibid., 1:433.

19. Ibid., 1:447, 449.

20. Ibid., 1:458–59.

21. "Operations of Tank Corps A.E.F.," 5.

22. Blumenson, 1:455; and Macksey, 22–23.

23. Jones, Rarey, and Icks, 157.

24. "Operations of Tank Corps A.E.F.," 4.

25. Ibid., 6.
26. U.S. War Department, Office of the Chief of Tank Corps, *Report of the Chief of the Tank Corps* (Washington, D.C., 1919), 4375.
27. Nenninger, "Development of American Armor," 33; Blumenson, 1:465–66; and *Report of the Chief of the Tank Corps* (1919), 4373.
28. "Operations of Tank Corps A.E.F.," 6.
29. Nenninger, "Development of American Armor," 34, 37.
30. "Operations of Tank Corps A.E.F.," 7.
31. Ibid.
32. Ibid., 3, 4.
33. U.S. War Department, *Infantry and Tank Co-operation and Training*, Document no. 804 (Washington, D.C., 1918), 1.
34. Ibid., 17.
35. American Expeditionary Forces, *Tanks: Organization and Tactics*, A.E.F. no. 1432, G-5 (General Headquarters, American Expeditionary Forces, France, 1918), 6.
36. Ibid., 1.
37. "Operations of Tank Corps A.E.F.," appendix 3, pp. 1–2; Nenninger, "Development of American Armor," 44–46; Jones, Rarey, and Icks, 106. The 344th and 345th Tank Battalions were originally designated the 366th and 327th Tank Battalions, respectively. Their final designations are used throughout this study.
38. Jones, Rarey, and Icks, 108; and Nenninger, "Development of American Armor," 46.
39. *United States Army in the World War*, 12:42.
40. Blumenson, 1:618–19.
41. Blumenson, 1:619–20; Nenninger, "Development of American Armor," 46–49; and Jones, Rarey, and Icks, 109–14.
42. U.S. War Department, *Final Report of Gen. John J. Pershing, Commander-in-Chief, American Expeditionary Forces* (Washington, D.C., 1920), 76.
43. Nenninger, "Development of American Armor," 49–50.
44. "The Role of Tanks in Modern Warfare," 1, 2.
45. Ibid., 3.
46. Ibid., 2, 6.
47. Ibid., 2. Emphasis in original.
48. "Report of Superior Board," 29.
49. Ibid.
50. Congress, House, Committee on Military Affairs, *Army Reorganization: Hearings before the Committee on Military Affairs*, 2 vols., 66th Cong., 1st sess., 1919, 1:59.
51. Rockenbach, "The Tank Corps," 7. Emphasis in original.
52. House, *Army Reorganization Hearings*, 1:285, 1437–38.
53. U.S. War Department, *Acts and Resolutions Relating to the War Department Passed during the Sixty-sixth Congress, Second Session, December 1, 1920* (Washington, D.C., 1920), 436.
54. U.S. War Department, Office of Chief of Tank Corps, *Report of the Chief of the Tank Corps* (Washington, D.C., 1920), 1893.

CHAPTER 3

1. Juliette A. Hennessy, *The United States Army Air Arm, April 1861 to April 1917* (Washington, D.C., 1985), 1–13.
2. R. Earl McClendon, "A Checklist of Significant Documents Relating to the Position of the United States Army Air Arm in the System of National Defense" TMs, p. 1,

239.04–17 (Feb. 1949), in USAF Collection, U.S. Air Force Historical Research Agency (USAFHRA), Maxwell Air Force Base, Ala.

3. Hennessy, 15–16.

4. Maurer Maurer, *Aviation in the U.S. Army, 1919–1939* (Washington, D.C., 1987), 371–75; and Maurer Maurer, ed., *Combat Squadrons of the Air Force: World War II* (1969; Washington, D.C., 1982), 3, 10, 18.

5. Hennessy, 20–21, 23–28, 221–25.

6. McClendon, 2, 4.

7. "Legislative Proposals for Change in Internal Relationship of Air Branch to Army," p. 1, in "Legislation on: A Separate Air Force; a Department of Aviation; a Department of National Defense, 1916–1943," February 1944, 168.04–14 (1916–1943), USAFHRA.

8. Congress, House, Committee on Military Affairs, *Hearings before the Committee on Military Affairs in Connection with H.R. 5304 May 16, 1913, Entitled "An Act to Increase the Efficiency of the Aviation Service of the Army, and for Other Purposes,"* 63rd Cong., 1st Sess., August 12, 14, 15, and 16, 1913, 51, 73–93.

9. Hearings before the Committee on Military Affairs, House of Representatives, *Aeronautics in the Army, (1919)*, in Maurer Maurer, ed., *The U.S. Air Service in World War I*, 4 vols. (Washington, D.C., 1978–79), 2:8–9.

10. Hearings, H.R. 5304, 77.

11. McClendon, 5; and "Legislative Proposals for Change in Internal Relationship of Air Branch to Army," 1.

12. War College Division, *Military Aviation* (Washington, D.C., 1916), in Maurer, *U.S. Air Service in World War I*, 2:41.

13. 39 Stat. 166 (1916), in Maurer, *U.S. Air Service in World War I*, 2:65.

14. McClendon, 5, 8.

15. I. B. Holley Jr., *Ideas and Weapons: Exploitation of the Aerial Weapon by the United States during World War I: A Study in the Relationship of Technological Advance, Military Doctrine, and the Development of Weapons* (1953; Washington, D.C., 1983), 37; and Hennessy, 196. Holley states that the number of airplanes was "200-odd," while Hennessy gives an estimate of "less than 300."

16. Hennessy, 197; Edgar S. Gorrell, *The Measure of America's World War Aeronautical Effort* (Burlington, Vt.: Lane Press, 1940), 2; and Holley, *Ideas and Weapons*, 103–4. Hennessy makes a valiant effort to untangle the conflicting aircraft delivery figures cited by a number of sources, arriving at 314 as the number delivered to the Army before April 7, 1914. Gorrell states that the number was 224. These numbers are largely irrelevant; what is important is the state of the American aircraft industry on the eve of war, as analyzed by Holley.

17. Holley, *Ideas and Weapons*, 67.

18. Alex Roland, *Model Research: The National Advisory Committee for Aeronautics, 1915–1958* (Washington, D.C., 1985), 45–46; Holley, *Ideas and Weapons*, 66–67.

19. Roland, 45–47, 394; and Holley, *Ideas and Weapons*, 66–67.

20. Hughes, 121–22.

21. Coffman, *War to End All Wars*, 15–16; and Richard B. Morris, *Encyclopedia of American History* (New York: Harper, 1953), 276.

22. Holley, *Ideas and Weapons*, 65–68.

23. Ibid., 68–69.

24. Ibid., 42.

25. Coffman, *War to End All Wars*, 190. The cable used by the Joint Army and Navy Technical Board to determine the May 29, 1917, American aircraft program differed from that actually received in the French embassy in Washington in that the 1918 time limit was added and the desire that the American contribution be split between

bombers and fighters was deleted. For a discussion of the basis for the Ribot message and for an analysis of the impact caused by the changes in the text of the cable, see Holley, *Ideas and Weapons*, 42–45.

26. Report of Joint Army and Navy Technical Board to the Secretary of War, May 29, 1917, in Maurer, *U.S. Air Service in World War I*, 2:105.

27. Coffman, *War to End All Wars*, 191.

28. Gorrell, 3.

29. *Final Report of the Chief of Air Service, AEF*, in Maurer, *U.S. Air Service in World War I*, 1:53, 54.

30. Holley, *Ideas and Weapons*, 59–60.

31. Coffman, *War to End All Wars*, 192–93; and Holley, *Ideas and Weapons*, 126.

32. Holley, *Ideas and Weapons*, 121.

33. Ibid., 124–26.

34. *Final Report of the Chief of Air Service, AEF*, in Maurer, *U.S. Air Service in World War I*, 1:85–86; and Holley, *Ideas and Weapons*, 143–45.

35. *Final Report of Chief of Air Service, AEF*, in Maurer, *U.S. Air Service in World War I*, 1:60.

36. Gorrell, 4.

37. Holley, *Ideas and Weapons*, 143–45.

38. *Final Report of the Chief of Air Service, AEF*, in Maurer, *U.S. Air Service in World War I*, 1:54, 69.

39. Gorrell, 35.

40. Hennessy, 243.

41. Spiller, Dawson, and Williams, 772; Hennessy, 165, 185–86; and Coffman, *War to End All Wars*, 193–94.

42. Memoranda, Major William Mitchell to Chief of Staff, U.S. Expeditionary Forces, in Maurer, *U.S. Air Service in World War I*, 2:107, 108, 111.

43. Board of Officers, Recommendations, July 4, 1917, in Maurer, *U.S. Air Service in World War I*, 2:123. Emphasis in original.

44. 59-Squadron Plan, July 10, 1917, in Maurer, *U.S. Air Service in World War I*, 2:127.

45. Maurer, *U.S. Air Service in World War I*, 1:391–92.

46. Restatement of 260-Squadron Plan, June 5, 1918, and 202 Squadrons, August 16, 1918, in Maurer, *U.S. Air Service in World War I*, 2:196, 228.

47. *Final Report of the Chief of Air Service, AEF*, in Maurer, *U.S. Air Service in World War I*, 1:67, 72, 83, 99–112.

48. War Department, *Field Service Regulations, United States Army, 1914, Corrected to July 31, 1918 (Changes Nos. 1 to 11)* (Washington, D.C., 1918), in Maurer, *U.S. Air Service in World War I*, 2:23–24. Maurer states that no changes in the aviation sections were made between 1914 and 1918.

49. George P. Scriven, *The Service of Information,* Circular no. 8, Office of the Chief Signal Officer (Washington, D.C., 1915), in Maurer, *U.S. Air Service in World War I*, 2:33.

50. Ibid., 2:35.

51. *Final Report of the Chief of Air Service, AEF*, in Maurer, *U.S. Air Service in World War I*, 1:51, 399; and Holley, *Ideas and Weapons*, 36–37.

52. Hearings before the Committee on Military Affairs, House of Representatives, *Army Appropriation Bill, 1917*, in Maurer, *U.S. Air Service in World War I*, 2:72.

53. Hearings before the Committee on Military Affairs, House of Representatives, *Army Appropriation Bill, 1918*, in Maurer, *U.S. Air Service in World War I*, 2:99.

54. Memorandum, Major Mitchell for Chief of Staff, U.S. Expeditionary Forces, n.d. [June 1917], in Maurer, *U.S. Air Service in World War I*, 2:108.

55. Ibid., 2:111.

56. Note, Major Townsend Dodd to Chief of Staff, AEF, June 20, 1917, in Maurer, *U.S. Air Service in World War I*, 2:113.

57. I. B. Holley Jr., "An Enduring Challenge: The Problem of Air Force Doctrine," in *The Harmon Memorial Lectures in Military History, 1959–1987*, ed. Harry R. Borowski (Washington, D.C., 1988), 426.

58. "The Role and Tactical and Strategical Employment of Aeronautics in an Army," in Maurer, *U.S. Air Service in World War I*, 2:119.

59. Maj. R. C. Bolling to Chief Signal Officer, August 15, 1915, in Maurer, *U.S. Air Service in World War I*, 2:131–33.

60. For strategic bombing plans prepared by Lt. Col. Edgar S. Gorrell, see "The Future Role of American Bombardment Aviation," by E. S. Gorrell, n.d. [1918], 248.222–78, USAFHRA; and Maurer, *U.S. Air Service in World War I*, 2:141–57.

61. Maurer, *U.S. Air Service in World War I*, 2:191.

62. *Final Report of the Chief of Air Service, AEF*, in Maurer, *U.S. Air Service in World War I*, 1:85–86.

63. Ibid., 1:17, 29–37.

64. Coffman, *War to End All Wars*, 187.

65. "Report of Superior Board," 81–82.

66. The four-volume document collection cited throughout this chapter, *The U.S. Air Service in World War I*, edited by Maurer, is based largely on Gorrell's 280-volume history and Patrick's *Final Report*.

67. Major General Mason M. Patrick to Commander-in-Chief, American E.F., May 19, 1919, 167.404.5, USAFHRA. A copy of the report submitted by the Foulois Board is attached to the basic document.

68. Brigadier General Benjamin D. Foulois, "Air Service Lessons Learned during the Present War," January 1919, in Maurer, *U.S. Air Service in World War I*, 4:25, 26.

69. McClendon, 21; and "Aeronautics in America," *New York Times*, August 14, 1919, p. 8.

70. Coffman, *Hilt of the Sword*, 205.

71. Maurer, *Aviation in the U.S. Army*, 41. Although the 1919 New and Curry Bills were the first seriously considered by Congress, earlier efforts to create an independent air organization included the first, H.R. 13838, submitted in March 1916 by Representative Charles Lieb of Indiana. The Lieb Bill set a precedent—virtually every session of Congress would have before it a similar bill until the 1947 establishment of the U.S. Air Force. See McClendon, 7; and "Digest of Legislative Proposals for a Department of Aviation and/or Department of National Defenses," p. 1–2, and "Legislation on: A Separate Air Force; a Department of Aviation; a Department of National Defense, 1916–1943," February 1944, Tab A:1–4: 168.04–14 (1916–1943), USAFHRA.

72. "Baker Opposes Single Air Bureau," *New York Times*, August 13, 1919, p. 15.

73. McClendon, 22; and Maurer, *Aviation in the U.S. Army*, 40.

74. McClendon, 22.

75. Senate, *Reorganization of the Army*, 2:1301–2.

76. Ibid., 1:300.

77. Ibid., 2:1258–98.

78. Ibid., 1:182–83.

79. Ibid., 2:1686, 279, 287.

80. *Acts and Resolutions Relating to the War Department Passed during the Sixty-sixth Congress, Second Session*, 424, 426, 435; Maurer, *Aviation in the U.S. Army*, 44; and McClendon, 26.

81. Maurer, *Aviation in the U.S. Army*, 108–11.

82. *Acts and Resolutions Relating to the War Department Passed during the Sixty-sixth Congress, Second Session*, 644.

CHAPTER 4

1. Lawrence Goodwyn, "Organizing Democracy: The Limits of Theory and Practice," *democracy* 1 (January 1981): 41–60.

2. See George C. Marshall, "Profiting by War Experiences," *Infantry Journal* 18 (January 1921): 34–37. Major Marshall was one of the few officers to argue, although with deference to the American contribution to victory, that the American experience in the war could be misleading: "It is not intended by this discussion to belittle our efforts in the later part of the war, for what we actually accomplished was a military miracle, but we must not forget that its conception was based on a knowledge of the approaching deterioration of the German army, and its lessons must be studied accordingly. We remain without modern experience in the first phases of war and must draw our lessons from history" (37).

3. Weigley, 394–400.

4. "Oppose an Army of 576,000," *New York Times,* September 4, 1919, p. 4.

5. *War Department Annual Report, 1919,* 60–61; and "March Defends Army Plan," *New York Times,* August 18, 1919, p. 18.

6. Mark S. Watson, *Chief of Staff: Prewar Plans and Preparations,* U.S. Army in World War II (1949; Washington, D.C., 1985), 33.

7. "General M'Andrew's Figures," *New York Times,* September 24, 1919, p. 16.

8. Bernardo and Bacon, 385.

9. *War Department Annual Report, 1920,* 254–255; and *War Department Annual Report, 1921,* 9–19.

10. Weigley, *History of the United States Army,* 599. Before World War I, the officer corps generally made up less than 6 percent of the total Army; during the interwar period, officer strength was usually more than 10 percent of the Army.

11. "General M'Andrew's Figures," *New York Times,* September 24, 1919, p. 16.

12. U.S. War Department, *Official Army Register for 1916* (Washington, D.C., 1916), 670 (hereafter cited as *Army Register*); and *Army Register, 1921,* 1402. On December 1, 1916, the War Department had legislative support for thirty-seven general officers. By 1921 the authorization had risen to ninety-four (sixty-eight general officers of the line and twenty-six in the various arms, services, and departments).

13. See John W. Killigrew, *The Impact of the Great Depression on the Army* (New York: Garland Publishing, 1979), appendix, p. 2. Killigrew encloses a letter by Secretary of War Woodring, dated May 28, 1940, that notes that from 1925 to 1940 the Army spent 86.1% of its budget on "recurring charges and improvement of plant," leaving the remaining small percentage for "augmentation, modernization, and replacement of arms and equipment." The War Department eventually received congressional approval to sell surplus property to fund housing construction (*War Department Annual Report, 1925,* 19).

14. Ralph E. Jones, "The Recent Factors," *Infantry Journal* 28 (February 1926): 148.

15. Spiller, Dawson, and Williams, 922; and Hennessy, 167–176.

16. *War Department Annual Report, 1919,* 473, 474.

17. Wrapper Indorsement, G.H.Q., A.E.F, forwarding "Report of A.E.F. Superior Board on Organization and Tactics," June 16, 1920, AEF Records, AEF Board of Officers, Loose Papers, Box 2206, AEF Records, RG 120/23, NA, 1, 2, 8.

18. Ibid., 7, 6.

19. *Final Report of Gen. John J. Pershing,* 76. See also Holley, *Ideas and Weapons,* 160.

20. *Final Report of Gen. John J. Pershing,* 76.

21. Bernardo and Bacon, 386.

22. Ralph E. Jones, "The Weak Spot in the Military Progress," *Infantry Journal* 34 (March 1929): 290. Emphasis in original.

23. Memorandum, Major General W. A. Holbrook, Chief of Cavalry, for Director, War Plans Division, "Duties and Responsibilities of the Chiefs of Combatant Arms," September 8, 1920, File 323.362/316, OCC, Box 7a, RG 177, NA; and U.S. War Department, *Army Regulations No. 70–5: Chiefs of Combatant Branches* (Washington, D.C., 1927), 1–3.

CHAPTER 5

1. Robert H. Ferrell, *American Diplomacy: The Twentieth Century* (New York: W. W. Norton, 1988), 155.
2. Sally Marks, *The Illusion of Peace: International Relations in Europe: 1918–1933* (New York: St. Martin's, 1976), 24.
3. Thomas A. Bailey, *A Diplomatic History of the American People*, 8th ed. (New York: Appleton-Century-Crofts, 1969), 627.
4. Ferrell, *Woodrow Wilson and World War I*, 166, 172–73.
5. *Annual Report, 1919*, 22–25; and Charles A. Beard and Mary R. Beard, *A Basic History of the United States* (New York: Doubleday, Doran, 1944), 436.
6. Department of State, *Papers Relating to the Foreign Relations of the United States, 1919*, vol. (Washington, D.C., 1934), 866, 873.
7. Woodrow Wilson, "The United States and the Armenian Mandate: Message of President Wilson to the Congress, May 24, 1920," *International Conciliation* 151 (June 1920): 13–16.
8. Bailey, 624–25.
9. Beard and Beard, 436; and Morris, 311.
10. John Maynard Keynes, *The Economic Consequences of the Peace* (1920; New York: Penguin, 1988).
11. Bailey, 625.
12. Ferrell, *American Diplomacy*, 235; and Morris, 331–32.
13. Morris, 331, 511.
14. Ferrell, *American Diplomacy*, 176.
15. "Disarmament Feelers Are Well Received," *New York Times*, June 11, 1921, p. 3.
16. Bailey, 633–48; and Morris, 319.
17. Bailey, 646.
18. "Harding Moving for World Conference, but Lodge in Senate Opposes Borah Plan and Majority Will Block the Proposal," *New York Times*, December 28, 1922, p. 1.
19. "Coolidge Suggests New Naval Parley on Auxiliary Ships to Four Powers; Might Also Include Curb on Aircraft," *New York Times*, February 19, 1925, p. 1.
20. Bailey, 648–49.
21. Morris, 323–24.
22. Robert H. Ferrell, *Peace in Their Time: The Origins of the Kellogg-Briand Pact* (New Haven: Yale University Press, 1952), 219, 263–65.
23. Morris, 322.
24. J. G. Harbord, "Universal Military Training," *Infantry Journal* 18 (January 1921): 4–8.
25. Hunter Liggett, "Universal Military Training—A Patriotic Obligation," *Infantry Journal* 18 (March 1921): 217–18.
26. Robert L. Bullard, "Military Training: Its Effect on the Citizen," *Infantry Journal* 19 (July 1921): 7–11.
27. George W. Hinman Jr., "Citizen's Military Training Camps." *Infantry Journal* 18 (June 1921): 579–83; and "Resolutions," *Infantry Journal* 19 (December 1921), 602–7.
28. "Disarmament," *Infantry Journal* 18 (February 1921): 186–88.

29. Robert L. Bullard, "The U.S. Should Not Lead in Disarmament—Because!" *Infantry Journal* 18 (June 1921): 559.

30. "Pershing Favors 5-Power Disarming," *New York Times*, February 3, 1921, p. 5.

31. "New Army Policy Fixed by Harding," *New York Times*, July 25, 1921, p. 4; and "Disarmament Feelers Are Well Received," *New York Times*, June 11, 1921, p. 3.

32. "Pershing Demands Economy in Army," *New York Times*, July 3, 1921, p. 15.

33. "Says Army Officers Must Not Criticize," *New York Times*, June 25, 1922, p. 21.

34. "Military Preparedness and Public Speaking," *Cavalry Journal* 31 (October 1922): 404, 403.

35. U.S. Bureau of the Census, *Historical Statistics of the United States, Colonial Times to 1970*, pt. 2 (Washington, D.C., 1975), 1141.

36. See *Annual Reports, 1921–1930*; "Foundations of Sand," *Infantry Journal* 20 (May 1922): 576–77; "Menace to National Defense," *Infantry Journal* 21 (August 1922): 214–16; "Weeks and Pershing Urge Larger Army," *New York Times*, October 17, 1922, p. 18; "Shortage of Officers," *Infantry Journal* 24 (January 1924): 86; "Officers Are Alarmed at Low State of Army," *New York Times*, March 9, 1924, p. 10 (IX); "Pershing's Final Report," *New York Times*, November 30, 1924, p. 6 (II); and "Next Year's Regular Army," *Infantry Journal* 25 (December 1924): 686–88.

37. "Officers Are Alarmed at Low State of Training," *New York Times*, March 9, 1924, p. 10 (IX).

38. *Annual Report, 1924*, 6–7.

39. *Annual Report, 1924*, 30; and *Annual Report, 1925*, 19–26.

40. *Annual Report, 1924*, 31.

41. "Coolidge Unmoved by Bureaus' 'Alarm' Over Budget Cuts," *New York Times*, August 26, 1925, p. 1.

42. "Text of President's Address to the Legion in Omaha," *New York Times*, October 7, 1925, p. 2.

43. "Coolidge Demands Tolerance for All as Basis for Peace at Home and Abroad; Attacks Propaganda by Army Officers," *New York Times*, October 7, 1925, p. 1. The controversy surrounding Mitchell's views on the Shenandoah crash and his court-martial are discussed in chapter 7.

44. "Davis to Enforce Strict Discipline on Army Factions," *New York Times*, December 21, 1925, p. 1.

45. "Assails Army Economy," *New York Times*, October 12, 1927, p. 23.

46. "Coolidge Halted Summerall Trip," *New York Times*, October 14, 1927, p. 52.

47. "Summerall Awaits Call," *New York Times*, October 19, 1927, p. 27.

48. "A Warning as to Suggestions," *New York Times*, October 30, 1927, p. 2 (III).

49. "Notes from the Chief of Infantry," *Infantry Journal* 21 (August 1922): 196.

50. J. L. Bradley, "Reorganization of the Infantry," *Infantry Journal* 37 (August 1930): 138.

51. J. L. Bradley to "Chyn," September 8, 1930, in Bradford Grethen Chynoweth Papers (Chynoweth Papers), U.S. Army Military History Institute (USAMHI), Carlisle Barracks, Pa.

52. Major General Stephen O. Fuqua to Brig. Gen. Campbell King, August 21, 1930, in Chynoweth Papers, USAMHI.

53. J. L. Bradley to "Chyn," September 8, 1930, in Chynoweth Papers, USAMHI.

54. See B. G. Chynoweth, "Tank Infantry," *Infantry Journal* 18 (May 1921): 504–7; "Mechanical Transport," *Infantry Journal* 18 (June 1921): 561–65; and "Cavalry Tanks," *Cavalry Journal* 30 (July 1921): 247–51.

55. B. G. Chynoweth to "Koch," May 17, 1930, in Chynoweth Papers, USAMHI.

56. Major B. G. Chynoweth to President of Infantry Board, April 3, 1930, in Chynoweth Papers, USAMHI.

57. Major B. G. Chynoweth to Chief of Infantry, April 1, 1930, in Chynoweth Papers, USAMHI.

58. B. G. Chynoweth to Col. George S. Pappas, October 24, 1967, in Chynoweth Papers, USAMHI.

59. Ibid.

60. Major B. G. Chynoweth to Major General C. D. Rhodes, April 10, 1930; and Major B. G. Chynoweth to Chief of Infantry, April 10, 1930, in Chynoweth Papers, USAMHI.

61. Major General Stephen O. Fuqua to Major B. G. Chynoweth, April 29, 1930, in Chynoweth Papers, USAMHI.

62. Raymond G. O'Connor, *American Defense Policy in Perspective* (New York: John Wiley, 1965), 215, quoted in *The Military and American Society*, ed. Stephen E. Ambrose and James A. Barber (New York: Free Press, 1972), 301.

CHAPTER 6

1. See "Remarks of Brigadier General S. D. Rockenbach, Chief of Tank Corps, U.S. Army, At Conference of Department and Division Commanders, Held in Washington, D.C., January 12–19, 1920," in *Tanks with Infantry*, n.p., n.d. [1920–1924], USAMHI.

2. U.S. War Department, *Tank Combat* (Washington, D.C., 1920), 7.

3. S. D. Rockenbach, "American Tanks since the World War, 1923," TMs, p. 1, USAMHI; *Report of the Chief of the Tank Corps (1920)*, 1891; Nenninger, *Development of American Armor*, 56; and Jones, Rarey, and Icks, 157.

4. *Course of Study*, vol. 3. (Camp Benning: Infantry School Press, 1921), 3:1, 2.

5. *Tank Combat*, 7.

6. 11th Ind. to AG 473.1 (3-31-22), Adjutant General through Chief of Infantry to Chief of Ordnance, April 3, 1922, File 470.8, Records of the Chiefs of Arms, Office of the Chief of Infantry, Correspondence, 1921–1942, OCI, Box 90, RG 177, NA.

7. Ibid.

8. *Report of the Chief of the Tank Corps (1920)*, 1893–94.

9. See S. D. Rockenbach, "Tanks and Their Cooperation with Other Arms," *Infantry Journal* 16 (January 1920): 533–45.

10. George S. Patton Jr., "Tanks in Future Wars," *Infantry Journal* 16 (May 1920): 958–62.

11. B. G. Chynoweth, "Tank Infantry," *Infantry Journal* 18 (May 1921): 504–7; and B. G. Chynoweth, "Mechanical Transport," *Infantry Journal* 18 (June 1921): 561–65.

12. Bradford G. Chynoweth, "Cavalry Tanks," *Cavalry Journal* 30 (July 1921): 247–51.

13. D. D. Eisenhower, "A Tank Discussion," *Infantry Journal* 17 (November 1920): 453–54.

14. Dwight D. Eisenhower, *At Ease: Stories I Tell to Friends* (Garden City, N.Y.: Doubleday, 1967), 173, 178–79. Eisenhower wrote this account of his confrontation with Farnsworth nearly fifty years after the fact, and it is probably embellished. The court-martial threat seems somewhat dramatic, but it might have been Eisenhower's way of rationalizing his decision to abandon tanks, even to the point of declining a chance for tank battalion command in 1924 (198). Still, his assertion that he was silenced is very plausible, given the 1920s climate of the Army.

15. Patton, "Tanks in Future Wars," 962.

16. Blumenson, 1:741.

17. A. W. Lane, "Tables of Organization," *Infantry Journal* 18 (May 1921): 503.

18. "Notes from the Chief of Infantry," *Infantry Journal* 21 (August 1922): 196.

19. See, for example, Isaac Gill Jr., "Value of Tanks in Action," *Infantry Journal* 18 (March

1921): 248–50; and George H. Rarey, "The Tank in the World War," *Infantry Journal* 30 (January 1927): 43–50. Gill's article is typical of the writing strategy employed by some officers. Although Gill is critical of the disregard for tank capabilities by many officers, he is careful to frame his argument to meet the central criterion for sanctioned discourse: "The *raison d'être* of the tank was, and still is, to facilitate the progress of the Infantry." Rarey relies on an even more subtle approach, using an analysis of the wartime value of the tank as an argument to awaken the readership to its future potential. Until the advent of the mechanized force in the late 1920s, discussed in chapter 8, articles by American tank advocates generally followed these patterns.

20. Brigadier General S. D. Rockenbach to Adjutant General, December 7, 1926, File 470.8, OCI, Box 94, RG 177, NA.

21. 1st Ind., Adjutant General to Chief of Infantry, AG 473.1 (12–7–26), December 7, 1926; 3d Ind., Adjutant General to Commanding General, District of Washington, AG 473.1 (12–7–26), December 15, 1926; Major General R. H. Allen to Brigadier General S. D. Rockenbach, December 10, 1926; and S. D. Rockenbach to General Allen, December 11, 1926, File 470.8, OCI, Box 94, RG 177, NA.

22. "Mission of Tanks," *Instructors' Summary of Military Articles [Military Review]*, no. 5 (May 1922), 12–14. This article is a reprint of "Notes from the Chief of Infantry," *Infantry Journal* 20 (May 1922): 559. The *Instructors' Summary of Military Articles* was the predecessor to the *Military Review*. The journal had a number of names during the 1920s and 1930s; all are referred to as the *Military Review* throughout this book. As implied by its title, this journal contained summarized versions of military articles prepared by the instructors at Fort Leavenworth. The scope was broad and included selections from the journals of other American and foreign services. As early as 1924 the thoughts of J. F. C. Fuller, the British "tank enthusiast," began appearing in this journal. See J. F. C. Fuller, "The Influence of Fast-Moving Tanks on the Encounter of Battle," *Instructors' Summary of Military Articles [Military Review]*, no. 13 (April 1924), 5.

23. D. D. Eisenhower, "Tanks in Cooperation with Other Infantry Weapons during the World War," in *Tanks with Infantry*, USAMHI, 7.

24. U.S. War Department, *Field Service Regulations, United States Army, 1923* (Washington, D.C., 1924), 13.

25. See *Course of Study*, vol. 3 (Fort Leavenworth: General Service Schools Press, 1925); and *Tanks* (Fort Riley: Cavalry School, 1926).

26. Lane, "Tables of Organization," 494, 500; Nenninger, *Development of American Armor*, 65–68; and Jones, Rarey, and Icks, 275–77.

27. Incl. 1 to memorandum, Major Thompson Lawrence for Chief of Infantry, November 2, 1929, File 470.8, OCI, Box 90, RG 177, NA.

28. John Walter Christie was the exception. Although he offered designs to the Army as early as 1919, his major involvement did not begin until 1928. See George F. Hofmann, "Rejection of Christie's Armored Fighting Vehicles: A Study of the Christie-Army Relationship" (M.A. thesis, University of Cincinnati, 1970).

29. Office of the Chief of Ordnance, *History of the Development of the Light Tank*, July 10, 1929, File 470.8, OCI, Box 92, RG 177, NA. Emphasis in original.

30. 1st Ind., Office of the Tank Board to Chief of Infantry, T.B. 470.8/Med., February 21, 1928, File 470.8, OCI, Box 90, RG 177, NA.

31. John H. Hughes to Adjutant General, CI-470.8/2164-B, September 14, 1923, File 470.8, OCI, Box 90, RG 177, NA.

32. 1st Ind., Ordnance Office to Adjutant General, O.O.451.25/1870, September 19, 1923, File 470.8, OCI, Box 90, RG 177, NA.

33. 2d Ind., Chief of Engineers to Adjutant General, 470.8-E-4, September 25, 1923, File

470.8, OCI, Box 90, RG 177, NA. One can only speculate that tank development might have been much different if the requirement for the divisional bridge had been stated subsequent to that for a medium tank instead of vice versa. Instead, bridge capacity determined tank design.

34. 3d Ind., Adjutant General to Chief of Infantry, AG 473.1 (9–14–23), October 18, 1923, File 470.8, OCI, Box 90, RG 177, NA.

35. Colonel O. S. Eskridge to Chief of Infantry, TB470.8/226, December 12, 1928, File 470.8, OCI, Box 92, RG 177, NA.

36. Chief of Infantry to President, Tank Board, CI 470.8/6403-B, December 26, 1928, File 470.8, OCI, Box 92, RG 177, NA.

37. Memorandum, Colonel L. B. Gasser for IV Section, Office of the Chief of Infantry, February 11, 1930, File 470.8, OCI, Box 94, RG 177, NA.

38. Nenninger, *Development of American Armor*, 79–81.

39. Jones, Rarey, and Icks, 153–68.

CHAPTER 7

1. Robert T. Finney, *History of the Air Corps Tactical School, 1920–1940*, USAF Historical Studies no. 100 (Maxwell Air Force Base: Air University, 1955), 5.

2. "War Department Committee Report on the Organization of the Air Service [Lassiter Board]," March 27, 1923, p. 3, 167.404–6 (April 24, 1923), USAFHRA (hereafter referred to as the "Lassiter Board Report"); and Lane, 488.

3. James P. Tate, "The Army and Its Air Corps: A Study of the Evolution of Army Policy Towards Aviation, 1919–1941," (Ph.D. diss., Indiana University, 1976), 9–10.

4. Maurer, *Aviation in the U.S. Army*, 70–72. Observation units performed the air service mission, which consisted of the reconnaissance, artillery spotting, and liaison functions. Pursuit, attack, and bombardment units provided air force, or offensive aviation.

5. Brig. Gen. Wm. Mitchell, "Tactical Application of Military Aeronautics," p. 1, 167.603–7 (1919), USAFHRA.

6. Ibid., 12–13.

7. Senate, *Reorganization of the Army*, 1:300.

8. "Declares America Helpless in Air War," *New York Times*, August 29, 1920, p. 6.

9. Tate, 22–23.

10. Isaac D. Levine, *Mitchell: Pioneer of Air Power* (Cleveland: World Publishing Company, 1943), 206–11.

11. "Statement Regarding the Necessity of the Air Service," pp. 4, 15, 16, 20, 167.404–9 (1921), USAFHRA.

12. Maurer, 115.

13. Levine, 228–31; Maurer, 115–16.

14. Maurer, 116.

15. "Weeks Tries to End Rift in Air Service," *New York Times*, June 11, 1921, p. 3.

16. "Weeks Will Decide Mitchell Case Today," *New York Times*, June 17, 1921, p. 3.

17. Maurer, 119–20. The *Ostfriesland* was one of a number of ex-German ships the U.S. Navy had received in the aftermath of World War I.

18. Ibid., 120–21.

19. U.S. Navy Department, *Report of the Joint Board on Results of Aviation and Ordnance Tests Held during June and July, 1921 and Conclusions Reached* (Washington, D.C., 1921), 7. See also Lieutenant Commander H. B. Grow, "Bombing Tests on the 'Virginia' and 'New Jersey,'" extract from *U.S. Naval Institute Proceedings*, pp. 1995–96, 248.222–69,

USAFHRA. Grow used these later bombing tests to make a clever argument for an increase in naval aviation so that it could protect the important battleships.

20. *Report of the Joint Board on Results of Aviation and Ordnance Tests*, 5, 7.

21. Memorandum, Brigadier General Wm. Mitchell for Chief of Air Service, August 29, 1921, 248.222–69 (April–August 1921), USAFHRA. See also Flugel, 33–36. Flugel argues convincingly that the principal source of Mitchell's air power theories was General Sir Hugh Trenchard, the World War I commander of the British Royal Flying Corps.

22. Maurer, 121.

23. "Mitchell Attacks Bomb Test Findings," *New York Times*, September 14, 1921, p. 1.

24. "Menoher to Quit Army Air Service," *New York Times*, September 17, 1921, p. 3. See also "Menoher Succeeds Shanks at Dix," *New York Times*, October 26, 1921, p. 4.

25. "Gen. Patrick to Head Air Service," *New York Times*, September 22, 1921, p. 4; and Robert F. Futrell, *Ideas, Concepts, Doctrine: A History of Basic Thinking in the United States Air Force, 1907–1964*, 2 vols. (Maxwell Air Force Base: Air University, 1971), 1:37, quoted in Tate, 27.

26. H. H. Arnold, *Global Mission* (New York: Harper, 1949), 106; and Tate, 27–28.

27. *War Department Annual Report, 1922*, 261.

28. Adjutant General to Chief of Air Service, AG 319.12 (9–9–22), December 18, 1922, in "Lassiter Board Report," appendix 1, p. 2.

29. 1st Ind., Major General Mason M. Patrick to Adjutant General, AG 319.12 (9–9–22), January 19, 1923, in "Lassiter Board Report," appendix 1, pp. 2–3.

30. 2d Ind., Adjutant General to Chief of Air Service, AG 319.12 (12–18–22), January 26, 1923, in "Lassiter Board Report," appendix 1, p. 3.

31. 3d Ind., Major General Mason M. Patrick to Adjutant General, AG 319.12 (12–18–22), February 7, 1923, in "Lassiter Board Report," appendix 1, p. 4.

32. Adjutant General to Major General William Lassiter, March 17, 1923, "Lassiter Board Report," 2.

33. Tate, 30; and "Lassiter Board Report," 5.

34. "Lassiter Board Report," 6.

35. "Warns Army Faces Failure in Air War," *New York Times*, October 19, 1923, p. 5.

36. Congress, House, Select Committee of Inquiry Into Operations of the United States Air Services, *Report of Select Committee of Inquiry into Operations of the United States Air Services*, 68th Cong., 2d sess., report no. 1653 (Washington, D.C., 1925), 18. Hereafter cited as *Lampert Committee Report*.

37. "Says Navy Conceals Real Aircraft Facts," *New York Times*, February 1, 1925, p. 27.

38. "Discipline Threat for Gen. Mitchell for Aviation Views," *New York Times*, February 4, 1925, p. 1.

39. See "Moffett's Removal as Naval Air Chief Said to Be Planned," *New York Times*, February 5, 1925, p. 1; "Moffett and Mitchell," *New York Times*, February 6, 1925, p. 16; "Mitchell Defiant, Widens His Attack on Aviation Policy," *New York Times*, February 7, 1925, p. 1; "Weeks Indirectly Assails Mitchell," *New York Times*, February 8, 1925, p. 25; and "No Mitchell Rebuke, He Renews Attacks," *New York Times*, February 20, 1925, p. 1.

40. "Intolerable Charges," *New York Times*, February 22, 1925, p. 4 (II). See also "An Indiscreet General," *New York Times*, February 14, 1925, p. 12.

41. "Mitchell Dropped; Col. Fechet Named to Take Air Post," *New York Times*, March 7, 1925, p. 1.

42. "General Mitchell Demoted," *New York Times*, March 7, 1925, p. 12.

43. "Mitchell Charges Force Davis to Act," *New York Times*, September 6, 1925.

44. Maurer, 129.

45. Komons, 75–76.

46. "America at Mercy of Air, Mitchell Asserts," *New York Times*, September 30, 1925, p. 1.

47. "Plans and Recommendations Submitted to the Morrow Commission of Inquiry," TMs, p. 10, USAMHI.
48. *Report of President's Aircraft Board* (Washington, D.C. 1925).
49. Ibid., 8–9; 18.
50. Levine, 345.
51. "The Intense Drama of the Mitchell Trial," *New York Times,* November 15, 1925, p. 3 (IX).
52. See oral history interview of Lieutenant General Ira C. Eaker by Arthur Marmor, January 1966, pp. 28–29, K239.0512–626, USAFHRA; oral history interview of General Carl A. Spaatz by Alfred Goldberg, May 19, 1965, p. 9, K239.0512–755, USAFHRA; and Arnold, 120. Eaker's comments are representative. He recalled: "We did, however, all of us—Arnold and Spaatz and Hickam, Kilner, Frank, Weaver—we realized that Mitchell had deliberately set about disobeying regulations in order to attract attention to himself and to the cause of airpower, the degraded condition of military aviation at that time. So we realized that from a purely military standpoint—from the standpoint of discipline and morale—that the War Department had no alternative but to take disciplinary action against him."
53. "Mitchell Is Found Guilty on All Counts," *New York Times,* December 18, 1925, p. 1.
54. Maurer, 129. See also "Mitchell Charges Force Davis to Act," *New York Times,* September 6, 1925, p. 6.
55. The 1955 motion picture *The Court Martial of Billy Mitchell* is perhaps the most compelling manifestation of the Mitchell myth. As played by Gary Cooper, Mitchell is a heroic figure who willingly sacrifices himself in the cause of trying to provide America with a sound air policy.
56. Arnold, 157–58.
57. Eaker oral history interview (K239.0512–626), 28.
58. Arnold, 122; and "Orders Inquiry into Air Service," *New York Times,* February 9, 1926, p. 27.
59. Roland, *Model Research,* 395.
60. Alex Roland, "The Impact of War upon Aeronautical Progress: The Experience of NACA," in *Air Power and Warfare: The Proceedings of the 8th Military History Symposium, United States Air Force Academy, 18–20 October 1978,* ed. Alfred F. Hurley and Robert C. Ehrhart (Washington, D.C., 1979), 371.
61. Congress, Senate, Committee on Military Affairs, *The Army Air Service: Hearings before the Committee on Military Affairs,* 69th Cong., 1st sess., May 10, 1926, 1–49; David L. Hardee, "The Air Corps and the Infantry," *Infantry Journal* 30 (March 1927): 265–74. I. B. Holley Jr., *Buying Aircraft: Matériel Procurement for the Army Air Forces,* U.S. Army in World War II (1964; Washington, D.C., 1989), 48–63; and Bernardo and Bacon, 394.
62. Roland, *Model Research,* 395–96.
63. Roland, "Impact of War upon Aeronautical Progress," 371.
64. Roland, *Model Research,* 99; and Roland, "Impact of War upon Aeronautical Progress," 371–73.
65. Arnold, 127.
66. Roland, "Impact of War upon Aeronautical Progress," 373.
67. Arnold, 127.
68. "Notes on the Characteristics, Limitations, and Employment of the Air Service," in Maurer, *U.S. Air Service in World War I,* 2:303.
69. "Sherman: Tentative Manual for the Employment of Air Service," in Maurer, *U.S. Air Service in World War I,* 2:313.
70. Thomas H. Greer, *The Development of Air Doctrine in the Army Air Arm, 1917–1941,* U.S. Air Force Historical Studies, no. 89 (1955; Washington, D.C., 1985), 16.
71. "Fundamental Conceptions of the Air Service," 167.404–10 (1923), USAFHRA, 2–3.

72. Ibid., 1–2, 9. See also *War Department Annual Report, 1922,* 261, where Patrick stated that the air force should constitute 80 percent of the air service.

73. "Fundamental Conceptions of the Air Service," 13.

74. Ibid., 2, 9.

75. Ibid., 3.

76. Air Service Tactical School, *Bombardment* (Langley Field: Air Service Tactical School, 1924), 2. Hereafter, all Air Service and Air Corps Tactical School texts are cited with the course name and year.

77. *Bombardment, 1926,* 72, 78, 20.

78. Pursuit, 1926, 53.

79. 3d Ind., Major O. Westover to Chief of Air Service, July 14, 1925, File 385, Office of the Chief of Air Corps, Secret and Confidential Correspondence (OCAC), Box 20, RG 18, NA.

80. Lieutenant Colonel C. C. Culver to Chief of Air Corps, September 3, 1928, 248.121–1 (1926 and 1928), USAFHRA.

81. Memorandum, Captain Charles W. Walton for Assistant Commandant, Air Corps Tactical School, May 1, 1929, 248.211–16F (May 1, 1929), USAFHRA.

82. *Bombardment, 1931,* 69. Emphasis in original.

83. Lieutenant Colonel W. S. Wuest to Chief of Air Corps, March 4, 1930, 248.101–9 (1930), USAFHRA.

CHAPTER 8

1. *Annual Report, 1922,* 13–16.

2. *Annual Report, 1924,* 6–7; and "Pershing's Final Report," *New York Times,* November 30, 1924, p. 6.

3. "Progress in Matériel," *Infantry Journal* 30 (May 1927): 53.

4. U.S. War Department, *Training Regulations No. 10-5: Doctrines, Principles, and Methods* (Washington, D.C., 1921), 1, 2, 3.

5. U.S. War Department, *Field Service Regulations, United States Army, 1923* (Washington, D.C., 1924), 11.

6. U.S. War Department, *FM 100-5, Tentative Field Service Regulations: Operations* (Washington, D.C., 1939), 1.

7. Mildred H. Gillie, *Forging the Thunderbolt: A History of the Development of the Armored Force* (Harrisburg, Pa.: Military Service Publishing Co., 1947), 20; *History of the Armored Force, Command and Center,* Study no. 27 (Washington, D.C., 1946), 1–2; and Nenninger, "Development of American Armor," 84–85.

8. Nenninger, "Development of American Armor," 85–86.

9. Nenninger, "Development of American Armor," 85–86. See also "The Army to Have a Mimic War of Machines," *New York Times,* March 4, 1928, p. 3 (X).

10. "The Army to Have a Mimic War of Machines," 3 (X).

11. Nenninger, "Development of American Armor," 87–88.

12. *Annual Report, 1930,* 125–26. For an interesting contrast to Summerall's condemnation of Ordnance Department efforts, see "Ordnance Chief Lauds Quality of Our Tanks," *New York Times,* November 10, 1930, p. 21.

13. Memorandum, Brigadier General Frank Parker for Chief of Staff, G-3/18677, March 20, 1928, File 84-17, USAMHI, 19, 6.

14. Memorandum, Chief of Infantry for Assistant Chief of Staff, G-3, 537.3 (3-20-28), March 26, 1928, RG 94; quoted in Nenninger, "Development of American Armor," 95–96.

15. Memorandum, Brigadier General Frank Parker for Chief of Staff, G-3/18677, March 20, 1928, File 84-17, USAMHI, 21.

16. "Proceedings of a War Department Board of Officers on 'A Mechanized Force,' October 1, 1928," G-3 Course no. 24, U.S. Army War College, 1928–29, File 352-A-24, USAMHI, 1, 3, 5–6. Emphasis in original.

17. Ibid., 11, 14, 29–30.

18. Ibid., 32.

19. "Proceedings of a War Department Board of Officers on 'A Mechanized Force,' " 33.

20. Nenninger, "Development of American Armor," 95; and "Mechanized Unit Urged for Army," *New York Times,* December 14, 1928, 9.

21. Nenninger, "Development of American Armor," 100–106; and Arthur Wilson, "The Mechanized Force: Its Organization and Equipment," *Infantry Journal* 38 (May–June 1931): 252–56.

22. Daniel Van Voorhis, "Address at the Army War College on the Subject of 'Mechanization,' 13 October 1937," TMs, p. 3, Mechanized Cavalry Board Maneuvers, 1929–39, Box 1, RG 177, NA.

23. "Study by Lieutenant Colonel Adna R. Chaffee, General Staff, December 12, 1930, 'Mechanization in the Army,' " 84–28/AWC (12–12–30), USAMHI, 3.

24. *Training Regulation No. 10-5 (1921),* 3, 5.

25. *Field Service Regulations, 1923,* 21–23.

26. "Fundamental Conceptions of the Air Service," 1923, 3; Maurer, *Aviation in the U.S. Army,* 72.

27. U.S. War Department, *Training Regulations No. 440–15: Fundamental Principles for the Employment of the Air Service* (Washington, D.C., 1926), 11.

28. "The McNair Board and the Auxiliary Reports, Data and Correspondence, Part I, The McNair Report, the Panama Canal Report," 248.82-70, pt. 1 (1923–24), USAFHRA, 27. In March 1924 the department commander, Charles P. Summerall, approved the report.

29. Major General Mason M. Patrick to Adjutant General AG 353 (2–12–25), February 12, 1925, File 321, Army Ground Forces, Headquarters, Commanding General, General Decimal File, 1940–44 (McNair File), Box 5, RG 337, NA.

30. Brigadier General H. A. Drum, "War Department Statement Presented before the Board of Aviation Inquiry," October 13, 1925, 248.211–16D, pt. 2 (October 13 1925), USAFHRA, 22.

31. Ibid., 1, 15. Emphasis in original.

32. This fixation on independence for the air arm and the criticality of its being directed by air officers is a common thread that runs through the oral histories of the many Air Force generals who eventually did come to control military aviation. See USAFHRA oral history interviews of Lieutenant General James H. Doolittle (K239.0512–623), Lieutenant General Ira C. Eaker (K239.0512–626), General Carl A. Spaatz (K239.0512–755), and Major General Donald Wilson (K239.5012–878).

33. "War Department Statement Presented before the Board of Aviation Inquiry," 6.

34. Ibid., 7, 6.

35. "Army Must Transfer 1,200 Men to Air Arm," *New York Times,* December 18, 1926, p. 2; "Infantry Shifted into Air Service," *New York Times,* August 21, 1929, p. 4; "First Engineers Lose Unit to Air Service," *New York Times,* September 2, 1929, p. 9; "Filling Air Corps from Ground Forces," *New York Times,* November 16, 1930, p. 2 (II); and *Annual Report, 1929,* 104.

36. "War Department Statement Presented before the Board of Aviation Inquiry," 7.

37. Oral history interview of Major General Donald Wilson by Hugh Ahmann, December 10–11, 1975, p. 78, K239.5012–878, USAFHRA. See also oral history interview of General Laurence S. Kuter by Hugh N. Ahmann and Tom Sturm, September 30–October 3, 1974, p. 49–50, K239.0512–810, USAFHRA.

CHAPTER 9

1. *Hard Times* and *The Good War* are books by Studs Terkel on, respectively, the Great Depression and World War II.
2. Beard and Beard, 452.
3. Robert H. Ferrell, *American Diplomacy in the Great Depression: Hoover-Stimson Foreign Policy, 1929–1933* (New Haven: Yale University Press, 1957), 138–39.
4. H. C. Engelbrecht and F. C. Hanighen, *Merchants of Death: A Study of the International Armament Industry* (New York: Dodd, Mead, 1934), 9; and Robert Dallek, *Franklin D. Roosevelt and American Foreign Policy, 1932–1945* (1979; New York: Oxford University Press, 1981), 85, 95, 102–3; and Weigley, *History of the U.S. Army*, 402. Quote is from Engelbrecht and Hanighen.
5. Dallek, 85.
6. Bailey, 670.
7. Morris, 328.
8. Ibid., 357; and Bailey, 706.
9. Dallek, 186–88.
10. U.S. War Department, *Biennial Report of the Chief of Staff of the United States Army, July 1, 1939, to June 30, 1941, to the Secretary of War* (Washington, D.C., 1941), 2. All hereafter cited as *Biennial Report* and ending year date.
11. *Public Opinion Quarterly* 4: 102, quoted in Bailey, 711.
12. Robert A. Divine, *Roosevelt and World War II* (1969; Baltimore: Penguin, 1971), 28.
13. Ibid., 31, 36–37.
14. Dallek, 229.
15. Department of State, *Peace and War: United States Foreign Policy, 1931–1941* (Washington, D.C., 1943), 549–53, quoted in Divine, 33.
16. Beard and Beard, 477.
17. Dallek, 243–47; and Bailey, 718–19.
18. Morris, 364.
19. Ibid., 256–57.
20. Mark S. Watson, *Chief of Staff: Prewar Plans and Preparations, U.S. Army in World War II* (1950; Washington, D.C., 1985), 367–410.
21. Morris, 366.
22. Elliot Roosevelt, *As He Saw It* (New York: Duell, Sloan & Pearce, 1946), 19–46.
23. Larry I. Bland and Sharon R. Ritenour, eds., *The Papers of George Catlett Marshall*, 2 vols. (Baltimore: Johns Hopkins University Press, 1981–86), 1:426. For postwar reminiscences about officer lifestyles during the depression, see Lucian K. Truscott Jr., *The Twilight of the U.S. Cavalry: Life in the Old Army, 1917–1942* (Lawrence: University Press of Kansas, 1989); and oral history interview of General Hunter Harris Jr. by Hugh N. Ahmann, November 14–15, 1974 and March 1–2, 1979, p. 16, K239.0512–811, USAFHRA.
24. *War Department Annual Report, 1931*, 40–41.
25. Bethanie C. Grashof, *A Study of United States Army Family Housing Standardized Plans*, 6 vols. (Washington, D.C.: Office of the Chief of Engineers, 1986), 1:146–47.
26. Adjutant General to All Chiefs of Branches and Bureaus, AG 333 E.P. (7-30-29), August 1, 1929, File 333, OCC, Box 12, RG 177, NA.
27. Ibid.
28. Ibid.
29. Killigrew, 2:10–11.
30. Ibid., conclusion, p. 3.
31. Ibid., 3:4.

32. *War Department Annual Report, 1932,* 1–2. See also chapter 5 in Killigrew.

33. Killigrew, 5:8.

34. "Size of the Army," *New York Times,* December 1, 1932, p. 20.

35. *Hearings,* War Department Appropriations Bill, 1933 (December 21, 1931), 3, cited in Killigrew, 5:6.

36. Killigrew, 5:24–25. See also Watson, 31–32.

37. U.S. War Department, *Report of the Chief of Staff U.S. Army, 1934 (Extract from Annual Report of the Secretary of War, 1934)* (Washington, D.C., 1934), 7. Emphasis in original.

38. Ibid., 2, 5.

39. Ibid., 11, 34.

40. Ibid., 8–11.

41. Ibid., 11, 34.

42. *War Department Annual Report, 1935,* 42–43.

43. *Annual Report of the Chief of Staff,* 10.

44. Watson, 29–30.

45. *War Department Annual Report, 1936,* 40.

46. Weigley, *History of the U.S. Army,* 416.

47. Weigley, 416; and Watson, 42–43

48. Colonel Steven L. Conner, quoted in Constance M. Green, Harry C. Thomson, and Peter C. Roots, eds., *The Ordnance Department: Planning Munitions for War.* U.S. Army in World War II (1955; Washington, D.C., 1990), 183–85.

49. *Biennial Report, 1941,* 10.

50. Watson, 299–329.

51. Weigley, *History of the U.S. Army,* 599.

CHAPTER 10

1. Incl. 1, General Douglas MacArthur, May 1, 1931, in Adjutant General to Commanding Generals of All Corps Areas and Departments; Commandants of All General and Special Service Schools; Superintendent, U.S. Military Academy; Chiefs of All Arms, Services, and Bureaus; and War Department General Staff, AG 537.3 I.R. (12–18–34), File 322.012, OCC, Box 7a, RG 177, NA.

2. *War Department Annual Report, 1931,* 42–43.

3. Memorandum, Major R. W. Grow for Colonel Kent, December 21, 1936, File 322.02, OCC, Box 6, RG 177, NA.

4. Memorandum, Brigadier General George P. Tyner for Chief of Staff, G-3/21500, October 25, 1937, File 470.8, OCI, Box 82, RG 177, NA.

5. See Ralph E. Jones, "The Tactical Influence of Recent Tank Developments," *Infantry Journal* 32 (May 1928): 457–67; Ralph E. Jones, "The Weak Spot in Military Progress," *Infantry Journal* 34 (March 1929): 290–92; and George H. Rarey, "United States Tank Requirements," *Tank Notes,* March 1932, 31–39.

6. See K. B. Edmunds, "Defense against Tanks," *Infantry Journal* 38 (January 1931): 38–41; and W. L. Roberts, "Tanks, a G.H.Q. Weapon," *Tank Notes,* March 1932, 16–18.

7. William C. Lee, "Fast Tanks as Leading Tanks and Exploiting Tanks," *Tank Notes,* March 1932, 3.

8. U.S. War Department, *Infantry Field Manual,* vol. 2, *Tank Units* (Washington, D.C.: 1931).

9. Ibid., i; and Jones, Rarey, and Icks, v.

10. *Infantry Field Manual,* 2:181.

11. Severne S. MacLaughlin, "History of the Tank School," *Tank Notes,* May 1932, 20–29.

12. "Major General Stephen O. Fuqua, Chief of Infantry, before Subcommittee of House Committee on Appropriations," *Infantry Journal* 39 (July–August 1932): 251.

13. Ibid., 255.

14. Memorandum, Major General Stephen O. Fuqua for Deputy Chief of Staff, CI-470.8/550-B-1931, June 13, 1931, File 470.8, OCI, Box 83, RG 177, NA.

15. Hofmann, 81, 84.

16. Jones, Rarey, and Icks, 168.

17. Hofmann, 119–21.

18. J. W. Stilwell, "Annual Maneuvers at Benning," *Infantry Journal* 40 (July–August 1933): 254.

19. Major General Edward Croft to President, Infantry Board, CI-470.8/550-B, August 8, 1933, File 470.8, OCI, Box 83, RG 177, NA.

20. Colonel F. L. Munson to Chief of Infantry, IB-470.8, August 25, 1933, File 470.8, OCI, Box 83, RG 177, NA.

21. Major General Edward Croft to President, Infantry Board, CI-470.8/550-B, September 5, 1933, File 470.8, OCI, Box 83, RG 177, NA.

22. Memorandum sheet, Office of the Chief of Infantry, October 28, 1933, File 470.8, OCI, Box 83, RG 177, NA.

23. Colonel G. A. Herbst to President, Infantry Board, CI 470.8/550-B XII "B", March 10, 1936, File 470.8, OCI, Box 82, RG 177, NA.

24. Adjutant General to Commanding Generals of All Corps Areas and Departments, AG 451 (7–8–37), July 28, 1937, File 470.8, OCI, Box 83, RG 177, NA.

25. Brigadier General Asa L. Singleton to Chief of Infantry, IB-470.8/51, September 11, 1937, File 470.8, OCI, Box 88, RG 177, NA.

26. Ibid.

27. George A. Lynch, "Current Infantry Developments," *Infantry Journal* 45 (January–February 1938): 5–6.

28. Ibid., 7.

29. George A. Lynch, "Some Reflections on Infantry Matériel and Tactics," *Infantry Journal* 45 (July–August 1938): 294. Emphasis in original.

30. Chamberlain and Ellis, *The Great Tanks*, 69, 119–120.

31. 1st Ind., Adjutant General to Chief of Infantry, AG 320.2 (6–20–38), August 10, 1938, in the Willis D. Crittenberger Papers (Crittenberger Papers), USAMHI.

32. George A. Lynch, "The Tactics of the New Infantry Regiment," *Infantry Journal* 46 (March–April 1939): 101.

33. Colonel J. B. Woolnough to President, Infantry Board, CI 470.8/550-B XVII, February 28, 1939, File 470.8, OCI, Box 89, RG 177, NA.

34. 1st Ind., Colonel Edwin Butcher to Chief of Infantry, IB-470.8/51 (2–28–39), March 9, 1939, File 470.8, OCI, Box 89, RG 177, NA.

35. John K. Christmas to Chief of Ordnance, O.O. 451.25/9112, APG 451.21/180–80 A, July 21, 1939, File 470.8, OCI, Box 88, RG 177, NA.

36. Lieutenant Colonel E. W. Fales to Chief of Ordnance, CI 470.8/550-B XVII T-5 (12–5–39), February 1, 1940, File 470.8, OCI, Box 88, RG 177, NA.

37. Lieutenant Colonel E. W. Fales to Adjutant General, CI 470.8/550 XXI, May 20, 1940, File 470.8, OCI, Box 90, RG 177, NA.

38. Lieutenant Colonel E. W. Fales to Chief of Ordnance, CI 470.8/550 XVII, June 5, 1940, File 470.8, OCI, Box 81, RG 177, NA.

39. Sub-Committee on Automotive Equipment to Ordnance Committee, Technical Staff, June 10, 1940, File 470.8, OCI, Box 81, RG 177, NA.

40. Major General C. M. Wesson to Adjutant General, June 19, 1940, File 470.8, OCI, Box 81, RG 177, NA.

41. Lieutenant Colonel E. W. Fales to Chief of Ordnance, CI 470.8/550 XVII, June 24, 1940, File 470.8, OCI, Box 81, RG 177, NA.
42. John K. Herr and Edward S. Wallace, *The Story of the U.S. Cavalry, 1775–1942* (Boston: Little, Brown, 1953), 243–44.
43. *War Department Annual Report, 1919*, 480.
44. "Pleads to Maintain Cavalry Strength," *New York Times*, April 17, 1921, p. 11 (ii).
45. George S. Patton Jr. "What the World War Did for Cavalry," *Cavalry Journal* 31 (April 1922): 172.
46. Herr and Wallace, 247.
47. See Kuter oral history interview (K239.0512–810).
48. Major General Herbert B. Crosby, "Our New Cavalry Organization," September 19, 1928, 325-B-6/AWC (9–19–28), USAMHI, 15. See also Duncan Crow and Robert J. Icks, *Encyclopedia of Tanks* (Seacaucus, N.J.: Chartwell, 1975), 17. "Tankettes" were small tanks with a one- or two-man crew.
49. Brigadier General George Van Horn Moseley to Maj. Gen. H. B. Crosby, December 9, 1927, File 322.02, OCC, Box 7a, RG 177, NA.
50. Adjutant General to All Chiefs of Branches and Bureaus, AG 333 E.P. (7–30–29), August 1, 1929, File 333, OCC, Box 12, RG 177, NA.
51. Major General H. B. Crosby to Adjutant General, 334/Army Survey, September 21, 1929, File 333, OCC, Box 12, RG 177, NA.
52. Ibid.
53. Ibid. Emphasis in original.
54. Lieutenant Colonel K. B. Edmunds, "Tactics of a Mechanized Force: A Prophecy," *Cavalry Journal* 39 (July 1930): 410, 411.
55. George S. Patton Jr., "Motorization and Mechanization in the Cavalry," *Cavalry Journal* 39 (July 1930): 331–48.
56. Nenninger, *Development of American Armor*, 104.
57. Krisman, 302.
58. Gillie, 39.
59. Lieutenant Colonel Adna R. Chaffee, "Mechanization in the Army," December 12, 1930, 84–28/AWC (12–12–30), USAMHI.
60. See Nenninger, *Development of American Armor*, 107–10; Gillie, 46–49; Blumenson, 1:884; Killigrew, 4:13–19; and James D. Clayton, *The Years of MacArthur*, 3 vols. (Boston: Houghton Mifflin, 1970), 1:358.
61. George S. Patton Jr. to Colonel Pierre Lorillard Jr., May 14, 1931, in Blumenson, 1:885.
62. Memorandum, Major R. W. Grow for Colonel Kent, December 21, 1936, File 322.02, OCC, Box 6, RG 177, NA.
63. Incl. 1, General Douglas MacArthur, May 1, 1931, in Adjutant General to Commanding Generals of All Corps Areas and Departments; Commandants of All General and Special Service Schools; Superintendent, U.S. Military Academy; Chiefs of All Arms, Services, and Bureaus; and War Department General Staff, AG 537.3 I.R. (12–18–34), File 322.012, OCC, Box 7a, RG 177, NA.
64. Ibid.
65. U.S. War Department Press Release, "Chief of Staff Sets Forth General Principles to Govern the Extension of Mechanization and Motorization Throughout the Army," May 5, 1931, in Guy V. Henry Jr. Papers (Henry Papers), USAMHI.
66. Colonel Aubrey Lippincott to Commandant, Cavalry School, 320.2/1st Cav. M., October 10, 1931, File 320, OCC, Box 3, RG 177, NA; and memorandum, Brigadier General John H. Hughes for Chief of Staff, AG 537.3 I.R. (12–18–34), G-3/33047, January 21, 1935, File 322.02, OCC, Box 7a, RG 177, NA.

67. Adjutant General to Commanding Generals of All Corps Areas; Chiefs of War Department Arms and Services; Commandants of All General and Special Service Schools; and Superintendent, U.S. Military Academy, AG 537.3 (5–13–31), Misc. C., October 3, 1931, File 322.02, OCC, Box 7c, RG 177, NA.
68. Memorandum, Major General Leon B. Kromer for Assistant Chief of Staff, G-1, and Assistant Chief of Staff, G-3, December 19, 1934, File 322.02, OCC, Box 6, RG 177, NA.
69. "History of the Seventh Cavalry Brigade (Mecz), n.d., File 314.7, OCC, Box 3, RG 177, NA; and Gillie, 55–58.
70. Major General Guy V. Henry, "The Trend of Organization and Equipment in the Principal World Powers and Its Probable Role in Wars of the Near Future," *Infantry Journal* 39 (March–April 1932): 100.
71. 1st Ind., Brigadier General A. G. Lott to Chief of Cavalry, 363.162, January 16, 1933, File 320.2, OCC, Box 6, RG 177, NA.
72. Colonel Selwyn D. Smith to Chief of Cavalry, 353.162, December 10, 1932, File 320.2, OCC, Box 6, RG 177, NA.
73. 2d Ind., Major General Guy V. Henry to Commandant, Cavalry School, 320.2/2nd Cav. (12–10–32), March 21, 1933, File 320.2, OCC, Box 6, RG 177, NA. Emphasis in original.
74. George Van Horn Moseley to Colonel Daniel Van Voorhis, OCS 20640–14, February 16, 1933, File 322.012, OCC, Box 6, RG 177, NA.
75. Guy V. Henry, "Autobiography (Duplicate but with New Supplement), n.d. [1945?]," TMs, p. 68, in Henry Papers, USAMHI.
76. "Address of Major General Leon B. Kromer, Chief of Cavalry, at Fort Riley, Kansas, during the April–May Maneuvers," *Cavalry Journal* 43 (May–June 1934): 46.
77. Memorandum, Major General Leon B. Kromer for Assistant Chief of Staff, G-1, and Assistant Chief of Staff, G-3, December 19, 1934, File 322.02, OCC, Box 6, RG 177, NA.
78. Memorandum, Major General Leon B. Kromer for Assistant Chief of Staff, G-3, Attention: Major Gilbert R. Cook, February 1, 1935, File 322.02, OCC, Box 6, RG 177, NA.
79. 1st Ind., Brigadier General John H. Hughes to Chief of Cavalry, February 11, 1935, File 322.02, OCC, Box 6, RG 177, NA.
80. 2d Ind., Major General Leon B. Kromer to Assistant Chief of Staff, G-3, 320.2/Gen. (2–1–35), February 27, 1935, File 322.02, OCC, Box 6, RG 177, NA.
81. Memorandum, Brigadier General John H. Hughes for Chief of Staff, G-3/21500, April 17, 1936, File 322.02, OCC, Box 6, RG 177, NA.
82. Adjutant General to Commanding Generals of All Corps Areas and Departments; Commandants of all General and Special Service Schools; Superintendent, U.S. Military Academy; Chiefs of All Arms, Services, and Bureaus; and War Department General Staff, AG 537.3 I.R. (12–18–34), April 5, 1935, File 322.012, OCC, Box 7a, RG 177, NA.
83. Ibid.
84. Memorandum, L. B. K. [Major General Leon B. Kromer] for Deputy Chief of Staff, April 25, 1935, File 322.02, OCC, Box 6, RG 177, NA.
85. Van Voorhis, "Address at the Army War College on the Subject of 'Mechanization,' 13 October 1937," 6; and Chamberlain and Ellis, 69.
86. Memorandum, Major General Leon B. Kromer for the Executive [Col. A. M. Miller Jr.], March 26, 1936, File 333, OCC, Box 11, RG 177, NA.
87. Memorandum, Colonel A. M. Miller Jr. for Col. A. R. Chaffee, April 25, 1936, File 333, OCC, Box 11, RG 177, NA.
88. Colonel A. M. Miller Jr. to Commandant, Cavalry School, May 4, 1936, File 322.02, OCC, Box 17, RG 177, NA.
89. "History of the Seventh Cavalry Brigade."
90. Memorandum, Colonel A. M. Miller Jr. for Assistant Chief of Staff, G-3, December 28, 1936, File 322.02, OCC, Box 6, RG 177, NA.

91. Memorandum, Colonel Guy Kent for General Kromer, December 15, 1936, File 322.02, OCC, Box 6, RG 177, NA.

92. Major General Leon B. Kromer to Commanding General, 7th Cavalry Brigade (Mecz.), December 7, 1936, in Crittenberger Papers, USAMHI.

93. Brigadier General Daniel Van Voorhis to Chief of Cavalry, February 12, 1937, in Crittenberger Papers, USAMHI.

94. "History of the Seventh Cavalry Brigade."

95. See, for example, Bruce Palmer, "Mechanized Cavalry in the Second Army Maneuvers," *Cavalry Journal* 45 (November–December 1936): 461–78; "Tactical Employment of the Mechanized Division," *Quarterly Review of Military Literature [Military Review]*, no. 65 (June 1937), 203–31; R. W. Grow, "Mechanized Cavalry," *Cavalry Journal* 47 (January–February 1938): 30–31; and R. W. Grow, "One Cavalry," *Cavalry Journal* 47 (March–April 1938): 150.

96. Brigadier General Daniel Van Voorhis to Adjutant General, July 23, 1937, File 680.2, OCC, Box 80, RG 177, NA.

97. Ibid.

98. Palmer, "Mechanized Cavalry in the Second Army Maneuvers," 461.

99. "Necessity for Horse Cavalry under Modern Conditions," *Cavalry Journal* 46 (May–June 1937): 251.

100. Herr and Wallace, 242, 248.

101. "My Greeting to All Cavalrymen," *Cavalry Journal* 47 (March–April 1938): 5.

102. H. S. Hawkins, "Imagination Run Wild," *Cavalry Journal* 47 (November–December 1938): 491.

103. "Remarks Re Conference with Assistant Chief of Staff, G-3," October 10, 1938, File 334.3, OCC, Box 13, RG 177, NA.

104. Memorandum, Major General J. K. Herr for Chief of Staff, October 17, 1938, File 322.02, OCC, Box 6, RG 177, NA.

105. Memorandum, Lieutenant Colonel Willis D. Crittenberger for Chief of Cavalry, November 22, 1938, in Crittenberger Papers, USAMHI.

106. "What of the Future?" *Cavalry Journal* 48 (January–February 1939): 3–6.

107. "Cavalry Affairs before Congress," *Cavalry Journal* 48 (March–April 1939): 130–35.

108. Ibid.

109. "Training of Modern Cavalry for War: Polish Cavalry Doctrine," *Cavalry Journal* 48 (July–August 1939): 298–305.

110. "Cavalry in Poland," *Cavalry Journal* 39 (July–August 1939): 315.

111. John K. Herr, "Lecture at the Army War College, 19 September 1939, 'The Cavalry'," TMs, MSS G-3 #5-A, 1940/AWC (9–19–39), USAMHI.

112. Lieutenant Colonel H. J. M. Smith to Chief of Cavalry, September 21, 1939, with handwritten noted signed "H. S." at bottom, File 320.02, OCC, Box 6, RG 177, NA.

113. Adna R. Chaffee, "Address at the Army War College on the Subject of 'Mechanized Cavalry,' 29 September 1939," TMs, p. 31, Mechanized Cavalry Board Maneuvers, 1929–1939, Box 1, RG 177, NA.

114. Ibid., 34.

115. Ibid., 31.

116. Ibid., 30–31.

117. Hamilton S. Hawkins, "General Hawkins' Notes: Obvious Conclusions," *Cavalry Journal* 48 (November–December 1939): 516.

118. "Time to Wake Up," *Cavalry Journal* 48 (November–December 1939): 507.

119. Memorandum, Brigadier General F. M. Andrews for Chief of Cavalry, G-3/42070, February 23, 1940, File 322.02, OCC, Box 7b, RG 177, NA.

120. Memorandum, Major General J. K. Herr for Assistant Chief of Staff, G-3, 322.02, February 28, 1940, File 322.02, OCC, Box 7b, RG 177, NA. Emphasis in original.

121. Memorandum, Major General J. K. Herr for Chief of Staff, 322.02, April 10, 1940, File 322.02, OCC, Box 7, RG 177, NA.

122. Colonel K. S. Bradford to Colonel Arthur H. Wilson, May 13, 1940, File 322.02, OCC, Box 7, RG 177, NA.

123. *History of the Armored Force*, 6–7; Blumenson, 1:949; and Nenninger, *Development of American Armor*, 182–84. The Provisional Tank Brigade contained all infantry tank units except one tank company assigned to Fort Lewis, Washington, and one company in Hawaii (*History of the Armored Force*, 6).

124. *History of the Armored Force*, 7; and Blumenson, 1:948–50.

125. "Editorial Comment," *Cavalry Journal* 55 (May–June 1946): 38.

126. *History of the Armored Force*, 7.

127. Memorandum, Brigadier General F. M. Andrews for Chief of Cavalry, G-3/41665, June 1, 1940, File 322.02, OCC, Box 8, RG 177, NA.

128. Memorandum, Major General George A. Lynch for Assistant Chief of Staff, G-3, June 2, 1940, File 322.02, OCC, Box 8, RG 177, NA. Emphasis in original. General Lynch underlined the sections of the quote from *Time* magazine in this memorandum for Andrews.

129. Ibid. One can only speculate about the deeper meaning of the Air Corps analogy used by Lynch, since Andrews was an Air Corps officer and had commanded the General Headquarters Air Force.

130. Memorandum, Major General J. K. Herr for Assistant Chief of Staff, G-3, June 3, 1940, File 322.02, OCC, Box 8, RG 177, NA.

131. Memorandum, Major General J. K. Herr for Chief of Staff, 322.02, June 5, 1940, File 322.02, OCC, Box 8, RG 177, NA.

132. Letter, Major General J. K. Herr to Commanding General, 7th Cavalry Brigade, 322.02, June 7, 1940, and Major General J. K. Herr to General. C. L. Scott, 322.02, June 7, 1940, File 322.02, OCC, Box 8, RG 177, NA.

133. Note, K. S. B. [Colonel K. S. Bradford] to General Herr, June 7, 1940, File 322.02, OCC, Box 8, RG 177, NA.

134. Memorandum, Brigadier General F. M. Andrews for A.C. of S., G-1; A.C. of S., G-2.; A.C. of S., G-4; A.C. of S., WPD; Chief of Infantry; Chief of Cavalry; Chief of Field Artillery; Chief of Coast Artillery; Chief of Air Corps; Chief of Engineers; Chief of Ordnance; Chief of Chemical Warfare; Chief of Signal Corps; Quartermaster General; and Surgeon General, June 7, 1940, File 322.02, OCC, Box 8, RG 177, NA.

135. *History of the Armored Force*, 8.

136. Memorandum, Brigadier General Adna R. Chaffee for Chief of Infantry, Chief of Cavalry, Chief of Field Artillery, Chief of Chemical Warfare Service, Chief of Engineers, Quartermaster General, Surgeon General, and Chief of Air Corps, June 13, 1940, File 322.02, Office of the Chief of Cavalry, Correspondence, 1921–1942, Box 8, RG 177, NA. Brigadier General Chaffee (cavalry, president), Brigadier General Charles L. Scott (cavalry), Colonel Gladeon M. Barnes (ordnance), Colonel Sereno M. Brett (infantry), and Major Ingemar M. Oseth (infantry, recorder) were the members.

137. Memorandum, Brigadier General C. L. Scott for General Andrews, June 12, 1940, File 322.02, OCC, Box 8, RG 177, NA.

138. Ibid.

139. Memorandum, Brigadier General C. L. Scott, June 17, 1940, File 322.02, OCC, Box 8, RG 177, NA. See also draft memorandum, Lieutenant Colonel W. M. Grimes for Chief of Staff, n.d. [June 20, 1940], File 322.02, OCC, Box 8, RG 177, NA.

140. Draft memorandum, Lieutenant Colonel W. M. Grimes for Chief of Staff, n.d. [June 20, 1940], File 322.02, OCC, Box 8, RG 177, NA.

141. Memorandum, Lieutenant Colonel Willis D. Crittenberger for Chief of Cavalry, June 21, 1940, File 322.02, OCC, Box 8, RG 177, NA.

142. Memorandum, Major General George A. Lynch for Chief of Staff, June 22, 1940, File 322.02, OCC, Box 8, RG 177, NA.

143. Memorandum, Brigadier General F. M. Andrews for Adjutant General, G-3/ 41665, July 5, 1940, File 322.02, OCC, Box 8, RG 177, NA.

144. Ibid.; and memorandum, Brigadier General F. M. Andrews for Chief of Cavalry, July 5, 1940, File 322.02, OCC, Box 8, RG 177, NA.

145. Brigadier General Bruce Magruder for Adjutant General, AG 320.2 AF, October 2, 1940, File 322.02, OCC, Box 8, RG 177, NA.

146. *History of the Armored Force*, 45.

147. Robert W. Grow, "The Ten Lean Years: From the Mechanized Force (1930) to the Armored Force (1940), 1969," TMs, p. 90, in Robert W. Grow Papers (Grow Papers), USAMHI.

148. *Biennial Report, 1941*, 6.

149. Robert R. Palmer, Bell I. Wiley, and William R. Keast, *The Procurement and Training of Ground Combat Troops*, U.S. Army in World War II (1948; Washington, D.C., 1973), 250.

150. *History of the Armored Force*, 17.

151. U.S. War Department, *FM 100-5, Field Service Regulations: Operations* (Washington, D.C., 1941), 278.

152. *History of the Armored Force*, 44.

153. Adjutant General to Chief of Armored Force; Commanding General I Armored Corps; Chief of Infantry; and Chief of Staff, GHQ, AG 320.2 (1–21–41) M (Ret) M-C, April 3, 1943, File 320.2, OCI, Box 15, RG 177, NA.

154. *History of the Armored Force*, 45.

155. *FM 100-5*, 1941, 278–79.

156. George A. Lynch, "Current Infantry Developments," *Infantry Journal* 45 (January–February 1938): 5–7.

157. *History of the Armored Force*, 18, 33, 44, 47. See also Shelby L. Stanton, *Order of Battle: U.S. Army, World War II* (Novato: Presidio Press, 1984), 19.

158. Chaffee, "Address at the Army War College on the Subject of 'Mechanized Cavalry,' 29 September 1939," 32.

159. Major General Charles L. Scott to Maj. Gen. John K. Herr, August 7, 1940, quoted in *History of the Armored Force*, 9, 16–17.

160. *History of the Armored Force*, 29.

161. *FM 100-5*, 1941, 263. Emphasis in original.

162. Ibid., 273.

163. Larry H. Addington, *The Blitzkrieg Era and the German General Staff, 1865–1941* (New Brunswick, N.J.: Rutgers University Press, 1971), 44–45; and B. H. Liddell Hart, *The German Generals Talk* (New York: Quill, 1979), 95. In Liddell Hart's interview with General Ritter von Thoma, he asked von Thoma to elaborate on the major reasons behind the success of the German armored breakthroughs. The first element in von Thoma's list was "the concentration of all forces on the point of penetration in co-operation with bombers."

164. *FM 17-10*, 1942, 11.

165. Ibid., 12.

166. *FM 100-5*, 1941, 264.

167. Ibid., 269–70.

168. Major General Adna R. Chaffee to Representative David L. Terry, cited in *History of the Armored Force*, 12.

169. D. L. McCaskey, *The Role of Army Ground Force in the Development of Equipment,* Study no. 34 (Washington, D.C., 1946), 37.

170. Chamberlain and Ellis, 69–72; and *History of the Armored Force,* 12.

171. McCaskey, 37; and *History of the Armored Force,* 35.

172. Lt. Col. E. W. Fales for Chief of Ordnance, CI 470.8/550 XVII, June 5, 1940, File 470.8, OCI, Box 81, RG 177, NA.

173. Charles M. Baily, *Faint Praise: American Tanks and Tank Destroyers during World War II* (Hamden, Conn.: Archon Books, 1983), 4–5; Chamberlain and Ellis, 121–25; *History of the Armored Force,* 87; and R. P. Hunnicut, *Sherman: A History of the American Medium Tank* (Belmont, Calif.: Taurus Enterprises, 1978), 559, 562.

174. Chamberlain and Ellis, 128–31; *History of the Armored Force,* 12; and Hunnicut, 525. Production of the M4 medium tank, known as the Sherman, did not begin until July 1942.

175. *History of the Armored Force,* 144–45.

176. Blumenson, 2:34–36, 41.

177. Ibid., 2:42–43; and Christopher R. Gabel, *Seek, Strike, and Destroy: U.S. Army Tank Destroyer Doctrine in World War II,* Leavenworth Papers no. 12 (Fort Leavenworth: U.S. Army Command and General Staff College, 1985), 14–15.

178. Gabel, 15–16.

179. Watson, 240.

180. Gabel, 16–17; and "GHQ Comments on North Carolina Maneuvers," *Command and General Staff School Quarterly [Military Review],* no. 83 (January 1942), 115.

181. Christopher R. Gabel, "Evolution of US Armor Mobility," *Military Review* 64 (March 1984): 59–61; and *History of the Armored Force,* 29–31.

182. *New York Times,* September 15, 1941, quoted in Gabel, "Evolution of US Armor Mobility," 59. For an examination of the Army maneuver program, see Christopher R. Gabel, *The U.S. Army GHQ Maneuvers of 1941* (Washington, D.C., 1991).

183. Major General George A. Lynch to Assistant Chief of Staff, G-3, AG 320.2 (7–3–40) M-C, July 3, 1940, McNair Files, Box 8, RG 337, NA.

184. 2d Ind., Brigadier General L. J. McNair to Adjutant General, AG 320.2 (7–3–40) M-C, July 29, 1940, McNair Files, Box 8, RG 337, NA.

185. Gabel, *Seek, Strike, and Destroy,* 14–18.

186. Ibid., 1.

187. U.S. War Department, *FM 18-5, Tank Destroyer Field Manual: Organization and Tactics of Tank Destroyer Units* (Washington, D.C., 1942), 7.

188. Ibid.

189. Ibid. See also *Gabel, Seek, Strike, and Destroy,* 27–28; Hunnicut, 563, 564; and Lida Mayo, *The Ordnance Department: On Beachhead and Battlefront,* U.S. , Army in World War II (Washington, D.C., 1968), 322, 327, 335, 336, 340.

190. Memorandum, Colonel K. B. Edmunds for Commandant, July 22, 1940, McNair Files, Box 8, RG 337, NA.

191. K. B. Edmunds, "Antimechanized Defense: Comments at the Conclusion of a Map Exercise at the Command and General Staff School," *Command and General Staff School Quarterly [Military Review],* no. 81 (June 1941): 102. Emphasis in original.

192. Major General Jacob L. Devers to Lieutenant General Lesley J. McNair, December 18, 1941, McNair Files, Box 9, RG 337, NA.

193. Lieutenant General L. J. McNair to Major General J. L. Devers, May 9, 1942, McNair Files, Box 9, RG 337, NA.

194. Major General Jacob L. Devers to Lieutenant General Lesley J. McNair, July 18, 1942, McNair Files, Box 9, RG 337, NA.

195. Ibid. See handwritten note at top of letter, "Talked fonecon this," with McNair's initials.

196. Draft reply to General Devers [July 18, 1942] to General McNair, n.d. [July 1942], McNair Files, Box 9, RG 337, NA.

197. Ray S. Cline, *Washington Command Post: The Operations Division,* U.S. Army in World War II (1951; Washington, D.C., 1970), 92–93.

CHAPTER 11

1. *Bombardment, 1931,* 6921, 68–71. (quote on page 69) Emphasis in original.

2. Wesley F. Craven and James L. Cate, eds., *The Army Air Forces in World War II,* 7 vols. (1948–58; Washington, D.C., 1983), 1:161–62.

3. *War Department Annual Report, 1931,* 38, quoted in Craven and Cate, 1:62.

4. Maurer, *Aviation in the U.S. Army,* 289.

5. Jean H. Dubuque and Robert F. Gleckner, "The Development of the Heavy Bomber, 1918–1944, U.S. Air Force Historical Study No. 6, 1951," TMs, pp. 101–6, USAFHRA (Manhattan: Sunflower University Press, n.d.), 70–72.

6. Ibid., 73, 146.

7. Maurer, *Aviation in the U.S. Army,* 388–89.

8. Finney, 15.

9. Lieutenant Colonel John F. Curry to Chief of Air Corps, April 8, 1932, 248.192 (1929–1936), USAFHRA.

10. Ibid.

11. Lieutenant H. L. George, "Lecture Given at the Marine Corps School, 'Bombardment Aviation'," 248.2202 A-3 (1932–33), USAFHRA. See also Haywood S. Hansell Jr., "Harold L. George: Apostle of Air Power," in *Makers of the United States Air Force,* USAF Warrior Studies, ed. John L. Frisbee (Washington, D.C., 1987), 73–97.

12. Ibid.

13. Memorandum, 1st Lt. Kenneth N. Walker for Assistant Commandant, Air Corps Tactical School, September 24, 1932, 248.211–13, USAFHRA.

14. *Bombardment, 1933.*

15. Finney, 56–59.

16. C. L. Chennault, "The Role of Defensive Pursuit," p. 7, 248.282–4 (1933), USAFHRA.

17. Ibid., 12.

18. Ibid., 11; and C. L. Chennault, "The Role of Defensive Pursuit, Part II: Interceptions," p. 13, 248.282–4 (1933), USAFHRA.

19. *Pursuit Aviation, 1933,* 6, 11.

20. Captain Claire L. Chennault to Assistant Commandant, December 4, 1934, 248.282–11 (1937), USAFHRA.

21. Memorandum, Brigadier General L. W. Miller for Commanding General, Army Air Forces, April 15, 1943, File "B-17 History," Henry H. Arnold Papers (Arnold Papers), Box 39, Library of Congress (LC), Washington, D.C. See also Robert W. Krauskopf, "The Army and the Strategic Bomber, 1930–1939," *Military Affairs* 22 (Summer 1958): 83–94, and "The Army and the Strategic Bomber, 1930–1939," pt. 2, *Military Affairs* 22 (Winter 1958): 208–15.

22. Tate, 173–74. The figure of 1,800 airplanes came from the authorization in the 1926 Air Corps Act. The plans under consideration were those for a war with Britain (Red), with a coalition of Britain and Japan (Red-Orange), or with Mexico (Green).

23. Ibid., 176–78.

24. Ibid., 178.

25. Major R. M. Jones to Adjutant General, AG 452.1 (7–5–34), July 5, 1935, File 452.1, Army Adjutant General (AG), Box 2584, RG 407, NA.

26. I. B. Holley Jr., *Buying Aircraft: Matériel Procurement for the Army Air Forces,* U.S. Army in World War II (1964; Washington, D.C., 1989), 54.

27. "Report of Special Committee, General Council, on Employment of Army Air Corps under Certain Strategic Plans," AG 580 (8–11–31), RG 407, NA; cited in Tate, 177.

28. *Report of the Chief of Staff, 1934,* 13.

29. Tate, 177–82.

30. See Holley, *Buying Aircraft,* 55; and Tate, 182.

31. John F. Shiner, *Foulois and the U.S. Army Air Corps, 1931–1935,* United States Air Force General Histories (Washington, D.C., 1983), 125–27.

32. Ibid., 148. See also Tate, 168–70.

33. Holley, *Buying Aircraft,* 55–56.

34. U.S. War Department, *Final Report of War Department Special Committee on Army Air Corps* (Washington, D.C., 1934), 31, 75.

35. Memorandum, Brigadier General C. E. Kilbourne for Chiefs of General Staff Divisions, Chiefs of Arms and Services, and Individual Officers Who Worked on This Report, September 11, 1934, File 334.8, OCC, Box 13, RG 177, NA.

36. U.S. Congress, Senate, *Report of the Federal Aviation Commission,* 74th Cong., 1st sess., 1935, Senate Document no. 15, 248.211–53 (January 1935), USAFHRA, 119.

37. "Testimony Presented by Major Donald Wilson, Capt. Robert Olds, Capt. Harold Lee George, Capt. Robert M. Webster, 1st Lieut. K. N. Walker before the Federal Aviation Commission," 248.121–3 (May 7–9, 1935), USAFHRA.

38. Craven and Cate, 1:31.

39. "Lecture: Principles of War Applied to Air Force Action, 28 May 1934," in *Air Force Lectures, 1933–1934,* USAMHI. See also oral history interview of Maj. General Donald Wilson (K239.0512–878).

40. "Lecture: The Air Force, 16 May 1934," in *Air Force Lectures, 1933–1934,* USAMHI.

41. "A Study of Proposed Air Corps Doctrine, Made by the Air Corps Tactical School, Based upon Information Furnished by the War Plans Division, General Staff, in Memorandum, Dated December 21, 1934," January 31, 1935, 145.91–418 (December 1934–December 1940), USAFHRA.

42. Captain R. M. Webster to Commanding General, 2d Corps Area, June 27, 1935, 248.211–28, pt. 1, USAFHRA.

43. 3d Ind., Major F. V. Hemenway to Captain R. M. Webster, Air-201 Webster, R.M., July 25, 1935, 248.211–8, pt. 1, USAFHRA.

44. Webster's project consists of eight sections and is contained in 248.211–28, pts. 1–8, USAFHRA.

45. Maurer, *Aviation in the U.S. Army,* 354. See also Dubuque and Gleckner, 72–104.

46. Craven and Cate, 1:66.

47. Colonel Wm. T. Carpenter to Adjutant General, AG 452.1 (11–8–35), November 8, 1935, File 452.1, AG, Box 2583, RG 407, NA.

48. Memorandum, Colonel Wm. T. Carpenter for Chief of Staff, AG 452.1 (10–1–35), G-4/29217–29, October 18, 1935, File 452.1, Army AG, Box 2583, RG 407, NA.

49. Maurer, *Aviation in the U.S. Army,* 354.

50. Brigadier General O. Westover for Adjutant General, AG 452.1 (11–8–35), November 8, 1935, File 452.1, AG, Box 2583, RG 407, NA.

51. Ibid.

52. Memorandum, Colonel Wm. T. Carpenter for Chief of Staff, AG 452.1 (11–8–35) G-4/29217–29, November 14, 1935, File 452.1, AG, Box 2583, RG 407, NA.

53. Ibid. See also Maurer, *Aviation in the U.S. Army,* 354; and Craven and Cate, 1:66.

54. Maurer, *Aviation in the U.S. Army,* 354–55.

55. Memorandum, Brigadier General L. W. Miller for Commanding General, Army Air

Forces, April 15, 1943, File "B-17 History," Arnold Papers, Box 39, LC; Maurer, *Aviation in the U.S. Army*, 360–61; and Holley, *Buying Aircraft*, 142.

56. Memorandum, Brigadier General Geo. R. Spalding for Chief of Staff, AG 452.1 (8–8–36), G-4/27277–12, August 8, 1936, File 452.1, AG, Box 2583, RG 407, NA.

57. Memorandum, Brigadier General Geo. R. Spalding for Chief of Staff, AG 452.1 (9–14–36), G-4.27277–12, September 14, 1936, File 452.1, AG, Box 2583, RG 407, NA.

58. U.S. War Department, *Training Regulations No. 440-15, Air Corps: Employment of the Air Forces of the Army* (Washington, D.C., 1935), 5.

59. Major Harold L. George, "Principles of War," in *Annual* (Montgomery, Ala.: Air Corps Tactical School, 1937), 11.

60. *Bombardment, 1935*, 37.

61. Michael J. H. Taylor, ed., *Jane's Encyclopedia of Aviation* (New York: Portland House, 1989), 173.

62. *Bombardment, 1935*, 40. See also Kuter oral history interview (K239.0512–810), 114, 131–32.

63. Dubuque and Gleckner, 72, 73.

64. Major General F. M. Andrews to Adjutant General, AF 452.1 (8–27–36), September 15, 1936, File 452.1, AG, General Files, Box 2581, RG 407, NA.

65. Memorandum, Colonel Wm. T. Carpenter for Chief of Staff, AG 452.1 (10–1–35) G-4/29217–29, October 18, 1935, File 452.1, AG, Box 2583, RG 407, NA. See also I. B. Holley Jr., "An Enduring Challenge: The Problem of Air Force Doctrine," and William R. Emerson, "Operation POINTBLANK: A Tale of Bombers and Fighters," in *The Harmon Memorial Lectures in Military History, 1959–1987*, United States Air Force Special Studies, ed. Harry R. Borowski (Washington, D.C., 1988), 425–72.

66. Henry H. Arnold, "Address at the Army War College, 'The Air Defense Problem as Studied by the First Wing, G.H.Q. Air Force,' [ca. 1936]," TMs, p. 8, File "Speech: Air Defense Problem," Arnold Papers, Box 277, LC. See also William W. Welsh, "Research on Maneuver Rules—Bombardment Losses to Pursuit, 22 May 1937," TMs, 248.222–65A, USAFHRA.

67. See Kuter oral history interview, 112–14.

68. 2d Ind., Office of the Chief of Air Corps to Adjutant General, AG 452.1 (6–1–37), June 9, 1937, File 452.1, AG, Box 2580, RG 407, NA.

69. Brigadier General Haywood S. Hansell, "Lecture Presented at the Air War College, 'The Development of the United States Concept of Bombardment Operations,' 16 February 1951," TMs, p. 7, K239.716251–75 (February 16, 1951), USAFHRA.

70. Kuter oral history interview, 111.

71. Ibid., 112.

72. *Pursuit Aviation, 1939*, 4, 40. See also Colonel M. F. Harmon to Brigadier General B. K. Yount, November 25, 1939, 145.91–418 (December 1934–December 1940), USAFHRA.

73. *Air Operations—Immediate Support of Ground Forces, 1937–1938*, 2.

74. *Training Regulations 440-15, 1926*, 12.

75. *Attack Aviation, 1935*, 1.

76. 2d Wrapper Ind., Colonel John H. Pirie to Chief of Air Corps, October 28, 1938, File 385, OCAC, Box 20, RG 18, NA.

77. George Fielding Elliot, *Bombs Bursting in Air*, in Eugene M. Emme, *The Impact of Air Power* (Princeton, N.J.: Van Nostrand, 1959), 67. See also Barry R. Posen, *The Sources of Military Doctrine: France, Britain, and Germany between the World Wars* (Ithaca, N.Y.: Cornell University Press, 1984).

78. Department of State, Eu 862.248/179, September 27, 1938, File 385, OCAC, Box 20, RG 18, NA.

79. Forrest C. Pogue, *George C. Marshall*, 4 vols. (New York: Viking, 1963), 1:321–22.

80. Ibid., 1:322–23; and Watson, 136–37.
81. Watson, 136–39.
82. Arnold, 179.
83. Pogue, 1:323.
84. Arnold, 180. See also Major General H. H. Arnold, "Address at the Army War College, 'Air Power Related to Hemisphere Defense, and Procurement and Training of Personnel,' September 18, 1939," p. 15, 248.211–19A (September 18, 1939), USAFHRA.
85. Pogue, 1:323–26.
86. Arnold, 178.
87. Pogue, 1:323.
88. Dallek, 173.
89. Michael S. Sherry, *The Rise of American Air Power: The Creation of Armageddon* (New Haven: Yale University Press, 1987), 80.
90. Dallek, 173.
91. Watson, 139–45, 299.
92. A. Craig Baird, *Representative American Speeches, 1939–1940,* in Emme, 71.
93. Tate, 230. The Second Aviation Objective for eighty-four groups was approved in March 1941.
94. Watson, 280–91.
95. Letters to Chairmen of Senate and House Military Affairs Committees, June 20, 1941, made public in WD Press Release, June 21, 1941, quoted in "Organization of the Army Air Arm, 1935–1943," Army Air Forces Historical Studies no. 10, July 1944, p. 18, Arnold Papers, Box 267, LC.
96. Franklin D. Roosevelt to Secretary of War, July 9, 1941, File "1934–1941," Arnold Papers, Box 273, LC.
97. Cline, 59; and Thomas H. Greer, *The Development of Air Doctrine in the Army Air Arm, 1917–1941,* USAF Historical Study no. 89 (1955; Washington, D.C., 1985), 124.
98. A-WPD/1, Munitions Requirements of the Army Air Forces To Defeat Our Potential Enemies, table 2, section 2, pt. 3, appendix 2, p. 1, in Joint Board 355 (Serial 707) (National Archives Microfilm Publication M1080), NA. Hereafter cited as AWPD-1.
99. Greer, 124. For examples of how the work of this group of air officers has been mystified see Haywood S. Hansell Jr., *The Air Plan That Defeated Hitler* (Atlanta: Higgins-McArthur/Longino and Porter, 1972); and James C. Gaston, *Planning the American Air War: Four Men and Nine Days in 1941* (Washington, D.C.: National Defense University Press, 1982).
100. AWPD-1, table 4, section 2, pt. 3, appendix 2, p. 1. Emphasis in original.
101. Ibid., chart 2, section 1, pt. 3, appendix 2.
102. "AWPD-1: File of informal notes in AWP Division HQ AAF, Office of Chief of the Air Staff, Washington," August 25, 1941, p. 18, File "1934–1941," Arnold Papers, Box 273, LC.
103. AWPD-1, chart 2, section 1, pt. 3, appendix 2.
104. Ibid., table 2, section 2, pt. 3, appendix 2, p. 10. Emphasis in original.
105. Ibid., table 4, section 2, pt. 3, appendix 2, pp. 1–2.
106. Ibid. See also Thomas A. Fabyanic, "A Critique of United States Air War Planning, 1941–1944" (Ph.D. diss., Saint Louis University, 1973), 40–48; and Bernard Boylan, "Development of the Long-Range Escort Fighter, U.S. Air Force Historical Study No. 136, 1955," TMs, pp. 101–36, USAFHRA.
107. This is a chapter title from Paul Fussell, *Wartime: Understanding and Behavior in the Second World War* (New York: Oxford University Press, 1989), 13–19.
108. AWPD-1, table 2, section 2, pt. 3, appendix 2, p. 2.
109. AWPD-1, table 17, section 2, pt. 3, appendix 2, p. 3. Emphasis in original.

110. Ibid., table 1, section 2, pt. 3, appendix 2, p. 1; and Tate, 231. See also Holley, *Buying Aircraft*, 209–573.

111. Fabyanic, 75.

112. Office of the Chief of Naval Operations for General G. C. Marshall, Op-10-MD, August 19, 1941, File "Separate Air Force," Arnold Papers, Box 46, LC.

113. Major General H. H. Arnold to Warren Atherton, September 3, 1941; and Major General H. H. Arnold to Norman M. Lyon, September 3, 1941, File "Separate Air Force," Arnold Papers, Box 46, LC.

114. Memorandum, Major General H. H. Arnold for General Marshall, X–57–2, A.C., September 2, 1941, File "Separate Air Force," Arnold Papers, Box 46, LC.

115. "Organization of the Army Air Arm, 1935–1943," Army Air Forces Historical Studies no. 10, July 1944, pp. 19–20, Arnold Papers, Box 267, LC.

116. Ibid., 27.

117. Military Intelligence Division, U.S. War Department, "Tentative Lessons Aviation: Notes on British Bombsights and Bombing Tactics," no. 29, G-2/183–345, September 11, 1941, 248.222–50 (July 10, 1941), USAFHRA.

118. "Summaries of B-17's (Fortress I) Bombing Operations," September 12, 1941, 167.6-45 (September 12, 1941), USAFHRA.

119. Ibid. See also Retired U.S. Army Air Corps Officer to Lt. Hansell, September 14, 1937, 248.211–24 (1937), USAFHRA; Henry J. Reilly to General Arnold, May 13, 1938, File 385, OCAC, Box 20, RG 18, NA; Lieutenant Colonel Ralph Royce to Adjutant General, July 17, 1939, 248.211–24 (1935), USAFHRA; and memorandum, Brigadier General Sherman Miles for Chief of Staff, AG 452.1 (5–22–40), G-2/183-Z-376, May 22, 1940, File 452.1, AG, Box 810, RG 407, NA. These documents are a sampling of reports from combat observers that question many of the fundamental premises of American bombardment doctrine, particularly bomber invulnerability and accuracy.

120. Max Hastings, *Bomber Command* (1979; New York: Touchstone, 1989), 123–40.

121. Memorandum, L. S. K. [Laurence S. Kuter] for Chief of Staff, January 13, 1942, 168.7012 (1942–1943 SL-3), USAFHRA.

122. Lieutenant General H. H. Arnold to Air Chief Marshall Sir Charles F. A. Portal, March 9, 1942, File "Correspondence—Commanders in the Field," Arnold Papers, Box 38, LC.

123. Craven and Cate, 1:612–54.

124. Memorandum, Lieutenant General H. H. Arnold for Chief of Staff, July 29, 1942, File "Bomber Command to Great Britain," Arnold Papers, Box 149, LC; memorandum, Lieutenant. General H. H. Arnold for Harry Hopkins, September 3, 1942, File "Mr. Hopkins," Arnold Papers, Box 43, LC; memorandum, Lieutenant. General H. H. Arnold for Honorable Harry L. Hopkins, October 7, 1942; File "Mr. Hopkins," Arnold Papers, Box 43, LC; and memorandum, Lieutenant General H. H. Arnold for Harry Hopkins, December 18, 1942, File "Mr. Hopkins," Arnold Papers, Box 43, LC.

125. Brigadier General Ira C. Eaker to Lieutenant General H. H. Arnold, August 8, 1942, File "Bomber Command to Go to Great Britain," Arnold Papers, Box 49, LC.

126. Major General Carl Spaatz to Arnold, August 11, 1942, File "Bomber Command to Go to Great Britain," Arnold Papers, Box 49, LC.

127. Kit C. Carter and Robert Mueller, comps., *The Army Air Forces in World War II: Combat Chronology, 1941–1945* (Washington, D.C., 1973), 33–34.

128. Major General Carl Spaatz to Arnold, August 21, 1942, File "Bomber Command to Go to Great Britain," Arnold Papers, Box 49, LC.

129. Major General Carl Spaatz to Arnold, August 24, 1942, File "Correspondence—Commanders in the Field," Arnold Papers, Box 38, LC.

130. Memorandum, Lieutenant General H. H. Arnold for Harry Hopkins, September 3, 1942, File "Bombers," Arnold Papers, Box 41, LC.

131. Lieutenant. General H. H. Arnold to Major General Carl A. Spaatz, September 3, 1942, File "Correspondence—Commanders in the Field," Arnold Papers, Box 38, LC. Emphasis in original. See also Fabyanic, 79–130.

132. Memorandum, Lieutenant General H. H. Arnold for Harry Hopkins, October 29, 1942, File "Mr. Hopkins," Arnold Papers, Box 43, LC.

133. Major General Ira C. Eaker to Lieutenant General H. H. Arnold, October 20, 1942, File "Bomber Command to Great Britain," Arnold Papers, Box 149, LC.

CHAPTER 12

1. *Biennial Report, 1941*, 1–2.

2. Lieutenant Colonel H. J. M. Smith to Chief of Cavalry, September 21, 1939, File 320.02, OCC, Box 6, RG 177, NA.

3. Pogue, 2:290.

4. Marshall Statement, September 5, 1945, *Patch-Simpson Board Proceedings, 1945*, OCS, RG 110 58–85, quoted in ibid., 2:289.

5. Cline, 10.

6. Memorandum, Major General George A. Lynch for Assistant Chief of Staff, G-3, June 2, 1940; and memorandum, Major General J. K. Herr for Assistant Chief of Staff, G-3, June 3, 1940, File 322.02, OCC, Box 8, RG 177, NA.

7. Memorandum, Brigadier General F. M. Andrews for Chief of Staff, AG 320.2 (10-2-40), G-3/41665, November 19, 1940; and memorandum, Major General J. K. Herr for Assistant Chief of Staff, G-3, 320.2, December 7, 1940, File 322.02, OCC, Box 8, RG 177, NA.

8. Pogue, 2:81–83; and Watson, 206.

9. Watson, 206.

10. *Biennial Report, 1941*, 8.

11. Watson, 207.

12. Unused memorandum, WPD for CofS, n.d., WPD 4618, quoted in Cline, 70.

13. Cline, 68–72.

14. Notes on Conferences in OCS, II, 424C, WDCSA records, quoted in Cline, 73.

15. Memorandum, AAF/A-WPD for Chief of Staff, n.d. [November 1941], 145.96–104 (WP-III-B-7), USAFHRA.

16. Cline, 73; and memorandum, Major C. K. Gailey for Secretary General Staff, WPD 4614, November 28, 1941, 145.96–104 (WP-III-B-7), USAFHRA.

17. Pogue, 2:293.

18. *Pearl Harbor Attack: Hearings before the Joint Committee on the Investigation of the Pearl Harbor Attack*, pt. 14, pp. 1328–30, quoted in Cline, 76–77.

19. Cline, 77–78, 90; and Gordon W. Prange, *At Dawn We Slept: The Untold Story of Pearl Harbor* (New York: Penguin, 1982), 402–13, 599, 652, 686–88.

20. Prange, 592, 599–600, 823.

21. *Hearings before the Joint Committee on the Investigation of the Pearl Harbor Attack*, pt. 39, pp. 1–21, quoted in ibid., 599.

22. Franklin D. Roosevelt to Secretary of War, January 3, 1942, File 452.1, AG, Box 807, RG 407, NA.

23. Ibid.

24. Bernardo and Bacon, 424.

25. Prange, 594.

26. Pogue, 2:292, 293.

27. Cline, 91.

28. Memorandum, Major General McNarney for Chief of Staff, January 31, 1942, OCS records, WDCSA 020 (1942), quoted in ibid.

29. Memorandum, Chief of Cavalry, "Memorandum of My Conversation with the Chief of Staff on the Afternoon of Thursday, February 5, 1942," February 5, 1942, File 322.02, OCC, Box 8, RG 177, NA.

30. Herr, 248–49; *Field Service Regulations, 1941*, 8; and *FM 2-5, Cavalry Field Manual: Horse Cavalry* (Washington, D.C., 1940), 112–13.

31. Memorandum, Chief of Cavalry, February 5, 1942, File 322.02, OCC, Box 8, RG 177, NA.

32. Cline, 92.

33. Memorandum, Major General McNarney for Major General A. D. Surles, February 27, 1942, quoted in ibid., 95.

34. Cline, 92–93.

35. B. G. Chynoweth, "Modernization, n.d." (1935), TMs, in Chynoweth Papers, USAMHI.

36. See, for example, Military Attaché Report no. 15,596 (Major Truman Smith, Berlin), November 24, 1937, G-2 Report no. 25,345-W (Lieutenant Colonel Sumner Waite, Paris), August 28, 1939, and "The German Panzer Division," 614.25/.4, October 15, 1939, all in Crittenberger Papers, USAMHI; G-2 Report no. 6910 (Maj. W. D. Hohenthal, Berlin), January 10, 1940, 248.211–5 (1939), USAFHRA; Adolf von Shell, "Antitank Defense," *Infantry Journal* 43 (July–August 1936): 339–44; "Tank Tactics," *Quarterly Review of Military Literature [Military Review]* no. 65 (June 1937), 15–31; Heinz Guderian, "Armored Forces," pts. 1 and 2, *Infantry Journal* 44 (September–October and November–December 1937); Lieutenant Colonel von Wedel, "The German Campaign in Poland," *Infantry Journal* 46 (November–December 1939): 542–47; and "International Military Survey: German Tanks, Organization, and Equipment," *Infantry Journal* 46 (November–December 1939): 595–97.

CHAPTER 13

1. Minutes of General Council meetings, March 17, 1942, DC of S records, quoted in Cline, 112–13.

2. Cline, 107–19.

3. Green, Thomson, and Roots, 20–29; Holley, *Buying Aircraft*, 247; and Kent Roberts Greenfield, Robert R. Palmer, and Bell I. Wiley, *The Organization of Ground Combat Troops*. U.S. Army in World War II (1947; Washington, D.C., 1983), 40, 189–90.

CHAPTER 14

1. Freeland A. Daubin, "The Battle of 'Happy Valley,' 1948," TMs, p. 8, USAMHI.

2. Ibid., 1–2.

3. Ibid., 3.

4. George F. Howe, *Northwest Africa: Seizing the Initiative in the West*, U.S. Army in World War II (Washington, D.C., 1957), 299–302; and Paul M. Robinett, *Armor Command* (Washington, D.C.: McGregor & Werner, 1958), 65–66.

5. "Report of the Mission Headed by Lieutenant General Jacob L. Devers to Examine the Problems of Armored Force Units in the European Theatre of Operations, n.d. [January 1943]," File "Inspections," Arnold Papers, Box 43, LC.

6. Ibid.

7. Ibid.

8. G. MacLeod Ross, *The Business of Tanks, 1933 to 1945* (Elms Court, England: Arthur H. Stockwell, 1976), 40–41.

9. Devers Report.

10. Ibid.

11. Howe, 401–77; and Thomas E. Griess, ed., *The Second World War, Europe and the Mediterranean*, West Point Military History Series (Wayne, N.J.: Avery, 1984), 173–75.

12. Griess, 175.

13. U.S. War Department, *Lessons from the Tunisian Campaign* (Washington, D.C., 1943), quoted in Dennis J. Vetok, *Lessons Learned: A History of US Army Lesson Learning* (Carlisle Barracks: U.S. Army Military History Institute, 1988), 61.

14. Lieutenant General L. J. McNair to Major General A. D. Bruce, February 19, 1943, File A-B, McNair File, Box 9, RG 337, NA.

15. Jonathan M. House, *Toward Combined Arms Warfare: A Survey of Tactics, Doctrine, and Organization in the 20th Century*, Combat Studies Institute Research Survey no. 2 (Fort Leavenworth: U.S. Army Command and General Staff College, 1984), 108–10; *History of the Armored Force*, 29, 46–47; and Baily, 51.

16. *FM 17-100 (Tentative): Employment of the Armored Division and Separate Armored Units, 1943*, 1, 8, 13.

17. Baily, 76.

18. *History of the Armored Force*, 29, 34–35, 47.

19. Baily, 83–85.

20. Memorandum, CG AGF for Requirements Division AGF, November 19, 1943, Binder 1, AGF McNair file 470.8, quoted in Green, Thomson, and Roots, 280.

21. Baily, 99.

22. Lieutenant General G. S. Patton Jr. to Lieutenant General L. J. McNair, April 10, 1944, File P-Q, McNair File, Box 10, RG 337, NA.

23. Baily, 106–7.

24. Omar N. Bradley, *A Soldier's Story* (1951; Chicago: Rand McNally, 1978), 322–23.

25. Mayo, 323.

26. Major General I. D. White, "A Report on United States vs. German Equipment, 1945," TMs, exhibit 3, p. 37, USAMHI.

27. Mayo, 325.

28. White Report, exhibit 3, p. 30.

29. Mayo, 323–27.

30. Baily, 116.

31. Hanson W. Baldwin, "The German Blow—III," *New York Times*, January 5, 1945, in "My Little Green Book," George B. Jarrett Papers [Jarrett Papers], Box 6, USAMHI.

32. "U.S. Ordnance Is Defended," *The Sun (Baltimore)*, February 3, 1945, in "My Little Green Book," Jarrett Papers, Box 6, USAMHI.

33. Sidney Shalett, "Ordnance Head Backs U.S. Tank; Calls Heavier Types Not Wanted," *New York Times*, February 3, 1945, in "My Little Green Book," Jarrett Papers, Box 6, USAMHI. See also George S. Patton Jr., *War as I Knew It* (Boston: Houghton Mifflin, 1947), 263. Patton was concerned that the "rumors" about German tank superiority would negatively affect the morale of his soldiers on the fighting front and that of American workers producing tanks on the home front.

34. Shalett.

35. Dwight D. Eisenhower to Brigadier General I. D. White, March 18, 1945, in White Report; Dwight D. Eisenhower to General Rose, March 18, 1945, and Major General Maurice Rose to General Dwight D. Eisenhower, March 21, 1945, in DDE Pre-Presidential Papers, "Rose, Maurice," Eisenhower Library. Hereinafter referred to as Rose Letter.

36. Ibid.

37. Brigadier General I. D. White to General Eisenhower, March 20, 1945, in White Report, 1, 5.
38. White Report, exhibit 1, p. 1.
39. Ibid.
40. Ibid., exhibit 2, p. 9.
41. Ibid., exhibit 2, p. 1.
42. Ibid., exhibit 3, p. 8.
43. Ibid., exhibit 3, p. 40.
44. Ibid.
45. Ibid., exhibit 3, p. 41.
46. Rose Letter, 1.
47. Ibid., 3.
48. Ibid., 4.
49. Dwight D. Eisenhower to Brigadier General Isaac D. White, March 27, 1945, in White Report, and Dwight D. Eisenhower to Major General Maurice Rose, March 27, 1945, in Rose Letter.
50. Baily, 52; and Mayo, 139–40.
51. *Biennial Report, 1945,* 94–95. See also N. T. Kenney, "Some German Weapons Topped Ours, Marshall Admits," *Evening Sun (Baltimore),* October 10, 1945, in "My Little Green Book," Jarrett Papers, Box 6, USAMHI.

CHAPTER 15

1. Draft memorandum, General Arnold for Harry L. Hopkins, AFABI (10–28–42), File "Bomber Command to Great Britain," Arnold Papers, Box 49, LC. See also Craven and Cate, 2:221–22. The number of enemy fighters claimed to have been destroyed on the Lille mission was grossly inflated. In January 1943 the numbers were revised to 21 destroyed, 21 probably destroyed, and 15 damaged, for a total of 57. The actual figure was much lower. A postwar review of German Air Ministry records indicated that only 2 fighters had been lost during the engagement. These inflated claims continued throughout the war, although they were received with increasing skepticism by the air planners. There were two basic reasons for these exaggerations: First, in a formation of bombers, every gunner who was firing on an incoming fighter thought it was his bullet that damaged or destroyed the plane. In the intense, high-speed environment of aerial combat, claims were bound to be distorted. Second, gunners had an incentive to claim victories—they received medals for destroying enemy aircraft. See also Kenneth P. Werrell, "The Tactical Development of the Eighth Air Force in World War II" (Ph.D. diss., Duke University, 1969), 57. Werrell notes: "The significance of the claims' problem was its influence on intelligence, for GAF [German Air Force] attrition was used, along with estimates of production and order of battle, to figure the GAF's strength and capabilities." Quite simply, these grossly inflated figures during the early months of air operations over Europe led the air planners to some overly optimistic expectations about the effort required to eliminate the Luftwaffe.
2. Lieutenant General H. H. Arnold to Major General Carl Spaatz, November 15, 1942, File "Bomber Command to Great Britain," Arnold Papers, Box 149, LC.
3. John Steinbeck, *Bombs Away: The Story of a Bomber Team* (New York: Viking, 1942), 185. See also Sherry, 125–38.
4. Lieutenant General H. H. Arnold to Major General Ira C. Eaker, November 18, 1942, File "VIII Bomber Command, Volume II," Ira C. Eaker Papers [Eaker Papers], Box 16, LC.

5. Craven and Cate, 2:229–241, 3:340–42; and Holley, *Buying Aircraft*, 552–56.

6. James Parton, *"Air Force Spoken Here": General Ira Eaker and the Command of the Air* (Bethesda, Md.: Adler & Adler, 1986), 215.

7. Ibid., 218–20.

8. Major General Ira C. Eaker to Major General George Stratemeyer, January 30, 1943, File "8th Air Force, Correspondence with Generals Eubank & Stratemeyer," Eaker Papers, Box 17, LC.

9. "Casablanca Questions: Replies by General Eaker, January 1943," 614.201–2 (January–May 1943), USAFHRA.

10. Ibid.

11. Parton, 220–21; and Winston Churchill, *The Second World War*, 6 vols. (Boston: Houghton Mifflin, 1950), 4:678–79.

12. Churchill, 4:678–79.

13. CCS 166/1/D, quoted in Craven and Cate, 2:305.

14. Carl A. Spaatz, "Strategic Air Power in the European War," *Foreign Affairs* (April 1946), in Emme, 230.

15. See "Casablanca Questions: Replies by General Eaker." The question of what constituted "unacceptable losses" eludes a precise answer. Eaker's notes from the Casablanca Conference provide what is probably as good a definition as any: "It is believed very unwise to operate at a rate faster than we can make good our losses in planes and crews. The law of diminishing returns will seize us and we will be going down-hill instead of up. Do not worry, therefore, that we will not operate at a rate which will consume against the enemy all the stores of planes and crews you send to us, providing always a small margin for a steady build-up in the size of the force, which I am convinced is the wise thing to do."

16. Churchill, 4:679.

17. DeWitt S. Copp, *Forged in Fire: Strategy and Decisions in the Air War over Europe, 1940–1945* (Garden City, N.Y.: Doubleday, 1982), 357–58.

18. Werrell, 66.

19. Major General Ira C. Eaker to Major General George E. Stratemeyer, January 30, 1943, File "8th Air Force, Correspondence with Generals Eubank & Stratemeyer," Eaker Papers, Box 17, LC.

20. Headquarters, Army Air Forces, Statistical Control Division, Office of Management Control, "Eighth Air Force Heavy Bomber Operations by Month (July, 1943–March, 1944), April 28, 1944," 520.164, vol. 2 (1942–1945), USAFHRA.

21. For the Luftwaffe response to the Eighth Air Force's bombing campaign, see Williamson Murray, *Strategy for Defeat: The Luftwaffe, 1933–1945* (Maxwell Air Force Base: Air University Press, 1983); Adolf Galland, *The First and the Last: The Rise and Fall of the Luftwaffe, 1939–1945*, trans. Mervin Savill (1954; New York: Ballantine, 1971); and David Irving, *The Rise and Fall of the Luftwaffe: The Life of Field Marshal Erhard Milch* (Boston: Little, Brown, 1973).

22. Craven and Cate, 2:843.

23. Memorandum, Lieutenant General H. H. Arnold for General Stratemeyer, February 26, 1943, File "BC to GB," Arnold Papers, Box 48, LC.

24. Major General Ira C. Eaker to Commanding General, Eighth Air Force, October 8, 1942, File "VIII Bomber Command, Volume II," Eaker Papers, Box 16, LC.

25. Murray, 175–76.

26. Major General Ira C. Eaker to Lieutenant General Frank M. Andrews, February 27, 1943, File "BC to GB 7–'44 to," Arnold Papers, Box 48, LC.

27. General H. H. Arnold to Lieutenant General Frank M. Andrews, March 24, 1943, File "Correspondence—Commanders in the Field," Arnold Papers, Box 38, LC.

28. Memorandum, General H. H. Arnold for Harry Hopkins, March 27, 1943, File "Mr. Hopkins," Arnold Papers, Box 43, LC. Emphasis in original.

29. Murray, 175–76.

30. General H. H. Arnold to Lieutenant General Frank M. Andrews, April 26, 1943, File "Bomber Command to Great Britain," Arnold Papers, Box 149, LC.

31. Major General Ira C. Eaker to Gen. H. H. Arnold, May 13, 1943, File "BC to GB 7-'44 to," Arnold Papers, Box 48, LC.

32. Major General Ira C. Eaker to General Henry H. Arnold, May 18, 1943, File "Bomber Command to Great Britain," Arnold Papers, Box 149, LC.

33. Lieutenant General Carl Spaatz to General H. H. Arnold, May 24, 1943, in "Policy File, 8th Air Force, Volume II," p. 91, 520.164, vol. 2 (1942–1945), USAFHRA.

34. Dubuque and Gleckner, 112.

35. For an analysis of the YB-40 program, and the effort to develop long-range escorts, see Boylan.

36. Major General Barney M. Giles to Major General Ira C. Eaker, June 11, 1943, File "8th Air Force, Correspondence with Major General Barney Giles," Eaker Papers, Box 17, LC.

37. Memorandum, Major General Barney M. Giles for General Arnold, June 10, 1943, File "BC to GB 7-'44 to," Arnold Papers, Box 48, LC.

38. Major General Barney M. Giles to Major General Ira C. Eaker, June 11, 1943, File "8th Air Force, Correspondence with Major General Barney Giles," Eaker Papers, Box 17, LC.

39. Memorandum, Robert A. Lovett for Commanding General, Army Air Forces, June 19, 1943, File "8th Air Force, Correspondence with Honorable Robert A. Lovett," Eaker Papers, Box 17, LC.

40. General H. H. Arnold to Major General Ira C. Eaker, June 28, 1943, File "Bomber Command to Great Britain," Arnold Papers, Box 149, LC. See also Major General Ira C. Eaker to General H. H. Arnold, July 20, 1943, File "Bomber Command to Great Britain," Arnold Papers, Box 149, LC.

41. General H. H. Arnold to Major General Ira C. Eaker, June 29, 1943, File "BC to GB 7-'44 to," Arnold Papers, Box 48, LC. Emphasis in original.

42. Robert A. Lovett to Major General Ira C. Eaker, July 1, 1943, File "8th Air Force Correspondence with Honorable Robert A. Lovett," Eaker Papers, Box 17, LC.

43. Major General Ira C. Eaker to General H. H. Arnold, June 29, 1943, File "8th Air Force, Volume I," Eaker Papers, Box 16, LC.

44. General H. H. Arnold to Major General Ira C. Eaker, July 7, 1943, File "8th Air Force, Volume II," Eaker Papers, Box 16, LC.

45. General H. H. Arnold to Major General Ira C. Eaker, August 1, 1943, File "BC to GB 7-'44 to," Arnold Papers, Box 48, LC.

46. Martin Middlebrook, *The Schweinfurt-Regensburg Mission* (New York: Charles Scribner's Sons, 1983), 295–303; and Craven and Cate, 2:848.

47. Craven and Cate, 2:683; and Middlebrook, 262.

48. Middlebrook, 307–11.

49. Robert A. Lovett to Major General Ira C. Eaker, August 21, 1943, File "8th Air Force, Correspondence with Honorable Robert A. Lovett," Eaker Papers, Box 17, LC.

50. Message no. A-3517, September 8, 1943, in General Arnold's Briefs of Messages, 1942–1945, #19, Air Adjutant General, Message and Cable Division, Box 8, RG 18, NA.

51. Command Informational Intelligence Series, no. 43-124, September 17, 1943, "Interview with Brigadier General H. S. Hansell, 9 August 1943," 142.05 (1942–43), USAFHRA.

52. Message no. R-3350, in General Arnold's Briefs of Messages, 1942–1945, #19, Air Adjutant General, Message and Cable Division, Box 8, RG 18, NA.

53. Craven and Cate, 2:849–50.

54. Ibid.

55. Command Information Intelligence Series, no. 43-121, "German Day-Fighter System," August 31, 1943, 142.034–3 (August 31, 1943), USAFHRA.

56. Lieutenant General Ira C. Eaker to General H. H. Arnold, October 15, 1943, File "Bomber Command to Great Britain," Arnold Papers, Box 149, LC.

57. Headquarters, Eighth Air Force, Operational Analysis Section, "An Evaluation of Measures Taken to Protect Heavy Bombers from Loss and Damage," November 1944, p. 6, USAMHI. Lieutenant General James H. Doolittle, commander of the Eighth Air Force after Eaker, approved this report in November, noting that "the conclusions are considered sound." The conclusions about unescorted bomber penetrations into Germany were compelling: "Various studies of operations during 1943 demonstrated that . . . by the fall of 1943, growing enemy fighter power precluded bomber operations to targets deep in Central or Southern Germany until long-range fighters were available to provide full escort." The report also noted the impact of escort fighters on bomber survivability: "Their efforts in the main are responsible for cutting the loss rate to fighters to a fraction of what it was, and thus saving thousands of bombers."

58. Excerpts from file no. 519,332, "Press Releases and Telegrams, Schweinfurt—Oct. 14, 1943," 520.056–230 (October 14, 1943), USAFHRA.

59. United States Strategic Bombing Survey, *The German Anti-Friction Bearing Industry*, January 1947, p. 2, 520.056–224 (January 1947), USAFHRA.

60. Memorandum, Lieutenant Colonel C. V. Whitney for General Kuter, September 11, 1943; and memorandum, Brigadier General L. S. Kuter for Colonel Whitney, September 11, 1943, 168.7012–1 (1942–1945 SL-1), Kuter Papers, USAFHRA. See also Brigadier General Haywood S. Hansell, "Lecture Presented at the Air War College, 'The Development of the United States Concept of Bombardment Operations,' February 16, 1951," p. 12, K239.716251–75 (February 16, 1951), USAFHRA. Hansell noted: "Actually Germany was able to get from Switzerland and from Sweden enough ball bearings to get her out of her embarrassment and difficulty."

61. Lieutenant General Ira C. Eaker to Major General Barney M. Giles, December 13, 1943, File "8th Air Force, Correspondence with Major General Barney Giles," Eaker Papers, Box 17, LC.

62. Memorandum, General H. H. Arnold for Chief of Staff, December 27, 1943, File "BC to GB 7-'44 to," Arnold Papers, Box 48, LC.

63. "Evaluation of Measures Taken to Protect Heavy Bombers," 4.

64. Major General Ira C. Eaker to General H. H. Arnold, June 29, 1943, File "8th Air Force, Volume I," Eaker Papers, Box 16, LC.

CHAPTER 16

1. Martin Blumenson, *Breakout and Pursuit*, U.S. Army in World War II (1961; Washington, D.C., 1984), 185.

2. Russell F. Weigley, *Eisenhower's Lieutenants: The Campaign of France and Germany, 1944–1945* (Bloomington: Indiana University Press, 1981), 142–43.

3. John J. Sullivan, "The Botched Air Support of Operation Cobra," *Parameters* 18 (March 1988): 97–98.

4. Blumenson, 215.

5. Oral history interview of Lieutenant General Elwood R. Quesada by Steve Long and Ralph Stephenson (senior officers, Debriefing Program), 1975, p. 35, USAMHI; and Omar N. Bradley, *A Soldier's Story* (1951; Chicago: Rand McNally, 1978), 337–38.

6. Bradley, 337.

7. Howe, 492.

8. Brigadier General L. S. Kuter to Commanding General, Army Air Forces, May 12, 1943, 614.201–2 (January–May 1943), USAFHRA.

9. Ibid.

10. Memorandum, McCloy for General Lear, May 15, 1943, 353/283 (Air-Gnd), quoted in Kent Roberts Greenfield, *Army Ground Forces and the Air-Ground Battle Team Including Light Aviation*. Historical Section, Army Ground Forces, Study no. 35 (Fort Monroe: Historical Section, Army Ground Forces, 1948), 49–50.

11. "Statement by Brigadier General Laurence S. Kuter, 'Lessons in Air Force Organization Learned from the North African War,' 22 May 1943," 614.505 (May 1943), USAFHRA.

12. "N.A.T.A.F. Planning Notes, 22 May '43," 614.321 (22 May 1943), USAFHRA.

13. Greenfield, 47.

14. *FM 100-20, Field Service Regulations: Command and Employment of Air Power*, 1.

15. Brigadier General L. S. Kuter to Air Marshal Sir A. Coningham, June 26, 1943, Public Records Office (Jew, England) 23/7439, cited in Richard G. Davis, *Tempering the Blade: General Carl Spaatz and American Tactical Air Power in North Africa, November 8, 1942–May 14, 1943*, Air Staff Historical Study (Washington, D.C., 1989), 117.

16. General H. H. Arnold to Commanding Generals, All Air Forces, All Independent Army Air Forces Commands, Commandant Army Air Forces School of Applied Tactics, 9/23, File "Employment of Air Forces," Arnold Papers, Box 42, LC.

17. *FM 100-20*, 2.

18. Ibid., 8–12.

19. Lieutenant Colonel B. B. Troskoski to Major John P. Crowder, 3AF 337 (May 15, 1944), May 15, 1944, 248.122 (1944), USAFHRA.

20. Major General Westside T. Larson to Commanding General, Army Air Forces, 3AF 373 (May 22, 1944) SOGU, May 22, 1944, File "SAS 373.21," Arnold Papers, Box 110, LC.

21. Brigadier General R. E. Nugent to Commanding General, Army Air Forces, Adv.AEAF/24241, July 20, 1944, 168.161–3 (1943–1945), USAFHRA.

22. Major A. J. Bochicchio to COC-in-Chief, 21 A Gp Main, 452.1(C), July 17, 1944, 168.161–3 (1943–1945), USAFHRA.

23. Brigadier General R. E. Nugent to Commanding General, Army Air Forces, Adv.AEAF/24241, July 20, 1944, 168.161–3 (1943–1945), USAFHRA.

24. Bradley, 339.

25. Blumenson, 220.

26. Omar N. Bradley and Clay Blair, *A General's Life* (New York: Simon & Schuster, 1983), 276; and memorandum, ColonelW. J. Paul for Acting Commanding General, Air University, 5AC, April 16, 1951, 520.453(A) (24 July 1944), USAFHRA.

27. "Report of Investigation of Tactical Bombing, 25 July 1944," 168.6005–110 (July 25, 1944), USAFHRA; Bradley, 340–41; and Blumenson, 220.

28. Bradley, 346–54; Bradley and Blair, 276; Quesada oral history interview, 5; Craven and Cate, 3:231; "Report of Investigation of Tactical Bombing"; and *FM 100-20*, 1–2, 8–9.

29. "Report of Investigation of Tactical Bombing"; Craven and Cate, 3:228–30; and Blumenson, 228–29.

30. Blumenson, 233; Bradley, 346–48.

31. Craven and Cate, 3:232–33; and Blumenson, 234–36.

32. Bradley, 347; Quesada oral history interview, 5; Blumenson, 233; and "Report of Investigation of Tactical Bombing."

33. *FM 100-20*, 9.

CONCLUSION

1. Winton, 224.
2. Katzenbach, 649.
3. John S. Wood, "Memories and Reflections," quoted in Hanson W. Baldwin, *Tiger Jack* (Fort Collins: Old Army Press, 1979), 75.
4. See Thomas S. Kuhn, *The Structure of Scientific Revolution*, 2d ed. (1962; Chicago: University of Chicago Press, 1970), particularly the 1969 postscript (pp. 174–210). I rely heavily on the definitions of the term *paradigm* Kuhn gives on page 175: "the term paradigm is used in two different senses. On the one hand it stands for the entire constellation of beliefs, values, techniques, and so on shared by the members of a given community. On the other it denotes one sort of element in that constellation, the concrete puzzle-solutions which, employed as models or examples, can replace explicit rules as a basis for solution of the remaining puzzles of normal science."
5. Johnson Hagood, *The Services of Supply* (Boston: Houghton Mifflin, 1927), 22ff; quoted in Watson, 63.
6. See Alex Roland, *Underwater Warfare in the Age of Sail* (Bloomington: Indiana University Press, 1978). Roland's comments on the U.S. Navy's traditionalism and its effects on retarding the potential of the early technologies of underwater warfare are analogous to the infantry and cavalry's response to the tank: "In many respects this [conservatism] was simply a special case of the general rule that those in power tend to resist change because they are not likely to risk their positions for an uncertain future. This behavior is especially important in military circles where tradition plays such a powerful role in the group mentality" (180). Similarly, an insight into the success of the airplane, like that eventually enjoyed by the submarine, is offered: "Once military professionals adopt a weapon as their own, it gathers an independent existence" (181).
7. 1st Ind. Major General J. K. Herr, chief of cavalry, to Commanding General, Washington Provisional Brigade, February 9, 1940, File 322.02, OCC, RG 177, Box 7b, NA.
8. John W. Masland and Laurence I. Radway, *Soldiers and Scholars: Military Education and National Policy* (Princeton, N.J.: Princeton University Press, 1957), 88.
9. Harry P. Ball, *Of Responsible Command: A History of the U.S. Army War College*, rev. ed. (Carlisle Barracks: Alumni Association of the U.S. Army War College, 1994), 253.
10. Ibid.
11. Martin Blumenson, "Kasserine Pass, 30 January–22 February 1943," in *America's First Battles, 1776–1965*, ed. Charles E. Heller and William A. Stofft (Lawrence: University Press of Kansas, 1986), 231.
12. Masland and Radway, 88.
13. Brigadier General L. J. McNair to Adjutant General, August 31, 1939, in U.S. Army Command and General Staff College Library Collection; and oral history interview of Major General Donald Wilson by Hugh Ahmann, December 10–11, 1975, K239.5012–878, USAFHRA, 74. See also oral history interview of General Laurence S. Kuter by Hugh N. Ahmann and Tom Sturm, September 30–October 3, 1974, K239.0512–810, USAFHRA, 130. Kuter was even more blunt, noting that "it [the Command and General Staff School course] was a wasted year. . . . It was, again, good if you wanted to know how to patrol the trenches, how Gettysburg should have been fought." See also Timothy K. Nenninger, "Leavenworth and Its Critics: The U.S. Army Command and General Staff School, 1920–1940," *Journal of Military History* 58 (April 1994): 224. Nenninger notes that the representation of air officers in the Leavenworth courses increased over the interwar period. He believes the reason for the higher attendance was "linked to the Air Corps' organizational expectations and agenda. Officers who were not graduates of the CGSS could not be named to the General Staff Eligible List,

and thus could not serve on the War Department General Staff. If the Air Corps wanted representation on the General Staff, one means to enhance its organizational status as a branch within the Army or to influence War Department policy to increase branch autonomy, it had to qualify officers by sending them to Leavenworth."

14. Larry I. Bland and Sharon R. Ritenour, eds., *The Papers of George Catlett Marshall*, 4 vols. (Baltimore: Johns Hopkins University Press, 1981), 702–3.

15. See Morris Janowitz, *The Professional Soldier: A Social and Political Portrait* (New York: Free Press, 1971), 90–93. Janowitz presents evidence that the majority of the officer leadership of the interwar era had its origins in the upper and upper middle social classes of American society (more than 70 percent between 1910 and 1935).

16. Citation from Herr and Wallace, 254; and Orville Z. Tyler Jr., *The History of Fort Leavenworth, 1937–1951* (Fort Leavenworth: U.S. Army Command and General Staff College, 1951), 1–2.

17. Brigadier General L. J. McNair to Adjutant General, August 31, 1939, Subject: Annual Report, School Year 1938–39, in U.S. Army Command and General Staff College Library collection.

18. *Instruction Circular No. 1, 1939–1940* (Fort Leavenworth: U.S. Army Command and General Staff School, 1939), 10.

19. McNair, Annual Report, 1938–39. See also Ira C. Eaker, "The Air Corps Tactical School: As Seen by an Air Corps Officer," *Air Corps News Letter* 19 (April 15, 1936), 10. Eaker wrote that in the 1936 course at the Air Corps Tactical School, students were required to participate in one hour of equitation instruction every other day, although there was "considerable agitation on the part of the present class to make riding optional."

20. Huntington, 311, 310, 309.

21. *Infantry Journal* 43 (1936): 237–38; quoted in Huntington, 310.

22. Huntington, 304.

23. U.S. Forces, European Theater, General Board, Air Section, *The Tactical Air Force in the European Theater of Operations*. Study no. 54 (n.p., n.d. [1946]), foreword.

24. *12th Army Group Report of Operations (Final After Action Report)*, vol. II, (n.p., 1945), 11:61.

25. General Board, Armored Section, *Organization, Equipment, and Tactical Employment of the Armored Division*. Study no. 48 (n.p., n.d. [1946]), 22; and General Board, Armored Section, *Organization, Equipment, and Tactical Employment of Separate Tank Battalions*. Study no. 50 (n.p., n.d. [1946]), appendix 2, p. 1.

26. General Board, Air Section, *The Control of Tactical Aircraft in the European Theater of Operations*. Study no. 55 (n.p., n.d. [1946]), 1.

27. General Board, Armored Section, *Tank Gunnery*. Study no. 53 (n.p., n.d. [1946]), 29. Emphasis in original.

28. General Board, Armored Section, *Organization, Equipment, and Tactical Employment of Separate Tank Battalions*. Study no. 50 (n.p., n.d. [1946]), 12.

29. General Board, study no. 48, p. 22.

30. General Board, study no. 50, appendix 2, p. 2.

31. U.S. Strategic Bombing Survey, *The United States Strategic Bombing Surveys (European War) (Pacific War)* (1945–46; Maxwell Air Force Base: Air University Press, 1987), 37.

32. Ibid., 8, 13.

33. Ibid., 113, 116.

34. Message, Personal Eyes Only to Spaatz from Marshall, no. WAR 45991, August 8, 1945, Public Relations Division (War Department General and Special Staff Correspondence File, 1944–46), File II and III-1945, Box 3, RG 165, NA.

35. Message, Personal Eyes Only to Marshall from Spaatz, no. 1589, August 9, 1945,

Public Relations Division (War Department General and Special Staff Correspondence File, 1944–46), File II and III-1945, Box 3, RG 165, NA.

36. Message, Personal Eyes Only to Spaatz from Marshall.

37. *Strategic Bombing Surveys*, 115.

38. Weigley, *History of the U.S. Army*, 501.

Primary Sources

ARCHIVE AND MANUSCRIPT COLLECTIONS

Library of Congress, Washington, D.C., Manuscript Division

Henry H. Arnold Papers
Ira C. Eaker Papers

National Archives (NA), Washington, D.C.

Record Group 18 (NM 6), Army Air Forces, Air Adjutant General, Message and Cable
　　Division, General Arnold's Briefs of Messages, 1942–45
Record Group 18, Office of the Chief of Air Corps, Secret and Confidential Correspon-
　　dence, 1935–38
Record Group 165, War Department General and Special Staff, Correspondence File,
　　1944–46
Record Group 177, Records of the Chiefs of Arms
Record Group 337, Army Ground Forces, Headquarters, Commanding General (McNair
　　Files)
Record Group 407, Office of the Adjutant General

The U.S. Air Force Historical Research Agency (USAFHRA), Maxwell Air Force Base, Ala.

Personal papers
Charles Pearre Cabell Papers
Muir Stephen Fairchild Papers
Laurence Sherman Kuter Papers
Guido Rinaldo Perera Papers

Oral history interviews
General Samuel E. Anderson, K239.0512–905
Lieutenant General James H. Doolittle K239.0512–623; 793
Lieutenant General Ira C. Eaker, K239.0512–626; 627

Lieutenant General Barney M. Giles, K239.0512–779; 814
Major General Haywood Hansell Jr., K168.051; K239.0512–628; 629
Major General Russell L. Harmon, K239.0512–1758
General Hunter Harris Jr., K239.0512–811
General Laurence S. Kuter, K239.0512–810
Justice Lewis F. Powell Jr., K239.0512–1754
Lieutenant General Joseph Smith, K239.0512–906
Brigadier General Ralph A. Snavely, K239.0512–1223
General Carl A. Spaatz, K239.0512–754; 755
ColonelReade F. Tilley, K239.0512–1757
General Nathan F. Twining, K239.10512–634
General O. P. Weyland, K239.0512–813
Major General Donald Wilson, K239.5012–878

U.S. Army Center of Military History, Washington, D.C.

Committee 17, Armor Officer Advanced Course. "A Critical Analysis of the History of
    Armor in World War II." Typed manuscript (TMs). Armored School, Fort Knox, Ky.,
    May 1950.
United States Forces, European Theater, General Board Reports, n.d. [1946].

U.S. Army Military History Institute (USAMHI), Carlisle Barracks, Pa.
U.S. Army War College Curricular Files

Government reports
"American Tanks since the World War, February 1, 1923." Typed manuscript (TMs).
    U.S. Army Military History Institute, Carlisle Barracks, Pa.
Army Air Forces Statistical Digest: World War II. Washington, D.C.: Army Air Forces
    Office of Statistical Control, 1945.
Bradley, Omar N., and the Air Effects Committee, 12th Army Group. *Effect of Air
    Power on Military Operations, Western Europe.* Wiesbaden: 12th Army Group, 1945.
Chief of Infantry to Adjutant General, April 30, 1941, "Final Report" 319.12 (4–30–41).
    TMs. U.S. Army Military History Institute, Carlisle Barracks, Pa.
Combat Operations Data, First Army: Europe 1944–1945. Governors Island, N.Y.: Head-
    quarters, First Army, 1946.
Coox, Alvin D., and L. Van Loan Naisawald. *Survey of Allied Tank Casualties in World
    War II.* Washington, D.C.: Operations Research Office, Johns Hopkins University,
    Fort Lesley J. McNair, 1951. ORO-T-117.
ETO Ordnance Technical Intelligence Report no. 273, May 8, 1945. In George B. Jarrett
    Papers. U.S. Army Military History Institute, Carlisle Barracks, Pa.
Hardison, David C. *Data on W.W. II Tank Engagements Involving the U.S. Third and
    Fourth Armored Divisions.* Aberdeen Proving Ground: Ballistic Research Laborato-
    ries, 1954. BRL MR-798.
Headquarters, Eighth Air Force, Operational Analysis Section. "An Evaluation of Mea-
    sures Taken to Protect Heavy Bombers from Loss and Damage." November 1944.
"9th Bombardment Division in Cooperation with the Ground Forces (10 April–31
    March 1945): A Study of Medium Bombardment in Air Activity Coordinated with
    Ground Forces for the Conquest of Germany, April 1945." TMs. U.S. Army Military
    History Institute, Carlisle Barracks, Pa.
"Plans and Recommendations Submitted to the Morrow Commission of Inquiry,
    1925." TMs. U.S. Army Military History Institute, Carlisle Barracks, Pa.

Report of the G.H.Q. Air Force (Provisional), 1933. N.p., 1933.

Rockenbach, S. D. "Operations of Tank Corps A.E.F. at St. Mihiel, in the Meuse-Argonne Operation, and with the British E.F., 27 December 1918." TMs. U.S. Army Military History Institute, Carlisle Barracks, Pa.

———. "Weight and Dimensions of Tanks, February, 1923." TMs. U.S. Army Military History Institute, Carlisle Barracks, Pa.

12th Army Group Report of Operations (Final After Action Report). Vol. 11, *Antiaircraft Artillery, Armored, Artillery, Chemical Warfare, and Signal Sections.* N.p., 1945.

U.S. War Department. *Report of Chief of the Tank Corps.* Washington, D.C., 1919.

———. *Report of Chief of the Tank Corps.* Washington, D.C., 1920.

White, I. D. "A Report on United States vs. German Equipment, 1945." TMs. U.S. Army Military History Institute, Carlisle Barracks, Pa.

Personal papers

Bradford Grethen Chynoweth Papers

Willis D. Crittenberger Papers

Robert W. Grow Papers

Guy V. Henry Jr. Papers

George B. Jarrett Papers

Leon B. Kromer Papers

Oral history interviews

Ira C. Eaker

Elwood R. Quesada

PUBLIC DOCUMENTS

Final Report of War Department Special Committee on Army Air Corps. Washington, D.C., 1934.

Mitchell, William, Clayton Bissell, and Alfred Verville. *Report of Inspection Trip to France, Italy, Germany, Holland, and England, Made during the Winter of 1921–1922.* Washington, D.C., 1923.

Report of President's Aircraft Board. Washington, D.C., 1925.

U.S. Congress. House. *A Bill to Create a Department of Aeronautics.* 68th Cong., 2d sess., H.R. 10147, December 3, 1924.

———. *A Bill to Create a Department of Air.* 68th Cong., 1st sess., H.R. 12285, February 13, 1925.

———. *A Bill to Establish a Department of Air.* 77th Cong., 1st sess., H.R. 4192, March 26, 1941.

———. *A Bill to Increase the Efficiency of the Air Service of the United States and for Other Purposes.* 69th Cong., 1st sess., H.R. 9220, February 11, 1926.

———. Committee on Military Affairs. *Army Reorganization: Hearings before the Committee on Military Affairs.* 2 vols. 66th Cong., 1st sess., September 3–November 12, 1919.

———. *Housing Bill: Hearings before the Committee on Military Affairs.* 69th Cong., 1st sess., March 20, 1926.

———. *Hearings before the Committee on Military Affairs in Connection with H.R. 5304 May 16, 1913, Entitled "An Act to Increase the Efficiency of the Aviation Service of the Army, and for Other Purposes."* 63rd Cong., 1st sess., August 12, 14, 15, and 16, 1913.

———. Committee on Naval Affairs. *Proposed Coordination between the Army and Navy Air Services: Hearings before the Committee on Naval Affairs.* 68th Cong., 1st sess., 1924.

——. Select Committee of Inquiry into Operations of the United States Air Services. *Report of Select Committee of Inquiry into Operations of the United States Air Services.* 68th Cong., 2d sess., Report no. 1653. Washington, D.C., 1925.

U.S. Congress. Senate. Committee on Military Affairs. *The Army Air Service: Hearings before the Committee on Military Affairs.* 69th Cong., 1st sess., 10 May 1926.

——. *A Bill to Increase the Efficiency of the Air Service of the United States Army: Hearing before the Committee on Military Affairs.* 69th Cong., 1st sess., February 5, 1926.

——. *Construction at Army Posts: Hearings before the Committee on Military Affairs.* 69th Cong., 1st sess., April 16, 1926.

——. Special Committee Investigating the National Defense Program. *Progress of the National Defense Program.* 77th Cong., 1st sess., pt. 1, April 15–25, 1941.

——. Subcommittee of the Committee on Military Affairs. *Reorganization of the Army: Hearings before the Subcommittee of the Committee on Military Affairs.* 2 vols. 66th Cong., 1st sess., August 7, 1919, to March 1, 1920.

——. *Report of the Federal Aviation Commission.* 74th Cong., 1st sess., Senate Document no. 15. Washington, D.C., 1935.

U.S. Navy Department. *Report of the Joint Board on Results of Aviation and Ordnance Tests Held during June and July, 1921 and Conclusions Reached.* Washington, D.C., 1921.

U.S. War Department. *Acts and Resolutions Relating to the War Department Passed during the Sixty-sixth Congress, Second Session, December 1, 1920.* Washington, D.C., 1920.

——. *Acts and Resolutions Relating to the War Department Passed during the Sixty-sixth Congress, Third Session, December 6, 1920, to March 4, 1921.* Washington, D.C., 1921.

——. *Biennial Report of the Chief of Staff of the United States Army, July 1, 1939, to June 30, 1941, to the Secretary of War.* Washington, D.C., 1941.

——. *Biennial Report of the Chief of Staff of the U.S. Army, General George C. Marshall, July 1, 1943, to June 30, 1945, to the Secretary of War.* Washington, D.C.: U.S. News Publishing Corp., 1945.

——. *Final Report of General John J. Pershing, Commander-in-Chief, American Expeditionary Forces.* Washington, D.C., 1920.

——. *Report of the Chief of Staff of the U.S. Army, 1934.* Washington, D.C., 1934.

——. *Report of the Secretary of War to the President, 1921–1940.* Washington, D.C., 1921–1940.

——. *"Victory Is Certain," Being the Biennial Report of the Chief of Staff of the U.S. Army, General George C. Marshall, July 1, 1941, to June 30, 1943, to the Secretary of War.* New York: National Educational Alliance, 1943.

——. *War Department Annual Reports, 1920.* Vol. 1. Washington, D.C., 1921.

FIELD MANUALS, REGULATIONS, TRAINING PUBLICATIONS, AND SERVICE SCHOOL TEXTS

War Department Publications

U.S. War Department. *Army Regulations No. 95-5: Army Air Forces: General Provisions.* Washington, D.C., 1941.

——. *Army Regulations No. 75-60: Infantry Tank Board.* Washington, D.C., 1926.

——. *Field Service Regulations, United States Army, 1923 (War Department Document No. 1120).* Washington, D.C., 1924.

——. *FM 1-5, Air Corps Field Manual: Employment of Aviation of the Army.* Washington, D.C., 1940.

——. *FM 1-5, Army Air Force Field Manual: Employment of Aviation of the Army.* Washington, D.C., 1943.

————. *FM 1-10, Air Corp Field Manual: Tactics and Technique of Air Attack.* Washington, D.C., 1940.

————. *FM 1-10, Army Air Force Field Manual: Tactics and Technique of Air Fighting.* Washington, D.C., 1942.

————. *FM 2-5, Cavalry Field Manual: Horse Cavalry.* Washington, D.C., 1940.

————. *FM 2-10, Cavalry Field Manual: Mechanized Elements.* Washington, D.C., 1941.

————. *FM 2-15, Cavalry Field Manual: Employment of Cavalry.* Washington, D.C., 1941.

————. *FM 17, Armored Force Field Manual: Employment of Armored Units (The Armored Division).* Washington, D.C., n.d. [1940].

————. *FM 17-10, Armored Force Field Manual: Tactics and Technique.* Washington, D.C., 1942.

————. *FM 17-33, Armored Force Field Manual: The Armored Battalion, Light and Medium.* Washington, D.C., 1942.

————. *FM 17-100 (Tentative): Employment of the Armored Division and Separate Armored Units.* Fort Knox: Armored School, 1943.

————. *FM 18-5, Tank Destroyer Field Manual: Organization and Tactics of Tank Destroyer Units.* Washington, D.C., 1942.

————. *FM 18-5, War Department Field Manual: Tactical Employment, Tank Destroyer Unit.* Washington, D.C., 1944.

————. *FM 31-35, War Department Basic Field Manual: Aviation in Support of Ground Forces.* Washington, D.C., 1942.

————. *FM 100-5, Tentative Field Service Regulations: Operations.* Washington, D.C., 1939.

————. *FM 100-5, War Department Field Service Regulations: Operations.* Washington, D.C., 1941.

————. *FM 100-5, War Department Field Manual: Field Service Regulations, Operations.* Washington, D.C., 1944.

————. *FM 100-20, War Department Field Service Regulations: Command and Employment of Air Power.* Washington, D.C., 1943.

————. *Infantry and Tank Co-operation and Training, Document No. 804.* Washington, D.C., 1918.

————. *Infantry Field Manual.* Vol. 2, *Tank Units.* Washington, D.C., 1931.

————. *A Manual for Commanders of Large Units (Provisional).* Vol. 1, *Operations.* Washington, D.C., 1930.

————. *Tank Combat.* Washington, D.C., 1920.

————. *Tank Corps Combat.* N.p., 1919.

————. *Training Circular No. 17: Air-Ground Liaison.* Washington, D.C., 1945.

————. *Training Circular No. 32: Employment of the Cavalry Regiment, Horse and Mechanized (Corps Reconnaissance Regiment).* Washington, D.C., 1941.

————. *Training Circular No. 42: Employment of Cavalry Mechanized Reconnaissance Elements.* Washington, D.C., 1942.

————. *Training Circular No. 52: Employment of Aviation in Close Support of Ground Troops.* Washington, D.C., 1941.

————. *Training Circular No. 70: Army Air Forces—Basic Doctrine.* Washington, D.C., 1941.

————. *Training Circular No. 107: Employment of Mechanized Cavalry Units.* Washington, D.C., 1943.

————. *Training Circular No. 108: Employment of Tank Destroyer Units.* Washington, D.C., 1943.

————. *Training Regulations No. 10-5: Doctrines, Principles, and Methods.* Washington, D.C., 1921.

————. *Training Regulations No. 420-250: Infantry Drill, the Light Tank, Platoon, and Company.* Washington, D.C., 1925.

[281]

————. *Training Regulations No. 420-255: Infantry Drill, the Heavy Tank, Platoon, and Company.* Washington, D.C., 1925.
————. *Training Regulations No. 440-15: Air Service: Fundamental Principles for the Employment of the Air Service.* Washington, D.C., 1926.
————. *Training Regulations No.440-15: Air Corps: Employment of the Air Forces of the Army.* Washington, D.C., 1935.
————. *Unofficial Revision of Pages 1 to 54 in the 1923 Edition of Field Service Regulations, United States Army.* West Point, N.Y.: U.S. Military Academy Printing Office, 1927.

Service School Publications

Ground Doctrine

American Expeditionary Forces. *Tanks: Organization and Tactics, A.E.F. No. 1432, G-5.* General Headquarters, American Expeditionary Forces, France, 1918.
Infantry in Battle. Fort Leavenworth: U.S. Army Command and General Staff College, n.d.
U.S. Army Cavalry School. *Armored Cars.* Fort Riley: Cavalry School, 1926.
————. *Cavalry Combat.* Harrisburg, Pa.: Telegraph Press, 1937.
————. *The Employment of Tanks in Combat.* Fort Leavenworth: General Service Schools Press, 1925.
————. *Mechanized Cavalry.* Fort Riley: Cavalry School, 1932.
————. *Tanks.* Fort Riley: Cavalry School, 1926.
U.S. Army Command and General Staff School. *Instruction Circular No. 1, 1939–1940.* Fort Leavenworth: U.S. Army Command and General Staff School, 1939.
U.S. Army Infantry School. *Course of Study.* Vol. 3, *Drill and Command, and Tanks.* Camp Benning: Infantry School, 1921.

Air Doctrine

Air Corps Tactical School. *Air Force Basic Tactical Functions.* Maxwell Field: Air Corps Tactical School, 1938.
————. *Air Force: The Employment of Combat Aviation.* Maxwell Field: Air Corps Tactical School, 1939.
————. *Air Force Lectures, 1933–1934.* Maxwell Field: Air Corps Tactical School, 1934.
————. *Air Force.* Pt. 1, *Air Warfare.* Maxwell Field: Air Corps Tactical School, 1936.
————. *Air Operations—Immediate Support of Ground Forces, 1937–1938.* Maxwell Field: Air Corps Tactical School, 1937.
————. *Air Warfare.* Maxwell Field: Air Corps Tactical School, 1938.
————. *Annual.* Maxwell Field: Air Corps Tactical School, 1937.
————. *Annual.* Maxwell Field: Air Corps Tactical School, 1938.
————. *Attack Aviation.* Maxwell Field: Air Corps Tactical School, 1935.
————. *Bombardment.* Maxwell Field: Air Corps Tactical School, 1933.
————. *Bombardment.* Maxwell Field: Air Corps Tactical School, 1935.
————. *Bombardment Aviation.* Langley Field, Virginia: Air Corps Tactical School, 1931.
————. *Bombardment Aviation.* Maxwell Field: Air Corps Tactical School, 1938.
————. *Genesis of Bombardment Aviation.* Maxwell Field: Air Corps Tactical School, 1938.
————. *Light Bombardment Aviation.* Maxwell Field: Air Corps Tactical School, 1940.
————. *Program of Instruction for the Air Corps Tactical School, Maxwell Field, Montgomery, Ala., 1936–1937.* Maxwell Field: Air Corps Tactical School, 1936.
————. *Pursuit Aviation.* Maxwell Field: Air Corps Tactical School, 1933.
————. *Pursuit Aviation.* Maxwell Field: Air Corps Tactical School, 1939.
Air Service Tactical School. *Bombardment.* Washington, D.C., 1924.
————. *Bombardment.* Washington, D.C., 1926.

———. *Pursuit.* Washington, D.C., 1926.
Montgomery, B. L. *Some Notes on the Use of Air Power in Support of Land Operations and Direct Air Support.* N.p., 1944.
U.S. Army Command and General Staff School. *Tactical Employment of the Air Corps (Tentative).* Fort Leavenworth: Command and General Staff School Press, 1937.

MEMOIRS, PUBLISHED INTERVIEWS, AND PUBLISHED PAPERS

Arnold, H. H. *Global Mission.* New York: Harper, 1949.
Bland, Larry I., and Sharon R. Ritenour, eds. *The Papers of George Catlett Marshall.* 4 vols. Baltimore: Johns Hopkins University Press, 1981–96.
———Blumenson, Martin. *The Patton Papers.* 2 vols. Boston: Houghton Mifflin, 1972–74.
Bradley, Omar N. *A Soldier's Story.* 1951; Chicago: Rand McNally, 1978.
Bradley, Omar N., and Clay Blair. *A General's Life.* New York: Simon & Schuster, 1983.
Daubin, Freeland A. "The Battle of 'Happy Valley', 1948." TMs. U.S. Army Military History Institute, Carlisle Barracks, Pa.
Eisenhower, Dwight D. *At Ease: Stories I Tell to Friends.* Garden City, N.Y.: Doubleday, 1967.
———. *Crusade in Europe.* Garden City, N.Y.: Doubleday, 1948.
Foulois, Benjamin D., and C. V. Glines. *From the Wright Brothers to the Astronauts: The Memoirs of Major General Benjamin D. Foulois.* New York: McGraw-Hill, 1968.
Hansell, Haywood S., Jr. *The Strategic Air War against Germany and Japan: A Memoir.* USAF Warrior Studies. Washington, D.C., 1986
Harmon, E. N., Milton MacKaye, and William Ross MacKaye. *Combat Commander: Autobiography of a Soldier.* Englewood Cliffs, N.J.: Prentice-Hall, 1970.
Howze, Hamilton H. *A Cavalryman's Story: Memoirs of a Twentieth-Century Army General.* Washington, D.C.: Smithsonian Institution Press, 1996.
Kohn, Richard H., and Joseph P. Harahan, eds. *Air Superiority in World War II and Korea: An Interview with General James Ferguson, General Robert M. Lee, General William Momyer, and Lieutenant General Elwood R. Quesada.* USAF Warrior Studies. Washington, D.C., 1983.
———. *Strategic Air Warfare: An Interview with Generals Curtis E. LeMay, Leon W. Johnson, David A. Burchinal, and Jack J. Catton.* USAF Warrior Studies. Washington, D.C., 1988.
LeMay, Curtis E., and MacKinlay Kantor. *Mission with LeMay.* Garden City, N.Y.: Doubleday, 1965.
March, Peyton C. *The Nation at War.* Garden City, N.Y.: Doubleday, Doran, 1932.
Patton, George S., Jr. *War as I Knew It.* Boston: Houghton Mifflin, 1947.
Seymour, Charles. *The Intimate Papers of Colonel House.* 2 vols. Boston: Houghton Mifflin, 1926.
Truscott, Lucian K., Jr. *Command Missions: A Personal Story.* 1954; Novato: Presidio Press, 1990.
———. *The Twilight of the U.S. Cavalry: Life in the Old Army, 1917–1942.* Lawrence: University Press of Kansas, 1989.
Zuckerman, Solly. *From Apes to Warlords.* New York: Harper & Row, 1978.

Index

Air Commerce Act, 90
Air (Service, Corps, Forces), Army: and Air
    Corps Act, 90, 102; and air mail fiasco,
    158–59; and American Legion, 171–72;
    AWPD-1 proposed, 169–71; and bomb-
    ings, 93–94, 100–101, 112, 153, 155–56;
    and Drum, 101, 102, 158; and GHQ Air
    Force, 158, 161, 169; vs. ground officers,
    102–3, 225–26; and ground support,
    166–67; independent Air Service, 50–53,
    61, 81–82, 84, 91, 101–2, 160, 171–72,
    222; and Marshall, 168; and Naval Air,
    53, 153–54; and NYC vulnerability,
    162; officer qualifications for, 102;
    pre–World War I, 40–45; publicity and
    record setting, 91; pursuit role of,
    156–57, 165–66; and Red-Orange Plan,
    158; and Roosevelt, 168–69; World War
    I, 41, 43–45, 47–50. *See also* aircraft, U.S.;
    production/procurement.
  interwar period, 50–53, 61, 81–94; vs.
    battleship, 83; vs. coast artillery, 101;
    independence of, conflicts regarding,
    50–53, 61, 81–82, 84, 91, 101–2, 160,
    171–72, 222. *See also* disarmament;
    isolationism, U.S.; Mitchell, Billy;
    strategic bombing
  World War II: Arnold seeks publicity for,
    203–4, 207–8; and B-17 mission over
    France, 174; and bomber losses, 206,
    211; VIII Bomber Command estab-
    lished, 173; and German air campaign,
    207–11; and long-range escort fighters,
    207–10; losses and results, 210; and un-
    escorted bomber doctrine, 188; and

YB-40 gunship, 207, 208. *See also* strate-
    gic bombing; tactical air support
Air Corps Tactical School, 154–55, 160–61
aircraft, U.S.: interwar, 154, 157–58, 162–65;
    in World War I, 40–41, 43–45; in World
    War II, 207, 208

Air Service Tactical School, 91–94
Allen, R. H., 97–98
Andrews, Frank M., 140–41
Armored Force, U.S., 141–49, 192, 221–22;
    and cavalry, 124–40; division structure,
    missions defined, 143, 222; performance
    of, 226–27. *See also* mechanized forces,
    U.S.; tank doctrine; tanks, U.S.; unpre-
    paredness, U.S.
Army, U.S., active-duty strength of, 95,
    110, 188. *See also* mechanized forces,
    U.S.; modernization, military; tank
    doctrine, U.S.
Army War College, 223
Arnold, Henry H. "Hap," 175, 202–3, 205–10;
    lobby, 171–72

Baker, Newton D., 22, 51
Baker-March Bill, 28
ballooning, military, 40
Beck, Ludwig, 10–11
Bolling, Raynal C., 43–45
bombing, aerial. *See* Air Corps, Army;
    strategic bombing; tactical air support
Borah, William E., 64–65
Bradley, J. L., 69
Bradley, Omar, 212, 216
Briand, Aristide, 65

Cornell Studies in Security Affairs

edited by Robert J. Art, Robert Jervis,
and Stephen M. Walt

Bombing to Win: Air Power and Coercion in War, by Robert A. Pape

A Question of Loyalty: Military Manpower in Multiethnic States, by Alon Peled

Inadvertent Escalation: Conventional War and Nuclear Risks, by Barry R. Posen

The Sources of Military Doctrine: France, Britain, and Germany between the World Wars,
    by Barry Posen

Dilemmas of Appeasement: British Deterrence and Defense, 1934–1937, by Gaines Post, Jr.

Crucible of Beliefs: Learning, Alliances, and World Wars, by Dan Reiter

Eisenhower and the Missile Gap, by Peter J. Roman

The Domestic Bases of Grand Strategy, edited by Richard Rosecrance and Arthur Stein

Societies and Military Power: India and Its Armies, by Stephen Peter Rosen

Winning the Next War: Innovation and the Modern Military, by Stephen Peter Rosen

Vital Crossroads: Mediterranean Origins of the Second World War, 1935-1940,
    by Reynolds Salerno

Fighting to a Finish: The Politics of War Termination in the United States and Japan, 1945,
    by Leon V. Sigal

Alliance Politics, by Glenn H. Snyder

The Ideology of the Offensive: Military Decision Making and the Disasters of 1914, by Jack Snyder

Myths of Empire: Domestic Politics and International Ambition, by Jack Snyder

The Militarization of Space: U.S. Policy, 1945–1984, by Paul B. Stares

The Nixon Administration and the Making of U.S. Nuclear Strategy, by Terry Terriff

The Ethics of Destruction: Norms and Force in International Relations, by Ward Thomas

Causes of War: Power and the Roots of Conflict, by Stephen Van Evera

Mortal Friends, Best Enemies: German-Russian Cooperation after the Cold War,
    by Celeste A. Wallander

The Origins of Alliances, by Stephen M. Walt

Revolution and War, by Stephen M. Walt

The Tet Offensive: Intelligence Failure in War, by James J. Wirtz

The Elusive Balance: Power and Perceptions during the Cold War, by William Curti Wohlforth

Deterrence and Strategic Culture: Chinese-American Confrontations, 1949–1958,
    by Shu Guang Zhang